Heinrich Hussmann, Gerrit Meixner, and Detlef Zuehlke (Eds.)

Model-Driven Development of Advanced User Interfaces

T0180634

Studies in Computational Intelligence, Volume 340

Editor-in-Chief

Prof. Janusz Kacprzyk
Systems Research Institute
Polish Academy of Sciences
ul. Newelska 6
01-447 Warsaw
Poland
E-mail: kacprzyk@ibspan.waw.pl

Further volumes of this series can be found on our
homepage: springer.com

Vol. 318. Oscar Castillo, Janusz Kacprzyk,
and Witold Pedrycz (Eds.)
*Soft Computing for Intelligent Control
and Mobile Robotics,* 2010
ISBN 978-3-642-15533-8

Vol. 319. Takayuki Ito, Minjie Zhang, Valentin Robu,
Shaheen Fatima, Tokuro Matsuo,
and Hirofumi Yamaki (Eds.)
*Innovations in Agent-Based Complex
Automated Negotiations,* 2010
ISBN 978-3-642-15611-3

Vol. 320. xxx

Vol. 321. Dimitri Plemenos and Georgios Miaoulis (Eds.)
Intelligent Computer Graphics 2010
ISBN 978-3-642-15689-2

Vol. 322. Bruno Baruque and Emilio Corchado (Eds.)
Fusion Methods for Unsupervised Learning Ensembles, 2010
ISBN 978-3-642-16204-6

Vol. 323. Yingxu Wang, Du Zhang, and Witold Kinsner (Eds.)
Advances in Cognitive Informatics, 2010
ISBN 978-3-642-16082-0

Vol. 324. Alessandro Soro, Vargiu Eloisa, Giuliano Armano,
and Gavino Paddeu (Eds.)
*Information Retrieval and Mining in Distributed
Environments,* 2010
ISBN 978-3-642-16088-2

Vol. 325. Quan Bai and Naoki Fukuta (Eds.)
Advances in Practical Multi-Agent Systems, 2010
ISBN 978-3-642-16097-4

Vol. 326. Sheryl Brahnam and Lakhmi C. Jain (Eds.)
*Advanced Computational Intelligence Paradigms in
Healthcare 5,* 2010
ISBN 978-3-642-16094-3

Vol. 327. Slawomir Wiak and
Ewa Napieralska-Juszczak (Eds.)
*Computational Methods for the Innovative Design of
Electrical Devices,* 2010
ISBN 978-3-642-16224-4

Vol. 328. Raoul Huys and Viktor K. Jirsa (Eds.)
Nonlinear Dynamics in Human Behavior, 2010
ISBN 978-3-642-16261-9

Vol. 329. Santi Caballé, Fatos Xhafa, and Ajith Abraham (Eds.)
*Intelligent Networking, Collaborative Systems and
Applications,* 2010
ISBN 978-3-642-16792-8

Vol. 330. Steffen Rendle
Context-Aware Ranking with Factorization Models, 2010
ISBN 978-3-642-16897-0

Vol. 331. Athena Vakali and Lakhmi C. Jain (Eds.)
New Directions in Web Data Management 1, 2011
ISBN 978-3-642-17550-3

Vol. 332. Jianguo Zhang, Ling Shao, Lei Zhang, and
Graeme A. Jones (Eds.)
Intelligent Video Event Analysis and Understanding, 2011
ISBN 978-3-642-17553-4

Vol. 333. Fedja Hadzic, Henry Tan, and Tharam S. Dillon
Mining of Data with Complex Structures, 2011
ISBN 978-3-642-17556-5

Vol. 334. Álvaro Herrero and Emilio Corchado (Eds.)
Mobile Hybrid Intrusion Detection, 2011
ISBN 978-3-642-18298-3

Vol. 335. Radomir S. Stankovic and Radomir S. Stankovic
From Boolean Logic to Switching Circuits and Automata, 2011
ISBN 978-3-642-11681-0

Vol. 336. Paolo Remagnino, Dorothy N. Monekosso, and
Lakhmi C. Jain (Eds.)
Innovations in Defence Support Systems – 3, 2011
ISBN 978-3-642-18277-8

Vol. 337. Sheryl Brahnam and Lakhmi C. Jain (Eds.)
*Advanced Computational Intelligence Paradigms in
Healthcare 6,* 2011
ISBN 978-3-642-17823-8

Vol. 338. Lakhmi C. Jain, Eugene V. Aidman, and
Canicious Abeynayake (Eds.)
Innovations in Defence Support Systems – 2, 2011
ISBN 978-3-642-17763-7

Vol. 339. Halina Kwasnicka, Lakhmi C. Jain (Eds.)
Innovations in Intelligent Image Analysis, 2010
ISBN 978-3-642-17933-4

Vol. 340. Heinrich Hussmann, Gerrit Meixner, and
Detlef Zuehlke (Eds.)
Model-Driven Development of Advanced User Interfaces, 2011
ISBN 978-3-642-14561-2

Heinrich Hussmann, Gerrit Meixner, and
Detlef Zuehlke (Eds.)

Model-Driven Development of Advanced User Interfaces

 Springer

Prof. Dr. Heinrich Hussmann
Ludwig-Maximilians-Universität München
Lehr- und Forschungseinheit
Medieninformatik
Amalienstr. 17
80333 München
Germany
E-mail: Hussmann@ifi.lmu.de

Prof. Dr. Detlef Zuehlke
Deutsches Forschungszentrum für
Künstliche Intelligenz (DFKI)
Innovative Fabriksysteme (IFS)
Trippstadter Str. 122
67663 Kaiserslautern
Germany
E-mail: zuehlke@dfki.de

Dr. Gerrit Meixner
Deutsches Forschungszentrum für
Künstliche Intelligenz (DFKI)
Innovative Fabriksysteme (IFS)
Trippstadter Str. 122
67663 Kaiserslautern
Germany
E-mail: Gerrit.Meixner@dfki.de

ISBN 978-3-642-26686-7   ISBN 978-3-642-14562-9 (eBook)

DOI 10.1007/978-3-642-14562-9

Studies in Computational Intelligence   ISSN 1860-949X

Typeset & *Cover Design*: Scientific Publishing Services Pvt. Ltd., Chennai, India.

Printed on acid-free paper

9 8 7 6 5 4 3 2 1

springer.com

Preface

Model-Driven Development (MDD) has become an important paradigm in software development. The approach claims to provide a solution for systematic and efficient software development for the highly complex systems developed nowadays. It uses models, i.e. abstract representations of certain aspects of a system, as primary artifacts in the development process. Models are often visual models, like Unified Modeling Language (UML) models, but can also be represented in textual formats like the Extensible Markup Language (XML). A model-driven development process usually makes use of different models on different levels of abstraction. Model transformations are used to transform a model (semi) automatically into another (usually less abstract) model and finally into implementation code. MDD provides a large number of powerful concepts and tools to deal with models, meta-models, and model transformations.

Model-driven development of user interfaces applies the principles of MDD to the target domain of user interfaces. Modern user interface development requires the usage of extensive pre-fabricated software libraries and frameworks and has a strong tendency that the code becomes rather platform-specific. Therefore, MDD is a highly interesting technology for user interface development. MDD can help to hide the complexity of libraries and frameworks by using adequate abstractions, and MDD can achieve some degree of platform-independence through abstract interface models. The fact that different models of the same system may describe different views of the same system is also helpful, for instance, to separate the content (what is displayed) from the design (how it is displayed) into distinct models. Also for the emerging the paradigm of ubiquitous computing MDD is an interesting technology. Ubiquitous computing requires user interfaces which run on diverse target platforms in a consistent way, can adapt at runtime to the current application context or even migrate at runtime between different devices. Platform-independent, abstract models provide an excellent base to address such requirements.

The topics discussed in this book are intended to give a broad overview of the currents state of research in MDD for user interface development, in particular for advanced user interface concepts. Topics include, e.g., foundations and principles of models required for modeling (specific aspects of) advanced or non-standard user interfaces, tools supporting model-driven development of advanced user interfaces, adaptation and customization mechanisms for model transformations leading to tailored advanced user interfaces with a high degree of usability, the combination of models and informal design knowledge in a model-driven development process and project experience on user interface development using a model-driven development approach.

The specific chapters in this book cover a relatively broad spectrum of detailed research topics concerning, e.g., method engineering, formal description techniques, multi front-end engineering, development of multimodal user interfaces, models at development-time and at run-time, business process modeling, task modeling languages (e.g., useML, CTT, AMBOSS), user interface description languages (e.g., DISL, UIML, UsiXML, XAML), model transformation languages (e.g., ATL, QVT, T:XML), optimization of automatic generated user interfaces, informal design knowledge, user-centered software engineering and mixed interaction.

The idea of this book is based on the very successful workshop series of "Model-Driven Development of Advanced User Interfaces (MDDAUI)". The MDDAUI workshops were organized initially at the MODELS conference (2005, 2006 and 2007) mainly attracting software engineers and HCI researchers with a strong technical background. In 2009, the workshop took place at the Intelligent User Interfaces (IUI) conference, focusing topics at the intersection between HCI and Artificial Intelligence (AI). The last workshop up to now, in 2010, was conducted at the conference on Human Factors in Computing Systems (CHI) which focused more on user experience related aspects rather than pure technological innovations in model-driven development. Based on the contributions to this workshop, the editors have invited selected authors to contribute timely and original research papers to this book.

This book provides an outstanding overview as well as deep insights into the area of model-driven development of advanced user interfaces, which is an emerging topic in the intersection of Human-Computer-Interaction and Software-Engineering. Besides aiming to be the reference in its area, this book is intended as a very significant and valuable source for professional researchers as well as senior and post-graduate computer science and engineering students.

This book could not be completed without the help of many people. We would like to thank all the authors for their contribution to the book and their effort in addressing reviewers' and editorial feedback. Thanks also go to all the other participants and program committee members of former MDDAUI workshops. Finally, we would like to thank Eva Hestermann-Beyerle and Birgit Kollmar-Thoni at Springer (Heidelberg, Germany) for their assistance in publishing this book in a timely fashion.

October 2010   Heinrich Hussmann
                                                                                           Gerrit Meixner
                                                                                           Detlef Zuehlke

Contents

Authors Biography

Sahin Albayrak
Prof. Dr.-Ing. Sahin Albayrak is the chair of the professorship on Agent Technologies in Business Applications and Telecommunication (AOT) at the Technische Universität Berlin. He is the founder and head of the DAI-Labor, currently employing about 100 researchers and support staff. He is member of "The Institute of Electrical and Electronics Engineers" (IEEE), "Association for Computing Machinery" (ACM), "Gesellschaft für Informatik" (German Computer Science Society, GI), and "American Association for Artificial Intelligence" (AAAI). Prof. Albayrak is one of the founding members of Deutsche Telekom Laboratories (T-Labs) and currently member of the steering board. He was the initiator of many reputable research projects, e.g., E@MC2, Sun-Trec, in which he has been supervising research networks at national and international levels. He is also a member of various industrial and political advisory committees, e.g., Impulskreis "Vernetzte Welten".

Marco Blumendorf
Dr. Marco Blumendorf is leading the HCI working group of the DAI-Labor of the Technische Universität Berlin. He participated in several research projects funded by the German government, the Deutsche Telekom, Sun Microsystems and others. His current research interests include multimodal human computer interaction, focussing on model-based development of user interfaces for smart home environments. He is a member of different organisations, including the "Association for Computing Machinery" (ACM) and "Gesellschaft für Informatik" (German Computer Science Society, GI).

Goetz Botterweck
Goetz Botterweck is a Senior Research Fellow at Lero, the Irish Software Engineering Research Centre, were he leads two projects in Software Product Line Engineering and Model-driven Software Engineering. Further research interests include Model-driven User Interface Engineering, Model-based Evolution of Software Systems, Model-based Engineering of Embedded Systems, Consistency in Model-driven Approaches, and Domain-specific Languages. Goetz is Workshop Chair of the 14th International Software Product Line Conference (SPLC 2010). He co-organized several workshops at international conferences, including workshops on Automated Configuration and Tailoring (ACOTA at ASE), Visualization in Product Line Engineering (VISPLE at SPLC), Product Line Approaches in SE (PLEASE at ICSE), Model-driven Product Line Engineering (MAPLE at SPLC),

Model-driven Engineering of Embedded Systems (MOMPES at ASE), and Consistency Management ("Living with Inconsistencies" at ASE). Goetz holds a Diploma in Computer Science (Diplom-Informatiker) and a PhD in Computer Science both from the University of Koblenz-Landau, Germany.

Paolo Bottoni
Paolo Bottoni, Ph.D. in Computer Science from University of Turin, is an associate professor at the Department of Computer Science of the Sapienza University of Rome. His research interests are in the area of interactive computing, and include: definition of pictorial and visual languages, visual simulation, formal models of visual interactive computing, multimedia applications for creative processes and fruition of cultural heritage. On these topics, he has published 150 scientific papers in international journals, contributed volumes and conference proceedings. He participated as partner, responsible or consultant in many international EC projects and national projects. He has been in the program committee and reviewer of several conferences and international journals, program chair of several workshops and guest editor of special issues of international journals. He is in the Steering Committee of the ICGT and AVI international conference series and a member of the Editorial Board of the Journal of Visual Languages and Computing. His e-mail address is bottoni@di.uniroma1.it and his web-page is http://w3.uniroma1.it/dipinfo/scheda_docente.asp?cognome=Bottoni\&nome=Paolo

Kai Breiner
Kai Breiner holds a diploma degree in Computer Science of the University of Kaiserslautern. Since August 2006, he has been working as a scientist at the Software Engineering Research Group at the computer science department of the University of Kaiserslautern as well as at the Fraunhofer-Institute for Experimental Software Engineering (IESE) with focus on Usability and Requirements Engineering. He is involved in teaching and research activities in the field of Software Engineering. Since 2008, he has been lecturer of a distant study course concerning Software Engineering for Embedded Systems. He was co-organizer of the workshop on Intelligent User Interfaces for Ambient Assisted Living (IUI4AAL) at IUI 2008, the MDDAUI workshop at IUI 2009, co-organizer of the MDDAUI workshop at CHI 2010 and a session on Ambient Assisted Living at USAB 2009.

Karin Coninx
Karin Coninx is full professor at Hasselt University, leading the Human-Computer Interaction group of the Expertise Centre for Digital Media (EDM). Her research interests include Context-Aware User Interfaces, Model-Based and User-Centered Software Engineering, Mobile Guides, Ubiquitous Computing, Multimodal interaction and flexible development of Virtual Environments. An overview of publications can be found at http://www.edm.uhasselt.be/karin.coninx.

Sylvain Degrandsart
Sylvain Degrandsart is a Ph.D. candidate at the Ansymo research group of the University of Antwerp. He is mainly interested in applying software engineering techniques in the domain of context-sensitive interactive application. This leads

him to make his research between the Software Engineering Lab of University of Mons where he obtained his Master degree in 2007, the Expertise Centre for Digital Media of University of Hasselt and the Ansymo group.

Serge Demeyer

Serge Demeyer is a professor at the University of Antwerp (Department of Mathematics and Computer Science) where he leads a research group investigating the theme of "Software Reengineering" (LORE - Lab On REengineering). His main research interest concerns software engineering (more precisely, reengineering in an object-oriented context) but due to historical reasons he maintains a heavy interest in hypermedia systems as well. He is an active member of the corresponding international research communities, serving in various conference organization and program committees. He has written a book entitled "Object-Oriented Reengineering" and edited a book on "Software Evolution". He also authored a considerable amount of peer reviewed articles, some of them in highly respected scientific journals. He completed his M.Sc. in 1987 and his Ph.D. in 1996, both at the "Vrije Universiteit Brussel". After his Ph.D., he worked for three years in Switzerland, where he served as a technical coordinator of an European research project. During 2009-2010 he had a sabbatical leave at the University of Zurich in the research group SEAL.

Emmanuel Dubois

Emmanuel Dubois received a Ph.D. in Computing Science from the University of Grenoble in 2001. He is now Assistant Professor at the University of Toulouse – Tarbes (France). His research domain is the Design and Engineering of Human Computer Interaction and more specifically advanced forms of HCI, including Tangible and Augmented Reality systems. During the last decade, he has been working on the definition of methods and models for the design of user's interaction with Mixed Interactive Systems, i.e. systems combining physical and digital artifacts.

Juergen Falb

Juergen Falb joined the Institute of Computer Technology in 1999. He was involved in many projects where he gained experiences in the software development of distributed systems, communication systems and user interface frameworks. His current research interests include bridging the gap between software engineering and human-computer interaction, and model-driven development in the human-computer interaction area. He received his Dr. techn. from the Vienna University of Technology with a thesis on a model-driven development method for nomadic interactive systems.

Guillaume Gauffre

Guillaume Gauffre received a Ph.D. in Computing Science from the University of Toulouse in 2009. His research domain is Human Computer Interaction and more specifically tangible and augmented user interfaces. His primary research focus is on the coupling of abstract design resources, used in the early stages of such interactive system developments, with concrete implementation resources such as API and software components. His approach is largely based on Model Driven Engineering methods and tools.

Pascual González

He got his Ph.D in Computer Science from the University Polytechnic of Madrid in 1999. Currently, he is the general manager of the Science and Technology Park of Albacete, which fosters technology transferring between research institutes and companies. He has worked as an analyst and a project manager for different companies. Since 1991, he has been a teacher and a researcher at the University of Castilla-La Mancha teaching courses related with Software Engineering and Human-Computer Interaction. He is the head of the research group (Laboratory of User Interfaces and Software Engineering - LoUISE) and he is the leader of several national and regional projects. He is the author of different papers in relevant international conferences and journals indexed in JCR regarding user interfaces design including, but not limited to, XML-based user interfaces description languages and user interfaces generation for different target platforms following a model-driven approach.

Esther Guerra

Esther Guerra got her Ph.D. in Computer Science from Universidad Autónoma (Madrid). From 2010, she is working as an assistant professor in the Computer Science Department of the Universidad Autónoma in Madrid. Previously, she worked in the Computer Science Department at Carlos III University in Madrid. She has been a doctoral researcher at the Institute of Theoretical Computer Science (TU Berlin) and at the University of Rome Sapienza, as well as a post-doctoral researcher at the University of York (UK). Her research interests focus on formal techniques in model-driven development primarily for model transformation, meta-modeling, and formalization of software patterns. Her e-mail address is Esther.Guerra@uam.es and her web-page is http://www.ii.uam.es/~guerra.

Mieke Haesen

Mieke Haesen is a Ph.D. student at Hasselt University, where she is a member of the Expertise Centre for Digital Media (EDM). In 2007, she started her Ph.D. which concerns user-centred software engineering techniques that support the co-operation within multidisciplinary teams. Besides these topics, her research interests include model-based user interface development and multimedia content retrieval. More on her research can be found at http://research.edm.uhasselt.be/mhaesen.

Heinrich Hussmann

Heinrich Hussmann holds a diploma degree in Computer Science from Munich University of Technology and a doctoral degree from University of Passau. He did research and education work at universities in Munich, Passau and Dresden. For several years, he worked as a systems engineer and team leader in the telecommunications industry. From 1997 to 2002, he was full professor for Computer

Science at Dresden University of Technology, and since March 2003, he is full professor for Computer Science (Media Informatics) at Ludwig Maximilians University of Munich (LMU). He is member of the program committee of the UML/MODELS conferences since 1999 and currently chairman of the steering committee for this conference. During the last five years, the focus of his work has become the border area between software technology and human-computer interaction, leading to a number of publications in the HCI community, also at the CHI conference.

Hermann Kaindl

Hermann Kaindl joined this institute at the Vienna University of Technology in early 2003 as a full professor. In the same year, he was elected as a member of the University Senate. Prior to moving to academia, he was a senior consultant with the division of program and systems engineering at Siemens AG Austria. There, he has gained more than 24 years of industrial experience in software development. His current research interests include software and systems engineering focusing on requirements engineering and architecting, and human-computer interaction as it relates to interaction design and automated generation of user interfaces. He has published four books and more than a hundred refereed papers in journals, books and conference proceedings. He is a Senior Member of the IEEE, a Distinguished Scientist member of the ACM, Fellow of the IARIA and a member of the INCOSE, and is on the executive board of the Austrian Society for Artificial Intelligence.

Sevan Kavaldjian

Sevan Kavaldjian was born in the year 1979 in Vienna, Austria. After he finished the Fachhochschulstudiengang in Electronics at the Technikum Wien, he started studying at the Vienna University of Technology in 2003. Since October 2005, he is a research assistant at the Institute of Computer Technology and deals with model-driven generation of user interfaces within the projects ONTOUCP and REDSEEDS.

Juan de Lara

Juan de Lara is an associate professor at the Computer Science Department of the Universidad Autónoma in Madrid, where he teaches Software Engineering, Model-Driven Development, and Automata Theory. He holds a Ph.D. degree in Computer Science, and works in areas such as modeling and simulation, meta-modeling, visual languages and graph transformation. He has been a post-doctoral researcher at the MSDL lab (McGill University), the institute of theoretical computer science (TU Berlin), the department of computer science of the University of Rome Sapienza and the University of York (UK). His e-mail address is Juan.deLara@uam.es and his web-page is http://www.ii.uam.es/~jlara.

Grzegorz Lehmann

Grzegorz Lehmann is a Ph.D. student at the DAI-Labor of the Technische Universität Berlin. His research focuses on the model based development and design of multimodal user interfaces. In his Ph.D. thesis, Grzegorz intends to thoroughly explore the benefits and disadvantages of the application of executable models to user interface development, which he started to investigate in his diploma thesis titled "Model Driven Runtime Architecture for Plastic User Interfaces". As the gap between the design and run time is being closed, he is particularly interested in the impact of this process on topics such as end-user development, self-adaptive UIs and UI plasticity.

Víctor López-Jaquero

Víctor López-Jaquero got his Ph.D in Computer Science from the University of Castilla-La Mancha in 2005. He is a teacher and a researcher at the University of Castilla-La Mancha teaching courses related with Data Bases and Human-Computer Interaction. His research activities are focused on human-computer interaction and more specifically on adaptable and adaptive user interface design following a model-driven approach and multi-agent systems to support the adaptation facilities. He is author of more than 40 papers in relevant conferences and journal indexed in JCR regarding user interfaces design including, but not limited to, XML-based user interfaces description languages and user interfaces generation for different target platforms following a model-driven approach, adaptive and adaptable user interfaces and multi-agent systems.

Kris Luyten

Kris Luyten is a professor at Hasselt University, where he is a member of the Expertise Centre for Digital Media (EDM). His main research interests are Context-Aware User Interfaces, User Interface Description Languages, Model-Based and User-Centered Interface Development, Multi-touch Interaction, Mobile Guides, Ubiquitous Computing and Social and Collaborative Software. More on his research can be found at http://research.edm.uhasselt.be/kris.

Célia Martinie

Célia Martinie is Ph.D. candidate in Informatics at the University Paul Sabatier (2009 -). Previously, she has been at Motorola Mobile Devices for 8 years (2001-2009) working as a software engineer in the design and development of embedded services and innovative technologies for mobile systems. She holds a Master degree in Electronics and Telecommunications from the EPF Engineering School, Sceaux, France (2001) and a Master of Philosophy in Digital Telecommunications Systems from the Telecom ParisTech School, France (2001). Her current research interests focus on model-based approaches to design and evaluate interactive systems. Other topics of interest include software engineering, formal methods and safety critical systems. Further information at: http://www.irit.fr/~Celia.Martinie/

Gerrit Meixner

Gerrit Meixner got his diploma and his Master degree in Computer Science from the University of Applied Sciences Trier and a doctoral degree in Mechanical Engineering from the University of Kaiserslautern. Currently, he is a senior researcher and group supervisor for Human-Machine-Interaction at the German

Research Center for Artificial Intelligence (DFKI) in Kaiserslautern, Germany. His main research interests are in the field of model-driven development of user interfaces and usability-engineering. On these topics, he has published more than 45 scientific papers in journals, contributed volumes and conference proceedings. He has been in the program committee and reviewer of several conferences and international journals. Furthermore, he co-organizes the workshop series on Model-Driven Development of Advanced User Interfaces and is co-workshop chair at the EICS 2011. Actually, he is a member of the W3C "Model-based User Interfaces" Incubator Group and a member of different organizations, including the "Association for Computing Machinery" (ACM), "Gesellschaft für Informatik" (German Computer Science Society, GI) and the "German Usability Professionals Association" (German UPA).

Jan Meskens
Jan Meskens is a Ph.D. researcher at the Expertise Centre for Digital Media (EDM), a research institute of Hasselt University. Jan has been working with the User Interface Markup Language (UIML) since 2006, and created the Gummy multi-device design tool on top of UIML. His research interests revolve mainly around model-driven UI design, multi-device user interface design tools and automatic user interface generation. More on his research can be found at http://research.edm.uhasselt.be/jmeskens.

Francisco Montero
He got his Ph.D in Computer Science from the University of Castilla-La Mancha in 2005. He is a teacher and a researcher at the University of Castilla-La Mancha teaching courses related with Software Engineering and Human-Computer Interaction. His research activities are focused on human-computer interaction, and more specifically on usability and the generation of user interfaces following a model-driven approach considering a quality model to improve the overall usability and accessibility of the systems. He is author of more than 40 papers in relevant conferences and journal indexed in JCR regarding user interfaces design including, but not limited to, XML-based user interfaces description languages and user interfaces generation for different target platforms following a model-driven approach, quality models and usability.

Philippe Palanque
Philippe Palanque Palanque is Professor in Computer Science at the University Toulouse 3 and is head of the Interactive Critical Systems research group in Toulouse. He has been and is still involved in research projects dealing with the notations and tools for the formal description of real-time interactive systems (including Command and Control systems for drones, multimodal interfaces for military cockpits, new civil interactive cockpits, …) as well as air traffic control and satellite ground segments. He edited and co-edited twelve books or conference proceedings. As for conferences, he is general chair of HCI in Aeronautics (HCI Aero 2010) and of IFIP INTERACT 2011. He is member of the Executive Committee and of the Conference Management Committee of ACM SIGCHI as well as

French representative in the IFIP TC 13 on HCI. He is the author and co-author of more than 100 international peer-reviewed publications (available at http://www.irit.fr/~Philippe .Palanque/publications.html).

Fabio Paternò

Fabio Paternò is Research Director at CNR-ISTI, where he leads the HIIS Laboratory. He has long been working on model-based design and evaluation of interactive applications. In 2000, he published a book on this topic. He has been the scientific coordinator of five European Projects. He is currently working in the exploitation of model-based approaches for ubiquitous multi-device applications. He is an ACM Distinguished Scientist and the Chair of the IFIP WG Group 2.7/13.4 on User Interface Engineering. He has been member of the Programme Committee of the main international HCI conferences, including ACM EICS 2011.

Andreas Pleuss

Andreas Pleuss holds a diploma in computer science from the Technical University of Dresden and a doctoral degree from University of Munich. From 2002 to 2008, he worked as research and teaching associate at the Media Informatics Group at University of Munich (LMU). Since 2009, he is a Research Fellow at Lero - The Irish Software Engineering Centre at University of Limerick in Ireland. His main research interests lie in model-driven development, software product lines, and user interface engineering. He is in particular interested in approaches integrating software engineering and human-computer interaction principles, leading to a systematic engineering of high quality interactive applications. He co-organizes the workshop series on Model-Driven Development of Advanced User Interfaces and is involved in different events in both areas software engineering and human-computer interaction.

Roman Popp

Roman Popp was born 1976 in Vienna, Austria. He studied electrical engineering and specialized later on in computer science. He received his MS-Degree from the University of Technology Vienna in March 2003 with distinction. In January 2003, he joined the Institute of Computer Technology as a research assistant and is currently working in the field of "Communication Platforms" and "User Interface Generation".

David Raneburger

David Raneburger was born in the year 1982 in Vienna, Austria. He studied electrical engineering at the Vienna University of Technology. He specialized later on in the field of computer technology. He graduated with the degree MSc. from the Vienna University of Technology in January 2009. He wrote his thesis on the topic of automated user interface generation. Since October 2008, he is working as a research assistant at the Institute of Computer Technology. His main research interest is in the field of model driven UI development.

Dirk Roscher
Dirk Roscher is a researcher and Ph.D. student at the DAI-Labor of the Technische Universität Berlin. He is working in the HCI group of the DAI-Labor and participated in several research projects funded, e.g., by the German government or the Deutsche Telekom. His research focuses on the model based specification of ubiquitous user interfaces and their runtime adaptation in smart environments. Dirk currently examines issues of runtime distribution of user interfaces between different interaction devices and modalities, the fusion of user input at runtime as well as topics regarding meta user interfaces.

Carmen Santoro
Carmen Santoro is a researcher for the HIIS Laboratory of CNR in Pisa, Italy. She graduated in Computer Science from the University of Pisa, and gained a Ph.D. in Computer Science from University of Toulouse 1, France in 2004. Her research interests include methods and tools for the analysis, design, development and evaluation of interactive multimodal and multi-platform applications. She has published papers for international conferences and journals on HCI, and she has been reviewer for international HCI journals. Currently, she is Program Committee Member for EICS 2011 conference, and Editorial board member of "International Journal of Handheld Computing Research" journal.

Stefan Sauer
Stefan Sauer is senior researcher and executive manager of the Software Quality Lab (s-lab), a joint private-public research institute for software engineering at the University of Paderborn, Germany. Before he got this position in 2005, he worked as a research and teaching associate in the computer science department of the same university. He received a Diplom-Informatiker degree in 1997 from the University of Oldenburg, Germany. While he was a computer science student, he spent one year as a visiting scholar at the University of Southern California, USA. His main areas of work are model-centric software engineering, meta-modeling, domain-specific languages, software specification techniques, user-oriented software engineering, software processes, and method engineering.

Marc Seissler
Marc Seissler received his diploma in 2009 from the University of Kaiserslautern, in which he introduced a semi-automatically process for transforming task-models into dialog models. Since July 2009, he works as a researcher at the Center for Human-Machine-Interaction (ZMMI) at the University of Kaiserslautern where his focus is on the integration of knowledge representations within the model-based development of user interfaces.

Kenia Sousa
Kênia Sousa has a Ph.D. in Economics and Management Sciences from Louvain School of Management at Université catholique de Louvain, Belgium where she worked with the definition of a methodology for the alignment of user interfaces with business processes aiming to optimize processes and improve user

experience. She has a Master degree in Applied Computing at University of Fortaleza, Brazil with emphasis on a software development process that encompasses usability aspects. She also has a Bachelor's degree in Computer Science at University of Fortaleza, Brazil. She has been working with Human-Computer Interaction (HCI) since 2002, specializing in the integration of HCI with Software Engineering and Business Process Management, contributing with around 30 publications in journals, scientific and industrial international conferences. In the industry, she has provided consulting services for software organizations in the areas of software development process and software quality. During her Ph.D., she has done applied research, interacting with large organizations in the banking and telecommunications sectors for the application of the proposed methodology. As a recognition of the results achieved by this work, she has received the IBM PhD Fellowship Award in 2009.

Lucio Davide Spano
Lucio Davide Spano was born in 1983, in Tempio Pausania, Italy. He graduated cum laude in Computer Science Tecnologies at the University of Pisa in 2009 and he is currently a Ph.D. student at the Computer Science Department of the University of Pisa. He belongs to the research staff at the Human Interface in Information System laboratory of the ISTI-CNR in Pisa and is involved in the EU project ServFace and in the development of the UIDL MariaXML.

Veit Schwartze
Veit Schwartze is a Ph.D. student at the DAI-Labor of the Technische Universität Berlin, currently working in a project focused on the design and development of user friendly multimodal user interfaces for the home environment. His main focus is the model-based development of user interfaces, especially the context aware adaptation of graphical user interfaces.

Gerd Szwillus
Gerd Szwillus studied Computer Science in the 1970's at the University of Dortmund. In 1984, he finished his Ph.D. in Computer Science with a dissertation about an efficient scanning algorithm. In 1990, he was habilitated at the University of Dortmund for his work on generating graphical structure editors. He was appointed to a professorship at the University of Paderborn in 1991 and since then has worked in the field of modeling user interfaces, tools for user interface development and usability engineering. A strong emphasis of his working group is on task modeling and its use for evaluating, specifying, and simulating user interface software and web sites. Other modeling levels have been worked on as well intensively, including interface builders, dialog modeling tools, and modeling tools for the special area of user interfaces of safety-critical systems. Since recently the group works intensively in the field of innovative clients for document management systems, including multi-touch table user interfaces.

Jan Van den Bergh

Jan Van den Bergh is a senior researcher at Hasselt University, where he is a member of the Expertise Centre for Digital Media (EDM). He obtained his Ph.D. at transnationale Universiteit Limburg in 2006. His main research interests are context-aware user interfaces, model-driven and user-centered development of user interfaces and social and collaborative interactive software. An overview of publications can be found at http://www.edm.uhasselt.be/jan.van_den_bergh.

Jean Vanderdonckt

Jean Vanderdonckt is Professor of Computer Science at the Louvain School of Management of Université catholique de Louvain, Belgium where he leads the Belgian Laboratory of Computer-Human Interaction (BCHI- http://www.isys.ucl.ac.be/bchi). This laboratory is conducting research, development, and consulting services in the domain of user interface engineering. This domain is located at the crossroads of software engineering, human-computer interaction, and usability engineering of multimodal interfaces. Current topics of interest include: user interface forward and reverse engineering, context-aware computing, multimodal interaction, mixed reality systems, user interface adaptation, model-driven engineering. He is coordinating the UsiXML Consortium (www.usixml.org) supported by the Similar network of excellence (www.similar.cc), in which he is coordinating the HCI activities. He is also a member of the COST n°294 European action.

Marco Antonio Alba Winckler

Marco Antonio Alba Winckler is lecturer in Computer Science at the University Toulouse 3. He came to Toulouse, France in 2000 to work in his Ph.D. thesis (completed in 2004) whose main focus is the navigation modeling of complex Web applications. During the master thesis, he worked on remote usability evaluation methods to support the assessment of Web-based interactive systems. His current research mingles Human-Computer Interaction methods and Software Engineering methods applied to the development of Web-based interactive systems. His goal is to propose models, methods and techniques to support the development of usable, sound and effective Web applications. Most recent projects include methods to design and evaluate e-services applications for e-Government initiatives and formal description techniques to deal with navigation modeling of Web applications. Other topics of interest are: Automation of guidelines inspection; Model-based usability evaluation; Navigation and dialogue formal modeling; Task models. Further information at: http://www.irit.fr/~Marco.Winckler

Model-Driven Useware Engineering

Gerrit Meixner, Marc Seissler, and Kai Breiner

Abstract. User-oriented hardware and software development relies on a systematic development process based on a comprehensive analysis focusing on the users' requirements and preferences. Such a development process calls for the integration of numerous disciplines, from psychology and ergonomics to computer sciences and mechanical engineering. Hence, a correspondingly interdisciplinary team must be equipped with suitable software tools to allow it to handle the complexity of a multimodal and multi-device user interface development approach. An abstract, model-based development approach seems to be adequate for handling this complexity. This approach comprises different levels of abstraction requiring adequate tool support. Thus, in this chapter, we present the current state of our model-based software tool chain. We introduce the use model as the core model of our model-based process, transformation processes, and a model-based architecture, and we present different software tools that provide support for creating and maintaining the models or performing the necessary model transformations.

1 Introduction

Considering the interaction with technical devices such as a computer or a machine control panel, the users actually interact with a subset of these hardware and software components, which, in their entirety, make up the user interface [1]. Unfortunately, today's developers often disregard the most important component of

Gerrit Meixner
German Research Center for Artificial Intelligence (DFKI), Trippstadter Str. 122, 67663, Kaiserslautern, Germany
e-mail: Gerrit.Meixner@dfki.de

Marc Seissler
University of Kaiserslautern, Center for Human-Machine-Interaction, Gottlieb-Daimler Str. 42, 67663, Kaiserslautern, Germany
e-mail: Marc.Seissler@mv.uni-kl.de

Kai Breiner
University of Kaiserslautern, Software Engineering Research Group, Gottlieb-Daimler Str. 42, 67663, Kaiserslautern, Germany
e-mail: Breiner@cs.uni-kl.de

H. Hussmann et al. (Eds.): MDD of Advanced User Interfaces, SCI 340, pp. 1–26.
springerlink.com   © Springer-Verlag Berlin Heidelberg 2011

an interactive system – the user – because of their inability to put themselves into the position of a user. Since usability, which is perceived in a subjective way, depends on various factors such as skills or experience, the user interface will be perceived by each user in a completely different way.

Moreover, in a highly competitive market that brings forth technically and functionally more and more similar or equal devices, usability as an additional sales argument secures a competitive advantage. In order to put stronger emphasis on users' and customers' needs, wishes, working styles, requirements, and preferences, and in order to consider them right from the beginning in all phases of the device development process, the responsible professional organizations in Germany, i.e., GfA, GI, VDE-ITG, and VDI/VDE-GMA, coined the term "Useware" for the above-mentioned subset and intersection of hardware and software, back in 1998 already [2].

The development of user interfaces for interactive software systems is a time consuming and therefore costly task, which is shown in a study [3]. By analyzing a number of different software applications, it was found that about 48% of the source code, about 45% of the development time, about 50% of the implementation time, and about 37% of the maintenance time is required for aspects regarding user interfaces. Petrasch argues that the time effort needed for implementing user interfaces – even 15 years after the study by Myers et al. [3] – is still at least 50% [4]. He justifies that the spread of interactive systems as well as their requirements have drastically increased over the last years. To be able to enforce the development of user interfaces more efficiently, a methodical procedure with an early focus on user and task requirements was seen as necessary.

Therefore, the systematic Useware Engineering Process, which calls for a comprehensive user, task, and use context analysis preceding the actual development, was developed [5]. Later in the Useware Engineering Process, interdisciplinary teams composed, for instance, of computer scientists, mechanical engineers, psychologists, and designers, continue developing the respective device in close collaboration with the ordering customer and its clients by constantly providing prototypes even in the very early development phases, thereby facilitating continuous, parallel evaluation (as depicted in Fig. 1).

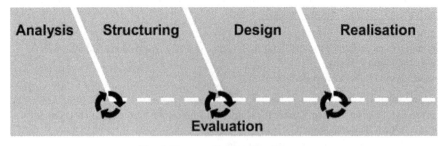

Fig. 1 Useware Engineering Process

The development process is determined by the procedure of ISO 13407 (user centered design) and follows the policy of ISO 9241-110 (dialog principles). In the analyzing phase, the characteristics and behaviors of current and prospective users are defined using different methods, i.e., interviews, observations, task analysis, or surveys. At first, individual task models as well as communalities and differences between the user groups are derived from the requirements and behaviors while the system is used. Additionally, such issues as environmental and working conditions, team and labor organizations, as well as domain-specific context are explored during the analysis. Data elicited during the analysis can be entered, saved, analyzed, and exported using appropriate tools [6]. First of all, the structuring phase concentrates on harmonization and manual conflation of the individual task models and user requirements in order to obtain a common, system comprehensive, platform-independent use model. This model describes, e.g., what kinds of tasks can be performed or are allowed, for example for user groups at specific locations with specific devices. On the basis of classification, prioritization, and temporal relation of the tasks, an abstract operating structure is specified initially and saved in the XML-based Useware Markup Language [6]. The structure evaluation is an important and determining part of this phase. It guarantees the conformity of the harmonized structure and temporal sequences with the mental models of the users. It is already possible to simultaneously generate first preliminary models as well as executable use models for evaluation goals based on the use models and to test them by having the user use the respective software tools [7]. After the structuring phase, the actual design takes place. With the help of the user requirements and the results of the analysis, concepts of visualization, navigation, and interaction are chosen and combined appropriately. The design of coarse mask layouts is finally followed by the fine design of the ergonomically designed user masks, with the focus being on providing efficient support for the user as well as information brokering in a quick and systematic way in order to offer the user adequate decision-making aids. In parallel to the fine design, the realization starts, meaning the concrete implementation of the developed concepts into a user interface using the selected hard- and software platforms. The parallel evaluation represents a continuation of the analysis phase [8], since the development results are tested and evaluated continuously with structural or executable prototypes in every phase of the development process by representative users. To ensure that each user evaluation is taken into account, the user interfaces are improved iteratively. Adjustments to the use model can be made by returning from later phases to earlier ones, for example.

Any process is useless if developers do not adhere to it or accidently execute the process in a wrong way. To support the correct execution of the Useware Engineering Process, tools are indispensable. Furthermore, the constantly increasing number of heterogeneous platforms (PC, smart phone, PDA, etc.) is another reason why user interfaces have to be kept consistent with each other in relation to user experience on such target platforms in order to guarantee intuitional handling and thus ensure usability [9]. Since usability is a subjectively experienced nonfunctional requirement, there is no such thing as a best user interaction concept. In order to reduce the recurrent development effort of individual solutions for specific platforms, modalities, or even context of use, a model-based approach – which facilitates reusability – can be taken, focusing on the needs and requirements of the users. This allows developers to generate prototypes of the user interface on the basis of the use model from the very beginning of their work.

In the subsequent sections, we will first discuss related work, followed by a section that focuses on supporting user interface developers during development time. Then we will introduce the CAMELEON Reference Framework as a meta architecture for model-based user interface development and subsequently present our derived model-based architecture. Furthermore, we will introduce useML 2.0 and the graphical useML-editor "Udit". Targeting the transition from the use model to the abstract user interface design, we present the Dialog and Interface Specification Language (DISL). Furthermore, we will introduce the User Interface Markup Language (UIML), which represents the concrete user interface. Additionally, we will introduce two mapping approaches: from useML to DISL and from DISL to UIML. Finally, we provide an outlook on currently developed as well as planned extensions to the tool chain.

2 Related Work

Many problems and limitations of current model-based architectures are a consequence of focusing too much on just one model [10]. For example, MECANO [11] and TRIDENT [12], [13] are architectures that do not integrate different discrete models.

TADEUS [14], [15] is an architecture and development environment for the development of user interfaces considering the application functionality as well as task modeling aspects. The dialog and the presentation model are generated from the task model on the basis of predefined classifications. The focus of TADEUS is on modeling application functionality. Regarding temporal operators, TADEUS only integrates a sequence operator.

GLADIS+ [16] and ADEPT [17] are architectures for model-based development on the basis of task models. The overall usability of these architectures is rather low. These architectures make use of classical formal models, such as entity relation (ER) models, to drive the greatest possible degree of automation regarding the user interface design process. As a consequence, only user interfaces with poor visual presentation can be generated [18].

In MOBI-D [19], an informal textual representation of the task and domain model is used to start the development process. MOBI-D is rather a set of tools than an architecture, and generates (semi-)automatic user interfaces [20]. MOBI-D cannot be used for developing multi-platform or multi-modality user interfaces.

One of the most recent architectures and XML-based development environments for multi-modal user interfaces is the Transformation Environment for inteRactivE Systems representAtions (TERESA) [21], [22]. Basically, TERESA consists of a task- and presentation model. On the basis of an abstract description of the task model in the ConcurTaskTree (CTT) notation [23], a developer is able to (semi-)automatically develop platform-specific task models, abstract presentation models, concrete presentation models, and finally HTML source code [24]. TERESA was developed as a monolithic development environment with an integrated simulator for evaluating models. The focus of TERESA, based on the task model specified with CTT, is on supporting developers by offering different tools [25], [20]. Besides the task model, the developers need to specify further design decisions in order to transform the task model into a presentation model (specified with TeresaXML [26]). Interaction tasks in CTT do not contain the necessary semantics for transforming tasks into abstract interaction objects fully automatically [20], [9]. Furthermore, transformation processes are integrated directly into the source code of TERESA, which reduces the flexibility of the transformation processes in terms of extension, modification, and maintenance [27]. In TERESA, finite state machines are used to describe the dialog model, which is therefore quite limited in its expressiveness [28]. Recent work has been about the development of MARIA [29], the successor of TERESA.

Similar to TERESA, DYGIMES (Dynamically Generating Interfaces for Mobile and Embedded Systems) [20] is an architecture for the development of user interfaces based on different XML-compliant languages. DYGIMES aims at simplifying the development process by clearly separating the user interfaces from the application functionality. Furthermore, DYGIMES aims at reducing the complexity of the different models used. The focus of DYGIMES is on the automatic generation of a dialog and presentation model from a task model specified with CTT at runtime. The dialog and presentation model is described with SeescoaXML (Software Engineering for Embedded Systems using a Component-Oriented Approach) [25]. Task models are also specified with CTT, which needs additional abstract UI descriptions [20] to transform the task model into a dialog and presentation model. Luyten adapts the Enabled Task Sets (ETS) approach from Paternò [23] and introduces an optimized ETS-calculation algorithm [9]. After ETS calculation, designers can specify spatial layout constraints, which allow expressing how the single UI building blocks are grouped and aligned at the user interfaces. Finally, the generated user interfaces are rendered by a light-weight runtime environment running, for example, on the target mobile device.

3 Useware Engineering at Development Time

In this section, we will give a short overview of the CAMELEON reference framework – which is a well-established refinement framework for the systematic development of user interfaces on the basis of different models. In accordance with the refinement steps of this particular framework, we will introduce our architecture as a concrete instantiation of the CAMELEON reference framework.

3.1 CAMELEON – A Reference Framework

For many years, there has been much intensive research on using model-based development methodologies in the development of user interfaces [30]. These methodologies are very similar to model-based approaches in the domain of software engineering. Key aspects like model abstraction and using transformations to automatically generate further models or source code (e.g., used in Model Driven Architecture (MDA) in software engineering) are also important factors in the development of consistent user interfaces [7].

The CAMELEON reference framework was developed by the EU-funded CAMELEON project [31]. It describes a framework that serves as a reference for classifying user interfaces that support multiple targets, or multiple contexts of use on the basis of a model-based approach. The framework covers both the design time and runtime phases of multi-target user interfaces. Furthermore, the CAMELEON reference framework provides a unified understanding of context sensitive user interfaces rather than a prescription of various ways or methods for tackling different steps of development.

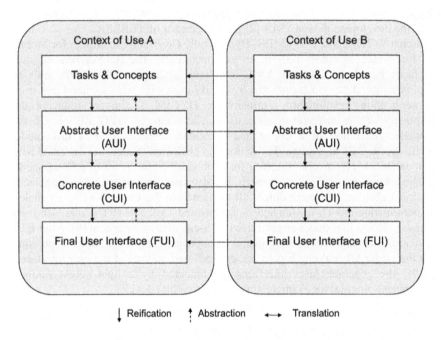

Fig. 2 The CAMELEON Reference Framework

As depicted in Fig. 2, the framework describes different layers of abstraction, which are important for model-based development of user interfaces, and their relationships among each other [32]:

- The **Task and Concepts level** considers, e.g., the hierarchies of tasks that need to be performed in a specific temporal order in order to achieve the users' goals (during the interaction with a user interface).
- The **Abstract User Interface** (AUI) expresses the user interface in terms of abstract interaction objects (AIO) [12]. These AIOs are independent of any platform or modality (e.g., graphical, vocal, haptic). Furthermore, AIOs can be grouped logically.
- The **Concrete User Interface** (CUI) expresses the user interface in terms of concrete interaction objects (CIO). These CIOs are modality

dependent but platform independent. The CUI defines more concretely how the user interface is perceived by the users.

• The **Final User Interface** (FUI) expresses the user interface in terms of platform-dependent source code. A FUI can be represented in any pro-gramming language (e.g., Java) or mark-up language (e.g., HTML). A FUI can then be interpreted or compiled.

Between these levels, there are different relationships: *reification* (forward engi-neering), *abstraction* (reverse engineering), and *translation* (between different contexts of use).

Fig. 3 shows an example (a simple graphical log-in screen) of the different lay-ers of the CAMELEON reference framework. Starting with the "task & concepts" layer modeling the log-in task, the AUI, CUI, and FUI layers can be (semi-) automatically derived via transformations.

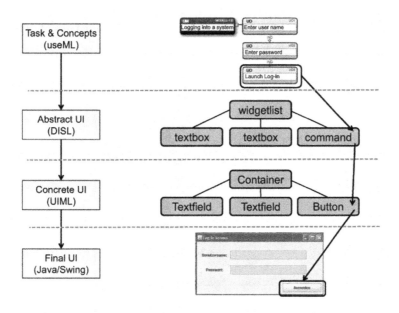

Fig. 3 A simple example showing the different layers

3.2 An Architecture for the Model-Based Useware Engineering Process

Different models are required in model-based development of user interfaces. The entity of models used is known as "interface model" and consists of different ab-stract and concrete models [30]. Abstract models are, e.g., the user model (represents different user groups, for example), the platform model (specifies target platforms), the context model (describes the context of use), as well as the task model (describes tasks and actions of the user). The visualization of the user interface is defined by the presentation model. It specifies how visual, haptic, or voice interaction objects of the user interfaces are specified. The dialog model is the link between the task model and the presentation model. It describes the operating sequence, the starting point, the goal, and the results that control the process of the user interface. Furthermore, the presentation model and the dialog model are divided into an abstract and a concrete model part. Especially the abstract presentation and dialog models are characterized by a lack of references to specific modalities and platforms. As a result, transformations into any modality or platform can be realized.

The CAMELEON reference framework is the starting point for developing and integrating our own model-based architecture. This reference framework leaves open aspects regarding the practical composition of models and how to use them in user-centered development processes (such as the Useware Engineering Process). Therefore, we adapted the framework and developed our own model-based architecture, which integrates perfectly into the different phases of the Useware Engineering Process (see Fig. 4).

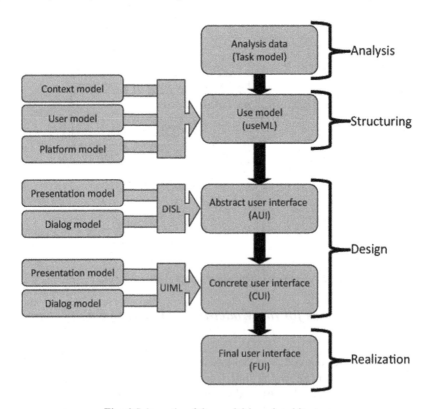

Fig. 4 Schematic of the model-based architecture

The first step consists of a survey of elicited analysis data, from which the task models of the individual users can be extracted. After harmonizing the analysis data, task models are combined (manually) during the structuring phase into a singular use model (see sections 3.3 and 3.4), which also integrates other abstract models (e.g., context, user, and platform model). Together, the analysis and structuring phases can be mapped to the "task & concepts" layer of the CAMELEON reference framework. The abstract user interface is built on the basis of the abstract presentation model and the abstract dialog model, which can be described using the Dialog and Interface Specification Language (DISL) (see section 3.5). With DISL, it is possible to describe platform- and modality-independent user interfaces during the design phase (abstract user interface). With the standardized User Interface Markup Language (UIML), concrete graphical user interfaces (design phase) can be described (see section 3.6). In our architecture, UIML covers the concrete presentation model as well as the concrete dialog model. By making use of an appropriate generic vocabulary [33], it is possible to transform UIML into a final user interface (realization phase) by generating source code or other markup languages (such as HTML) directly.

Although based on models and transformation processes, it is also necessary to integrate further models, transformations, tools, etc. into a holistic view and put them into order. As Schaefer shows, the overall architecture of model-based user interface processes consists of a number of further important components [28]. For the efficient development of user interfaces, respectively for the interactive processing of models, development teams additionally need software support, e.g., a model-based tool chain. This tool chain integrates model transformation engines (see sections 3.7 and 3.8), model editors, knowledge bases, as well as databases. Moreover, an execution environment is required, consisting of layout generators (e.g., for ordering graphical elements), HCI patterns (for reusing the designers' expert knowledge), and source code generators.

Finally, an application skeleton of the user interface can be generated via source code generators in the preferred programming language. This application skeleton can then be extended by functional characteristics until a complete vertical application prototype in a particular development environment is finished. This vertical application prototype can then again be tested iteratively by the users of the interactive system.

3.3 The Useware Markup Language 2.0

The Useware Markup Language (useML) 1.0 [34] was developed to support the user- and task-oriented Useware Engineering Process with a modeling language representing the results of the initial task analysis. Accordingly, the use model abstracts platform-independent tasks into use objects (UO) that make up a hierarchically ordered structure (see Fig. 5). Each element of this structure can be annotated by attributes such as eligible user groups, access rights, and importance. Further annotations and restrictions can be integrated by extending a dynamic part of the use model (e.g., for integrating information from the platform or context model). This functionality makes the use model more flexible than many other task models and their respective task modeling languages (cf. section 2). Furthermore, the leaf tasks of a use model are described with a set of elementary use objects (eUO) representing atomic interactive tasks: inform, trigger, select, enter, and change. In contrast to other task modeling languages such as CTT [23] (see section 2), an eUO refines an interaction task, i.e., an eUO can be mapped directly to a corresponding abstract interaction object in the abstract user interface.

The basic structure of the use model has not been changed since 2004 [34], but the development of a taxonomy for task models and its application to the use model have revealed certain shortcomings and potentials for enhancing the use model extensively [35]. All these enhancements have been incorporated into useML 2.0 as introduced below.

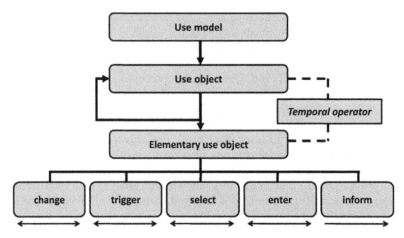

Fig. 5 Schematic of the use model

According to [36], the use model must differentiate between interactive user tasks (performed via the user interface) and pure system tasks requiring no active intervention by the user. System tasks encapsulate tasks that are fulfilled solely by the system – which, however, does not imply that no user interface must be presented, because the user might decide, for example, to abort the system task, or request information about the status of the system. Interactive tasks usually require the user(s) to actively operate the system, but still, there can be tasks that do not have to be fulfilled or may be tackled only under certain conditions. In any case, however, interactive tasks are usually connected to system tasks and the underlying application logic, which has been addressed recently by the newly introduced differentiation of user tasks and system tasks in useML 2.0.

To specify that a certain task is optional, the semantics of the use objects and the elementary use objects has been enhanced to reflect their importance. Their respective user actions can now be marked as "optional" or "required".

Similarly, only useML 2.0 can attribute cardinalities to use objects and elementary use objects. These cardinalities can specify minimum and maximum frequencies of utilization, ranging from 0 for optional tasks up to ∞. Further, respective logical and/or temporal conditions can now be specified, as well as invariants that must be fulfilled at any time during the execution (processing) of a task. Except for useML 2.0, only few task modeling languages are able to specify both logical and temporal conditions. Consequently, temporal operators (see [7]) have been added to useML, which is the most important and most comprehensive enhancement in version 2.0. These operators allow for putting tasks on one hierarchical level into certain explicitly temporal orders; implicitly, temporal operators applied to neighboring levels of the hierarchical structure can form highly complex, temporal expressions. In order to define the minimum number of temporal operators that allows for the broadest range of applications, the temporal operators of 18 task modeling languages were analyzed and compared [37]. Among others, Tombola [38], VTMB [39], XUAN [40], MAD [41], DIANE+ [42], GTA [43], and CTT [23] were examined closely. Based on their temporal operators' relevance and applicability in a model-based development process, the following binary temporal operators were selected for useML 2.0:

- **Choice** (CHO): Exactly one of two tasks will be fulfilled.
- **Order Independence** (IND): The two tasks can be accomplished in any arbitrary order. However, when the first task has been performed, the second one has to wait for the first one to be finalized or aborted.
- **Concurrency** (CON): The two tasks can be accomplished in any arbitrary order, even in parallel at the same time (i.e., concurrently).
- **Deactivation** (DEA): The second task interrupts and deactivates the first task.
- **Sequence** (SEQ): The tasks must be accomplished in the given order. The second task must wait until the first one has been fulfilled.

Since the unambiguous priority of these four temporal operators is crucial for the connection of the use model with a dialog model, their priorities (i.e., their order of temporal execution) have been defined as follows [9]:

Choice > Order Independence > Concurrency > Deactivation > Sequence

3.4   The Graphical useML 2.0-Editor

Editors, simulators, and model transformation tools are needed that allow creating, testing, as well as processing the user interface models. To address these demands, the useML-Editor (Udit) was introduced [7], which allows the graphical editing of useML 2.0 models. Udit enables the developer to create and manipulate use models easily and quickly via a simple, graphical user interface. It further provides a validation mechanism for ensuring the correctness of a use model and the integrity of a use model to be loaded from a useML file. In case of problems, Udit shows appropriate warnings, hints, and error messages (use models created and saved using Udit are always valid).

Using project-specific conditions and constraints, useML provides an external schema attribute definition that can be changed at any time, without necessitating changes to the core useML schema. For example, user group names, personas and roles, locations, device types and specifications, the devices' function models, etc., are highly variable. While these conditions and constraints are specified in an external XML file in useML, Udit provides a schema editor to edit them quickly and easily.

As can be seen in Fig. 6 (left part), the basic elements of the useML 2.0 specification, i.e., use model (root element, black), use objects (orange), active task elementary use objects (green), and elementary use objects of the passive "inform" type (blue), are displayed in different colors. This facilitates the developer's orientation and navigation, especially when a developer works with complex use models. Collapsing and expanding sub-trees of the use model is also possible. The temporal operators are displayed as part of the connection line between two neighboring (elementary) use objects.

Udit has been designed to support the features of the recently revised useML 2.0. Since then, the initial version of Udit has been consistently enhanced. Udit now implements the transformation process from the use model to the abstract user interface. An integrated filter mechanism can be used to automatically derive a specific use model from the basic use model. This specific use model can be refined by the developer, or it can be automatically exported. Additional features, such as drag&drop functionality, a model validation tool, and a zoom function, have been incorporated.

To visualize the dynamic behavior of the use model, a simulator has been integrated in Udit, which can be used to evaluate the behavior of the developed use model. As depicted in Fig. 6 (right part), the simulator is split into four main screens: On the left side of the window, the simulated use model is displayed. The eUOs that are enabled for execution are highlighted in this use model and listed in a box, located in the right upper window. Each of the listed eUOs can be executed by pressing the corresponding "execute" button, which triggers the simulator to load a new set of executable eUOs. Additional features of the simulator include an execution history and a window for displaying conditions.

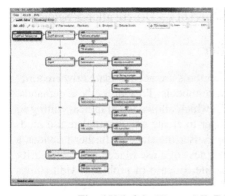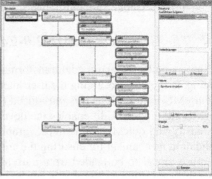

Fig. 6 Udit 2.0 - The useML Editor (left) and Simulator (right)

3.5 The Abstract User Interface

The abstract user interface is modeled with the Dialog and Interface Specification Language (DISL) [44], which was developed at the University of Paderborn (Germany) as a modeling language for platform- and modality-independent user interfaces for mobile devices. DISL focuses on scalability, reactivity, easy usability for developers, and low demands on processing power and memory consumption. An important precondition to the systematic development of user interfaces is the strict separation of structure, presentation, and behavior of a user interface. Since the User Interface Markup Language (UIML) [45] facilitates not only this separation, but also – by employing a XML-based file format – the easy creation of interpreters and development tools, UIML was used as a basis for the development of DISL. Therefore, the basic structure and the syntax of UIML were partially adapted. However, two UIML properties that shall be presented here in more detail did not fulfill the purpose of DISL. These are UIML's limited behavior model and its dependence on platform specifications.

UIML allows for the event-based behavior description of user interfaces. Events like pressing a key can lead to changes in the state of the respective user interface. Therefore, it is possible to specify the behavior of a user interface as a finite state machine in UIML. This is intuitive for simple user interfaces. In bigger projects, the developer is likely to lose track of the exponentially growing number of state transitions. In the past, this has been the reason why mechanisms and notations were introduced that significantly reduce the complexity of the state space, for example by employing parallel state transitions as in [46]. This, however, requires storing complex user interface states, such as "menu item 1 selected AND switch set to C". Instead of storing numerous complex states, DISL introduces state variables, resulting in state transitions being calculated from relevant state variable values at the occurrence of certain events. This also allows for setting state variables arbitrarily during a state transition. Finally, DISL also provides means for specifying time-dependent transitions, which is of high relevance for mobile applications where reactive user interfaces are to be designed even in unreliable networks, e.g., when a waiting period times out and an alternative interaction method must be provided to the user.

The second significant difference between DISL and UIML is the consequent abstraction of the DISL modeling language from any target platforms and modalities, which makes DISL a pure dialog modeling language. In UIML, on the contrary, abstract descriptions of the user interfaces are possible, but mapping between abstract items and concrete target platform items – the so-called "vocabulary" – is mandatory. DISL, however, uses only purely abstract interaction objects (AIO, see [10]); it is up to the implementation to either interpret AIOs directly on the target device (as presented, for example, in [44]), or to convert the abstract specification into a modality-dependent code using (external) transformations (see section 3.8). This supports DISL's objective of being scalable, since the abstract interaction objects possess only the minimal set properties that must be available on many systems. Fig. 7 shows as a proof of concept a simple interface for a media player modeled with DISL. The left part of Fig. 7 shows an emulated

Siemens M55 mobile phone, whereas the right part of Fig. 7 shows a real Siemens M55 mobile phone. Both mobile phones – the emulated and the real one – render the corresponding DISL document. The generated UI is functional but not very appealing; however, the AIOs could later be augmented during the transformation phase, e.g., by incorporating HCI patterns as design knowledge, in order to generate better interfaces on the respective end device.

Fig. 7 Simple User Interface for a Siemens M55 mobile phone generated from DISL

Adopting DISL into the Useware Engineering Process and linking it to the use models, finally completes the transformation-based, holistic Useware Engineering Process, as illustrated in [28]. For the development of DISL itself, not the whole user interface development process was taken into account, but, on purpose, only the dialog modeling and the presentation, either through direct interpretation on an end device or through transformation into a target format.

3.6 The Concrete User Interface

The concrete user interface is modeled with the User Interface Markup Language (UIML) [45]. UIML separates presentation components (e.g., widgets and layout), dynamic behavior (e.g., state transitions), and the content of a user interface (see Fig. 8). For instantiating a user interface in UIML, a UIML document and a specific vocabulary are required.

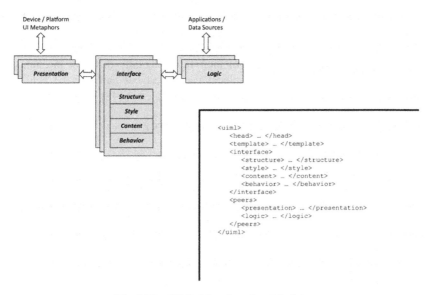

Fig. 8 The UIML Meta-Interface Model

The *interface* section of a UIML document consists of five components: structure, style, layout, content, and behavior:

- *Structure* describes a hierarchy of interaction objects and their relationships.
- *Style* specifies the properties of the components, e.g., text, color, or size.
- *Layout* defines how the components are arranged relative to each other (spatial constraints).
- *Content* separates the content of the interface from the other parts and is referenced in the components' properties.
- *Behavior* describes, for example, interaction rules or actions to be triggered under various circumstances (specifies the dialog model).

While the *interface* section describes the general appearance of the user interface, the *peers* section of a UIML document describes the concrete instantiation of the user interface by providing a mapping onto a platform-specific language (i.e., interface toolkits or bindings to the application logic).

- *Logic* specifies how the interfaces are bound to the application logic.
- *Presentation* describes the mapping to a concrete interface toolkit, such as Java Swing.

Furthermore, a UIML document includes an optional <head>-element for providing meta-information and a concept that allows the reuse of predefined components. These so-called "templates" are predefined interaction objects, which can be easily instantiated with concrete parameters derived from the application data model.

Since syntax and functionality of DISL were still close to UIML, several fundamental enhancements and improvements of DISL were incorporated into the new 4.0 version of UIML [47]. Since May 2009, UIML 4.0 is a standard of the Organization for the Advancement of Structured Information Standards (OASIS). DISL's abstractions accounting for platform and modality independence, however, are adopted by UIML 4.0 because of their fundamentally different mechanism. Still, platform independence of graphical user interfaces can now be achieved using UIML with a generic vocabulary, as demonstrated in [48].

3.7 Transformation of useML 2.0 into DISL

To support the developer in designing user interfaces, an automatic transformation process has been developed [49]. This process adapts the transformation process used in the TERESA development methodology [26] and consists of four phases depicted in Fig. 9. While in the (optional) first phase, the developer manually refines the use model – e.g., for the target platform or target user group – the subsequent phases gradually and automatically transform the use model into an abstract user interface.

While the transformation process introduced in [26] transforms a task model into a final user interface, we explicitly focus on mapping the use model onto an abstract user interface. Since this is compliant with the architecture proposed with the CAMELEON Reference Framework [31], it has the advantage that the generated user interface is independent from the later modality or platform.

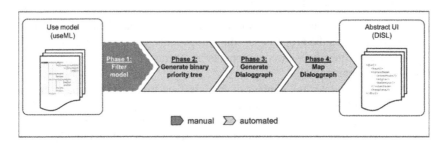

Fig. 9 The Transformation Process

Phase 1: Filtering the Use Model

In the optional first phase, developers can annotate the use model by applying assertions to the single UOs and eUOs. These assertions can be used to specify, for example, on which device a task can be executed or which user group is allowed to execute the task. After the developer has annotated the use model, filters can be set to generate the "system task-model" [26]. Whereas a standard set of assertions is specified in a separate XML-schema in useML, this schema can be individually extended with project-specific assertions.

Phase 2: Generating the Binary Priority Tree

The filtered use model is passed to the second process phase as input for the subsequent automated transformation steps. To simplify interpretation and to solve ambiguities between the temporal operators in this phase, the use model is transformed into a binary "priority tree" [25] representation. While in [25] the priority tree is used for grouping tasks with identical temporal operator priority on the same hierarchical level, a binary version of the priority tree has been used. The binary version of the priority tree has exactly two UOs – respectively eUOs – on each level of the tree. This significantly reduces the number of cases that have to be considered when generating the dialog graph in the next phase. In the left part of Fig. 10, a binary priority tree for a simple "pump" use model is depicted.

The hierarchical structure of the binary priority tree is derived from the temporal operator priorities. A recursive algorithm starts at the root level of the use model and selects those UOs that have the temporal operator with the highest priority. These two UOs are grouped with a new "abstract UO" that replaces both UOs. After that, the algorithm loops until only two UOs are left on the current level. Then the algorithm recursively descends into the next hierarchy level and starts grouping the children. The algorithm terminates when only two UOs/eUOs are left on each hierarchy level.

Phase 3: Generating the Dialog Graph

A dialog graph is generated based on the binary priority tree in the third phase of the transformation process. The dialog graph represents the dynamical character of the use model derived from the semantics of the temporal operators.

eUOs that can be executed by the user at the same point in time are grouped within the states of the dialog graph. Consequently, a state of the dialog graph represents an "Enabled Task Set" (ETS) [23]. The right part of Fig. 10 shows the corresponding dialog graph for the previously mentioned binary priority tree of a pump.

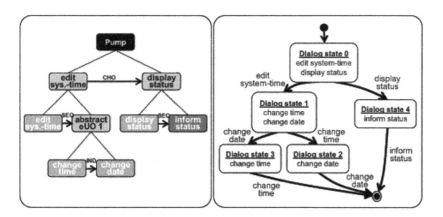

Fig. 10 The binary priority tree (left) and the generated dialog graph (right) of a simple pump use model

For each eUO of a dialog state, there is a corresponding directed transition that is labeled with the eUO and connected to a successor state. These transitions are used to describe the navigation between the single dialog states. The user can navigate through the dialog graph by executing one of the eUOs of a dialog state.

In [9], an algorithm is introduced that has been used in the DYGIMES framework to generate a dialog graph from a CTT task model. Since this algorithm has some shortcomings regarding the generation of parallel states, a new algorithm has been developed that solves these shortcomings and allows the parallel identification of successor states and transitions. The developed recursive algorithm generates the complete dialog graph by *virtually executing* the use model. For this execution, each UO and eUO is flagged with an *execution status* that denotes whether the object is currently executable or has already been executed.

The algorithm is divided into two subsequent phases: *Top-down analysis* for identifying the current dialog state and *bottom-up updating* for determining the new use model execution status.

In the top-down analysis, the use model is searched for executable eUOs. For this purpose, the use model is traversed from the root node of the use model to the leaves, which are represented by the eUOs. The semantics of the temporal operators and the execution status of the UOs are used to decide which branch of the binary priority tree has to be descended recursively. The algorithm terminates when the leaves of the use model have been reached and the executable eUOs have been identified. The result of one top-down-analysis is a unique dialog state that represents one ETS.

Following the top-down analysis, for each eUO stored in the identified dialog state, the successor dialog state as well as the transition to the successor dialog state has to be generated. This is where the identified eUOs are "virtually executed". Each eUO of the previously identified dialog state is selected and labeled by the algorithm as "executed". When the execution status of the selected eUO has been changed in the use model, the execution status of all other UOs/eUOs has to be updated. Beginning with the parent UO of the executed eUO, the tree nodes are recursively updated from the leaves up to the root of the use model. This is why this recursive algorithm is referred to as bottom-up updating.

To generate the whole dialog graph, these two recursive algorithms are nested within each other. When all eUOs in the binary priority tree are marked as "executed", the dialog graph has been generated.

Phase 4: Mapping the Dialog Graph

The final phase of the transformation process implements the mapping from the generated dialog graph onto a dialog model.

In contrast to the TERESA approach, a modality-independent target mapping language has been used for this mapping to support the generation of multi-modality and multi-platform user interfaces. For the specification of this abstract user interface we use DISL. Since DISL was initially designed for mobile devices, it supports a concept where the user interface is split into several modular interfaces. This concept is used in our transformation process for the presentation mapping. Here, the states of the dialog graph are mapped onto DISL interfaces.

Afterwards, each eUO of a dialog state is mapped onto its corresponding abstract interaction object. In Fig. 11, a mapping of the previously generated dialog graph of a pump is depicted.

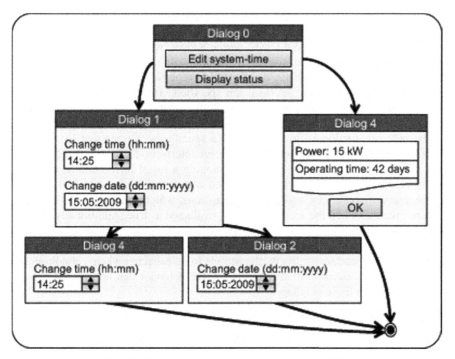

Fig. 11 The mapped dialog graph rendered as a GUI

Since the transitions of the dialog graph are used to move between the dialog states, they represent a dynamical aspect of the user interface. Therefore, the transitions are represented in the behavior part of the DISL user interface. By using a concept of rules and transitions for each AIO, a transition is specified that is fired when the user interacts with this AIO. This transition executes a "restructure" command, which triggers the DISL renderer to activate the new interface.

3.8 Transformation of DISL into UIML

According to the CAMELEON Reference Framework, the next step in a model-based user interface development process is the transformation of the abstract user interface into a modality-depended but platform-independent concrete user interface. Since UIML can be used to describe the user interface in terms of a platform-independent model, the language is used as the target mapping language. Therefore, in this step, the dialogs and interaction objects, as well as the behavior of the abstract UI have to be mapped onto the corresponding UIML elements.

In both languages (DISL and UIML), the user interface is separated into *structure*, *style,* and *behavior* descriptions. Starting by analyzing the user interface structure, the widgets that have to be mapped are identified in the first transformation step. This mapping is specified in a look-up table that expresses the relationship between the abstract DISL interaction objects and the concrete UIML widgets. One mapping can be, for example, that an abstract DISL *command* interaction object is mapped onto a UIML *button* widget, which is commonly used in graphical user interfaces to trigger a function. In the style section of the DISL and UIML user interfaces, the widget's properties that have an impact on the presentation of the user interface are specified. Therefore, DISL properties such as widget texts, descriptions, and visibility attributes are mapped onto the corresponding UIML properties.

The behavior section is primarily used to specify the actions that have to be executed when the user interacts with the user interface. These user interactions may result in opening a new window or changing a set of interaction objects. In DISL, the user interface behavior is described with a set of *rules*, which allow the specification of conditions, and a set of *transitions*, which specify a set of actions that are executed when the according rule is evaluated as true. Additionally, DISL supports the definition of events that allow the specification of time-triggered transitions. As in DISL, the behavior description in UIML is also specified using rules, conditions, and, accordingly, the actions to be executed when a condition is evaluated to true. Because of this similarity, the behavior can be mapped rather statically between those languages.

While those three categories are used in both languages to describe the UI, the languages have different characteristics that have an influence on the transformation process:

One aspect with an impact on the transformation is that an explicit classification of the interaction objects is used in DISL. The abstract interaction objects are classified as *output, interaction,* and *collection interaction objects*. While these classes have an impact on the interaction objects semantics, they are not expressed as an explicit property in the interaction objects style definition. Since UIML does not use such a widget classification, those properties have to be expressed as explicit properties in the UI style definition. For example, the *textfield* interaction object is an output element used for presenting large non-editable texts to the user [28]. Since there is no dedicated output-only widget in UIML, this property has to be expressed in the widget *style* definition by specifying the *editable* attribute of the respective *text* widget.

Another aspect that has to be considered in the mapping process is that the properties specified in the style description also have an influence on the mapping of the widgets. For example, in DISL there is an *incremental* property in the style definition that is used to specify a *variablebox* that accepts numerical input values. If this property is set, the variable box has to be mapped onto a *spinner* widget in UIML, while otherwise a *text* widget is used during the structure mapping phase.

The third aspect that has an influence on the transformation is that besides the explicit properties in the style section of the DISL document, additional information can be used in the mapping process. In DISL, some widget properties are specified in the behavior section. For example, DISL does not support the specification of a minimum or maximum value for a variable box that is set to be incrementally changeable. To emulate these boundaries, they have to be specified in the behavior section of the DISL document by using two variables and a set of rules and transitions that ensure that the values cannot exceed the limits. While this behavior can be mapped onto a UIML style property, the rules and transitions must be omitted when mapping the behavior section of the two languages.

While this phase of the transformation process benefits from the similar structure of the AUI and the CUI models, ambiguities in the mapping process may occur. These ambiguities stem from the fact that the abstract user interface model has to be enriched with additional, modality-specific information not contained in the source model. Since UIML is used as the target language for describing the CUI, attributes for the graphical user interfaces – such as widget size, layout, and color – have to be specified in this mapping that are, by definition, not contained in the AUI model.

Various strategies can be used to obtain this information and to use it as input in the transformation process. One approach is to derive the information from other models. Platform models [30] are used to specify information about the input and output capabilities of the target device and are therefore suitable as an input source. But while it has been shown that these models are suitable for partially deriving the layout [9], they are still not sufficient for automatically deriving a high fidelity user interface. Aspects such as the corporate identity of a user interface usually still have to be applied by the developer herself. Therefore, tools are needed in this transformation phase that allow manual intervention in the transformation phases.

Today, different languages – e.g., ATL [50], RDL/TT [51], and XSLT [52] – and tools are used for model transformation. A review of several transformation systems can be found in [53]. Since the models used in these transformation processes are based on XML, XML-based transformation languages and tools are needed. XSL Transformation (XSLT) is standardized by the W3C group and one of the most widespread languages for transforming XML-based documents. XSLT uses templates to match and transform XML documents into other XML structures, respectively output formats. Since XSLT is one of the most popular XML based transformation languages and offers a large set of generic transformation processors, it is used for the implementation of the DISL-to-UIML transformation process. To enable convenient handling of the XSLT templates, an additional tool has been built that allows selecting the input model (DISL), the transformation template (XSLT), and the output folder for transforming DISL into UIML. Following the generation of the CUI, the source code for the final user interface can be generated, or the user interface can be interpreted by a renderer. In order to enable early feedback of the resulting user interface, an UIML renderer has been integrated into the transformation tool DISL2UIML. Fig. 12 shows a screenshot of the DISL2UIML tool. In the left part, a developer can choose a DISL document and the transformation template (XSLT). After starting the transformation, the resulting UIML document is visualized in the right part of DISL2UIML. In the next step, UIML.net can be started for rendering the transformed UIML document.

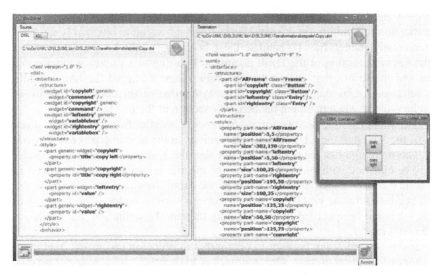

Fig. 12 Screenshot of DISL2UIML showing the transformation software as well as the rendered UIML document

This renderer is an enhanced and extended version of UIML.net [54] capable of rendering UIML 4.0 compliant user interfaces. Different vocabularies such as Gtk#, System.Windows.Forms and System.Windows.Forms for the Compact .Net Framework can be used to present the user interface with a different look and feel.

Besides offering tools for model transformation, tools for authoring and enhancing models are crucial. In recent years, a set of UIML authoring environments have been introduced that allow the design of multi-platform user interfaces. Gummy [55] is an authoring environment that supports the graphical editing of UIML 3.0 documents by offering a toolbox with a set of predefined widgets. After selecting the target platform, the tool loads the appropriate UIML widgets that are available on that platform. Jelly [56] has been recently introduced as a tool for designing multi-platform user interfaces. Although Jelly relies on a proprietary UI description language, it adapts the UIML structure. Harmonia Inc. LiquidApps [57] is the only known commercial UIML authoring environment that supports editing UIML 3.0 compliant documents. The tool has a graphical WYSIWYG editor for designing the user interface using drag&drop functionality. Besides adding and aligning the widgets, the behavior of the user interface can be specified in a different view. After the user interface has been specified, the code for the final user interface can be automatically generated by the tool for several target languages, e.g., Java, C++ Qt, and Web apps.

After generating the code for the final user interface, language-specific tools can be used by the developer to incorporate final design decisions and compile the user interface.

4 Summary and Outlook

In this chapter, we have presented the current status of our model-based user interface development environment. After discussing related work, we introduced the CAMELEON Reference Framework as a meta-architecture for model-based user interface development and subsequently presented the model-based architecture we derived from it. Furthermore, we introduced useML 2.0 and the graphical useML editor "Udit", which is targeted at the structuring phase of the Useware Engineering Process. Additionally, we introduced the Dialog and Interface Specification Language (DISL) and the User Interface Markup Language (UIML) as well as mapping processes from useML to DISL and from DISL to UIML.

Currently, we are investigating efforts to optimize the transformation approach from DISL to UIML by integrating platform models. For specifying platform models, we have analyzed the User Agent Profile (UAProf), which is a specification for capturing the capabilities of a mobile phone, including, e.g., screen size, multimedia capabilities, and character set support. Information about input and output capabilities, in particular, is relevant for transforming the abstract user interface into a concrete user interface. During this transformation process, information about target constraints is essential.

Furthermore, existing tools have to be extended and new tools have to be developed. Especially tools for tweaking the transformation process of useML to DISL have to be developed in conjunction with new DISL renderers, e.g., for the Apple iPhone or for the Google Android platform.

References

[1] Shneiderman, B.: Designing the user interface - strategies for effective human-computer interaction. Addison-Wesley, Boston (2005)
[2] Zuehlke, D., Wahl, M.: Hardware, Software – Useware. Elektronik 23, 54–62 (1999)
[3] Myers, B., Rosson, M.B.: Survey on User Interface Programming. In: Proc. of the 10thAnnual CHI Conference on Human Factors in Computing Systems, pp. 195–202 (1992)
[4] Petrasch, R.: Model Based User Interface Design: Model Driven Architecture und HCI Patterns. GI Softwaretechnik-Trends 27(3), 5–10 (2007)
[5] Zuehlke, D., Thiels, N.: Useware engineering: a methodology for the development of user-friendly interfaces. Library Hi Tech 26(1), 126–140 (2008)
[6] Meixner, G., et al.: Raising the Efficiency of the Use Context Analysis in Useware Engineering by Employing a Support Tool. In: Lee, S., Choo, H., Ha, S., Shin, I.C. (eds.) APCHI 2008. LNCS, vol. 5068, Springer, Heidelberg (2008)
[7] Meixner, G., et al.: Udit – A Graphical Editor For Task Models. In: Proc. of the 4thInternational Workshop on Model-Driven Development of Advanced User Interfaces (MDDAUI). CEUR Workshop Proceedings, Sanibel Island, USA, vol. 439 (2009)
[8] Boedcher, A.: Methodische Nutzungskontextanalyse als Grundlage eines strukturierten USEWARE-Engineering-Prozesses, Fortschritt-Berichte pak 14, Technische Universität Kaiserslautern, Kaiserslautern (2007)

[9] Luyten, K.: Dynamic User Interface Generation for Mobile and Embedded Systems with Model-Based User Interface Development. PhD thesis, TransnationaleUniversiteit Limburg (2004)

[10] Pribeanu, C., Vanderdonckt, J.: Exploring Design Heuristics for User Interface Derivation from Task and Domain Models. In: Proc. of the 4th International Conference on Computer-Aided Design of User Interfaces, pp. 103–110 (2002)

[11] Puerta, A.: TheMecano Project: Enabling User-Task Automation During Interface Development. In: Proc. of the Spring Symposium on Acquisition, Learning and Demonstration: Automating Tasks for Users, pp. 117–121 (1996)

[12] Vanderdonckt, J., Bodart, F.: Encapsulating Knowledge for Intelligent Automatic Interaction Objects Selection. In: Proc. of the 1st Annual CHI Conference on Human Factors in Computing Systems, pp. 424–429 (1993)

[13] Bodart, F., et al.: Key Activities for a Development Methodology of Interactive Applications. In: Benyon, D., Palanque, P. (eds.) Critical Issues in User Interface Systems Engineering, pp. 109–134. Springer, Heidelberg (1995)

[14] Schlungbaum, E.: Knowledge-based Support of Task-based User Interface Design in TADEUS. In: Proc. of the 16th Annual CHI Conference on Human Factors in Computing Systems (1998)

[15] Stary, C.: TADEUS: seamless development of task-based and user-oriented interfaces. IEEE Transactions on Systems, Man, and Cybernetics 30(5), 509–525 (2000)

[16] Ricard, E., Buisine, A.: Des tâches utilisateur au dialogue homme-machine: GLADIS++, une demarche industrielle. In: Proc. of Huitièmes Journéessurl'Ingénierie de l'Interaction Homme-Machine (1996)

[17] Markopoulos, P., et al.: On the composition of interactor specifications. In: Proc. of the BCS-FACS Workshop on Formal Aspects of the Human Computer Interface, London (1996)

[18] Abed, M., et al.: Using Formal Specification Techniques for the Modeling of Tasks and the Generation of Human-Computer User Interface Specifications. In: Diaper, D., Stanton, N. (eds.) The Handbook of Task Analysis for Human-Computer Interaction, pp. 503–529. Lawrence Erlbaum Associates, Mahwah (2003)

[19] Puerta, A.: A Model-Based Interface Development Environment. IEEE Software 14(4), 40–47 (1997)

[20] Clerckx, T., Coninx, K.: Integrating Task Models in Automatic User Interface Generation. EDM/LUC Diepenbeek, Technical Report TR-LUC-EDM-0302 (2003)

[21] Mori, G., et al.: Tool Support for Designing Nomadic Applications. In: Proc. of the 8th International Conference on Intelligent User Interfaces, pp. 141–148 (2003)

[22] Paternò, F., et al.: Authoring pervasive multi-modal user interfaces. International Journal on Web Engineering and Technology 4(2), 235–261 (2008)

[23] Paternò, F.: Model-based design and evaluation of interactive applications. Springer, London (1999)

[24] Mori, G., et al.: Design and Development of Multidevice User Interfaces through Multiple Logical Descriptions. IEEE Transactions on Software Engineering 30(8), 507–520 (2004)

[25] Luyten, K., et al.: Derivation of a Dialog Model from a Task Model by Activity Chain Extraction. In: Proc. of the 10th International Workshop on Interactive Systems: Design, Specification and Verification (2003)

[26] Berti, S., et al.: The TERESA XML language for the Description of Interactive Systems at Multiple Abstraction Levels. In: Proc. of the Workshop on Developing User Interfaces with XML: Advances on User Interface Description Languages, pp. 103–110 (2004)

[27] Limbourg, Q., Vanderdonckt, J.: Addressing the Mapping Problem in User Interface Design with UsiXML. In: Proc. of the 3rd International Workshop on Task Models and Diagrams for User Interface Design (2004)

[28] Schaefer, R.: Model-Based Development of Multimodal and Multi-Device User Interfaces in Context-Aware Environments. C-LAB Publication, 25. Shaker Verlag, Aachen (2007)

[29] Paternò, F., et al.: MARIA: A universal, declarative, multiple abstraction-level language for service-oriented applications in ubiquitous environments. ACM Transactions on Computer-Human Interaction (TOCHI) 16(4), 1–30 (2009)

[30] Puerta, A., Eisenstein, J.: Towards a General Computational Framework for Model-Based Interface Development Systems. In: Proc. of the 4th International Conference on Intelligent User Interfaces (1999)

[31] Calvary, G., et al.: A Unifying Reference Framework for Multi-Target User Interfaces. Interacting with Computers 15(3), 289–308 (2003)

[32] Cantera Fonseca, J.M., et al.: Model-Based UI XG Final Report, W3C Incubator Group Report, May 4 (2010), http://www.w3.org/2005/Incubator/model-based-ui/ XGR-mbui-20100504/ (accessed June 1, 2010)

[33] Ali, M.F., et al.: Building Multiplatform User Interfaces With UIML. In: Seffah, A., Javahery, H. (eds.) Multiple User Interfaces – Cross-Platform Applications and Context-Aware Interfaces, pp. 95–118. John Wiley & Sons, Chichester (2004)

[34] Mukasa, K., Reuther, A.: The Useware Markup Language (useML) - Development of User-Centered Interface Using XML. In: Proc. of the 9th IFAC Symposium on Analysis, Design and Evaluation of Human-Machine-Systems, Atlanta, USA (2004)

[35] Meixner, G., Goerlich, D.: Eine Taxonomie für Aufgabenmodelle. In: Proc. of Software Engineering 2009, Kaiserslautern, Germany. LNI P, vol. 143, pp. 171–177 (2009)

[36] Bomsdorf, B., Szwillus, G.: From task to dialogue: Task based user interface design. SIGCHI Bulletin 30(4), 40–42 (1998)

[37] Meixner, G.: Entwicklung einer modellbasierten Architektur für multimodale Benutzungsschnittstellen, Fortschritt-Berichte pak 21, Technische Universität Kaiserslautern, Kaiserslautern (2010)

[38] Uhr, H.: TOMBOLA: Simulation and User-Specific Presentation of Executable Task Models. In: Proc. of the International HCI Conference, pp. 263–267 (2003)

[39] Biere, M., et al.: Specification and Simulation of Task Models with VTMB. In: Proc. of the 17th Annual CHI Conference on Human Factors in Computing Systems, pp. 1–2. ACM Press, New York (1999)

[40] Gray, P., et al.: XUAN: Enhancing UAN to capture temporal relationships among actions. In: Proc. of the Conference on People and Computers, vol. IX, pp. 301–312. Cambridge University Press, Cambridge (1994)

[41] Scapin, D., Pierret-Golbreich, C.: Towards a method for task description: MAD. In: Proc. of the Conference Work with Display Units, pp. 27–34 (1989)

[42] Tarby, J.C., Barthet, M.F.: The Diane+ method. In: Proc. of the 2nd International Conference on Computer-Aided Design of User Interfaces, pp. 95–120 (1996)

[43] Van Der Veer, G., et al.: GTA: Groupware task analysis – modeling complexity. Acta Psychologica 91, 297–322 (1996)

[44] Mueller, W., et al.: Interactive Multimodal User Interfaces for Mobile Devices. In: Proc. of the 37th Annual Hawaii International Conference on System Sciences, Hawaii, USA (2004)

[45] Abrams, M., et al.: UIML: An Appliance-Independent XML User Interface Language. In: Proc. of the 8th International World Wide Web Conference, Toronto, Canada, pp. 1695–1708 (1999)

[46] Curry, M.B., Monk, A.F.: Dialogue Modeling of Graphical User Interfaces with a Production System. Behaviour and Information Technology 14(1), 41–55 (1995)

[47] Helms, J., et al.: User Interface Markup Language (UIML) Version 4.0. (2009), http://docs.oasis-open.org/uiml/v4.0/cd01/ uiml-4.0-cd01.pdf

[48] Ali, M.F., et al.: Building Multi-Platform User Interfaces with UIML. In: Proc. of the 4th International Conference on Computer-Aided Design of User Interfaces, pp. 255–266 (2002)

[49] Seißler, M., Meixner, G.: Entwicklung eines Transformationsprozesses zur modellbasierten Entwicklung von multimodalen Benutzungsschnittstellen. In: Proc. of the 8th Berliner Werkstatt Mensch-Maschine-Systeme, Berlin, Germany (2009)

[50] Jouault, F., Kurtev, I.: Transforming Models with ATL. In: Bruel, J.-M. (ed.) MoDELS 2005. LNCS, vol. 3844, pp. 128–138. Springer, Heidelberg (2006)

[51] Schaefer, R., et al.: RDL/TT - A Description Language for the Profile-Dependent Transcoding of XML Documents. In: Proc. of the International ITEA Workshop on Virtual Home Environments (2002)

[52] W3C Consortium, XSL Transformations (XSLT) Version 1.0. W3C Recommendation, November 16 (1999)

[53] Schaefer, R.: A survey on transformation tools for model based user interface development. In: Proc. of the 12th International Conference on Human-Computer Interaction: Interaction Design and Usability, Beijing, China, pp. 1178–1187. Springer, Heidelberg (2007)

[54] Luyten, K., Coninx, K.: UIML.Net: an Open UIML Renderer for the.Net Framework. In: Jacob, R.J.K., Limbourg, Q., Vanderdonckt, J. (eds.) Computer-Aided Design of User Interfaces, vol. IV, pp. 259–270. Kluwer Academic Publishers, Dordrecht (2006)

[55] Meskens, J., et al.: Gummy for multi-platform user interface designs: shape me, multiply me, fix me, use me. In: Proc. of the Working Conference on Advanced Visual Interfaces 2008, Napoli, Italy, pp. 233–240. ACM, New York (2008)

[56] Meskens, J., et al.: Jelly: A Multi-Device Design Environment for Managing Consistency Across Devices. In: Proc. of the Working Conference on Advanced Visual Interfaces 2010, Rome, Italy. ACM, New York (2010)

[57] Harmonia Inc. LiquidApps® - A Powerful Enterprise Mashup Solution, http://www.liquidappsworld.com/ (accessed June 1, 2010)

Multi Front-End Engineering

Goetz Botterweck

Abstract. Multi Front-End Engineering (MFE) deals with the design of multiple consistent user interfaces (UI) for one application. One of the main challenges is the conflict between commonality (all front-ends access the same application core) and variability (multiple front-ends on different platforms). This can be overcome by extending techniques from model-driven user interface engineering. We present the MANTRA approach, where the common structure of all interfaces of an application is modelled in an abstract UI model (AUI) annotated with temporal constraints on interaction tasks. Based on these constraints we adapt the AUI, e.g., to tailor presentation units and dialogue structures for a particular platform. We use model transformations to derive concrete, platform-specific UI models (CUI) and implementation code. The presented approach generates working prototypes for three platforms (GUI, web, mobile) integrated with an application core via web service protocols. In addition to static evaluation, such prototypes facilitate early functional evaluations by practical use cases.

1 Introduction

Multi Front-End Engineering (MFE) deals with the systematic design and implementation of multiple consistent user interfaces for one application.

One of the main challenges in MFE is the inherent conflict between commonality and variability. On the one hand, all front-ends provide access to the same application core. Hence, they share a common structure and provide similar functionality. On the other hand, each front-end has to take into account the specifics of the particular user interface platform. Hence, each front-end has to be adapted to these specific characteristics, e.g., when grouping interaction elements into logical presentation units of varying sizes.

Goetz Botterweck
Lero – The Irish Software Engineering Research Centre
University of Limerick, Limerick, Ireland
e-mail: goetz.botterweck@lero.ie

H. Hussmann et al. (Eds.): MDD of Advanced User Interfaces, SCI 340, pp. 27–42.
springerlink.com   © Springer-Verlag Berlin Heidelberg 2011

The challenges that arise from this conflict between commonality and variability can be overcome by adapting and extending techniques from model-driven user interface engineering. To support multiple user interfaces, however, we have to prepare by providing additional information that can guide an automatic or semi-automatic adaptation, for instance to take into account platform-dependent characteristics.

To illustrate how this can be done, we present the MANTRA[1] approach, where the abstract structure of all user interfaces of an application is modelled in an abstract UI model (AUI). This model is annotated with temporal constraints on the dialogue flow and the relative order of interaction tasks. Based on this information, we are able to adapt the user interface on an abstract level, for instance, by deriving and tailoring dialogue structures, which take into account constraints imposed by the particular user interface platform. The adaptation includes the clustering into presentation units and the insertion of control-oriented interaction elements. Based on this abstract model, we use model-to-model transformations to derive concrete, platform-specific UI models (CUI). Subsequently, we use model-to-text transformations to generate implementation code.

The presented approach is realized as a set of Eclipse-based tools and model transformations in ATL (Atlas Transformation Language). It generates working prototypes for three platforms: desktop GUI applications, dynamic web sites and mobile applications. These prototypes are integrated with an application core via web service protocols. Because of the *functional* integration with the application core, in addition to the evaluation of the static user interface (composition, layout and visual presentation of interaction elements), such prototypes also facilitate functional evaluations by performing and analysing practical use cases.

The remainder of this chapter is structured as follows: Section 2 summarises related work, Section 3 gives an overview of the presented approach, Section 4 explains the use of Abstract User Interface (AUI) models in the context of MFE, Section 5 deals with the adaptation of user interfaces on the AUI level, Section 6 describes the transformation from AUI to Concrete User Interface (CUI) Models and the generation of implementation artefacts, Section 7 explains the meta-models of the modelling languages used by our approach, and Section 8 concludes the chapter by discussing the presented approach and future work.

2   Related Work

Calvary et al. [1] define a reference framework for multi-target user interfaces. This is also known as the Cameleon reference framework after the European project of the same name. Calvary at al. define the challenges of "multi-targeting" and "plasticity", which are related to the problem addressed in this chapter. Also, the processes and artefacts in our approach are structured on abstraction levels similar to the Cameleon framework (see Section 3 for an overview).

---

[1] MANTRA stands for Model-driven Approach to UI-Engineering with Transformations.

The *mapping problem* [2] is the problem of defining mappings between abstract and concrete elements is one of the fundamental challenges in model-based approaches to User Interface Engineering. This challenge can occur in various forms and can be dealt with by various types of approaches [3]. One instance of this is the question of how we can identify concrete interaction *elements* that match a given abstract element and other constraints [4].

A similar challenge is the derivation of *structures* in a new model based on information given in another existing model. Many task-oriented approaches use requirements given by the task model to determine UI structures; for example, temporal constraints similar to the ones in our approach have been used to derive the structure of an AUI [5] or dialogue model [6].

Florins et al. [7] take an interesting perspective on a similar problem by discussing rules for splitting existing presentations into smaller ones. That approach combines information from the abstract user interface and the underlying task model - similar to our approach using an AUI annotated with temporal constraints which are also derived from a task model.

Many model-driven approaches to UI engineering have proposed a hierarchical organisation of interaction elements, which are grouped together into logical units. For instance, Eisenstein et al. [8] use such an structure when they aim to support designers in building user interfaces across several platforms.

A number of approaches to multiple user interfaces has been collected in a book edited by Seffah and Javahery [9].

Earlier work on MANTRA, the approach discussed in this chapter, has been presented in [10]. In current work [11], we adapt and specialize techniques taken from the MANTRA approach to support the configuration, derivation and tailoring of user interfaces for products in a product line.

3   Overview of the MANTRA Approach

Horizontally, the MANTRA approach (see Fig. 1) is structured by three tiers, *Front-Ends*, *Application Core*, and *Resources*. Vertically, the MANTRA activities and created artefacts are structured by abstraction levels similar to the CAMELEON framework [1]. They include Abstract User Interface (AUI), Adapted Abstract User Interface (Adapted AUI), Concrete User Interface (CUI), and Implemented User Interface (IUI).

The ultimate goal of MANTRA is to create multiple implemented front-ends of the application (see the IUI_w, IUI_m, and IUI_a at the bottom of Fig. 1). These front-ends are based on different platforms, but provide access to the same *Application Core* and indirectly to *Resources*, which are used by the application.

The MANTRA approach starts with the activity of *Abstract UI Modelling* ❶, which creates an abstract user interface AUI. Then, the interface is adapted on an abstract level ❷. The resulting adapted AUI models are then transformed ❸ into concrete platform-specific UI models (CUI) for three different platforms (Web,

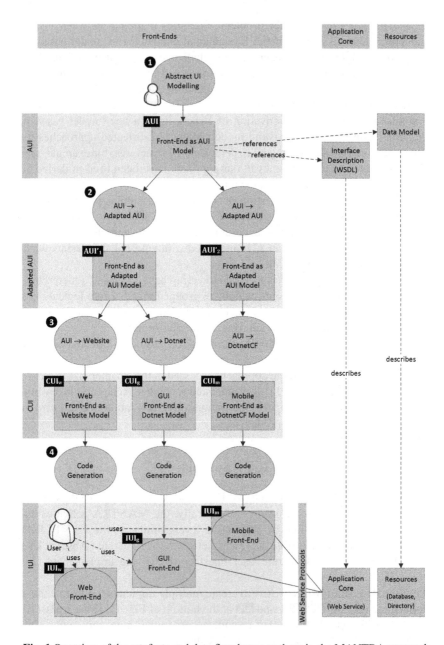

Fig. 1 Overview of the artefacts and data flow between them in the MANTRA approach

GUI, Mobile). Finally, the desired front-ends (implemented UI, IUI) are created by generating platform-specific code ❹.

The following sections will explain these activities and the processed artefacts in more detail.

4 Abstract Modelling of User Interfaces

We will now explain the subsequent activities of the MANTRA approach in more detail. For the illustration and discussion, we will use a simple time table application.

We start of with the activity of *Abstract UI Modelling* ❶, which creates an abstract user interface **AUI**. Fig. 2 shows the corresponding AUI model of our sample timetable application. The user can search for train and bus connections by specifying several search criteria like departure and destination locations, time of travel or the preferred means of transportation (lower part of Fig. 2).

Please note that in the context of the overall MANTRA approach the AUI model, which describes the front-ends of the application, references concepts in models describing other parts or aspects of the system (see AUI layer in the overview in Fig. 1). For instance, abstract UI elements can refer to web service operations to describe integration with the application core or data types defined in a data model.

In our sample shown in Fig. 2, one of the nodes refers to a web service operation *Timetable.getConnections()*, which retrieves connections from the *Timetable* web services and provides them to the subsequent presentation *Timetable Results* for display.

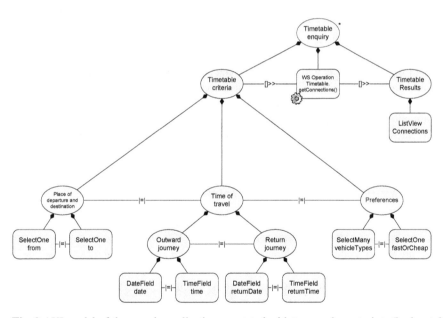

Fig. 2 AUI model of the sample application annotated with temporal constraints (horizontal lines)

At first, the AUI model only contains *UI Elements* (▢) and *UI Composites* (◯) organized in a simple composition hierarchy (indicated by ◆—— relations) and the web service operation necessary to retrieve the results. This model is the starting point of our approach (see **AUI** in Fig. 1) and captures the common essence of the multiple user interfaces of the application in one abstract UI. This AUI contains platform-independent interaction concepts like "Select one element from a list" or "Enter a date".

As an input for later adaptation techniques, the AUI is then further annotated by dialogue flow constraints based on the temporal relationships of the ConcurTaskTree approach [12]. For instance, we can describe that two interaction elements have to be processed sequentially (≫) or can be processed in any order (|=|).

5   Adaptation of Abstract User Interfaces

As a next step (❷ in Fig. 1), we augment the AUI by deriving dialogue and presentation structures. These structures are still platform-independent. However, they can be adapted and tailored to take into account constraints imposed, for instance, by platforms with limited display size or by inexperienced users. The result of this process step, the adapted AUI model, is shown in Fig. 3.

5.1   Clustering Interaction Elements to Generate Presentation Units

To derive this adapted AUI model, we cluster UI elements by identifying suitable UI composites. The subtrees starting at these nodes will become coherent presentations in the user interface (⌂). For instance, we decided that "Time of Travel" and all UI elements below will be presented coherently. This first automatic clustering is done by heuristics based on metrics like the number of UI elements in each presentation or the nesting level of grouping elements.

To further optimize the results, the clustering can be refined by the human designer by an interactive editors that operates on the adapted AUI model.

5.2   Inserting Control-Oriented Interaction Elements

Secondly, we generate the navigation elements necessary to traverse between the presentations identified in the preceding step. For this, we create triggers (▬). These are abstract interaction elements which can start an operation (*OperationTrigger*) or the transition to a different presentation (*NavigationTrigger*). In graphical interfaces, these can be represented as buttons, menus, or hyperlinks. In other frontends, they could for instance be implemented as speech commands.

To generate *NavigationTriggers* in a presentation p, we calculate *dialogueSuccessors*(p) which is the set of all presentations which can "come next" if we observe the temporal constraints. We can then create *NavigationTriggers* (and related Transitions) so that the user can reach all presentations in *dialogueSuccessors*(p). In addition to this, we have to generate *OperationTriggers* for all presentations which will trigger a web service operation, e.g., "Search" to retrieve matching train connections (see the lower right corner of Fig. 3).

These two adaptation steps (derivation of presentations, insertion of triggers) are implemented as ATL model transformations. These transformations augment the AUI with dialogue structures (e.g., presentations ⌒ and transitions ──▶ between them) which determine the paths a user can take through our application.

It is important to note that the dialogue structures are *not* fully determined by the AUI. Instead, we can adapt the AUI according to the requirements and create different variants of it (see the two adapted AUI models resulting from step ❷ in Fig. 1). For instance, we could create more (but smaller) presentations to facilitate viewing on a mobile device – or we could decide to have large coherent presentations, taking the risk that the user has to do lots of scrolling if restricted to a small screen.

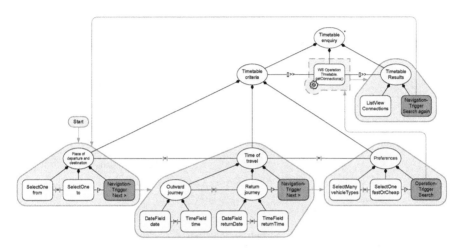

Fig. 3 Adopted AUI model with generated presentations and triggers

5.3 Selecting Content

To reflect limitations of the platform, e.g., limited screen estate, which only allows to show a limited number of interaction elements, can apply an additional adaptation step that filters content retrieved from the web service based on priorities.

For instance, if a user has a choice, higher priority is given to knowing when the train is leaving and where it is going before discovering whether it has a restaurant. This optional information can be factored out to separate "more details" presentations.

A similar concept are substitution rules which provide alternative representations for reoccurring content. A train, for example, might be designated as InterCityExpress, ICE, or by a graphical symbol based on the train category (for instance, ⚝⚝ to indicate a luxury train) depending on how much display space is available. These priorities and substitution rules are domain knowledge which cannot be inferred from other models. The necessary information can, for instance, be modelled as annotations to the underlying data model.

6 Generating Concrete Interface Models and Their Implementation

Subsequently, we transform the adapted AUI models into several CUIs using a specialized model transformation (❸ in Fig. 1) for each target platform. These transformations encapsulate the knowledge of how the abstract interaction elements are best transformed into platform-specific concepts. Hence, they can be reused for other applications over and over again.

As a result, we get platform-specific CUI models. These artefacts are still represented and handled as models, but now use platform-specific concepts like "HTML-Submit-Button" or ".NET GroupBox". This makes them more suitable to use them as a basis for the code generation (❹ in Fig. 1), which produces the implementations of the desired user interfaces in platform-typical programming or markup languages.

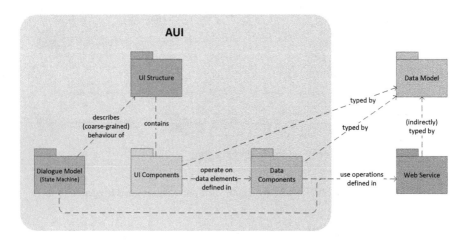

Fig. 4 Overview of the AUI metamodel

7 Modelling Languages

In this section, we will present the modelling languages (i.e., meta-models) used by the MANTRA approach. We will focus on the AUI level, where the common aspects of all front-ends are represented and differences between platforms are abstracted away. Fig. 4 shows an overview of the involved packages.

First, we will now introduce modelling elements that describe the overall user interface structure. Then, we will then focus on modelling elements for describing the dialogue structure. Finally, we will show how user interface elements can be bound to data components and how these data components are bound to the application core.

7.1   User Interface Structure

Fig. 5 shows a simplified excerpt from the AUI metamodel with metaclasses to describe UI structure (on the left) and metaclasses to describe dialogue structures (on the right). Please note that the sections "UI Structure" and "Dialogue" correspond to packages in the metamodel, which was shown earlier overview in Fig. 4.

The core structure of a user interface is given by the composition hierarchy of the various user interface components. In the AUI metamodel, this is modelled by a "Composite" design pattern [13] consisting of the classes *UIComponent*, *UIElement*, and *UIComposite* (see ❶ in Fig. 4).

There are two types of *UIComponents*: The first subtype are *UIElements* (see ❷ in the metamodel in Fig. 5) which cannot contain further *UIComponents*. Hence, they become the "leaves" of the hierarchy tree (see the ▭ symbols in the Timetable sample in Fig. 2). Subclasses of UIElement can be used to describe various abstract interaction tasks, such as the editing of a simple string value (*InputField*) or the selection of one value from a list (*SelectOne*). A special case of *UIElements* are Triggers which can start the transition to another presentation (*NavigationTrigger*) or start a (potential data modifying) transaction (*TransactionTrigger*). Please note that the AUI modelling language contains many more *UIElement* subclasses, but they have been omitted here to simplify the illustration.

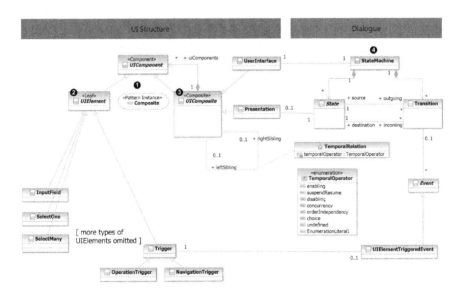

Fig. 5 Binding user interface elements to a data model

The second subtype of *UIComponents* are *UIComposites* (see ❸ in Fig. 5). *UIComposites* can contain other *UIComponents* via the association "uiComponents" and hence build up the "branches" of the hierarchy tree (see the ◯ symbols in the

Timetable sample in Fig. 2). A *UIComposite* can be connected to its left and right sibling by temporal relations (see the horizontal lines ——|=|—— in Fig. 2). In the metamodel, this is described by an instance of the association class *Temporal-Relation* which connects two *UIComposites leftSibling* and *rightSibling*. There are several kinds of temporal operators, such as *enabling*, *suspendResume* or *choice* (see the enumeration *TemporalOperator*).

There are two special cases of *UIComposites*: A *UserInterface* represents the whole user interface and is therefore the root of the hierarchy. In the Timetable sample, this is the node "Timetable enquiry" (see Fig. 2).

Another special case of an *UIComposite* is a *Presentation*. A *Presentation* is a hierarchy node that was selected during the adaptation process, because all *UIElements* contained in the subtree below it should be presented coherently. For instance, see the node "Time of travel" in the Timetable sample (Fig. 3): This node and the subtree below it are surrounded by a marked area to indicate that all *UICompo-nents* within that area will be presented in one coherent Presentation. Hence, this *UIComposite* will be converted into a Presentation in further transformation steps.

7.2   Dialogue Model

The dialogue model of an abstract user interface is described by a state machine (see ❹ in Fig. 5) which is based on UML Statecharts [14]. It consists of *States*, which are linked to *Presentations* generated in the adaptation process. As long as the *UserInterface* is one particular state, the related Presentation is displayed (or presented in different ways on non-visual interfaces).

When the *UserInterface* performs a Transition to a different State, the next Presentation is displayed. Transitions can be started by Events, for instance, by a *UIElementTriggeredEvent*, which fires as soon as the related *UIElement*, such as a Trigger, is triggered.

There are many other event types, which have been omitted here to simplify the metamodel illustration.

7.3   Binding UI Elements to Data Components

In the MANTRA metamodel, user interface elements are grouped into different categories depending on their main function, for instance structure-oriented (e.g., *UIComposite*, *UIComponentGroup*, see Section 7.1), control-oriented (e.g., *Trigger*, *Hyperlink*, *MenuItem*, see Section 7.2), and data-oriented (e.g., various forms of *Input*, various forms of *Select*, and the composite *DataTableView*).

For the latter category, data-oriented user interface elements MANTRA allows to describe corresponding data components that will hold and organize the corresponding processed data, which is presented (and potentially edited) via the data-oriented UI elements.

Fig. 6 shows both data-oriented user interface elements (left) and data components (right) as well as some of the mappings between them. For instance, each

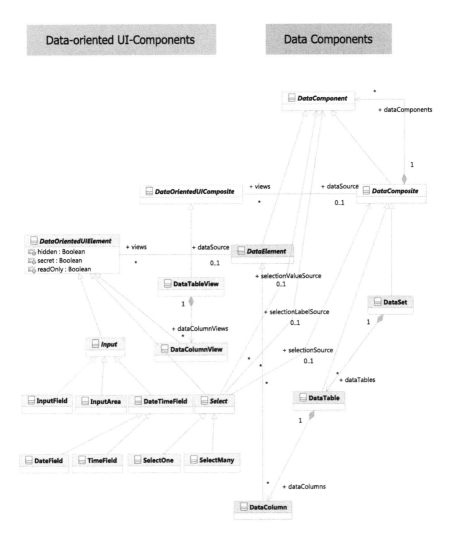

Fig. 6 Binding data-oriented UI elements to data components

DataOrientedUIElement (including specializations) has a *DataElement* as data source. Again the shown sections correspond to packages in the metamodel overview (Fig. 4).

7.4 Binding Data Components to the Application Core

As mentioned earlier, the front-end is integrated with the application core via web service protocols. To allow this integration, the AUI model references concepts in a web service model, which is based on a WSDL description.

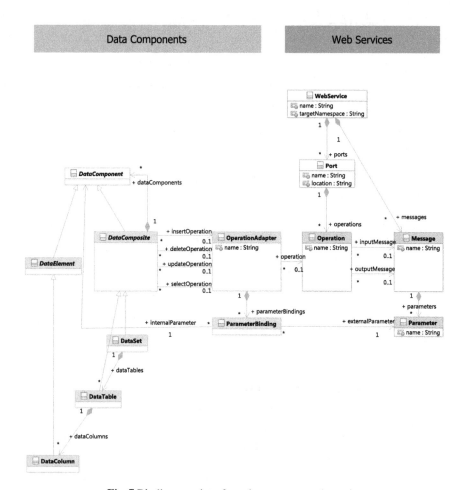

Fig. 7 Binding user interface elements to a web service

As an example of how this integration works on a metamodel level, Fig. 7 shows how data-oriented components are referring to the corresponding web service operations, which are used to retrieve or store data from/to the web service.

8 Discussion and Outlook

We have shown how our MANTRA approach can be used to generate several consistent user interfaces for a multi tier application (see Fig. 8).

We discussed how the user interface can be adapted on the AUI level by tailoring dialogue and logical presentation structures which take into account requirements

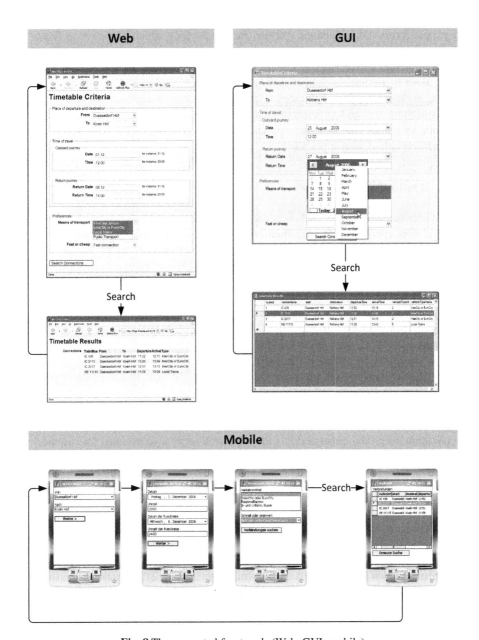

Fig. 8 The generated front-ends (Web, GUI, mobile)

imposed by front-end platforms or inexperienced users. For this, we used the hierarchical structure of interaction elements and constraints on the dialogue flow which can be derived from a task model.

The approach generates fully working prototypes of user-interfaces on three target platforms (GUI, dynamic website, mobile device), which can serve as front-ends to arbitrary web services. Such generated prototypes are beneficial in rapid prototyping and early evaluation of user interfaces, since they facilitate functional evaluations by performing and analysing practical use cases.

The approach is geared towards interaction patterns that are commonly found in electronic forms and hypertext-like applications. It would, for instance, be very difficult to model and generate applications like an image processing tool or a spreadsheet calculation application.

8.1 Applied Technologies

When implementing MANTRA, we described the meta-models (including platform-specific concepts) in UML and then converted these to Ecore, since we use the Eclipse Modeling Framework (EMF) [15] to handle all processed models and the corresponding meta-models.

The various model transformations (e.g., for steps ❷ and ❸ in Fig. 1) are described in ATL [16].

We use a combination of Java Emitter Templates and XSLT to generate (❹ in Fig. 1) arbitrary text-oriented or XML-based implementation languages (e.g., C-Sharp or XHTML with embedded PHP).

The coordination of several steps in the model flow is automated by Apache Ant [17] (integrated into Eclipse) and custom-developed "Ant Tasks" to manage the chain of transformations and code generation.

We use web services as an interface between the UIs and the application core. Hence, the UI models reference a WSDL-based description of operations in the application core. The generated UIs then use web service operations, for instance, to retrieve results for a query specified by the user.

8.2 Future Work

In the discussion of the AUI adaptation, it has been mentioned that the derived user interface structures (first the adapted AUI, then later the CUI) are not fully specified by the given input models (AUI with temporal constraints). In other words, when progressing down the MANTRA model workflow (see Fig. 2) and making decisions on how to *best* implement the given abstract specifications, we can choose among different potential solutions. This provides the opportunity for various optimisation approaches. We intend to explore this further.

Another aspect for future work is the modelling and handling of variability and commonality among the multiple front-ends of one application. On an *element* level, this can be addressed by abstraction, where one abstract element (e.g., "Select One" can describe multiple concrete solutions (e.g., "HTML Link List" and "'MS Windows ListBox"). This however, does not allow to describe variations among front-ends on a *structural* level. For instance, how do you represent that certain dialog structures and navigation paths are only available in some front-ends, but not all of them? Here, approaches from product line engineering and variability modelling could be beneficial [18, 19].

Related to this, feature modelling [20] could be applied to describe variation and configuration options. Then, techniques from product configuration [21, 22] could be applied and extend to describe how configuration options are chosen – potentially over multiple stages [23]. Finally, techniques from feature mapping [24] and variability realisation [25] could be used to describe how the chosen options influence the artefacts that actually describe the user interface.

In current work, we have take first steps towards such an integration of model-based user interface engineering and model-driven product line engineering approaches. In particular, we integrated feature models, which describe the variability and configuration choices of the product line, and abstract user interface models, which describe the common user interface structure of all products. More details are described in [11].

Acknowledgements. This work was partly supported, in part, by the Science Foundation Ireland (SFI) grant 03/CE2/I303_1 to Lero – The Irish Software Engineering Research Centre, http://www.lero.ie/.

References

1. Calvary, G., Coutaz, J., Thevenin, D., Limbourg, Q., Bouillon, L., Vanderdonckt, J.: A unifying reference framework for multi-target user interfaces. Interacting with Computers 15(3), 289–308 (2003)
2. Puerta, A.R., Eisenstein, J.: Interactively mapping task models to interfaces in MOBI-D. In: DSV-IS 1998 (Design, Specication and Verication of Interactive Systems), Abingdon, UK, June 3-5, pp. 261–273 (1998)
3. Clerckx, T., Luyten, K., Coninx, K.: The mapping problem back and forth: customizing dynamic models while preserving consistency. In: TAMODIA 2004 (Third Annual Conference on Task Models and Diagrams), Prague, Czech Republic, November 15-16, pp. 33–42. ACM Press, New York (2004)
4. Vanderdonckt, J.: Advice-giving systems for selecting interaction objects. In: UIDIS 1999 (User Interfaces to Data Intensive Systems), Edinburgh, Scotland, September 5-6, pp. 152–157 (1999)
5. Paternò, F.: One model, many interfaces. In: CADUI 2002 (Fourth International Conference on Computer-Aided Design of User Interfaces), Valenciennes, France, May 15-17 (2002)
6. Forbrig, P., Dittmar, A., Reichart, D., Sinnig, D.: From models to interactive systems – tool support and XIML. In: IUI/CADUI 2004 Workshop Making Model-Based User Interface Design Practical: Usable and Open Methods and Tools, Island of Madeira, Portugal (2004)
7. Florins, M., Simarro, F.M., Vanderdonckt, J., Michotte, B.: Splitting rules for graceful degradation of user interfaces. In: IUI 2006 (Intelligent User Interfaces 2006), Sydney, Australia, January 29 - February 1, pp. 264–266 (2006)

8. Eisenstein, J., Vanderdonckt, J., Puerta, A.R.: Applying model-based techniques to the development of UIs for mobile computers. In: IUI 2001 (6th International Conference on Intelligent User Interfaces), Santa Fe, NM, USA, January 14-17, pp. 69–76 (2001)
9. Seffah, A., Javahery, H.: Multiple user interfaces: cross-platform applications and context-aware interfaces. John Wiley & Sons, New York (2004)
10. Botterweck, G.: A model-driven approach to the engineering of multiple user interfaces. In: Auletta, V. (ed.) MoDELS 2006. LNCS, vol. 4364, pp. 106–115. Springer, Heidelberg (2007), doi:10.1007/978-3-540-69489-2_14
11. Pleuss, A., Botterweck, G., Dhungana, D.: Integrating automated product derivation and individual user interface design. In: Proceedings of the 4th International Workshop on Variability Modelling of Software-Intensive Systems (VAMOS 2010), pp. 69–76 (January 2010)
12. Paternò, F., Mancini, C., Meniconi, S.: ConcurTaskTrees: A diagrammatic notation for specifying task models. In: Howard, S., Hammond, J., Lindgaard, G. (eds.) Interact 1997 (Sixth IFIP International Conference on Human-Computer Interaction), Sydney, Australia, July 14-16, pp. 362–369. Chapman and Hall, Boca Raton (1997)
13. Gamma, E., Helm, R., Johnson, R., Vlissides, J.: Design patterns: Elements of reusable object-oriented software. Addison-Wesley, Reading (1995)
14. OMG: Uml 2.0 superstructure specification (formal/05-07-04). Object Management Group (2005)
15. Budinsky, F., Steinberg, D., Merks, E., Ellersick, R., Grose, T.J.: Eclipse modeling framework: a developer's guide. In: The Eclipse Series. Addison-Wesley, Boston (2003)
16. Jouault, F., Kurtev, I.: Transforming models with ATL. In: Bruel, J.-M. (ed.) MoDELS 2005. LNCS, vol. 3844, pp. 128–138. Springer, Heidelberg (2006)
17. Holzner, S., Tilly, J.: Ant: the definitive guide, 2nd edn. O'Reilly, Sebastopol (2005)
18. Clements, P., Northrop, L.M.: Software Product Lines: Practices and Patterns. In: The SEI series in software engineering. Addison-Wesley, Boston (2002)
19. Pohl, K., Boeckle, G., van der Linden, F.: Software Product Line Engineering: Foundations, Principles, and Techniques. Springer, New York (2005)
20. Kang, K., Cohen, S., Hess, J., Novak, W., Peterson, S.: Feature oriented domain analysis (FODA) feasibility study. SEI Technical Report CMU/SEI-90-TR-21, ADA 235785, Software Engineering Institute (1990)
21. Botterweck, G., Thiel, S., Nestor, D., bin Abid, S., Cawley, C.: Visual tool support for configuring and understanding software product lines. In: 12th International Software Product Line Conference (SPLC 2008), Limerick, Ireland (September 2008); ISBN 978-7695-3303-2.
22. Botterweck, G., Janota, M., Schneeweiss, D.: A design of a configurable feature model configurator. In: Proceedings of the 3rd International Workshop on Variability Modelling of Software-Intensive Systems (VAMOS 2009), pp. 165–168 (January 2009)
23. Czarnecki, K., Antkiewicz, M., Kim, C.H.P.: Multi-level customization in application engineering. Commun. ACM 49(12), 60–65 (2006)
24. Heidenreich, F., Kopcsek, J., Wende, C.: Featuremapper: Mapping features to models. In: ICSE Companion 2008: Companion of the 13th international conference on Software engineering, pp. 943–944. ACM, New York (2008)
25. Svahnberg, M., van Gurp, J., Bosch, J.: A taxonomy of variability realization techniques. Software - Practice and Experience (SP&E) 35, 705–754 (2005)

A Design Space for User Interface Composition

Fabio Paternò, Carmen Santoro, and Lucio Davide Spano

Abstract. Modern user interfaces are highly dynamic and interactive. They often compose in various ways user interface components. Thus, there is a need to understand what can be composed in user interfaces and how. This chapter presents a design space for user interface composition. The design space consists of five dimensions addressing aspects ranging from the UI abstraction level involved, the granularity of UI elements involved, the UI aspects that are affected by it, the time when such a composition occurs, and the type of web services involved. The design space is then analyzed with respect to the capabilities of the ConcurTaskTrees and MARIA languages in order to show how it is possible to compose user interfaces at various abstraction levels. In order to provide a deeper insight, in the paper, we also present a number of excerpts for several composition examples.

1 Introduction

The basic idea of user interface composition is to combine pieces of User Interface (UI) descriptions in order to obtain a new user interface description for a new interactive application. In the context of composition of user interfaces for emerging service-based applications, two main cases can be identified. On the one hand, we can compose services that do not have associated any UI. In this case, a strategy could be composing web services (using already existing and well-known techniques for orchestration of Web services) and then derive the UI of the service resulting from such composition. Examples of such approaches are WS-BPEL [9], a notation that is well known and used for representing and composing business processes, BPEL4people [1], which is an extension of BPEL to the standard WS-BPEL elements for modelling human interaction in business processes, and WS-Human Task [2], a notation for the integration of human beings in service-oriented applications. On the other hand, we can have the case when service-based applications have already associated user interfaces. They latter can be described through

Fabio Paternò · Carmen Santoro · Lucio Davide Spano
CNR-ISTI – HIIS Laboratory, Pisa, Italy

H. Hussmann et al. (Eds.): MDD of Advanced User Interfaces, SCI 340, pp. 43–65.
springerlink.com   © Springer-Verlag Berlin Heidelberg 2011

annotations (see for example [6]) providing some indications for the corresponding user interface specifications or they can be complete user interface descriptions composed to create new interactive applications, as it happens with mash-up applications. In this case, the focus is on composing the user interfaces descriptions and we will mainly discuss such aspects.

Many UI definition languages are XML-based, thus some work on user interface composition has aimed to apply the tree algebras for XML data system to the XML languages for user interface definition. A tree algebra for XML data systems can be found in [4]. A tree is as a set of nodes, each one with a single parent and many children. The trees have two types of operators: algebraic and relational. Another tree algebra definition can be found in [5], with a similar approach. The main difference is the focus of the definition: Jagadish et al. [5] aim to discuss a solution for creating data structures able to run efficient queries on XML trees and they define operators similar to the usual relational database. A similar tree-based approach, but specific for the concrete level of the UI has been applied for the USIXML Language [7]. In this chapter, we consider compositions that are mainly driven from the user interface perspective taking into account the support that they have to provide. In order to discuss comprehensively these issues, a systematic approach for analyzing this problem is advisable. To this aim, we have identified a design space based on various dimensions on which the composition of the UI can vary.

More specifically, this chapter describes a five-dimensional problem space for UI composition. In particular, in Section 2, we report an overview of the main characteristics of the problem space, showing a number of problem dimensions, and which aspects are modelled by each dimension. Afterwards, Section 3 is dedicated to describing how MARIA and ConcurTaskTrees support the different compositions identified in the problem space. For the various options, we provide some examples. Lastly, a final section summarises the main points covered.

2 The Design Space for Composition of UIs

User interfaces can be composed according to a number of aspects. In this section, we describe a design space referring to such aspects in order to identify the possible compositions that can occur. Up to now, five dimensions have been identified (see Figure 1):

- **Abstraction level** used to describe the user interface;
- **Granularity** of the user interface elements considered;
- **UI Aspects** addressed;
- **Time/Phase** when the composition occurs;
- The type of **Web Services** involved in the composition.

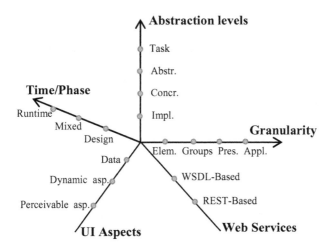

Fig. 1 The problem space for composition of UIs.

As we better see in the following sections, only on three (out of five) axis there is an ordering relationships between the contained values. In Figure 1, this has been highlighted by opportunely using arrows or plain lines for representing the different dimensions. In the next sub-sections (Section 2.1 – Section 2.5), we describe more in detail the characteristics of every axis of the problem space. Afterwards, in Section 3, we analyze how MARIA and ConcurTaskTrees support the composition options offered by the problem space.

2.1 Abstraction Levels

Since a UI can be described at various abstraction levels (task and objects, abstract, concrete, and implementation level), the user interface composition can occur at each of these levels. The abstraction levels usually considered are those of the CAMELEON Reference Framework [3], starting from the highest abstraction levels to the more concrete ones:

- **Task:** this level refers to activities performed to reach the users' goals;
- **Abstract:** this is the level of a platform-independent interface description;
- **Concrete:** an interface description referring to a specified platform, but in a manner that is independent from the implementation framework;
- **Implementation:** interface description referring to a specific implementation language.

Please note that with "platform" we mean a group of devices sharing a number of common interaction resources. Examples of different platforms are the graphical desktop platform, the graphical mobile platform, the vocal platform.

Moreover, transformations could be defined between the various user interface descriptions of the different levels. One example of such transformations could be the mapping that associate abstract interactors to concrete ones (through forward transformations). However, it could also be possible to have backward references (for instance, when it is possible to map abstract interactors to tasks).

Finally, an ordering relationship exists among the various values of this axis: the task level is the most abstract level, while the implementation level is the most concrete one.

2.2 Granularity

The granularity refers to the size of elements that can be composed. Indeed, we can compose single user interface elements or groups of objects, and we can join presentations in order to obtain the user interface for an entire application. Since it is also possible to compose user interfaces of applications (e.g., to obtain mash-ups), another value has been added on this dimension: "Applications". Therefore, below you can find the various values on this dimension, as they appear in the corresponding axis, starting from the most elementary ones to more complex objects (for instance, in a presentation, we can have compositions of groups, as well as in an application, we can have several presentations).

- **Elements:** Composing single user interface elements;
- **Groups:** Composing groups of elements;
- **Presentations:** Composing different presentations. A presentation is a set of UI-elements that are all perceivable at a certain moment. Therefore, a presentation can be seen in some sense as defining the current context where user actions can be performed. For instance, for a Web site, the page the user is currently visiting is an example of presentation;
- **Applications:** Composing different applications. For instance, with mash-up applications it is possible to add in a new composed application different (and generally smaller) applications (or 'gadgets'). An example of this is iGoogle (http://www.google.com/ig), where the user can create her personalized dashboard by grouping together 'gadgets', such as a weather application, a news feed, etc.

Again, also for this axis, the various values have been placed assuming an implicit underlying order (from the most elementary ones to the most structured/ comprehensive ones).

2.3 UI Aspects

With this dimension, we distinguish the different types of compositions depending on the main UI aspects the composition affects.

- **Data:** in this case the composition is carried out on the data manipulated by the UI elements considered;
- **Dynamic aspects:** in this case the composition affects the possible sequencing of user actions and system feedback;

- **Perceivable aspects:** this is the case when the composition acts on perceivable UI aspects.

No specific ordering relationship exists between the various values belonging to this axis.

2.4 Time/Phase

This dimension specifies when the composition occurs. It can be either a static composition, occurring at design time, in which case the elements we are going to compose are known in advance. It can also be a dynamic composition, occurring at runtime, during the execution of the application.

The latter composition (occurring at runtime) is especially significant in ubiquitous applications, since in such environments the context of use can vary a lot and then it may require different services according to such variations. Another option is the possibility of having types of composition that are a combination of the two possibilities. To summarize:

- **Runtime:** during application execution
- **Design Time:** when designing the application
- **Mixed:** when the composition is a mixed-up of the previous cases (e.g., when the composition occurs partially at design time and partially at runtime)

The time when the composition occurs can be assumed as the underlying order of this axis.

2.5 Web Services

A "Web service" is defined as "a software system designed to support interoperable machine-to-machine interaction over a network" [13]. Also, two basic classes of Web Services can be identified: REST-compliant Web services, and WSDL- (or SOAP-) based Web Services. On the one hand, SOAP (using WSDL) is a XML standard-based on document passing, with very structured formats for requests and responses. On the other hand, REST is lightweight, basically requiring just HTTP standard to work, and without constraining to a specific required format. In [12], there is an interesting comparison and discussion of strengths and weaknesses of both approaches.

3 How MARIA and ConcurtaskTrees fit the Problem Space

In this section, we mainly focus on how the MARIA [11] and ConcurTaskTrees [10] languages enable the composition mechanisms that are identified through the problem space. In order to concretely describe the support for the problem space, we also provide excerpts for some composition examples analyzed. We start our analysis by considering the highest abstraction level (task level, see Section 3.1) and then move to composition options at more concrete levels.

3.1 Task Level

In the following subsection, we show some examples of composition at the task level by exploiting the ConcurTaskTrees notation.

3.1.1 UI Composition at the Task Level Exploiting the ConcurTaskTrees Language

One example of composition at the task level involves the description of the activities to be performed in order to search for a DVD (using a web service like the Amazon AWSECommerce service) and then obtain the related trailer (using a movie trailer service like YouTube). A possible composition of these two tasks is exploiting the search service in order to find out which DVDs are available in store, allowing the user to watch the trailer of the search results. The starting point is having two separate task models describing the activities for searching for a DVD and getting a trailer (see Figure 2).

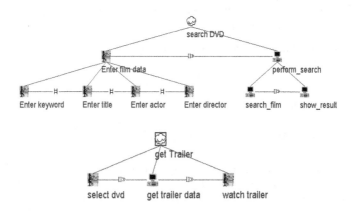

Fig. 2 Task models for accessing the DVD search and watch trailer services.

The composition is performed by specifying the temporal relationship between the two task models: the *"search DVD"* task enables the *"get Trailer"* task, by passing to it the information associated with the title of the selected DVD. In order to create such composition the designer has to:

1. Define an abstract task (the *"Compos dvd search"* task in Figure 3) that is the root of the composite task model (Step 1);
2. Add the *"search DVD"* task model as sub-task of the root specified at Step 1.
3. Add the *"get Trailer"* model as sub-task of the root specified at Step 1.

4. Connect the two models using the enabling with information passing operator (represented by this symbol: "[]>>")
5. Specify that the object of the search sub-task is used by the "*get Trailer*" service.

Figure 3 shows the result of the composition.

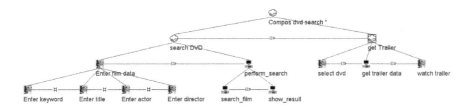

Fig. 3 The composition result.

In the five-dimensional space identified, this example can be represented as shown in Figure 4 (Abstraction level: task; Granularity: groups; UI Aspects: Dynamic aspects; Time/Phase: design time; Web Services: WSDL-based). Indeed, the abstraction level is the task because we are considering tasks for composition, the granularity is at the group level because we are composing parts of user interfaces associated with given services (we can suppose that the presentation might contain additional UI elements). Regarding the UI aspects, the composition in this example basically intervenes on dynamic aspects since it indicates that *after* executing the first service, the second one is enabled by receiving the result by the first one. In addition, through the CTT language it is possible to refer to

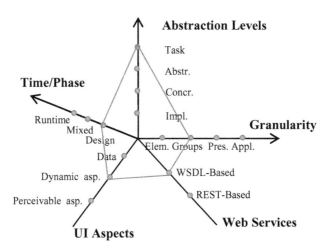

Fig. 4 The considered composition example referred to the problem space.

web services specified through WSDL descriptions, as it has been considered in this composition example. Finally, in the considered example, the composition occurs at design time.

3.2 Abstract Level

Figure 5 depicts how MARIA supports the problem space. In terms of abstractions, it covers both the abstract and the concrete level, as well as the implementation. At the abstract level, the UI is described using abstract elements and relationships, independent from a specific platform. Such relationships are *abstract composition operators*, which are provided by the language itself to combine together different interactors or, in turn, other composed expressions. Also the mechanisms used for composing together abstract presentations, by means of *abstract connections,* can be used for composition at this level. In addition, *mechanisms specified in the dialog model (at the abstract level)* can be used to specify compositions occurring within a single abstract presentation. While the first one (composition operators) is a composition that defines a static organization of the interactors, the other two mechanisms define dynamic compositions, which evolve over time. In the following sections, we better detail all such different cases, by devoting to each a separate section.

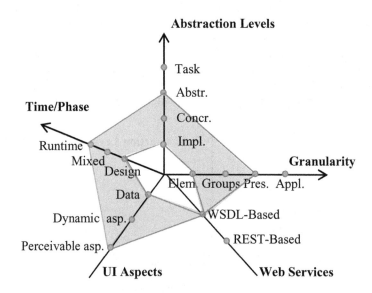

Fig. 5 The problem space supported by MARIA.

3.2.1 Abstract Composition Operators

The composition expressed through the abstract composition operators generally affects the presentation aspects of an interface. In MARIA, three composition operators have been identified: grouping, relation and repeater.

The composition operators allow for composing together (composition of) interactors. As it is indicated by the name, the objective of the grouping operator is to indicate that some interactors are logically grouped together: this information should be appropriately rendered in the UI. The definition of the Grouping operator in MARIA requires the specification of a number of attributes:

- **continuous_update.** Boolean type, optional. It is used to specify a continuous update of the content. The technique used for implementing such an update will depend on the specific technology that will be used at the implementation level.
- **hidden.** Boolean type, optional. It is True if the interactor is not displayed to the user.
- **hierarchy.** Boolean type, optional. If true, the grouped interactors have a hierarchical relation.
- **hierarchy_value.** String type, optional. Value for hierarchical presentation of the content.
- **id.** NMTOKEN type, required. It is the interactor composition identifier
- **ordering.** Boolean type, optional. If true, the grouped interactors have an ordering relation.
- **update_function.** String type, optional. The name of the function for a continuous_update.

A simplified example of grouping expression in the MARIA language is in the following XML-based excerpt in which three UI elements are grouped together: an interactor used for selecting a customer, an activator element for searching the quotations associated with the selected customer, and a description interactor showing the results. A more structured example of use of MARIA XML-based language will be presented later on in the Chapter.

```
<grouping id="Select_customer"hierarchy="false"
[...other attributes...]>
        <single_choice id="Specify_customer_ID" [...]>
          <choice_element value="item/id"/>
</single_choice>
        <activator id="Search_customer_quotations" [...]/>
        <description id="P3_Show_result" [...] />
</grouping>
```

Differently from the Grouping operator, which models a relationship between *several* abstract UI objects (or compositions of them), the *Relation* operator models a relationship between only two expressions of interactors. A typical example of Relation abstract operator is translated at the concrete level (for a graphical platform) in a UI *form*. In this case, the two expressions of interactors involved by the Relation are on the one hand, the N fields to be filled by the users, and, on the other hand, the button (generally labelled with "Submit") for transmitting the corresponding values to the application server. So, the Relation operator supports a N:1 relationship between the N elements appearing in the first expression, and the second expression involved in the composition.

3.2.2 Connections

The *connections* are mechanisms for composing together presentations, where a *presentation* is a set of UI elements that can be perceived at a certain time. Differently from what happens for the composition operators presented in the previous sections (which combine elements belonging to the same presentation), the compositions supported by the connections involve different presentations of the UI and generally affect the dynamic behaviour of the UI. A connection is generally defined by specifying a presentation, which is the current presentation, and an interaction element, which is generally a navigator element triggering the activation of another presentation (i.e., the target presentation) when it is selected. At the abstract level, the connections are defined in terms of abstract presentations and abstract interactors.

At the abstract level, three types of connections can be specified in MARIA:

- **Elementary connections:** connections linking together two presentations through one abstract interactor (e.g., by activating an interactor of type navigator). Thus, it is possible to move from a source presentation to a target presentation through an interactor.
- **Complex connections:** a more structured connection in which it is possible to specify a set of interactors composed by Boolean expressions able to activate the connection.
- **Conditional connections:** a more flexible mechanism for describing connections, in which it is possible to specify that, depending on the value currently assumed by a certain parameter, it is possible to move to different presentations. Therefore, a "conditional connection" is a connection that can activate more than one presentation, and the presentation that is finally activated depends on a specific value.

A simplified example of conditional connection in MARIA has the following specification:

```
<conditional_conn id="" interactor_id="" parameter_name="">
  <cond parameter_value="" presentation_to_load=""
      target_composition_operator=""
    target_presentation_name="">{1,unbounded}</cond>
</conditional_conn>
```

As you can see from the above excerpt, a conditional connection can have one or multiple child elements of type *cond*, whose definition has a number of attributes. In addition, the definition of the conditional connection includes some attributes, which are detailed below:

- **id.** Required, it is the unique identifier of the conditional connection

- **interactor_id.** Required, it is the identifier of the interactor which connects the current presentation with another one (generally refers to a navigator or an activator)
- **parameter_name.** Required, it is a string with the name of the variable to test for selecting the target presentation

In order to better illustrate how connections work, in the continuation of the Chapter, we will provide a more structured example in which they are exploited.

3.2.3 Dialog Model – Related Composition Mechanism (Abstract Level)

Another mechanism that can be used for composing UIs is the mechanism defined in the dialog model, which is an abstract model that is used to specify the structure of the dialogue between a user and an interactive computer system. The composition technique associated with the dialogue model involves dynamic aspects of a UI and it is generally used for specifying the dynamic behaviour occurring within a single presentation. Indeed, a presentation does not have just one single state, but it can move between different states depending on a number of events, which represents its dynamic behaviour. Therefore, the compositions intervening at the level of the dialog model allows for composing together over time the interactors that belong to the same presentation, by identifying different *states* within the same presentation.

For example, as a consequence of selecting a specific item in a list of cities in a part of a presentation, it can happen that some other UI elements in the presentation are disabled, since they are not possible for the specific item selected, while other elements are enabled. In this case, we have identified a first *state* of the presentation as the one in which a certain subset of interactors is disabled, and another state of the presentation as the one in which the same subset of interactors are enabled as a consequence of performing a certain selection in the UI (city selection). So, in this case, the mechanism for dynamically moving from the first state to the second state (in other terms: to compose together the two states or groups of interactors) is the UI element that supports the selection of a specific city. Another simple example would be a touristic web page with a list of cities, where the user selects a city in the countryside, and therefore, in the presentation, the part dedicated to reach this location by boat should be dynamically disabled.

The mechanism modelled by the dialog model is a consequence of the fact that the dynamic behaviour of an abstract presentation can evolve over time depending on some events that occur in the UI. In MARIA, the dialogue model is basically an event-based model in which the CTT temporal operators can be used for defining complex dialog expressions. As for the type of actions that can be performed in reaction to a change of state (the so-called *event handlers*), they can be i.e. to enable (or to disable) UI objects, as well as to support further, more flexible behaviour. To this aim, in MARIA, some more flexible constructs have been identified as useful for modelling the different activities that can be performed as a consequence of a change of state. For instance, a value change of an interactor attribute can be supported in MARIA through the *change_property* attribute. Other activities are: change of values of some elements in the data model, invocation of external functions, usage of typical programmatic operations on Strings, Numbers, and Boolean values, and the support for well-known programming language constructs like if-then-else and while. Finally, it is worth pointing out that at this level the composition will involve *abstract* events and *abstract event handlers (which are associated to abstract* interactors).

3.2.4 Abstract Composition Example

In this section, we focus on one example of composition at the abstract level and involving perceivable aspects of interactors belonging to a single presentation. In addition, the example considers composition occurring at design time. Therefore, the five-dimensional element identified by this example (see Figure 6) is: Abstraction level: abstract; Granularity: presentation; UI Aspects: perceivable aspects; Time/Phase: design time; Web Services: WSDL-Based.

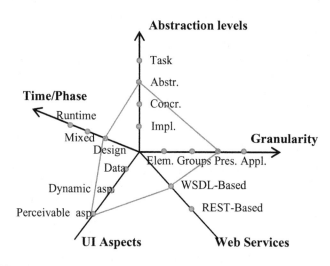

Fig. 6 The composition considered in the example, and referred to the problem space.

In order to provide an example of this kind of composition, we can consider a simple application with which the user interacts in order to search for a DVD within an online DVD database.

The application has three presentations. The first presentation ("Presentation_1", see excerpt below) provides the UI for specifying the data on which the search will be performed. As you can see in the MARIA excerpt below, in this presentation there are various interactors of type text_edit for specifying such information (e.g., title, actor, director, etc.):

```
<presentation name="Presentation_1">
      <grouping id="Specify dvd_search">
          <grouping id="Enter_film_data">
              <text_edit id="Enter_keyword"/>
              <text_edit id="Enter_title"/>
```

```
                <text_edit id="Enter_actor"/>
                <text_edit id="Enter_director"/>
                <activator id="search_film_activator"/>
            </grouping>
            <grouping id="perform_search">
                <activator id="show_result_activator"/>
            </grouping>
        </grouping>
    </presentation>
```

The second presentation shows the result of the search (see the description interactor "show_result" in the excerpt below). This result shows a list of possible movies satisfying the constraints specified in the search: from this list of results, the user can then select (see the single_choice interactor) a specific movie:

```
<presentation name="Presentation_2">
    <grouping id="Perform_dvd_search">
        <grouping id="perform_search">
            <description id="show_result"/>
            <navigator id="perform_search_navigator"/>
        </grouping>
        <grouping id="choose_dvd">
          <single_choice id="select_dvd"
cardinality="4"/>
        </grouping>
    </grouping>
</presentation>
```

Once the user has selected a specific trailer, in the third presentation the user can obtain the data about the trailer that has been selected by interacting with a navigator interactor.

```
<presentation name="Presentation_3">
    <grouping id="Get_Trailer">
        <navigator id="get_trailer_data_navigator"/>
    </grouping>
</presentation>
```

An example of composition for such UIs is to merge the three presentations into only one presentation. In such combined presentation there will be one part dedicated to entering the search keywords, one part for showing the results, and a remaining part for watching the selected trailer. In terms of the MARIA language, the resulting composition at the abstract level will produce the following result:

```
<presentation name="Composed_presentation">
    <grouping id="Composed_dvd_search">
        <grouping id="Specify_dvd_search">
            <grouping id="Enter_film_data">
                <text_edit id="Enter_keyword"/>
                <text_edit id="Enter_title"/>
```

```
            <text_edit id="Enter_actor"/>
            <text_edit id="Enter_director"/>
            <activator id="search_film_activator"/>
        </grouping>
        <grouping id="perform_search">
            <activator id="show_result_activator"/>
        </grouping>
    </grouping>
    <grouping id="Perform_dvd_search">
        <grouping id="perform_search">
            <description id="show_result"/>
            <navigator id="perform_search_navigator"/>
        </grouping>
        <grouping id="choose_dvd">
        <single_choice id="select_dvd" cardinality="4"/>
        </grouping>
    </grouping>
    <grouping id="get_Trailer">
        <navigator id="get_trailer_data_navigator"/>
    </grouping>
  </grouping>
<presentation>
```

The composition in this case has been exploited through a grouping operator composing the content of the involved presentations.

3.3   Concrete Level (Graphical Desktop Platform)

At the concrete level, the UI is expressed by referring to concrete elements and relationships. Differently from the abstract level, at this level the UI description refers to a specific *platform*. Therefore, at this level, we refer to a number of inter-action techniques that are *dependent* on a platform, but are *independent* of a specific implementation language. As an example, while on a vocal platform we use specific sounds for grouping together vocally rendered elements, on a graphical platform we can use a shared background colour for rendering the fact that some elements are grouped together. Then, the concrete composition mechanisms that have been identified are basically the concrete composition operators (which are refinements of grouping and relation abstract operators), the dialog model (defining the dynamic behaviour associated within a single concrete presentation), and the composition mechanisms that can be specified through the connections (expressing the dynamic behaviour between different concrete presentations).

3.3.1   Concrete Composition Operators

At this level, the composition mechanisms identified are refinements of the composition techniques identified at the abstract level, using references to a specific platform/modality. For instance, while at the abstract level we refer to abstract grouping relation between UI elements, at this level, we have to specify which concrete techniques we use on a specific platform/modality in order to render such a grouping relation between the various elements. At the concrete level, the composition operators inherit the attributes that they have at the abstract level, adding further concrete details. In particular, at the concrete level (e.g., the desktop platform), the composition operators have some default_settings.

For the grouping operator, they are the following, modelled as attributes of the grouping_settings element, as described in the excerpt below:

```
<grouping_settings bullet="" fieldset="" position="">
    <hierarchy_properties
visualization="">{0,1}</hierarchy_properties>
    <ordering_properties position=""
visualization="">{0,1}</ordering_properties>
    <background>{0,1}</background>
</grouping_settings>
```

- **bullet.** Optional, if the grouping is carried out by using bullets
- **fieldset.** Optional, for grouping the elements with a fieldset (yes/no)
- **position.** Required, the element position settings

As for the Relation operator, since this operator is generally used for modelling the relationships occurring between a set of interactors (possibly composed with some composition operators) and one interactor, it has the form as its default supporting mechanism at the concrete desktop level.

3.3.2 Connections

At the concrete level, the connections are defined in the same way as at the abstract level. The only difference is that, at this (concrete) level, the specification is done by referring to *concrete* interactors (and concrete presentations), since they are a mechanism that just refines the corresponding elements introduced at the abstract level (abstract connections) by just adding platform-specific details.

3.3.3 Dialog Model –Related Mechanism (Concrete Level)

As it happened at the abstract level, also at the concrete level it is possible to use composition techniques based on the dialogue model, in order to model a dynamic behaviour affecting a single concrete presentation. In order to do this, we use complex expressions of concrete events (associated with concrete interactors), which might trigger the activation of concrete event handlers. The main difference from the dialog model-related mechanisms in the abstract case is that now the composition (occurring in terms of dynamic behaviour) will be defined by means of concrete events (associated with concrete interactors), which trigger the activation of concrete event handlers. For example, in a graphical platform a "click" event is a refinement of the abstract "selection" event.

3.3.4 Concrete Composition Example (Graphical Desktop Platform)

At this level, we show an example of composition that involves dynamic aspects. In particular, we show how it is possible to group together three different presentations in such a way that, depending on the value held by a specific parameter that can be selected in the first presentation, different elements are dynamically activated in the other two presentations.

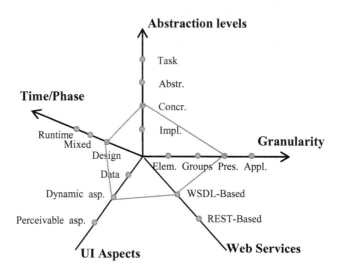

Fig. 7 The composition considered in the example, and referred to the problem space (concrete level, presentation granularity, dynamic aspects, design time, WSDL-based services).

We show how this behaviour can be modelled by using the "conditional connection" structure of MARIA language. Therefore, the five-dimensional element identified by this example is: Abstraction level: concrete; Granularity: presentations; UI Aspects: Dynamic aspects; Time/Phase: Design; Web Services: WSDL-based (see Figure 7). The considered example is drawn from an application that allows the user to present and edit home features. We can consider a first presentation ("presentation_1", see excerpt below), in which there is a grouping (implemented, in concrete terms, by a fieldset) of some pieces of information (textual elements) referring to a specific apartment. In addition, within this presentation, it is also possible to select the various rooms composing the flat.

```
<presentation name="presentation_1">
  ....
 <grouping id="deviceListGrouping">
 <properties position="row" bullet="false" fieldset="true">
  <background>
    <background_color>#D3D3D3</background_color>
  </background>
</properties>
<descriptionid="textRooms">
```

```
<text>  <string>Room List:</string>
    <font_settings style="" align="Center" size="20pt"
      color="#FF0000" name="Verdana"/>
  </text>
<description id="RoomDescription"><text>
  <string>The apartment is located in a seven-storey
building situated in the immediate outskirts of the town. It
consists of five rooms.</string></text>
    <font_settings style="" align="Center" size="20pt"
               color="#FF0000" name="Verdana"/>
  </description>
  <single_choicedata_reference="ArrayOfRooms"
id="roomSelection" selected="Bedroom" cardinality="5">
    <drop_down_list label="Room selection">
      <choice_element selected="false" value="Dining_room"
                 label="Dining room"/>
      <choice_element selected="false" value="Living_room"
                           label="Living room"/>
      <choice_element selected="false" value="Kitchen"
                           label="Kitchen"/>
      <choice_element selected="true" value="Bedroom"
                           label="Bedroom"/>
      <choice_element selected="false" value="Bathroom"
                           label="Bathroom"/>
    </drop_down_list>
  </single_choice>
  </grouping>
          ....
</presentation>
```

In addition to "presentation_1", we have other presentations that are devoted to describe the characteristics of each room in the apartment. More specifically, in the example presented, we have a second presentation ("presentation_2" in the excerpt below) dedicated to showing details of the bedroom, while the third presentation shows details of the bathroom (we do not include its XML specification for sake of brevity).

```
<presentation name="presentation_2">
          ...
<grouping id="bedroomGrouping">
  <properties position="column">
   <background>
     <background_color>#004466</background_color>
       <background_image></background_image>
     </background>
</properties>
<description id="title Image">
 <image width="100" height="100" horizontal_align="Left"
         alt="Bedroom image" source="img/bedroom.png"/>
 </description>
 <description id="titleText">
  <text><string>Bedroom</string>
```

```
    <font_settings style="italic" align="Left" size="30pt"
color="white" name="Arial"/>
      </text>
    </description>
    </grouping>
      ....
</presentation>
```

The idea is to have a new combined presentation in which, depending on the value that has been chosen between the set of rooms composing the flat, different presentations are activated. In the MARIA language, if we want to compose such presentations, in order to have a new UI with a dynamic behaviour that allows the activation of a specific presentation, depending on the value that is assumed by a specific interactor attribute, we can use the "conditional connection" construct. A "conditional connection" is a connection that can activate more than one presentation, and the presentation that is finally activated depends on a specific value. In the example, it is the value assumed by the drop-down list "roomSelection". Thus, if the value currently selected is "Bedroom", the "presentation_2" will be activated, and if the selected value is "Bathroom", the "presentation_3" will be activated.

Below is the related MARIA excerpt specifying the result of composition through conditional connection in "presentation_1" (only the part related to the connection specification has been described):

```
<presentation name="presentation_1">
 <connections>
  <conditional_conn id="id1" interactor_id="roomSelection"
parameter_name="roomSelection/selected">
    <cond parameter_value="Bedroom"
      target_presentation_name="presentation_2"
target_composition_operator="target_composition_operator1"
                presentation_to_load="presentation_1"/>
    <cond parameter_value="Bathroom"
              target_presentation_name="presentation_3"/>
  </conditional_conn>
 </connections>
<grouping id="deviceListGrouping">
   [ definition of  deviceListGrouping here ]
</grouping>
```

3.3.5 Example of Composition of Services at the Concrete Level

In this section, we show a possible composition of services at the concrete level. In particular, we consider the case when there is a first Web service used by a last minute tour agency, which, depending on the current time and location, delivers a list of cheap return flights (from the current location). We suppose that the user is currently in the area of London (Gatwick) and the service displays the flights currently available and departing from that airport from that moment onward, showing them in ascending order, from the cheapest flight to the most expensive one. A visualization of this service (for the desktop platform) is shown in Figure 8.

Price	Time/Date	To	Flight Number	Class
£ 291	09:35 9 Oct	Madrid	OP1456	Economy
	6:55 15 Oct	London Gatwick	OP1453	Economy
£ 295	12:30 9 Oct	Barcelona	TR1235	Economy
	6:55 15 Oct	London Gatwick	TR1665	Economy
£ 300	22:40 9 Oct	Barcelona	AA1466	Economy
	6:55 14 Oct	London Gatwick	AA1216	Economy
£ 350	10:35 8 Oct	Paris	PP4452	Economy
	6:55 15 Oct	London Gatwick	PP4452	Economy

Fig. 8 A possible graphical rendering of the UI for the first service providing information on flights (desktop platform).

Hotel Rex ★★★
Gran Via, 43, 01.Centro, Madrid
Centrally located, this elegant, traditional-style hotel provides a great base to visit Madrid's many cultural sights. It lies on Gran Vía, between the main squares of España and Callao.... More
Show rates

Il Castillas Madrid ★★★
Abada, 7, 01.Centro, Madrid
The Hotel Il Castillas has a fantastic central location, just 330 yards from Madrid's Puerta del Sol. It offers traditional style with modern facilities, including free Wi-Fi access.... More
Show rates

Ganivet ★★★
Toledo, 111, 01.Centro, Madrid
Hotel Ganivet has an ideal location in Madrid's La Latina district, a 10-minute walk from the Plaza Mayor. It offers good-value accommodation with free Wi-Fi access.... More
Show rates

Medium Cortezo ★★★
Doctor Cortezo, 3, 01.Centro, Madrid
The Medium Cortezo is set in the heart of Madrid, 800 metres from Atocha Train Station. It offers free Wi-Fi and 24-hour reception.... More
Show rates

Petit Palace Arenal Sol ★★★
Arenal, 16, 01.Centro, Madrid
Petit Palace Arenal is set in a pedestrian street by the Puerta del Sol. All rooms come with a flat-screen TV, a hydromassage shower and free Wi-Fi access.... More
Show rates

Suites Kris Aeropuerto ★★★
Campezo, 8, 20.San Blas, Madrid
The Suites Kris offers a 24-hour free shuttle service to nearby Barajas Airport and free transfer to IFEMA. It has a garden and a swimming pool, open seasonally.... More
Show rates

Fig. 9 A possible graphical rendering of the UI for the second service providing information on hotels (desktop platform).

The area given in input to this first service can vary, and can be specified, e.g., depending on the current position of the mobile user. In this case, a GPS receiver could provide this information. Then, the first service might be defined likewise: *flight_info=getFlightInfo(area)*, where *getFlightInfo* is the name of the service, *area* is the input parameter passed to the service, and *flight_info* is the output value returned by the service itself (it includes the city destination and departure/arrival times). Another service is also available, which, having in input a destination city and two dates (arrival/departure date), offers a list of available hotels for the considered period, also providing a visualization of each available hotel in a graphical map. The functionality of this second service can then be summarized with the following function: *hotels_info=provide_hotels_info(destination_city, arrival_date, departure_date)*, where *destination_city* is the city where to find an accommodation, while *arrival_date* and *departure_date* are the dates that identify the period during which the user will stay in that city.

This service delivers in output *hotels_info*, which is information about available hotels including name, address, rates, and also it provides a visualization of this hotel in a graphical map. A possible graphical rendering for this second service (for the graphical desktop platform) is visualized in Figure 9. These two UI services can be composed together on temporal aspects. Indeed, after the user selects a particular return flight in which s/he is interested from the currently available ones (depending on associated dates and destination selected), the second service will show the list of possible accommodation options in a graphical map. The composition of such services in the mobile device produces two presentations, which are displayed in Figures 10-11 below.

Price	Time/Date	To	Flight Number	Class
£ 291 ⊙	09:35 9 Oct	Madrid	OP1456	Economy
	6:55 15 Oct	London Gatwick	OP1453	Economy
£ 295 ⊙	12:30 9 Oct	Barcelona	TR1235	Economy
	6:55 15 Oct	London Gatwick	TR1665	Economy
£ 300 ⊙	22:40 9 Oct	Barcelona	AA1466	Economy
	6:55 14 Oct	London Gatwick	AA1216	Economy
£ 350 ⊙	10:35 8 Oct	Paris	PP4452	Economy
	6:55 15 Oct	London Gatwick	PP4452	Economy

Fig. 10 First presentation (mobile device) of the UI resulting from composing the two services.

More specifically, Figure 10 shows how the user can select the flight in which s/he is interested. Additionally, as soon as the user selects a particular hotel, this action triggers the visualization of a second presentation (visualized in Figure 11) in which the possible accommodation options are visualized. Depending on the

The Hotel II Castillas has a fantastic central location, just 330 yards from Madrid's Puerta del Sol. It offers traditional style with modern facilities, including free Wi-Fi access.

Fig. 11 Second presentation (mobile device) of the UI resulting from the composition

option selected by the user, the corresponding hotel is visualized in the graphical map, and its position will be highlighted in it by using an icon with a colour different from the one used for the other icons, to distinguish it from the other hotels in the same area. Also, in the mobile device, an adaptation step will generate an UI (see Figure 11) in which only a part of the information available for each hotel is immediately visible on the screen. Indeed, when the user selects a specific hotel, the application presents the overall description by displaying the picture and a part of the information in a textual manner, while the remaining information is vocally rendered.

As far as our problem space is concerned, in this case, the composition is carried out at the concrete level, involving groups of UI objects. Indeed, in this case, we are composing services, which can even provide data for only some parts of a presentation, and for this reason, we consider it as a composition involving groups of objects. In addition, the composition affects temporal aspects, since, after the user selects a particular item in the list different events are triggered in the other parts of the UI. The map shown in the right part of the UI changes its appearance since the selected item is highlighted with a different colour, and a vocal rendering of the remaining information about the selected hotel starts.

Therefore, the five-dimensional element identified by this example (see Figure 12) is: Abstraction level: Concrete; Granularity: groups of UI objects; UI Aspects: Dynamic aspects; Time/Phase: Runtime; Web Services: WSDL-Based.

The composition is done at runtime since we suppose that the service that provides information on hotels is not statically determined but it dynamically changes depending on the current position of the user. Regarding the level of composition, it occurs at the concrete level; the granularity is that of groups of UI objects, and

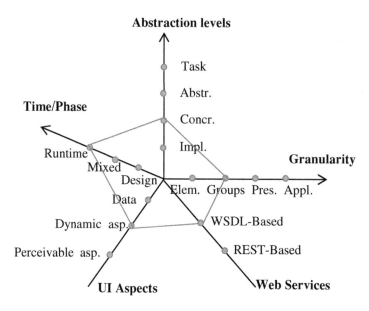

Fig. 12 The composition considered in the example, and referred to the problem space.

the aspects affected by the composition are the dynamic aspects (although also the perceivable aspects are affected as well).

4 Conclusions

This chapter presents a design space for user interface composition. In particular, we judged useful to propose a five-dimensional space for identifying the characteristics of the various user interface composition techniques that can be used. The five dimensions that have been identified are: granularity, abstraction level, UI-aspects affected by the composition, the phase when the composition occurs and the type of services that the composition involves.

Once we have defined such a problem space, we considered the support provides by the ConcurTaskTrees and MARIA languages, and to what extent they are able to cope with the composition options identified by the problem space. More specifically, currently MARIA neither provides support for composing together entire applications, nor for composing UIs at the task level.

In order to better illustrate relevant UI composition examples, we have provided and discussed a number of examples that cover the various parts of the proposed design space. Such examples have been provided by considering different levels of abstractions (also including the task level). Moreover, we have also provided relevant XML-based MARIA excerpts for some of them, in order to give the reader a more concrete idea of how in MARIA language it is possible to specify different composition cases.

Future work will be dedicated to further analysis of the proposed design space and to evaluating its validity and generality in identifying the possible situations that can occur in user interface composition.

Acknowledgments. This work has been supported by the ICT EU ServFace STREP project (http://www.servface.eu).

References

[1] Agrawal, A., Amend, M., Das, M., Ford, M., Keller, C., Kloppmann, M., König, D., Leymann, F., Müller, R., Pfau, G., Plösser, K., Rangaswamy, R., Rickayzen, A., Rowley, M., Schmidt, P., Trickovic, I., Yiu, A., Zeller, M.: Web Services Extension for People (BPEL4People), Version 1.0 (June 2007)

[2] Agrawal, A., Amend, M., Das, M., Ford, M., Keller, C., Kloppmann, M., König, D., Leymann, F., Müller, R., Pfau, G., Plösser, K., Rangaswamy, R., Rickayzen, A., Rowley, M., Schmidt, P., Trickovic, I., Yiu, A., Zeller, M.: Web Services Human Task (WS-HumanTask), Version 1.0 (June 2007)

[3] Calvary, G., Coutaz, J., Bouillon, L., Florins, M., Limbourg, Q., Marucci, L., Paternò, F., Santoro, C., Souchon, N., Thevenin, D., Vanderdonckt, J.: The CAMELEON reference framework. CAMELEON Project.Deliverable 1.1 (2002),
http://giove.isti.cnr.it/projects/cameleon/pdf/
CAMELEON%20D1.1RefFramework.pdf

[4] El bekai, A., Rossiter, N.: A Tree Based Algebra Framework for XML Data Systems. In: Proceedings of the Seventh International Conference on Enterprise Information Systems, ICEIS 2005, Miami, USA, May 25-28 (2005)

[5] Jagadish, H.V., Laks, V., Lakshmanan, S., Srivastava, D., Thompson, K.: TAX A Tree Algebra for XML. In: Proceedings of DBPL Conf. (2001)

[6] Janeiro, J., Preußner, A., Springer, T., Schill, A., Wauer, M.: Improving the Development of Service-Based Applications through Service Annotations. In: Proceedings of IADIS WWW/Internet (2009)

[7] Lepreux, S., Vanderdonckt, J., Michotte, B.: Visual Design of User Interfaces by (De)composition. In: DSV-IS 2006, pp. 157–170 (2006)

[8] Mori, G., Paternò, F., Santoro, C.: CTTE: Support for Developing and Analysing Task Models for Interactive System Design. IEEE Transactions on Software Engineering 28(8), 797–813 (2002)

[9] Oasis standard: Web Service Business Process Execution Language (April 2007)

[10] Paternò, F.: Model-Based Design and Evaluation of Inter-active Applications. Springer, Heidelberg (2000)

[11] Paternò, S.C., Spano, L.D.: MARIA: A Universal Language for Service-Oriented Applications in Ubiquitous Environment. ACM Transactions on Computer-Human Interaction 16(4), 19:1–19:30 (2009)

[12] Pautasso, C., Zimmermann, O., Leymann, F.: RESTful Web Services vs. Big Web Services: Making the Right Architectural Decision. In: Proc. of the 17th International World Wide Web Conference (WWW 2008), Bejing, China (April 2008)

[13] W3C, Web Services Glossary (2004), http://www.w3.org/TR/ws-gloss/

Applying Meta-Modeling for the Definition of Model-Driven Development Methods of Advanced User Interfaces

Stefan Sauer

Abstract. The user interfaces of interactive systems become increasingly complex due to new interaction paradigms, required adaptability, use of innovative technologies, multi-media and interaction modalities. Their development thus demands for sophisticated processes and methods, as they are deployed in software engineering. Model-driven development is a promising candidate for mastering the complex development task in a systematic, precise and appropriately formal way. Although diverse models of advanced user interfaces are deployed in a development process to specify, design and implement the user interface, it is not standardized which models to use, how to combine them, and how to proceed in the course of development. Rather, this has to be defined by methods in the context of organizations, domains, projects. To cope with the definition of model-driven development methods for advanced user interfaces, we propose a meta-method for method engineering. It can be used for modeling and tailoring such development methods. We show how to apply this meta-method for designing development methods in the domain of advanced user interfaces.

1 Introduction

The development of advanced interactive software systems demands for sophisticated engineering processes and methods, not only for the application functionality, but also for their increasingly sophisticated user interfaces. Model-driven development is a qualified approach for dealing with the complex development task of advanced user interface development in a systematic, precise and appropriately formal way. However, it needs to get along with the creative and less formal development techniques that are also used in user interface development.

Diverse models of advanced user interfaces are deployed in a development process to specify, design and implement the user interface. Among these models

Stefan Sauer
University of Paderborn, s-lab – Software Quality Lab
Warburger Straße 100, D-33098 Paderborn, Germany
e-mail: `sauer@s-lab.upb.de`

H. Hussmann et al. (Eds.): MDD of Advanced User Interfaces, SCI 340, pp. 67–86.
springerlink.com © Springer-Verlag Berlin Heidelberg 2011

are task models, dialog structure or navigation structure models, dialog flow or navigation models, dialog state and presentation state models, abstract and concrete user interface models, models of adaptation, device capability models, and so on. The concrete set of models that is used for a development depends on the domain, purpose, and nature of the interactive system and its user interface. In an integrated development approach, the set of models also has to be compatible with other models of the interactive system such as those regarding application functionality.

In order to cope with this complexity, it is necessary to define precise methods for model-driven development of advanced user interfaces (MDDAUI). It must be specified which models and artifacts are to be produced, how they are related and how to proceed from one to the other by the use of transformations. Such transformations can be executed as manual development tasks or by automated procedures (e.g. model transformations) as part of the development process.

We propose a meta-method for method engineering [1] as a solution for this challenge. It can be utilized for modeling and tailoring engineering methods. We show how to apply this meta-method for designing development methods in the domain of advanced user interfaces.

The meta-method consists of a product and a process part. The product part prescribes which elements must be defined for a development method (*product model*). The *process model* specifies what needs to be done (work model) and how to proceed to obtain the definition of the development method (workflow model).

Engineering a development method then means instantiating the meta-method's product model according to its process model, i.e., the method engineer performs the defined method engineering tasks of the work model and follows the meta-method's workflow model. The resulting development method – the product of method engineering – is an instance of the meta-method's product model.

In our approach, the development method itself contains a *model of domain concepts* from the MDDAUI domain as its first product. Such domain concepts are general concepts from the domain of human-computer interaction such as user, task (not to be confused with the concept "task" from the method engineering domain), dialog, presentation state, widget and so on, but also concepts that are specific to either advanced user interfaces or model-based and model-driven methods. Examples are multimodal interaction and adaptation, or domain-relevant – both general and domain-specific – types of models with their model elements and defined model transformations, respectively. The model of domain concepts defines these concepts, their relevant properties and the interrelationships between the concepts. The domain concepts are paired with notations for their representation to form the *artifact types* (artifact model) of the development method. (Their semantic relations are taken from the model of domain concepts.) The pairing provides us with an adequate, integrated set of (modeling) languages for advanced user interfaces. We thus combine method engineering and language engineering in our meta-method.

The tasks in the process dimension are described as *transformations* that act upon the artifacts of the method's artifact model. The model transformations of model-driven development are a specialization of this transformation concept. The activities of the workflow generally correspond to the tasks the UI developers have to accomplish, but may adapt them according to the situational context. It can be specified in a rule-based manner which effects a particular development task or activity has on the graph of artifacts. We use a notation based on graph transformation rules to describe the precondition, post-condition and effect of such development activities.

Tools can then be built that (1) use the model of domain concepts as the foundation of their artifact repository structure; (2) that use a representation that conforms to the defined notation of the method's artifact types in their interaction part, i.e., user interface, content and representation media, produced output documents and files; and (3) that use the work and workflow models as the basis for the supported functionality.

In the next section, we will analyze the method domain of MDDAUI in order to derive requirements for appropriate development methods from this analysis. These requirements transitively impose requirements on the meta-method, possibly requiring the specialization of the general meta-method for this class of methods. We structure our analysis according to the characteristics of user interfaces, advanced user interfaces, (advanced) user interface development, models of (advanced) user interfaces, and integrated model-driven development of advanced user interfaces. In Section 3, we give a general introduction into method engineering and the use of meta-modeling for method engineering. Our meta-method for method engineering is presented in Section 4. In Section 5, we show how to apply it for the MDDAUI method domain. We summarize our work in Section 6.

2 Model-Driven Development of Advanced User Interfaces

In this section, we give an overview of MDDAUI. We derive from this the requirements for model-driven development methods for advanced user interfaces. In particular, we look at both the characteristics of advanced user interfaces that impact their development from its product perspective and the inherent characteristics of the development approach from the process perspective.

2.1 User Interfaces

The user interface of interactive software systems is one of the key factors determining its success. Not surprisingly, the development of sophisticated user interfaces is gaining more and more attention not only in the human-computer interaction community, but eventually also in the software engineering community.

The *user interface* is the part of an interactive system where interaction between humans and computers occurs. Interaction is a bidirectional process of action and reaction, with the exchange of information between the human and the computer. User interfaces therefore provide means of input and/or output, thus allowing the users to manipulate a system and, vice versa, the system to indicate the effects of the users' manipulation. The user interface of a software-based system includes both hardware (physical) and software (logical) components. The term "computer" thereby stands for an increasing multitude of computing platforms, ranging from smart cards and wearable computing devices, across interactive embedded systems, appliances, mobile phones and mobile computers, to desktops and collaboration environments (cf.[2]).

2.2 Advanced User Interfaces

Advanced user interfaces represent the current state-of-the-art in human-computer interaction. It is an intricate task to precisely define the term advanced user interface, since there exists a wide range of user interfaces that are considered advanced. Their common qualification is that they go beyond traditional user interfaces of data-intensive or simple control systems. But this can be with respect to different aspects, e.g. supporting complex interactions, visualizations, multimedia representations, multimodality, context-dependent adaptability, or customization (see [3], [4]). Summarizing and extending the classification of [5], typical facets of advanced user interfaces are:

- they have to provide a high degree of usability,
- increasingly complex functionality is expected,
- more intuitive interaction techniques are built in,
- multimodal interaction is supported,
- tailored and customizable representations of information are offered,
- techniques like animation or 3D visualization are incorporated,
- speech or haptic output are used as additional perception channels,
- temporal media types, like video and audio, and the combination of different modalities require dealing with synchronization and dependency issues,
- different interaction devices are used for different purposes, even within a single modality,
- they use a broad spectrum of presentation, perception, and representation media,
- context-aware user interfaces and adaptation to the context of use by means of context-sensitive and multi-target user interfaces and user interface plasticity appear in ubiquitous computing [2].

2.3 (Advanced) User Interface Development

User interface development generally employs both creative and informal techniques of development such as storyboards and prototyping, and formal techniques such as dialog structure and dialog state models. The development of user interfaces of a software-based system is a multidisciplinary task. It typically involves knowledge (and experts) from areas such as usability engineering, interaction design, graphics and media design, user interface technologies and interaction devices, computer engineering, software engineering, human factors, ergonomics and even psychology. User interface development comprises tasks of specification, design, and implementation. The implementation of user interfaces often employs dedicated frameworks (e.g. Java AWT, SWT or SWING), toolkits, and tools (e.g. GUI builders).

Advanced user interface development covers a broader spectrum of aspects than traditional user interfaces development. This is due to two reasons: advanced user interfaces have additional aspects that need to be taken into account (product perspective); the development of advanced user interfaces comprises additional tasks, activities, methods and techniques that are not contained in traditional user interface development methods (process perspective).

We can thus distinguish between two different dimensions and interpretations of the term advanced user interface development, which can even be combined to build a third interpretation:

A) development of advanced user interfaces
B) advanced development of user interfaces
C) advanced development of advanced user interfaces

Model-driven development of user interfaces can be subsumed to category B, model-driven development of *advanced* user interfaces belongs to category C.

Advanced-user interface development naturally requires the combination of expertise from human-computer interaction and software engineering. One possible approach is to combine object modeling with user interface design [6]. A series of workshops on bridging the gaps between the software engineering and human-computer interaction communities was hold as an activity of IFIP WG 2.7/13.4 on User Interface Engineering during the last decade (http://www.se-hci.org/bridging/) and resulted in some interesting lines of research (see e.g. [7], [8], [9]) –MDDAUI being one of them!

It is our objective to integrate the knowledge from both domains and to apply the model-driven development paradigm to user interface development. We will look at this methodical integration from the perspective of models and modeling in the next section.

2.4 Models of (Advanced) User Interfaces

A *model* is, according to scientific theory, a representation of a natural or artificial original that focuses on those characteristics and properties of the original that are relevant for the given purpose of modeling, and abstracts from irrelevant properties. In an engineering process, models are used for specification, documentation, and communication. They are themselves objects of processing and transformation, and are a foundation for decision making, analysis, validation, verification, and testing. Models can be built upfront or retrospective in terms of forward engineering or reverse engineering, respectively.

The use of models has gained popularity in both software engineering and human-computer interaction over the years. Models have a long tradition in systems and software engineering. Eventually with the Unified Modeling Language (UML), model-based software development has become popular and common practice. Recently, model-driven development is attracting a lot of attention in the software engineering domain.

Likewise model-based user interface development has found its way into human-computer interaction design and user interface development. Models play an important role in today's user interface development. The purpose of models in the development of user interfaces has been stated in [4]:

> "Models shall act as a kind of bridge between input from various people involved in UI development (end users, domain experts, UI developers, management people, etc.) to integrate all this knowledge and to transfer it into the software engineering process."

However, although both communities make extensive use of models in their development methods, the modeling is still vastly independent.

As in software engineering, the modeling of user interfaces deals with different aspects and happens on different levels of abstraction. In addition, it may also be done with a different degree of detail. Therefore, a holistic model has to combine a set of partial models that are dedicated to modeling specific aspects on a defined level of abstraction. The required degree of detail should be part of an accompanying quality model.

For example, the CAMELEON reference framework for user interface models in [2] structures the development lifecycle in four *levels of abstraction*: tasks and concepts, abstract user interface, concrete user interface, final user interface.

Human-computer interaction and the development of advanced user interfaces naturally address a broad spectrum of *aspects* to be considered. They can be represented by a diversity of dedicated models. Different kinds of models have been widely used in the development of user interfaces. For example, task and dialog models are used in many developments, and traditional approaches for user interface development provide abstract and platform-independent models for basic widget-based user interfaces.

For example, the CAMELEON reference framework [2] proposes a set of models for the modeling of context-sensitive user interfaces. On the conceptual level, three groups of models are differentiated: domain, context, and adaptation. Domain concepts and tasks belong to the domain models. User, platform, and environment models are subsumed in the context models. Adaptation models comprise evolution and transition models. From these models, design models are derived. Among them are concepts and task models, abstract user interface and concrete user interface models and the final user interface model for a given configuration. A third group of models guide the adaptation process of the context-sensitive user interface at runtime. Obviously, there exist relationships between these models that call for systematic transformation.

In our method for object-oriented modeling of multimedia applications OMMMA [10], we use four different types of models in combination: presentation model (structure and layout), state model (interactive control), class model (media and application structure), and sequence model (temporal behavior). Our GuiBuilder method [11] uses a concrete user interface model consisting of a presentation model (structure and layout of user interface elements) and a dynamics model (interaction behavior). The GuiBuilder tool provides an editor and components for model validation, UI prototype generation and simulation.

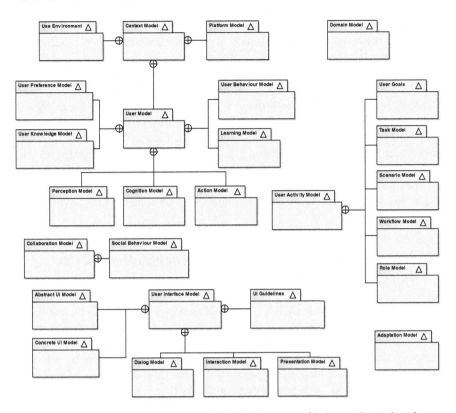

Fig. 1 A large variety of models is used in the development of (advanced) user interfaces

In [12], we have given a list of models and sub-models that are commonly used in user interface development. This list of models does not claim to be complete, but already shows the diversity of models being used. A partly extended set of models is shown in Fig. 1. Some of them may be even further decomposed, e.g. the dialog model into dialog structure, dialog flow, and dialog state models; or the presentation model into presentation structure, presentation layout, and presentation state models.

Which models are actually needed and best suited depends much on the given development task and context. In [5], we concluded that "it is very probable that there is no single set of models optimal for every kind of user interface".

However, not all of the aspects listed in Sections 2.1 and 2.2 can be easily represented by *formal* models in a user interface development method. Therefore, user interface development traditionally employs a number of informal techniques (see Section 2.3) to cover certain aspects, especially if development is performed on a higher level of abstraction. Their results can be considered to be *informal* models. Furthermore, development methods have not only to consider the system perspective, but also look from the perspective of the users.

Advanced user-orientation can be achieved by integrating methods of software engineering with (less formal) methods of user-centered design [8]. Therefore, the analysis and conceptual modeling of users, contexts of use, tasks and usage scenarios have to be covered by an advanced user interface development method as well.

Hence, it is our objective to provide a methodological framework that allows method engineers to define, flexibly select and customize (semi-)formal models and to integrate them with other artifacts to cover all relevant aspects of their advanced user interface development in a coherent set of models and artifacts. The resulting methods combine modeling with informal techniques of other design disciplines such as interaction design, creative design, graphics design, media design, to name but a few. We call the result of such a method development an *integrated method*.

2.5 Integrated Model-Driven Development of Advanced User Interfaces

The guiding principle of MDDAUI is "the demand for a flexible composition of various different models to support the model-driven development of user interfaces with a high degree of usability and customization" [13].

Model Driven Development (MDD) is an important paradigm in software engineering. The basic idea is to systematically specify software using (platform-independent) models, which are then gradually (i.e., using platform-specific models) and (semi-)automatically transformed into executable applications for different platforms and target devices.

MDD employs another core concept in addition to models: *model transformations*. Model transformations can be used to transform the content of a model or between models. Models can be (semantically) transformed or (syntactically) translated. Model transformations can also be used to check and restore consistency or other quality properties of models. The intention of MDDAUI is to apply this software engineering paradigm in the domain of user-interface development.

2.6 Requirements for Integrated MDD Methods for Advanced User Interfaces

From the aforementioned analysis, we can summarize important requirements for MDDAUI methods and, transitively, the method engineering meta-method. We classify the requirements by their origin: the product domain of (advanced) user interfaces (UI, AUI), the method domain of (advanced) user interface development (UID, AUID), and the development paradigms model-based development (MBD) and model-driven development (MDD). The requirements are listed in Table 1. They will be answered by the meta-method in Section 4.

Table 1 Requirements for model-driven development methods for advanced user interfaces that need to be covered by the meta-method

Requirement	Type
The method must be able to treat a user interface as part of an interactive system.	UI
The method must support typical user interface concepts such as user, goal, user interface, dialog, presentation, physical and logical user interface component, platform, device.	UI
The method must support typical concepts of advanced user interfaces and address the relevant aspects for the abstract user interface from the list in Section 2.2.	AUI
The method must allow user interface developers to use multiple methods and techniques that differ in formality and scope, such as creative techniques and formal techniques.	UID
The method must support a combination of different domains of knowledge in a multi-disciplinary development.	UID
The method must support multiple stages of development.	UID
The method must be able to account for implementation practices and techniques by specifying the use of technologies such as frameworks, toolkits, and tools.	UID
The method must account for usability and user needs.	UID
The method must support informal development techniques for user interfaces.	UID
The method must support multiple views.	UID
The method must produce a set of artifacts that are related to each other.	UID
The method must be able to distinguish different stages of development.	UID
The method must provide an integrated artifact model that combines formal and informal representations.	UID
The method must support different disciplines of user interface development.	UID
The method shall be integrated with software engineering practice.	UID
The method must provide restricted views for different developer roles.	UID
The method must include the necessary methods for developing the relevant aspects of advanced user interfaces.	AUID
The method must allow for the combination of methods from software engineering and human-computer interaction.	AUID
The method must be capable of using models in the development.	MBD
The method must support multiple models.	MBD
The method must support models for different purposes, such as specification, documentation, and communication (as indicated in Sect. 2.4).	MBD
The method must support the use of models for capturing development knowledge about the advanced user interface.	MBD
The method must support modeling on different levels of abstraction.	MBD
The method must support the selection of a set of different models that model different aspects.	MBD
The method must allow for the differentiation of degrees of detail in models.	MBD
The method must include the definition of elements of models.	MBD

Table 1 (*continued*)

Requirement	Type
The method must include the definition of relationships between models.	MBD
The method must support model-driven development, i.e., the specification of model transformations within and among models, operating on models and model elements.	MDD
It must be supported by the meta-method to specify model transformations.	MDD
The model shall provide notions of platform-independent and platform-specific models.	MDD

3   Method Engineering for Advanced User Interfaces

In this section, we will introduce the discipline of method engineering and will then discuss the use of meta-modeling for method engineering. This will lead us to the definition of our meta-method in the next section.

3.1   Method Engineering

Method engineering has been an active research area in the field of information systems engineering since the early 1990s. In general, method engineering is concerned with formalizing the use of methods for systems development [14]. More precisely, method engineering can be defined as the *engineering discipline to design, construct and adapt methods, techniques and tools for the development of (information) systems* (based on [15], [14]). The objective of method engineering is to develop a methodological approach for systems development in a given context (and situation) such as an organization or project.

Method engineering mainly addresses two perspectives: a) the systematic development of methods and b) the enactment and execution of methods. Both aspects may themselves be supported by dedicated tools, such as a method development environment and a method workflow engine.

Applying method engineering to the domain of advanced user interface development provides a number of advantages:

- method engineering provides a methodological framework and conceptual infrastructure for method knowledge,
- method engineering supports a systematic development of model-driven development methods for advanced user interfaces,
- by providing specific means for method adaptation, methods can be adapted to a particular situation and context of use *(cf. situational method engineering*, see ([14]) for a recent survey),
- concepts of method modularization, reuse and configuration can be used to assemble methods from method building blocks, such as *viewpoint templates* [16], *method fragments* [15], *method chunks* or *method services* [17],

- the meta-models that are used for the definition of methods enable analysis and comparison of methods, even quantitatively by the use of metrics,
- method engineering can ease reuse and provide means for compositional method development, and method integration,
- method engineering builds a sound basis for tool support, e.g. computer-aided software engineering (CASE) tools that may be built by using Meta-CASE tools.

The product of a method engineering process is a method. The users of this product are system and software engineers, and user interface developers in the case of MDDAUI.

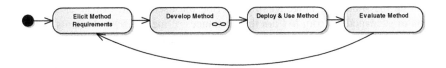

Fig. 2 The general overall method engineering lifecycle is similar to a software lifecycle

The lifecycle of a method is similar to the lifecycle of a software system. We can interpret a method as a conceptual system for system development. Method engineering manages and controls this method lifecycle and may even itself be computer-supported by its own software system, a computer-aided method engineering (CAME) tool [15]. The general overall process model of method engineering is depicted in Fig. 2. Once the domain of discourse has been identified (MDDAUI in our case), the requirements for the method are analyzed. It follows a multi-stage development process. Then the method is deployed, used, and evaluated in order to start another evolution cycle.

3.2 Meta-Modeling for Method Engineering

Meta-modeling has been identified as a promising means for method engineering. Several meta-models have been defined in the literature by different authors, see e.g.[18], [19], [20], [21]. Two standards also exist that use meta-models for the definition of software development methods: ISO 24744:2007 Software Engineering – Metamodel for Development Methodologies [22] and SPEM, the Object Management Group's (OMG) Software & Systems Process Engineering Meta-Model Specification [23]. The latter provides a meta-model as well as a UML profile for the specification of software development methods.

MOF, the OMG's Meta-Object Facility [24], has defined a four-layer meta-model architecture that is commonly used in object-oriented meta-modeling. In this hierarchy, elements of layer n-1 are instances of elements in layer n ($1 \leq n \leq 3$). According to this meta-model hierarchy, we can characterize the levels for the domain of method engineering:

M0 (Runtime layer) – M0 denotes the lowest level of the MOF 4-layer meta-model hierarchy. In this layer, objects of the real world are denoted that exist at execution time of the modeled system. More generally, M0 represents the area of concern, which may be business, software engineering, or method engineering. In the domain of method engineering, the M0 elements are the concrete objects that are produced or modified during a concrete development endeavor.

M1 (Model layer) – M1 is the layer where user models are located. Reality is modeled in a modeling language, such that elements of M0 are instances of elements in M1. In the domain of method engineering, the model of the method is allocated on this level.

M2 (Meta-model layer) – M2 is the layer where meta-modeling takes place. It contains meta-models (models of models) such as the UML meta-model or SPEM which define modeling languages to describe the user models of layer M1. Elements of user models from M1 are then instances of meta-model elements of layer M2. This level holds the meta-method's product model in the domain of method engineering.

M3 (Meta-meta-model layer) – M3 is the highest level of the 4-layer meta-model hierarchy. Meta-meta-models are defined on this layer. They are used to describe the meta-models on layer M2. In the MOF hierarchy, the Meta Object Facility itself is defined on this level. Defining method engineering within an object-oriented meta-model hierarchy, we use MOF for the domain of method engineering on this level as well.

We also build on meta-modeling in our meta-method for method engineering. However, we have discovered that simply employing object-oriented meta-modeling has some shortcomings. In particular, the restriction to solely have MOF's <<instanceOf>> relationship between meta-model layers, and to permit it only between directly neighboring layers, does not allow us to straightforwardly combine the product and the process parts within this framework. Yet for defining a method, we have to combine the method's product model with its process model, as depicted in Fig. 3.

The process model is composed of a work model and a workflow model. We apply this method pattern on both the meta-method level and the method level. However, while the meta-method process model must be an instance of a process meta-model to have execution semantics, all parts of the method are defined as an instance of the meta-method product model, since the complete method is the product of the method engineering process. Yet, the method process model must also be an instance of the process meta-model, since it is a process model itself. We solve this problem by bootstrapping the process meta-model into the meta-method product model with a <<merge>> relationship (see [24]), like this was done for MOF and UML, too. The method is engineered by instantiating the meta-method process model and enacting the thus instantiated process on the method level. This relation is represented by the dependency of type <<producedBy>> between the method and the instance of the meta-method process model. The same pattern applies on the M0 level for the production of the development project's artifacts. Further details on the formal background of our meta-modeling approach for method engineering can be found in [1].

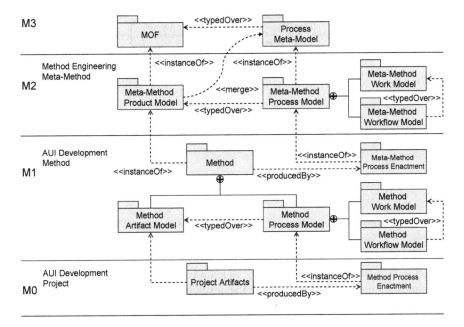

Fig. 3 Applying the meta-modeling approach for the engineering of methods

4 Meta-method for Engineering Development Methods

Conforming to the model presented in the previous section, the meta-method of our method engineering approach consists of a product and a process model. We will give an overview of both in this section. For the process part, we will focus on the workflow model.

4.1 Process Model of the Meta-Method

In Fig. 4, the workflow of the composite activity "develop method" from Fig. 2 is shown. While we describe the process workflow in a rather waterfall-like structure for the ease of presentation here, it may in practice be enacted in a more incremental and iterative fashion.

The meta-method's process combines activities of language engineering and method engineering. A first version of the process was published in [25]. There, we focused on the development of the domain model and artifact model together with language selection (steps 2 to 4 in the process depicted in Fig. 4). In [1], we provide a complete and revised description of the step 1-4, 6 and 7 of the above process in the context of the general method. However, in this work we have specialized and extended the general process for the domain of MDDAUI. We describe the specialized process in the following step by step.

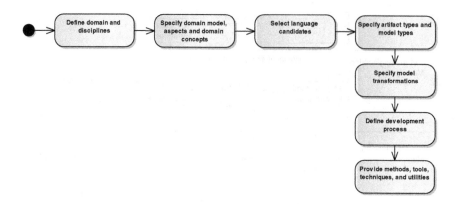

Fig. 4 High-level process model of the meta-method for model-driven development methods

1. **Define domain and disciplines:** The domain is MDDAUI in our case, and disciplines are used to further structure the development method into areas of concern, such as requirements elicitation, conceptual modeling, interaction design, abstract user interface modeling, concrete user interface modeling, user interface implementation, and so on.
2. **Specify domain model, aspects and domain concepts:** The model of domain concepts is set up and organized according to the identified disciplines (in the form of packages that may be hierarchically nested). The disciplines may also correspond to stages of development or levels of abstraction. From the requirements in Sect. 2.6, we have also derived the need for views that represent the perspective of a stakeholder or a particular aspect of the advanced user interface. Core tasks of this activity are the definition of domain concepts and assigning them to disciplines and views.

   Relationships between concepts are added such as composition and aggregation relationships, dependencies, associations.

   The meta-model representation is accompanied by a glossary that contains an entry for each meta-model class. It describes the semantics, purpose and properties of the concept and relationships to other concepts.
3. **Select language candidates:** In order to represent the domain concepts appropriately, languages, together with possible sub-languages (e.g., UML diagram types) and language elements must be identified as candidates.
4. **Specify artifact types and model types:** Candidate languages and language elements from step 3 are assigned to domain concepts from step 2 according to the properties of the domain concepts that need to be expressed. While the model of domain concepts defines the semantics of the method elements in the product model, languages define the syntax and notation for their representation. The artifact model then links language elements with domain concepts. If existing languages or symbols are used, then the method engineer has to take care that the given semantics of the proposed candidate language elements is conformant with the semantics imposed by the composition of step 3, and the

semantics of each language element shall still be unambiguous. Composition hierarchies in the model of domain concepts and the artifacts model must be compatible.

This step of the process is further extended in the domain of model-based development methods. In addition to general artifact types, models can be defined as specializations of the artifact concept. The required and allowed model elements are defined for each type of model, and relationships between models can be defined in the same way as for artifacts.

5. **Specify model transformations:** Since we address model-driven development methods for advanced user interfaces in our approach, this step is an extension to the standard method engineering process of the meta-method. If a model-driven development method is to be defined, the model transformations must be defined as transformation within or between models. This can be done in a rule-based manner.

6. **Define development process:** The definition of the development process reifies the definition of a roadmap through the network of development artifacts. Activities are defined and ordered into workflows that produce the required artifacts in the specified order.

   We have to define tasks, activities for accomplishing tasks, steps of activities and workflows containing an ordered set of activities in this step of the meta-method's process. The process structure contains activities, milestones and control-flow elements. The process model can be extended by object flows of input and output artifact types, and roles that are responsible for executing activities.

7. **Provide methods, tools, techniques, and utilities:** The selection or development and the provision of methods (method modules), tools, techniques, and utilities as well as the provision of tool mentors are required for guiding and simplifying the works of user interface development and producing the required artifacts. Tools are assigned to artifact types, languages or development techniques. Guidance on how to produce the artifacts of a particular type in the selected language shall be explicitly provided, e.g. in the form of guidelines, good and best practices, whitepapers, checklists, templates, examples, or roadmaps. However, even the assignment of languages to software engineering concepts in step 3 can be interpreted as partly associating a technique for the development artifact. Both languages and tools typically have implications on how to produce an artifact. Eventually, tools and utilities are thus related to the activities of the software engineering process model as well. By this, it is shown which activities are supported by tools and utilities and, in turn, which of them are to be used when accomplishing the task of the activity.

4.2 Product Model of the Meta-Method

The product meta-model for method engineering that we propose for model-driven development methods is depicted in Fig. 5. According to the meta-model, the domain is structured into disciplines. Artifacts are related to the disciplines, where they are used. An artifact is always related to a pair of concept and notation. All relevant concepts of the user-interface development domain are elements of the domain model. Furthermore, aspect views are defined on the domain model to cover particular views on selected aspects of the domain model, e.g. a modeling view such as for task modeling or a view for a given developer role or stakeholder (then possible relations to the respective classes `Model` and `Role` are not modeled as associations of this meta-model).

Models are an important concept in model-centered, i.e., model-based and model-driven, development paradigms. To account for that, we introduced the class `Model` as a specialization of the class `Artifact` in our meta-method's artifact model. Models contain model elements, as indicated by the composition relationship between the classes `Model` and `Model Element`. This allows method engineers to define model types and their element types directly as they commonly define artifact types in their methods.

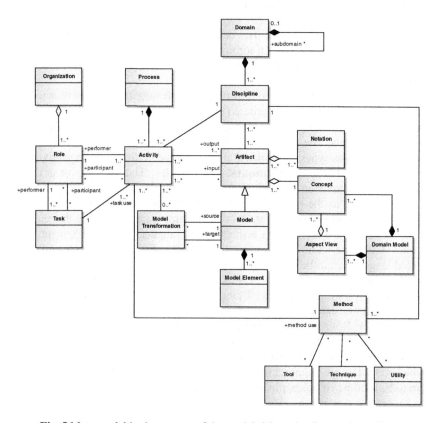

Fig. 5 Meta-model in the context of the model-driven development paradigm.

In the model-driven development paradigm, *model transformations* play a prominent role. They should therefore be considered as first-class citizens of any model-driven development method. Thus, for model-driven development methods, we have included the class `Model Transformation` which has source and target relations to class `Model`. A transformation rule then operates on the model elements (not modeled in this meta-model) of the related models. Activities are the binding element between the information and the process view of the method description. Activities are owned by disciplines and are the constituents of work-flow processes. They operate on artifacts which they use as their input and output parameter objects. Each activity uses a defined method to produce its output. Alike the activity, the method is also associated with a discipline. Such a method can provide tools, techniques and utilities that support the performers in accomplishing the task that is related to the activity. Each model transformation is related to one or more activities, meaning that the transformation is executed as part of the activities in order to transform the elements of the related models as specified by the transformation.

5   Applying the Meta-Method: Development of Model-Driven Development Methods for Advanced User Interfaces

After we have seen the product model and the general workflow model of the meta-method in the previous section, we will now look at some consequences when this approach for method engineering is applied in the MDDAUI domain. We will concentrate on some important aspects of such a method definition.

The first major result of the method engineering process that is released to user interface developers as the users of the method is a structured model of artifact and model types, together with their relationships. This is typically represented as a model of packages, sub-models (see Fig. 1 in Section 2.4) and classes. Such model can become quite large, therefore it is important to employ the described means of structuring. An excerpt from such a model of an advanced user interface is depicted in Fig. 6. It shows five types of models and three classes representing model elements.

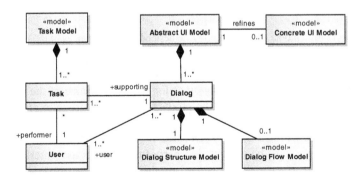

Fig. 6 Excerpt from the artifact model of a development method for user interfaces that is used as the type definition of a transformation rule

The definition of workflows does methodically not differ from the definition of workflows for the meta-method as shown in the previous section. We will therefore omit to present another example here. However, the use of transformations for the specification of development tasks and their effect on the product model was not shown there. The same approach can also be deployed for the specification of model transformations in model-driven development methods.

Effects of development tasks as well as model transformations on the models of the user interface can only be expressed in a limited way by using activity diagrams or composite structures [1]. Even if object flows are represented, they can only make reference to the state of individual objects. They are insufficient for modeling the effect of a task or transformation on the object structure, i.e., the graph of objects that are connected by association links, of the modeled system. We therefore included collaborations in our methodical framework that are interpreted as graph transformation rules [26]. These transformation rules are typed over the product model of the method.

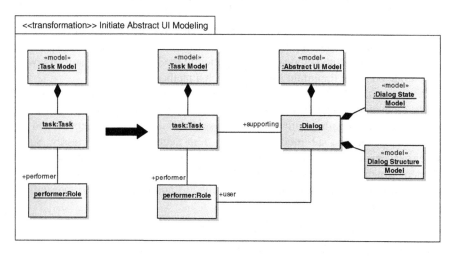

Fig. 7 Example for a model transformation rule defined on the instances of the meta-model

Fig. 7 gives an example of such a transformation rule. It states for the transformation "initiate abstract UI modeling" that for each occurrence of the pattern on the left-hand side in an instance of the product model, the structure on the right-hand side must be produced by the transformation. In particular, it states that if a task model contains a task that is performed by the instance performer of class Role, then a dialog must be generated as part of the abstract user interface model which supports the given task and is used by the performer:Role to accomplish the task. Furthermore, two more models have to be instantiated: a dialog state model and a dialog structure model, that are both associated to the generated dialog element. The rule can be interpreted as a visual contract stating pre- and post-conditions of the transformation [27].

6 Conclusions

We presented a meta-method for the development of systems, software and user interface development methods in this chapter. It builds on the concept of object-oriented meta-modeling based on the 4-layer MOF architecture, yet extends it to account not only for the product model, but also for the work definitions and workflows that form the process model.

We applied the concepts of method engineering in general and our meta-method in particular to the domain of model-driven development of advanced user interfaces (MDDAUI). Based on the analysis of requirements for such a development method stemming from both the product domain of (advanced) user interfaces and the method domain of integrated model-driven development, we adapted the general method engineering meta-method to cover models and model transformations as first-class citizens of the method description. Finally, we briefly showed some results of applying the meta-method to the target domain, especially graph transformation rules for the specification of tasks, activities and transformations in a user interface development process.

References

[1] Engels, G., Sauer, S.: A Meta-Method for Defining Software Engineering Methods. In: Engels, G., Lewerentz, C., Schäfer, W., Schürr, A., Westfechtel, B. (eds.) Graph Transformations and Model-Driven Engineering. LNCS, vol. 5765, pp. 411–440. Springer, Heidelberg (2010)

[2] Calvary, G., Coutaz, J., Thevenin, D., Limbourg, Q., Bouillon, L., Vanderdonckt, J.: A unifying reference framework for multi-target user interfaces. Interact with Comput. 15(3), 289–308 (2003)

[3] Pleuß, A., Van den Bergh, J., Sauer, S., Hußmann, H., Bödcher, A.: Model driven development of advanced user interfaces (MDDAUI) – MDDAUI'06 workshop report. In: Auletta, V. (ed.) MoDELS 2006. LNCS, vol. 4364, pp. 101–105. Springer, Heidelberg (2007)

[4] Pleuß, A., Van den Bergh, J., Sauer, S., Görlich, D., Hußmann, H.: Third international workshop on model driven development of advanced user Interfaces. In: Giese, H. (ed.) MODELS 2008. LNCS, vol. 5002, pp. 59–64. Springer, Heidelberg (2008)

[5] Pleuß, A., Van den Bergh, J., Sauer, S., Hußmann, H.: Workshop report: model driven development of advanced user interfaces (MDDAUI). In: Bruel, J.-M. (ed.) MoDELS 2005. LNCS, vol. 3844, pp. 182–190. Springer, Heidelberg (2006)

[6] Van Harmelen, M. (ed.): Object modeling and user interface design: designing interactive systems. Addison-Wesley, Longman (2001)

[7] Kazman, R., Bass, L.: Guest editors editorial: special issue on bridging the process and practice gaps between software engineering and human-computer interaction. Softw. Process Improv. Pract. 8, 63–65 (2003)

[8] Engels, G., Sauer, S., Neu, B.: Integrating software engineering and user-centred design for multimedia software developments. In: Proc. 2003 IEEE Symp. Human Centric Computing Languages and Environments (HCC 2003), pp. 254–256. IEEE Computer Society, Los Alamitos (2003)

[9] Seffah, A., Vanderdonckt, J., Desmarais, M.C.: Human-centered software engineering: software engineering models. In: Patterns and Architectures for HCI, Springer, London (2009)

[10] Engels, G., Sauer, S.: Object-oriented modeling of multimedia applications. In: Chang, S.K. (ed.) Handbook of Software Engineering and Knowledge Engineering, vol. 2, pp. 21–53. World Scientific, Singapore (2002)

[11] Sauer, S., Dürksen, M., Gebel, A., Hannwacker, D.: GuiBuilder – A tool for model-driven development of multimedia user interfaces. In: Van den Bergh, J., et al. (eds.) Model Driven Development of Advanced User Interfaces, MDDAUI 2006. CEUR-WS, vol. 214 (2006), http://CEUR-WS.org/Vol-214/

[12] Van den Bergh, J., Meixner, G., Sauer, S.: MDDAUI 2010 workshop report. In: Van den Bergh, J., et al. (eds.) Proc. 5th Intl. Workshop on Model Driven Development of Advanced User Interfaces MDDAUI 2010. CEUR-WS, vol. 617 (2010) urn:nbn:de:0074-617-8

[13] Meixner, G., Görlich, D., Breiner, K., Hußmann, H., Pleuß, A., Sauer, S., Van den Bergh, J.: Fourth international workshop on model driven development of advanced user interfaces. In: Proc. 13th Intl. Conf. Intelligent User Interfaces (IUI 2009), pp. 503–504. ACM, New York (2009)

[14] Henderson-Sellers, B., Ralyté, J.: Situational method engineering: state-of-the-art review. J. Univers. Comput. Sci. 16(3), 424–478 (2010)

[15] Brinkkemper, S.: Method engineering: engineering of information systems development methods and tools. Inf. Softw. Technol. 38, 275–280 (1996)

[16] Nuseibeh, B., Finkelstein, A., Kramer, J.: Method engineering for multi-perspective software development. Inf. Softw. Technol. 38, 267–274 (1994)

[17] Rolland, C.: Method engineering: towards methods as services. Softw. Process. Improv. Pract. 14, 143–164 (2009)

[18] Jeusfeld, A., Jarke, M., Mylopoulos, J. (eds.): Metamodeling for method engineering. MIT Press, Cambridge (2009)

[19] Bollain, M., Garbajosa, J.: A metamodel for defining development methodologies. In: Filipe, J., et al. (eds.) ICSOFT/ENASE 2007. CCIS, vol. 22, pp. 414–425. Springer, Heidelberg (2008)

[20] Gonzalez-Perez, C., McBride, T., Henderson-Sellers, B.: A metamodel for assessable software development methodologies. Soft. Qual. J. 13, 195–214 (2005)

[21] Henderson-Sellers, B., Gonzalez-Perez, C.: A comparison of four process metamodels and the creation of a new generic standard. Inf. Softw. Technol. 47, 49–65 (2005)

[22] ISO, ISO/IEC 24774:2007 Software engineering – metamodel for development methodologies. International Organization for Standardization, Geneva (2007)

[23] OMG, Software & systems process engineering meta-model specification, version 2.0. Object Management Group (2008), http://www.omg.org/specs/

[24] OMG, Meta object facility (MOF) core specification, version 2.0. Object Management Group (2006), http://www.omg.org/spec/MOF/2.0/PDF/

[25] Engels, G., Sauer, S., Soltenborn, C.: Unternehmensweit verstehen – unternehmensweit entwickeln: von der Modellierungssprache zur Softwareentwicklungsmethode. Inform. Spektrum 31(5), 451–459 (2008)

[26] Heckel, R., Sauer, S.: Strengthening UML collaboration diagrams by state transformations. In: Hussmann, H. (ed.) FASE 2001. LNCS, vol. 2029, pp. 109–123. Springer, Heidelberg (2001)

[27] Lohmann, M., Sauer, S., Engels, G.: Executable visual contracts. In: 2005 IEEE Symposium on Visual Languages and Human-Centric Computing (VL/HCC 2005), pp. 63–70. IEEE Computer Society, Los Alamitos (2005)

Using Storyboards to Integrate Models and Informal Design Knowledge

Mieke Haesen, Jan Van den Bergh, Jan Meskens, Kris Luyten,
Sylvain Degrandsart, Serge Demeyer, and Karin Coninx

Abstract. Model-driven development of user interfaces has become increasingly powerful in recent years. Unfortunately, model-driven approaches have the inherent limitation that they cannot handle the informal nature of some of the artifacts used in truly multidisciplinary user interface development such as storyboards, sketches, scenarios and personas. In this chapter, we present an approach and tool support for multidisciplinary user interface development bridging informal and formal artifacts in the design and development process. Key features of the approach are the usage of annotated storyboards, which can be connected to other models through an underlying meta-model, and cross-toolkit design support based on an abstract user interface model.

1 Introduction

The last few years, model-driven design of User Interfaces (UIs) is receiving an increasing amount of attention in the computer science and software engineering community. Model driven UI design can offer benefits in terms of quality, traceability, efficiency and consistency. However, this discipline has not been widely adopted in the field of Human-Computer Interaction (HCI). A major reason for this

Mieke Haesen · Jan Van den Bergh · Jan Meskens · Kris Luyten · Karin Coninx
Hasselt University - tUL - IBBT, Expertise Centre for Digital Media, Wetenschapspark 2, 3590 Diepenbeek, Belgium
e-mail: {mieke.haesen,jan.vandenbergh,jan.meskens}@uhasselt.be,
{kris.luyten,karin.coninx}@uhasselt.be

Sylvain Degrandsart · Serge Demeyer
Dept. Mathematics and Computer Science, Universiteit Antwerpen, Middelheimlaan 1, 2020 Antwerpen, Belgium
e-mail: {Sylvain.Degrandsart,Serge.Demeyer}@ua.ac.be

Sylvain Degrandsart
University of Mons - UMONS, Software Engineering Lab, 20 Place du Parc, 7000 Mons, Belgium

H. Hussmann et al. (Eds.): MDD of Advanced User Interfaces, SCI 340, pp. 87–106.

is that existing model-driven UI design approaches are not focused on UI design in multidisciplinary teams. Since this is the most common way UIs are created, model-driven approaches have to fit into an overall multidisciplinary design approach to become usable for HCI practitioners.

Fitting within an overall multidisciplinary design approach means that artifacts from other communities have to be incorporated into the model-driven design approach. Some challenges have already been tackled. User interface sketches can already be integrated into a model-driven approach, based on sketch recognition to recognize widgets within a sketch [1]. Furthermore, tools like Microsoft Expression Blend support the transition from early prototypes (SketchFlow) to final designs and integration with software development (through Visual Studio). But designers and other people involved in a user interface development process also use other, often informal, artifacts such as personas and scenarios (see section 2.1).

In this chapter, we present a model-driven development approach supporting a transition from informal to formal artifacts using the MuiCSer process framework [2]. This development approach has the advantage that experts in a multidiciplinary team can continue to use the artifacts that are most familiar to them, yet allows for a smooth transition between them. Consequently, we present several tools that support different roles in different stages of the development process as one possible way of achieving support. More specifically, we offer annotated storyboards, which can be connected to other models through an underlying meta-model and cross-toolkit design support based on a abstract user interface model expressed in UIML [3]. Finally, we compare our contribution with related work and provide some further discussion.

2   Artifacts for User Interface Design

The design and development of interactive systems require a deep understanding of various information sources and artifacts. Processing all information that is necessary to create a usable, appropriate and useful interactive system is often done in an engineering approach that processes this information gradually into the software and accompanying user interface. Designers need to know about the targeted end-users, the environment in which the software will be used, the devices on which it will run, the typical tasks that need to be supported and other non-functional requirements. A well-known approach that makes sure all this information does not interfere with striving for an optimal user experience, is user-centered design (UCD). Unfortunately, UCD is mostly a design approach and is hard to integrate with the actual engineering of the software. UCD is often employed by designers and delivers a user interface design, not an operational interactive system.

Connecting typical software engineering processes with UCD processes has been an ongoing challenge tackled by many researchers to date [4, 5, 6].

The gap between interface design and engineering interactive systems is mainly a matter of "design" language differences: an interface designer uses different artifacts than a software engineer. In fact, each domain of expertise uses its own vocabulary

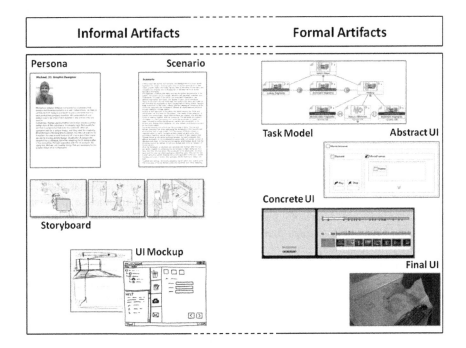

Fig. 1 Examples of informal and formal artifacts

which complicates collaboration between people having different backgrounds. We now give an overview of informal and formal (i.e. adhering to a meta-model) artifacts that are used in UCD processes and by software engineers to describe user interfaces. Fig. 1 shows examples of these informal and formal artifacts.

2.1 Informal Design Knowledge

Informal artifacts in UCD have the advantage that they can be understood by all team members, unregarded their expertise. Informal artifacts that are often used include personas, scenario descriptions and storyboards. Natural text or an unstructured graphical representation are two types of languages often used. Typically, informal artifacts are often presented in a narrative or sketched style so as to aid a universal comprehensability.

Personas are defined as hypothetical archetypes of actual users and usually result from a user analysis [7]. A persona describes a fictional person that represents a typical group of end-users and includes personal details (such as name, age, gender and photograph), roles, tasks, goals and skills. By personifying a group of end-users, team members are more likely to focus on the users and their needs, which may be beneficial for user experience of the resulting user interface [8].

Although personas are created in the beginning of a UCD process, they are supposed to be used during the entire process. Their primary goal is to communicate part of the user needs to all team members right after the user analysis. Furthermore, personas should be used as a guiding artifact in several other stages, such as UI design and development.

Personas contain a lot of information concerning user needs and requirements, but a similar type of informal artifacts that include user requirements are *Scenarios*. Scenarios are stories about people and their activities. A typical scenario describes a setting, includes a sequence of events or actions and represents the use of a system [9].

Both, personas and scenarios, have a narrative style, but in contrast to a scenario, a persona does not describe how a system is used. Consequently, personas and scenarios can be considered as complementary artifacts in UCD. In practice, personas can be included as the actors of a scenario. Both types of artifacts represent user requirements. Nevertheless, when personas or scenarios are poorly communicated or accepted by the leadership team, or when other team members do not know how to use them, a lot of information contained by these artifacts can get lost during a UCD process. Furthermore, it may be problematic for people with a technical background to translate narrative stories into technical specifications [10, 11].

The aforementioned types of informal artifacts are used as tools to communicate user requirements in a team and are presented in a narrative style. Another notation allows team members to communicate ideas visually through sketching. During many meetings or brainstorm sessions, diagrams and sketches are created or presented to express someone's ideas [12]. Sketching is very accessible, pen and paper suffice to start sketching, while even people with little drawing skills can present an insightful picture. Furthermore, sketches can be helpful to discover ideas that are very often invisible [13].

In UCD, sketches can have several shapes such as storyboards, diagrams or UI designs. *Storyboards*, originating from the film industry, can be considered as a visual representation of a scenario, and are often used to communicate ideas about a future system to stakeholders. The advantage of storyboards is that they provide a depiction of how a future system can be used that is less ambiguous than a scenario [14].

Another way to use sketches in UCD, is drawing the first *user interface mockups*. This technique is used to share ideas about what the UI should look like and to discuss several UI considerations. Furthermore, these UI mockups can be used to verify whether the first UI decisions meet the user needs. In practice, this can be done during stakeholder meetings, but also informal evaluations together with end-users can be conducted. When several screens in UI mockups are connected, they do not only present the look and feel of a UI, but also part of its behavior.

Storyboards and UI mockups do not always need to be sketched. These artifacts can also have a higher detail, depending on their aim. For instance, a storyboard or UI mockup may be more detailed and polished when presenting it to the management or at a later stage of UCD.

Although many of the artifacts discussed in this section can be classified as informal artifacts, part of their exact meaning is open for interpretation, they also contain unambiguous information. A notable example is the formalization of sketched interface designs using the formal specification language Z presented by Bowen and Reeves [15]. Our approach does not strive for this level of formality rather aims at structuring and extracting the information that can be linked to the models typically used in a model-driven engineering approach. The next section presents these models relevant for the design of (context-sensitive) user interfaces. This provides us with the required foundations to define a meta-model for informal artifacts such as the storyboard.

2.2   Formal Artifacts

Several models are commonly used in model-driven development of context-sensitive user interfaces. The reference framework for plastic user interfaces [16] lists the different kinds of models and their role in the development process. UsiXML [17] is a single language that integrates most of these models. They list the following abstractions of the user interface, from abstract to concrete.

Task models allow to express a hierarchical decomposition of a goal, into tasks and activities, that can be translated into actions at the lowest level. The COMM task model notation [18] illustrates this by allowing specification of modalities or interaction devices in *modal tasks*, which are leaves in the task tree. They are mostly used as a first step in designing an application to identify the tasks and later actions that have to be performed to reach a certain goal.

Abstract user interfaces are high-level descriptions of user interfaces that are independent of a modality. They consist of abstract interaction objects arranged in presentation units. An *Abstract Interaction Object* (AIO) is a part of the abstract user interface that supports the execution of a leave task; it allows the user to give input to the system (e.g enter a search term) or to start the execution of some function (e.g. start the search), or allows the system to present output to the user (e.g. "searching" or the search result). Abstract user interfaces usually also define the transitions between presentation units, although the latter fact is usually not emphasized in graphical representations of the abstract user interface. Most abstract user interface languages have a formal basis in the form of a meta-model, the Canonical Abstract Prototypes notation [19] was first defined to allow more abstract paper prototyping to encourage creativity and later integrated into a modeling environment with a proper meta-model [20].

Concrete user interfaces realize abstract user interfaces for a specific context of use, such as a desktop PC used by a journalist. It already represents the final look-and-feel (e.g. following the Windows User Experience Interaction Guidelines) but is independent of the user interface toolkit (e.g. Qt, MFC or GTK). A concrete user interface is especially useful to port user interfaces among different toolkits. Porting user interfaces between different platforms or modalities may require using a higher level of abstraction (such as the abstract user interface) to enable transition between radically different interaction objects.

Final user interfaces are instantiations of the concrete user interface for a specific toolkit (e.g. Qt on a HP PC running Windows 7). They can be interpreted or compiled to run on the target device. Final user interfaces are not considered in UsiXML or any other user interface description language supporting multiple abstractions.

Besides these abstractions, there are some other models that are important to user interface design, such as the domain model, describing concepts from the domain that are relevant to the user interface, and context models that capture the context of use in terms of user, platform and environment. Although UsiXML covers a wide range of models that describe various aspects of an interactive system, it has little support for typical informal artifacts. Besides the support for low-fidelity prototypes [1], other artifacts such as storyboards and personas are not covered by UsiXML. We think, a model-driven engineering approach for interactive systems needs to include other informal artifacts in the overall development process in order to support a complete design and development process.

Besides finding direct links between both informal and formal artifacts as to capture and reuse the information from the informal artifacts further down the engineering process, the process in which these artifacts are created is equally important. In the next section, we focus on a process framework that structures how artifacts, originating from UCD and software engineering, are created by a multidisciplinary team, and how these artifacts make the transition from informal and unstructured artifacts towards structured and formal artifacts that define the interactive system.

3   MuiCSer Process

In user-centered software engineering (UCSE), the traditional user-centered design (UCD) approach is extended towards the practical engineering (as in creation) of the software artifacts. MuiCSer[1] [2] is a process framework for *Mul*tidisciplinary user-*C*entered *S*oftware engin*eer*ing that explicitly focuses on the end-user needs during the entire software engineering (SE) cycle. MuiCSer embodies UCD with a structured SE approach and organizes the creation of interactive software systems by a multidisciplinary team. As such, it provides a way to define a process (based on the MuiCSer process framework) that describes when and how the transitions from informal to formal artifacts take place. The framework can be used to define a UCSE process and supports different formal models, where each model describes a specific aspect of an interactive system and represents the viewpoint of one or more specific roles in the multidisciplinary team.

Processes derived from MuiCSer typically start with a *requirements and user needs* analysis stage (Fig. 2-A) where the user tasks, goals and the related objects or resources that are important to perform these tasks are specified. Several notations are used to express the results of the analysis stage, but most of the results concern informal artifacts such as personas, scenarios and storyboards. Other artifacts that commonly result from this stage are use cases, which are more focused than scenarios but provide less context [21].

---

[1] Pronounced as "mixer".

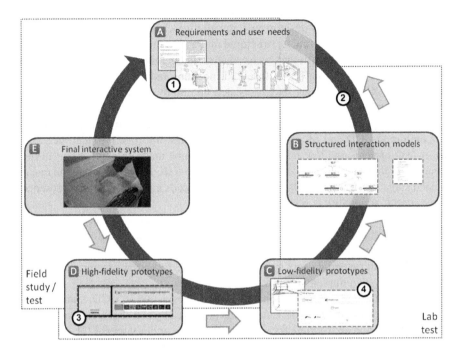

Fig. 2 The MuiCSer process that was used for the design and development of *News Video Explorer*. Extracts of the most important artifacts are presented for each stage of MuiCSer. In this diagram, informal artifacts have a solid border, while formal artifacts are distinguished by a dashed border

During the *structured interaction analysis* (Fig. 2-B), the results of the first analysis are used to proceed towards system interaction models, and a presentation model. These formal models are often expressed using the UML notation, thus keeping in pace with the traditional SE models. Both, the informal and formal artifacts, created so far, are used by user interface designers to create UI mockups during the *low-fidelity prototyping* stage (Fig. 2-C). In subsequent stages, low-fidelity prototypes are transformed into *high-fidelity prototypes* (Fig. 2-D), which on their turn evolve into the *final interactive system* (Fig. 2-E). For this evolution, informal artifacts as well as formal models are used.

Fig. 2 shows an overview of the stages of a MuiCSer process for the design and development of *News Video Explorer*, an application for TV researchers to browse a vast video archive in order to search suitable video fragments. We use this example throughout the remainder of this chapter to illustrate our approach. At the beginning of the process (stage *A*), requirements and user needs were captured by conducting user observations that involved several professional TV researchers. The results of this analysis were a scenario and a storyboard that among others defined that News

Video Explorer needs to be available in several situations: it should run on three different platforms, namely desktop pc, large multitouch display and mobile device. Based on these informal artifacts, structured interaction models (stage B), including a task model and a context model, were created. These models, as well as the other artifacts were used as input for sketched UI mockups and Canonical Abstract Prototypes (stage C), which were later translated into more detailed designs (stage D) and a final interactive system (stage E).

A MuiCSer process increases the traceability and visibility during the process. By combining UCD and SE in one integrated process, informal artifacts such as a list of requirements and low-fidelity prototypes can be made an explicit part of the process and their influence on other artifacts can be traced. By evaluating the result of each stage in the process, the support for user needs and goals and the presence of required functionality is verified.

Evaluation of informal and formal artifacts often differs: while team members have the background to read and understand the formal artifacts, informal artifacts can also be evaluated by end-users. Thus, the latter are suitable for verifying requirements with potential users and clients while the former are required to create the concrete system implementing these requirements.

A survey that involved practitioners of companies active in UCD, showed that there is insufficient support to translate artifacts created by non-technical team members into a notation appropriate for software engineers or developers [22]. Although the overall process to improve this situation is tackled by the MuiCSer framework, the different viewpoints of a multidisciplinary team and notations in UCSE still cause difficulties in the transition between some types of artifacts. From a study on the alignment of tools and models for multidisciplinary teams, we conclude that it is difficult to communicate informal artifacts on design decisions between designers and developers with existing tools [2]. There is a clear need for a well-defined approach linking informal and formal artifacts without requiring team members to get fully accustomed with each others' roles. In the next section, we present a model-driven approach to accomplish an elegant transformation between informal and formal artifacts without interrupting the typical team member activities.

4   From Informal to Formal Artifacts with Storyboards

One of the biggest challenges in integrating informal design knowledge and formal models is introducing a common language that enables multidisciplinary teams to collaborate in creating advanced user interfaces. We found inspiration in the intersection of storyboarding, comics and model-driven engineering. In this section, we describe a storyboarding approach and tools that take into account storyboards for the creation of more formal artifacts in MuiCSer processes. The proposed tools are the COMuICSer tool for creating storyboards (Fig. 2-1), mapping and transformation support for UsiXML (Fig. 2-2) and the Jelly high-fidelity prototyping tool (Fig. 2-3).

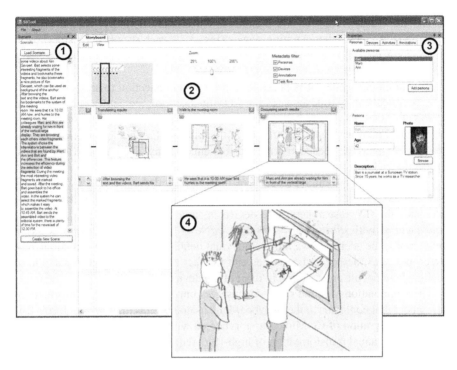

Fig. 3 Screenshot of the tool for COMuICSer. In the tool, it is possible to load a scenario (1), create scenes in the storyboard panel (2) and annotate scenes (3). One scene is enlarged (4) to exemplify what annotations and contextual information can be available

4.1 Storyboards: Graphical Narrative Models

COMuICSer[2] [23] is a tool we provide to support the integration of informal and formal models through usage of a common visual language. It supports the MuiCSer process framework and uses a natural, visual language. This is an effective and clear way for communication amongst a multidisciplinary team, given that no other universal languages for doing requirements engineering with multiple disciplines involved exist. The graphical notation, typical for storyboarding, makes complex details comprehensible and even allows to add contextual data.

In COMuICSer, a storyboard is defined as: *a sequence of pictures of real life situations, depicting users carrying out several activities by using devices in a certain context, presented in a narrative format.* This specific definition immediately provides us with a clear overview of the four primary pieces of information that can be found in a storyboard: users, activities, devices and context.

The accompanying COMuICSer tool is shown in Fig. 3. This tool is mainly used between the requirements and user needs specification and the creation of structured interaction models in the MuiCSer process, shown in Fig. 2-1.

---

[2] Pronounced as "comics-er".

The COMuICSer tool allows members of a multidisciplinary team to load a scenario (Fig. 3-1). When creating scenes (Fig. 3-2), each scene in the storyboard can be connected to a fragment of the scenario, and hence a connection between the storyboard and the scenario is provided.

By annotating scenes, it is possible to provide a connection to structured engineering models and UI designs. In the COMuICSer tool, rectangles can be drawn on top of scenes, to specify particular annotations (Fig. 3-2). These annotations are made in a similar way as the *photo tagging* features on Facebook or Flickr and can concern personas, devices, activities and free annotations. The tool provides forms to specify each annotation (Fig. 3-3).

Fig. 3-4 shows an enlarged scene of the storyboard that describes the use of News Video Explorer, introduced in section 3. In this scene, we can identify three personas: the TV researchers; one device: a large multitouch display; and two equivalent activities: browsing the videos in News Video Explorer. Besides these annotations, the scene shows more contextual details such as the connections between personas, device and activities and the fact that the scene takes place in a room, where people are standing in front of the device.

These annotations and the scenes themselves implicitly capture this information in a model that conforms to the storyboard meta-model. This meta-model forms the basis for integration of COMuICSer storyboards with other models. This avoids a completely manual transformation of high-level requirements that are contained in a storyboard but at the same time does not exclude the creative input that is often part of the storyboarding process.

4.1.1 A Storyboard Meta-Model

Our storyboard meta-model, shown in Fig. 4, is MOF-compliant[3]. There is one central element in the meta-model: the *Scene*. A scene is a graphical representation of a part of the scenario. A set of scenes that are related using *TemporalRelationShip* elements in a *Storyboard*. The TemporalRelationShip element is based on Allen's interval algebra [24]. The *before* relationship indicates one scene happened before another, and there is undefined time progress in between scenes. The *meets* relationship indicates that one scene is immediately followed by another scene, and the time progress between two scenes is virtually none. Although the most common relationships used in storyboarding are *before* and *meets*, we think, parallel activities should be supported since they are common in collaborative and multi-user activities. Defining more precise temporal relationships between scenes, allows us to exploit them later on, e.g. by mapping them on the temporal relationships that are used in the task model.

When constructing a storyboard, the drawings or photographs used, often contain a lot of contextual information. Dow et al. show storyboarding, especially contextual storytelling, is useful for context-aware application design (in their case ubicomp applications) but lacks a good way of formalizing the context data [10]. In

---

[3] MOF is an industry standard established by the Object Management Group.

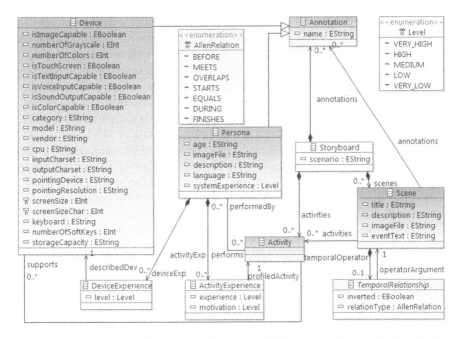

Fig. 4 Our initial COMuICSer storyboard meta-model. It contains the graphical depiction with the objects of interest (context), personas, devices and activities. Scenes are related using the Allen interval algebra operators

COMuICSer, a scene is annotated with different types of information: *Persona* specifies archetypical users, *Device* presents computing devices and systems, *Activity* represents what happens in a scene. By providing tagging of scenes, we support a rudimentary way of translating the context inferred from the graphical depiction of a scene into a readable format. We showed a graphical depiction could have high value to obtain a usable model of the context of use in previous work [25].

4.2 Mapping Storyboards to Models

In this section, we show a mapping from COMuICSer storyboards to UsiXml [17] as one instance of a transition from informal to formal artifacts. We selected UsiXml as the target model because it contains a consistent set of the models used in UCSE (e.g. task model, abstract user interface model, context model, ...) and because of the available tool support[4].

The two UsiXml models that can be partially generated from a COMuICSer storyboard are: the *task model*, describing task sequences required to reach the user's goal, and the *context model*, specifying the application's context of use.

---

[4] The UsiXML website (http://www.usixml.org) gives an overview of the avaible tools.

Tasks of the UsiXml task model are in direct relation with activities that are depicted in a scene of a storyboard. For each activity, the *activity2task* transformation (formalized in Fig. 5) creates a task in the task model with a *name* that corresponds to the activity *title*. Some domain-independent properties of an activity are also transformed into task properties through a one-to-one mapping. For example, the activity *importance* and *frequency* are directly mapped to their task equivalent, after a format adaptation. However, not all mappings are that straightforward: for instance, the type of task can be either a system task, a user task or an interactive task. The task *type* can be inferred by the number of devices and personas related to the activity. If an activity is performed by a persona using no device, the corresponding task is a user task, if no persona is performing the activity, the task is a system task, otherwise it is an interactive task. A task is set as *cooperative* if multiple personas are involved in the performance of corresponding activities. The scene shown in Fig. 3-4, includes a cooperative task which involves two personas carrying out the same activity: browsing the videos in News Video Explorer. The same reasoning on the number of devices is used to infer if a task is a *multi-device* task or not.

```
rule activity2task{
  from a : Mstoryboard3!Activity
   to task : MUsiXmlTask!Task (name <- a.title,
      importance <- a.getUsiXmlImportance(),
      multidevice <- (a.performedUsing->size()>1),
      frequency <- a.getUsiXmlFrequency(),
      cooperative <- (a.performedBy->size()>1),
      type <- if (a.performedBy->size()=0) then 'system'
       else if (a.performedUsing->size()=0) then 'user'
          else 'interactive' endif endif)
}
```

Fig. 5 Activity to task ATL transformation

Two other generative transformations, the *persona2userStereotype* and the *device2platform*, focus on the partial generation of a context model from information specified in a COMuICSer storyboard. Firstly, the *persona2userStereotype* transformation creates a new *userStereoType* element for each *Persona* element, with direct mapping of properties such as *DeviceExperience* and *ActivityExperience*. Secondly, each *Device* is transformed to new*hardwarePlatform* and *softwarePlatform* elements. All the device properties related to hardware are mapped to their hardwarePlatform equivalent: *category, cpu, inputCharset, isColorCapable, screenSize, storageCapacity, ...* The rest of the device properties (*osName, osVersion, isJavaEnabled, jvmVersion, ...*) are mapped to softwarePlatform properties.

The mapping to the context model, straightforward as it may seem, does not retrieve all the information available in the COMuICSer StoryBoard. Indeed, the StoryBoard model provides by definition a lot more context information mainly all the entities in the environment. We generate a new context model for every scene in a storyboard, even though it's likely that some of this context can be shared across scenes. Nevertheless, UsiXml does not allow to do this because variations are not possible within one context model.

4.3 Generation of Model Constraints from Storyboards

Since storyboard operators and task operators are expressed in different paradigms, a one-to-one mapping between the two is not desirable. Indeed, COMuICSer storyboards specify the relation between scenes using Allen interval algebra... [24] with operators such as *meets*, *after* and *overlaps*. However, task models, including the UsiXML task model, use LOTOS based temporal operators such as *enabling*, *choice* and *independent concurrency*. Consequently, the operators of the task models can not be generated directly. What we can do however, is provide support by restricting the choices to the ones allowed by the storyboard specification. We decided to express these restrictions using OCL constraints, in order to remain at the modelling level and exploit MOF-technology.

Below we list the transformations that take a COMuICSer storyboard instance as input and generate several OCL constraints:

- Each *after* relation between scenes requires that the tasks corresponding to the activities should have an *enabling* operator between them or between their parents.
- Each *meets* relation require is translated into a *enabling* operator. However, no task may be performed between performance of task related to operator arguments. We achieve this by computing all possible performance paths from one task to the other (after having removed all tasks that are achieved in parallel). Unfortunately, applying this complex rule has to be done manually, currently there is no simulator available for the UsiXml task model.
- Other Allen's algebra operators: *overlaps*, *starts*, *during*, *finishes* and *equals*, are all generating constraints that impose related tasks or parents of them to have a *ConcurrencyWithInfoPassing* or a *IndependentConcurrency* relation.

Finally, all activities within the same scene are also valid during the same period of time. Thus, we can define that all activities of a scene are mapped on tasks from the same *enabled task set*. An enabled task set is a definition from the ConcurTaskTrees language that specifies a set of tasks is valid during the same period of time. Unfortunately, it is not possible to generate an OCL specification of this constraint, the enabled task set computation has not yet been integrated in the UsiXml tools.

4.4 From Storyboard to High-Fidelity Prototype

Stage D of the MuICSer process framework (Fig. 2-D) involves the design of high-fidelity prototypes. In the MuICSer process of the News Video Explorer, high-fidelity prototypes were created using the multi-device Jelly [26] design tool (Fig. 6 (a)). Jelly allows designers to design a concrete user interface (concrete UI),

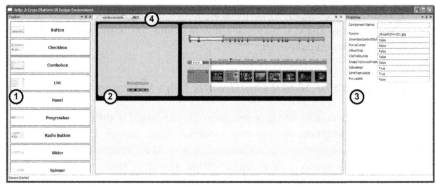

(a) The Jelly multi-device design environment

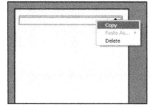

(b) copy widgets in one device-specific UI

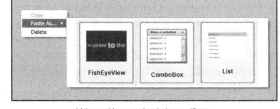

(c) Paste widgets to other device-specific UIs

Fig. 6 The Jelly multi-device design environment, showing a video browser design for a desktop computer (a). Jelly allows designers to copy widgets from one device (b) and to paste these widgets as a similar component on a different device (c)

while it automatically maintains an abstract UI presentation model for this concrete design. This allows designers to use a familiar notation, in this case a graphical user interface design, and to use this artifact in a model-driven engineering process without forcing them to change their working practices considerably. The abstract UI presentation model is a structured well-defined model (based on UIML [3]).

Jelly can use storyboards that are created by the COMuICSer tool. For every device that is *tagged* in the storyboard, Jelly provides a separate design workspace. This way, Jelly automatically takes the different contexts of devices into account as indicated by a storyboard. For example, loading the storyboard for News Video Explorer (Fig. 3) results in three design workspaces: desktop pc, large multitouch display and mobile device. In each of these workspaces, designers create User Interfaces (UIs) by placing widgets from the *toolbox* (Fig. 6 (a)-A) on the *canvas* (Fig. 6 (a)-B) and dragging them around until the resulting layout is visually appealing. These widgets' properties can be changed through the *properties panel* (Fig. 6 (a)-C). This usage model is very similar to traditional GuiBuilders, allowing designers to reuse their knowledge of single-platform UI design tools in a multi-device design environment. Under the hood, Jelly builds an underlying presentation model which can be connected with other artifacts included in the MuiCSer process.

The mappings between Jelly's underlying presentation model and formal artifacts such as Abstract Interaction Objects (AIOs, as introduced by the reference framework in section 2.2) also help designers during the creation of high-fidelity prototypes. It introduces the flexibility to *copy* a part of a UI on one device (Fig. 6 (b)) and to *paste* it *as* a similar part on another device (Fig. 6 (c)). A component is considered as similar if it has the same *AIO type* and *content datatype* as the given component [27]. We currently support four types of AIOs, differentiated according to the functionality they offer to the user: (1) *input* components allow users to enter or manipulate content; (2) *output* components present content to the user; (3) *action* components allow users to trigger an action; and finally (4) *group* components group other components into a hierarchical structure. As content datatypes, we currently support the five primitive types of XML Schema (e.g. decimal, string, void, etc.), a number of datatypes that are often used in user interfaces (e.g. Image, Colour, etc.) and container datatypes that group content items of a certain type together (e.g. a list of strings, a tree of images, etc.).

For example, assume we are looking for all Adobe Flex components that can represent a Windows Mobile combobox. Since the combobox is linked to an input AIO, the network is first searched for all Adobe Flex components that are linked to an input AIO. This returns a huge list of controls such as checkbox, spinbox, listbox, combobox, a custom fish-eye view container, etc. Secondly, this list is searched for all components that support the same datatype as the Windows Mobile combobox (i.e. a list of strings). This finally results in three Adobe Flex components: listbox, combobox and custom fish-eye view container. These components are then displayed in Jelly's *"paste as..."* menu (Fig. 6(c)).

5   Related Work

We are not the first to address the difference in "design language" between different roles in a multidisciplinary team and to bridge between informal and formal artifacts.

A study of Truong et al. [14] reports the need for a tool that offers all the functionality necessary to create storyboards. Existing storyboarding tools such as Comic Life[5], Celtx[6] and Kar2ouche[7] support the creation of storyboards, but do not take into account the characteristics of UCD processes.

Dow et al [10] present a speculative next generation storyboarding tool for ubiquitous computing. This concept of a tool provides a communication mechanism for different roles in a multidisciplinary team and supports the connection with other tools. This concept was implemented in ActivityDesigner [28], a tool that supports an activity-based prototyping process. One of the first steps supported by the tool, is the creation of a scene panel, based on everyday observations, accompanied by roles of users and activity models. These first models can contribute to the first

---

[5] http://www.comiclife.com/
[6] http://celtx.com/
[7] http://www.immersiveeducation.com/kar2ouche/

prototypes, that can include interaction sequences. Furthermore, the tool supports the evaluation of the prototypes created. This work overlaps stages *A* (Requirements and user needs), *B* (Structured interaction models), *D* (High-fidelity prototyping) in the MuiCSer process framework (Fig. 2).

SketchiXML [1] allows creating concrete user interface models through sketches by using sketch recognition. CanonSketch [29] offers different synchronized views on a user interface presentation model (UML class diagrams with Wisdom stereotypes [30], Canonical Abstract Prototypes [19] and final user interface). This approach allows immediate switching between the different views on the user interface presentation model. Both tools mainly address step *C* (low-fidelity prototypes) and the transition to *D* (high-fidelity prototypes) of the MuiCSer process framework in Fig. 2, but in different ways. While SketchiXML mainly focuses on informal specification of models, CanonSketch focuses on fluent transitioning between working styles; from detailed design to more high-level and abstract (re-)structuring of the user interface.

Some initial work has been proposed to support transitioning from informal artifacts to an initial task model. CTTE [31] has some limited support to identify tasks in a scenario description to ease the creation of a task model based on a scenario. Although this is a useful feature, it identifies only part of the information contained in a scenario; much information contained in the scenariomodel is not important to represent directly in a task model. Other types of information, such as contextual information is easily lost in this transition. While this work also addresses the transition from step *A* to *B* of the MuiCSer process framework (Fig. 2), it starts from a purely textual scenario to extract tasks, while the task and temporal relation extraction in our approach is more gradual, by first structuring a scenario in an annotated storyboard (section 3) and then guiding the transition to a task and context model using model transformation (section 4.2).

Denim [32] allows to specify important information, such as overall screen layout and navigation in a way that is easy to grasp for many people by using sketches that can be made interactive. It however does not make an attempt to go to the next step; there is no model-extraction nor code generation feature. This makes Denim a nice way to make quick prototypes and to discuss design ideas. The resulting artifact is however nearly as difficult to use in the remainder of the development cycle as a plain paper prototype.

Jelly is a design environment allowing designers to create high-fidelity prototypes for multi-device applications and to to exchange design parts across devices. This is complementary with Damask [33], a multi-device design extension for Denim [32], which is also oriented towards low-fidelity prototyping instead of designing high-fidelity UIs. Most other multi-device design approaches generate UIs automatically from a higher level model. It was shown that such approaches can be effective in some specific application domains (e.g. Supple [34] and PUC [35]). However, a major drawback of such tools is the lack of support for UI designers, which are not familiar with the models and algorithms that are used to generate the final UIs [36]. Jelly overcomes this problem by hiding the models from the designers and allowing them to work on the concrete representation of a UI.

6   Discussion

This chapter discussed the problem of integrating informal knowledge into a user-centered and model-driven process to design and develop user interfaces. This problem mainly occurs during the design and development of small-scale, context sensitive applications, which can benefit of the creativity of non-technical team members, but also need to take into account technical issues. To effectively integrate this informal design knowledge, an increased involvement of a multidisciplinary team during the entire process is recommended. This means that particular artifacts should be available to all team members in order to keep track of decisions made during the process. Nevertheless, a technique to translate informal design knowledge into more formal models is also necessary to improve communication within the team.

To accomplish this, we discussed three main tools that complement existing work: the COMuICSer tool, mapping and transformation support for formal models and Jelly. The COMuICSer tool enables the structuring and visualisation of narrative scenarios using annotated storyboards. Starting from an informal storyboard that visualizes a narrative scenario and gradually adding more structured infomation and annotations, assists all team members to understand and agree on the requirements for a future application. Furthermore, the annotations help in formalizing and augmenting the knowledge captured by the storyboard and translating into a formal model.

The model, obtained from the information extracted from the storyboard and its annotations, supports the creation of a task and context model that conforms with the storyboard through transformations that can create an initial set of tasks with temporal operators between them and constraints.

Jelly leverages the knowledge captured by the abstract interface objects (AIOs) and their relation to concrete and final interface objects to ease creation of multi-platform user interfaces. It does this without exposing the AIOs to designers, which stimulates designers' creativity. Furthermore, the possibility to keep an eye on a storyboard while using the Jelly tool, facilitates the possibility to keep in mind the user requirements during the creation and verification of UI designs.

In our current work, we are extending these tools, but are also extending the scope of our efforts to also include low-fidelity prototypes that include navigation. To enable this, we are extending the Canonical Abstract Prototypes notation [19] to also cover control and data flow. This extended notation (Fig. 2-4) will be supported by a meta-model and Eclipse-based tool support. In this way, we hope to make the abstract user interface model more accessible to designers, while encouraging creativity [19] but keeping the door open for automation.

Acknowledgements. This work is supported by the FWO project Transforming human interface designs via model driven engineering (G. 0296.08) and IWT project AMASS++ (SBO-060051).

References

1. Coyette, A., Schimke, S., Vanderdonckt, J., Vielhauer, C.: Trainable sketch recognizer for graphical user interface design. In: Baranauskas, M.C.C., Palanque, P.A., Abascal, J., Barbosa, S.D.J. (eds.) INTERACT 2007. LNCS, vol. 4662, pp. 124–135. Springer, Heidelberg (2007)
2. Haesen, M., Coninx, K., den Bergh, J.V., Luyten, K.: MuiCSer: A Process Framework for Multi-Disciplinary User-Centered Software Engineering processes. In: Proc. of Human-Centred Software Engineering, pp. 150–165 (2008)
3. Helms, J., Abrams, M.: Retrospective on ui description languages, based on eight years' experience with the user interface markup language (uiml). Int. J. Web Eng. Technol. 4(2), 138–162 (2008)
4. Brown, J., Graham, T.C.N., Wright, T.N.: The *Vista* environment for the coevolutionary design of user interfaces. In: Proc. of International Conference on Human Factors in Computing Systems, pp. 376–383 (1998)
5. Chatty, S., Sire, S., Vinot, J.L., Lecoanet, P., Lemort, A., Mertz, C.P.: Revisiting visual interface programming: creating gui tools for designers and programmers. In: Proc. of Annual ACM Symposium on User Interface Software and Technology, pp. 267–276. ACM, New York (2004)
6. Redmond-Pyle, D., Moore, A.: Graphical User Interface Design and Evaluation. Prentice Hall, London (1995)
7. Cooper, A.: The Inmates Are Running the Asylum: Why High Tech Products Drive Us Crazy and How to Restore the Sanity, 2nd edn. Pearson Education, Old Tappan (2004)
8. Pruitt, J., Adlin, T.: The Persona Lifecycle: Keeping People in Mind Throughout Product Design. Morgan Kaufmann Publishers, San Francisco (2006)
9. Carroll, J.M.: Making use: scenario-based design of human-computer interactions. MIT Press, Cambridge (2000)
10. Dow, S., Saponas, T.S., Li, Y., Landay, J.A.: External representations in ubiquitous computing design and the implications for design tools. In: Proc. of the Conference on Designing Interactive Systems, pp. 241–250
11. Johansson, M., Arvola, M.: A case study of how user interface sketches, scenarios and computer prototypes structure stakeholder meetings. In: Proc. of BCS Conference on Human-Computer Interaction, vol. (1), pp. 177–184, BCS (2007)
12. Buxton, B.: Sketching User Experiences getting the design right and the right design. Norman Kaufmann Publishers, San Francisco (2007)
13. Roam, D.: Back of the Napkin: Solving Problems and Selling Ideas with Pictures. Portfolio, New York (2008)
14. Truong, K.N., Hayes, G.R., Abowd, G.D.: Storyboarding: an empirical determination of best practices and effective guidelines. In: Proc. of the Conference on Designing Interactive Systems, pp. 12–21
15. Bowen, J., Reeves, S.: Formal refinement of informal gui design artefacts. In: Proc. of Australian Software Engineering Conference, pp. 221–230. IEEE Computer Society, Los Alamitos (2006)
16. Calvary, G., Coutaz, J., Thevenin, D., Limbourg, Q., Bouillon, L., Vanderdonckt, J.: A unifying reference framework for multi-target user interfaces. Interact. Comput. 15(3), 289–308 (2003)

17. Limbourg, Q., Vanderdonckt, J., Michotte, B., Bouillon, L., López-Jaquero, V.: USIXML: A language supporting multi-path development of user interfaces. In: Feige, U., Roth, J. (eds.) DSV-IS 2004 and EHCI 2004. LNCS, vol. 3425, pp. 200–220. Springer, Heidelberg (2005)
18. Jourde, F., Laurillau, Y., Nigay, L.: Comm notation for specifying collaborative and multimodal interactive systems. In: Proc. of Symposium on Engineering Interactive Computing Systems, pp. 125–134. ACM, New York (2010)
19. Constantine, L.L.: Canonical abstract prototypes for abstract visual and interaction. In: Jorge, J.A., Jardim Nunes, N., Falcão e Cunha, J. (eds.) DSV-IS 2003. LNCS, vol. 2844, pp. 1–15. Springer, Heidelberg (2003)
20. Nóbrega, L., Nunes, N.J., Coelho, H.: The meta sketch editor. In: Calvary, G., Pribeanu, C., Santucci, G., Vanderdonckt, J. (eds.) CADUI, pp. 201–214. Springer, Heidelberg (2006)
21. Harmelen, M.V. (ed.): Object Modeling and User Interface Design. The Component Software Series. Addison-Wesley, Reading (2001)
22. Haesen, M., Luyten, K., Coninx, K.: Get your requirements straight: Storyboarding revisited. In: Gross, T., Gulliksen, J., Kotzé, P., Oestreicher, L., Palanque, P., Prates, R.O., Winckler, M. (eds.) INTERACT 2009. LNCS, vol. 5727, pp. 546–549. Springer, Heidelberg (2009)
23. Haesen, M., Meskens, J., Luyten, K., Coninx, K.: Draw me a storyboard: Incorporating principles and techniques of comics to ease communication and artefact creation in user-centred design. In: Proc. of BCS Conference on Human Computer Interaction, Dundee (to appear, 2010)
24. Allen, J.F.: Maintaining knowledge about temporal intervals. Commun. ACM 26(11), 832–843 (1983)
25. Vanderhulst, G., Luyten, K., Coninx, K.: Photo-based user interfaces: Picture it, tag it, use it. In: Meersman, R., Herrero, P., Dillon, T. (eds.) OTM 2009 Workshops. LNCS, vol. 5872, pp. 610–615. Springer, Heidelberg (2009)
26. Meskens, J., Luyten, K., Coninx, K.: Jelly a multi-device design environment for managing consistency across devices. In: Santucci, G. (ed.) International Working Conference on Advanced Visual Interfaces, pp. 289–296. ACM Press, New York (2010)
27. Vermeulen, J., Vandriessche, Y., Clerckx, T., Luyten, K., Coninx, K.: Service-interaction descriptions: Augmenting services with user interface models. In: Proc. of Engineering Interactive Systems, Springer, Heidelberg (2007)
28. Li, Y., Landay, J.A.: Activity-based prototyping of ubicomp applications for long-lived, everyday human activities. In: Proc. of International Conference on Human Factors in Computing Systems, pp. 1303–1312
29. Campos, P.F., Nunes, N.J.: Towards useful and usable interaction design tools: Canonsketch. Interact. Comput. 19(5-6), 597–613 (2007)
30. Nunes, N.J.: Representing user-interface patterns in UML. In: Masood, A., Léonard, M., Pigneur, Y., Patel, S. (eds.) OOIS 2003. LNCS, vol. 2817, pp. 142–163. Springer, Heidelberg (2003)
31. Mori, G., Paternò, F., Santoro, C.: Ctte: Support for developing and analyzing task models for interactive system design. IEEE Trans. Software Eng. 28(8), 797–813 (2002)
32. Newman, M.W., Lin, J., Hong, J.I., Landay, J.A.: Denim: an informal web site design tool inspired by observations of practice. Hum. -Comput. Interact. 18(3), 259–324 (2003)

33. Lin, J., Landay, J.A.: Employing patterns and layers for early-stage design and proto-typing of cross-device user interfaces. In: Proc. of International Conference on Human Factors in Computing Systems, pp. 1313–1322
34. Gajos, K.Z., Weld, D.S., Wobbrock, J.O.: Automatically generating personalized user interfaces with supple. Artif. Intell. 174, 910–950 (2010)
35. Nichols, J., Chau, D.H., Myers, B.A.: Demonstrating the viability of automatically gen-erated user interfaces. In: Proc. of International Conference on Human Factors in Com-puting Systems, pp. 1283–1292. ACM, New York (2007)
36. Myers, B., Hudson, S.E., Pausch, R.: Past, present, and future of user interface software tools. ACM Trans. Comput.-Hum. Interact. 7(1), 3–28 (2000)

Optimized GUI Generation for Small Screens

David Raneburger, Roman Popp, Sevan Kavaldjian,
Hermann Kaindl, and Jürgen Falb

Abstract. More and more devices with small screens are used to run the same application. In order to reduce usability problems, user interfaces (UIs) specific to screen size (and related resolution) are needed, but it is time consuming and costly to implement all the different UIs manually.

Automated generation of UIs has the potential to reduce time and costs in case of many such devices. We extended the straight-forward approach to model-driven generation by including optimization according to maximum usage of available space on a small screen, minimum amount of clicks, and minimum scrolling. For these optimizations, we also use automated layouting and calculate the space needs of the possible variants. In effect, our new approach generates UIs optimized for small screens, in order to reduce related usability problems.

1 Introduction

Automated generation of UIs has certainly advanced in recent years, especially based on model-driven approaches. Still, such generated UIs pose many usability problems. We think that this is partly due to insufficient flexibility of the current generation approaches.

In particular, straight-forward model-driven generation only allows for matching a single transformation rule for each source pattern. We extend this approach by taking up means from rule-based programming, that have been around for a long time. We allow matching of several transformation rules for any source pattern, and we use so-called conflict resolution to determine which rule to apply (fire). Based on that, we implement a simple form of optimization in the context of model-driven UI generation.

It allows us to maximize the amount of information to be displayed on a small screen (with related resolution), to minimize the number of navigation clicks, and

David Raneburger · Roman Popp · Sevan Kavaldjian · Hermann Kaindl · Jürgen Falb
Institute of Computer Technology, Vienna University of Technology, Vienna, Austria
e-mail: {raneburger,popp,kavaldjian}@ict.tuwien.ac.at,
{kaindl,falb}@ict.tuwien.ac.at

H. Hussmann et al. (Eds.): MDD of Advanced User Interfaces, SCI 340, pp. 107–122.

to minimize scrolling. All this is important for reducing usability problems. Since more and more devices with small screens of different size are used to run the same application, we automatically optimize each generated UI for the given space available.

The remainder of this chapter is organized in the following manner. First, we present some background material in order to make our chapter self-contained. Then, we introduce our new rendering process for small screens that allows for certain optimizations. Based on that, we elaborate on our optimization approach in the context of model-driven generation of UIs. Finally, we discuss our new approach and relate it to previous work.

2 Background

In this section, we present our communication model, which is an interaction specification on a device-independent level of abstraction. Furthermore, we present our basic approach on how we transform such high-level interaction specifications into GUIs.

2.1 Our Communication Models

The input for our UI generation approach is a *communication model* [1], which is based on human communication theories and consists of three main parts. The most important part is the *discourse model* [2]. The other two parts are the *action model* and the *domain of discourse model*. The *discourse model* is inspired by the Speech Act Theory [3], Conversation Analysis [4] and Rhetorical Structure Theory (RST) [5].

Such a discourse model serves as an interaction design on a high level of abstraction based on concepts of human language theories. *Communicative acts* represent basic units of language communication. Thus, any communication can be seen as enacting of communicative acts, acts such as making statements, giving commands, asking questions and so on. Communicative acts indicate the intention of the interaction, e.g., asking a *question* or issuing a *request*.

A small excerpt of a larger discourse model for flight booking is shown in Fig. 1. Communicative acts typically refer to propositional content represented by text. The *Closed Question* communicative act on the left of Fig. 1 is for example about *select*ing a *departure airport*. The text "departure airport" represents a variable referring to an instance of the class *Airport* defined in the *domain of discourse model*. The Airport class has two attributes, a name and an airport code. For representing the *domain of discourse model*, we use a UML class diagram.[1]

The text *select* specifies the requested action to be taken by the user. Such requests are defined in the *action model*, which is only listed for completeness and

---

[1] At the time of this writing, the specification of UML is available at
http://www.omg.org.

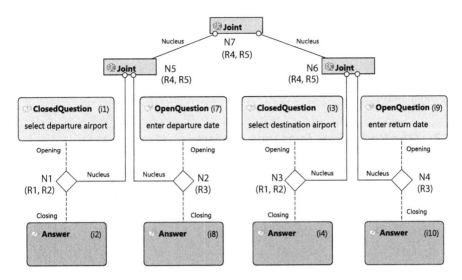

Fig. 1 A communication model excerpt for flight selection

not explained in detail, because it is not used in the optimization context for GUI generation per se.

Adjacency pairs are sequences of naturally-occurring "talk turns" to detect patterns that are specific to human (oral) communication, e.g., a *question* should have a related *answer*. Fig. 1 shows examples of adjacency pairs illustrated with a diamond symbol. The *Closed Question*, e.g., offers the human user a list of available *Airport*s and asks her to select one. The selected *Airport* is conveyed by the *Answer*. Such adjacency pairs are basic units for rendering a GUI.

RST relations specify relationships among text portions and associated constraints and effects. The relationships in a text are organized in a tree structure, where the rhetorical relations are associated with non-leaf nodes, and text portions with leaf nodes. In our work, we make use of RST for linking adjacency pairs and further structures made up of RST relations.

Adjacency pairs can be related with each other, resulting in a tree structure. In our example, the *Joint* relations N5 and N6 each relate two Question–Answer pairs. These *Joint* relations state that the Question–Answer pairs in both nucleus branches are of equal importance. The *Joint* relation N5 semantically connects the Closed Question to select a departure airport with the Open Question to enter a departure date, while the *Joint* relation N6 semantically connects the Closed Question to select a destination airport with the Open Question to enter a return date. The *Joint* relation N7 relates these two *Joint* relations N5 and N6.

A *Joint* relation means that each branch of the *Joint* relation has equal importance. Further, it does not imply a temporal order per se. For instance, both pieces of information can be presented in parallel if there is enough space on the screen. Otherwise, they can be uttered in a sequence. In contrast, a *Sequence* relation would imply a temporal order. In this case the nuclei would have to be performed sequentially.

The relations are used to define the dynamic behavior, the largest possible screens of a GUI, and the layouting of the GUI according to the semantics of the relations. A more detailed description of how the relations define the dynamic behavior can be found in [6].

2.2   Our Basic Transformation Process

We have developed a user interface generation process [7] that transforms communication models into WIMP-based (Windows, Icons, Menu and Pointers) GUIs. Our basic user interface generation process is illustrated in Fig. 2 and consists of two steps.

Fig. 2 Our basic transformation process

The first step transforms a *communication model* into a *Structural UI Model* [8] by applying transformation rules to communication model elements. The resulting Structural UI Model represents the user interface's widgets and their structure, but still abstracts from details of the final UI. We do not use a common UI description language (e.g., UsiXML[2]), because our runtime environment is based on the exchange of Communicative Acts. In our running example, some of the transformation rules listed in Table 1 are applied to elements of the discourse model excerpt shown in Fig. 1 for generating a model representing the structure of the final UI shown in Fig. 4. The following paragraphs explain in detail which transformation rules get applied in which order to the discourse model excerpt of our running example.

1. *Joint Rule* R4 gets applied three times, since it matches the three *Joint* relations N7, N5, N6 and it adds three panels to the Structural UI Model. The panel hierarchy is constructed according to the discourse tree. The panel resulting from the *Joint* relation N7 contains the two panels for the *Joint* relations N5 and N6. These panels act as containers each for one of the two radio button list and text box pairs shown in Fig. 4, each of which corresponds to the two nucleus branches of the *Joint* relations N5 and N6.

2. *Closed Question Rule* R1 gets applied twice, since it matches each of the two Question–Answer adjacency pairs N1 and N3. For each adjacency pair, a panel

---

[2] http://www.usixml.org

Table 1 Transformation rules applicable in the flight selection example

Rule	Rule Name	Description
R1	*Closed Question Rule*	matches a *Closed Question–Answer* adjacency pair and adds a panel containing a label for a heading, a list of radio buttons together with item labels, and a submit button at the bottom to the Structural UI Model.
R2	*Small Closed Question Rule*	matches a *Closed Question–Answer* adjacency pair and adds a combo box element and a submit button to the Structural UI Model.
R3	*Open Question Rule*	matches an *Open Question–Answer* adjacency pair and adds a panel containing a label for a heading, a text box and a submit button at the bottom to the Structural UI Model.
R4	*Joint Rule*	matches a *Joint* relation and adds a panel to the Structural UI Model.
R5	*Small Joint Rule*	matches a *Joint* relation and adds a tabbed pane to the Structural UI Model.

containing a label for a heading, a list of radio buttons together with item labels, and a submit button on the bottom are added to the Structural UI Model.

3. *Open Question Rule* R3 gets applied twice, since it matches each of the two Question–Answer adjacency pairs N2 and N4. For each adjacency pair, a panel containing a label for a heading, a text box and a submit button at the bottom are added to the Structural UI Model.

All information displayed in the Structural UI part created by the *Closed Question Rule* and the *Open Question Rule* is specified in the propositional content of the adjacency pairs' communicative acts. The messages displayed by the heading labels are derived from the action that is defined in the communication model's *action model*. The rest of the widgets is used to represent a single domain element (or a list of domain elements) that is specified in the *domain of discourse model*.

Each target device we render for, is characterized by an *abstract device specification* that contains all style data used by transformation rules. These style data specify default sizes for all widgets available on the target device, which can be overwritten in a transformation rule. These device-dependent sizes are used to set the size for each final UI element and allow calculating the exact size of each container (e.g., panel). For example, in our running example we set the size of list widgets explicitly. This makes them independent from the number of entries. If a list widget is not able to display all entries, it becomes scrollable.

At the end of this transformation step, we try to layout each generated screen to fit into the given space (with the given resolution). The layouting algorithm takes the relations into account and tries to visualize the semantics of the relations. However, we modify only the arrangement of the widgets that has not been fixed explicitly in a transformation rule. Therefore, we do not change the layout specified by the Closed Question Rule (i.e., the layout of the heading label, the radio button list and the submit button shown in Fig. 4). In our example, we modify the position of the complete radio button lists in the panel created by the *Joint* relation, since the Joint Rule does not contain any layout information.

In the second step of our transformation process, the Structural UI Model is used to generate source code for a particular target platform, e.g., Java Swing in our running example.

Our basic transformation process is a straight-forward model-driven generation that only allows for matching a single transformation rule for each source pattern. We are not aware of any optimization strategy in such a context. Therefore, we extend the straight-forward approach by allowing that several transformation rules may match for each source pattern, and by applying conflict resolution to select which rule to apply (fire) in the model-to-model transformation.

3   Rendering Process for Small Screens

Rendering of *communication models* on small devices brings up new challenges. For instance, the transformation process has to be capable of transforming multiple occurrences of relations of the same type with different transformation rules. Therefore, we need the ability to match multiple rules with the same discourse element type. Our approach allows the generation of optimized UIs for a continuous scale of screen sizes compared to a single-matching approach, where only a small subset of possible UIs can be generated by matching all relations of a particular type with the same rule. This involves a larger set of rules, where one discourse element can be matched by more than one rule. Furthermore, we need optimization objectives to identify an optimal solution.

3.1   Problem and Approach

The problem tackled by our extended approach is to fit a given amount of information optimally (according to the optimization objectives defined in Subsection 3.2) into small screens with limited resolution. It makes no sense to specify widget sizes in pixels on an abstract level as this makes the actual size on the screen dependent on the device's dpi value. Therefore, we support the definition of widget sizes in metric values (e.g., cm). These values are transformed into pixel values using the device's resolution (defined in dpi) during the generation process.

To solve the problem of how to find the optimal GUI according to our optimization objectives described in the next section, we studied approaches to heuristic search from the field of artificial intelligence [9, 10, 11]. However, we could not identify an algorithm that provided a complete solution for our problem, so we came up with an algorithm based on backtracking and branch-and-bound.

3.2 Optimization Objectives

We assume that the following optimization objectives improve the usability of the generated GUIs:

1. maximum use of the available space,
2. minimum amount of navigation clicks, and
3. minimum scrolling (except list widgets).

Whenever the information to be displayed does not fit into a single screen with default widgets, we try to display it with widgets that use less space (i.e., either not visualizing all information at the same time or even not rendering all information, which we will call "higher information loss" throughout this chapter). If the information still does not fit into a single screen, we split its display into two or more screens. Splitting increases the number of navigation clicks, but it minimizes scrolling. When we talk about scrolling in the optimization context, we do not consider whether list widgets are scrollable or not, because this depends on the number of entries the list displays during runtime. This information is not available during our rendering process.

It is hard, if not even impossible, to include all usability aspects in a cost function. Our optimization objectives reflect which aspects we consider in our approach and in which order we consider their importance. To be able to use a sum cost function, we treat the optimization objectives as independent from each other. Therefore, we assume that splitting always means a less usable GUI than one without. This means that we try to reduce the amount of used space before we split the screen, and we only rely on scrolling if we cannot find a rule combination representing a Structural UI Model that fits into the screen.

3.3 Our Extended Transformation Process

Our extended transformation process is presented in Fig. 3. It shows how we extended our basic transformation process in order to optimize the generated GUI to the given screen size. We achieve this by executing an optimization loop that transforms the *communication model* to a *Structural UI Model* with a different rule combination in each cycle until an optimal UI is generated. In our approach, the rules need not to be specifically designed for a particular screen size with a given resolution. It is the way the rules are applied, that achieves the given optimization objectives.

In order to implement such an optimization, the conflict resolution mechanism needs to select the rule combinations in a certain order. For achieving the optimization objectives given above, this selection order is defined according to the calculated costs of each rule combination. Therefore, all rules matching the same communication model element have to be classified by the designer according to their information loss. The information loss of a transformation rule is set to a higher value the fewer information is presented. Each rule that matches a discourse relation has to be classified according to whether it applies screen splitting or not. This

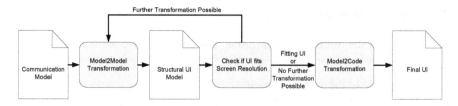

Fig. 3 Our extended transformation process

information is used to calculate the costs of a rule combination. The more rules with higher information loss, as well as splitting rules are included in a rule combination, the higher are its costs. Subsequently the rule combinations are sorted according to their calculated costs, starting with the lowest.

3.4 Optimization Strategy

The optimization strategy's purpose is to provide a list of possible rule combinations, sorted according to the optimization objectives defined in Subsection 3.2. Overall, the optimization strategy performs three major steps:

1. A list of possible rule combinations is created. This step requires the communication model, a set of applicable rules and the device specification as input. Its result is a list of rule combinations that might fit in the screen of the target device.
2. The second step calculates the costs for each rule combination. The costs reflect the violation of our optimization objectives. The lower the cost of a combination is, the closer it comes to an optimum according to our objectives. Subsequently, the combinations are sorted from cheapest to most expensive.
3. The third step tries to calculate a valid layout for each screen. Subsequently, the exact size for each screen can be calculated and thus can be checked whether the rule combination fits the screen size with the given resolution. If it does not fit, the next rule combination is checked. This process continues until a fitting rule combination (i.e., Structural UI Model) is found. As the costs represent the grade of violation of our optimization objectives, the fitting Structural UI Model is optimal with respect to the defined objectives.

In the following, we explain these optimization steps in more detail.

3.4.1 Create List of Possible Rule Combinations

At the beginning, we assign each discourse node a list of transformation rules that match this node. To uniquely identify each node in our communication model example in Fig. 1, we marked each node with an N and a unique number. Each transformation rule presented in Table 1 has been assigned an R and a unique number. The matching rules for each node in Fig. 1 are presented in parenthesis right beneath the node label. Nodes N1 and N3 are matched by the same rules R1 and R2 because

Table 2 Rule selection strategy execution example for a 4.2", 320×240 pixel display (see Fig. 7)

Discourse Node pre/post	Possible Rule Combinations
N7 pre	not calculated
N5 pre	not calculated
N1	{(N1,R1)},{(N1,R2)}
N2	{(N2,R3)}
N5 post	{~~(N5,R4)(N1,R1)(N2,R3)~~},{~~(N5,R4)(N1,R2)(N2,R3)~~}, {~~(N5,R5)(N1,R1)(N2,R3)~~},{(N5,R5)(N1,R2)(N2,R3)}
N6 pre	not calculated
N3	equal to N1
N4	equal to N2
N6 post	equal to N5
N7 post	{~~(N7,R4)(N5,R5)(N1,R2)(N2,R3)(N6,R5)(N3,R2)(N4,R3)~~}, {(N7,R5)(N5,R5)(N1,R2)(N2,R3)(N6,R5)(N3,R2)(N4,R3)}

both rules match an ClosedQuestion–Answer adjacency pair. Nodes N2 and N4 are matched by rule R3. Nodes N5, N6 and N7 are matched by rules R4 and R5 as both rules match a Joint relation.

Starting with the root node of the discourse, in our example the Joint relation N7, the list of possible rule combinations is calculated recursively. At each node we calculate all possible rule combinations of each subtree and combine them with all matching rules of the current node (post-order tree traversal). Applying this algorithm, the resulting set of possible rule combinations defines all possible rule combinations for the discourse tree part and grows exponentially at each node. An example of the calculation process is shown in Table 2 with the set of rule combinations in pre- and post-calculation state.

To reduce the solution space of possible rule combinations, we start the calculation with the leaf nodes, as predefined by the post-order tree traversal and reduce it at each node by applying branch-and-bound. After applying each matching rule to a communication model node, we calculate the size of the occupied screen space at the leaf nodes of the communication model tree. All rules leading to a GUI part that does not fit the screen are immediately omitted.

Next, at each inner node, we apply each matching rule and calculate an estimated size with a space-need assumption. The calculation of the space need assumption is done differently, depending whether the matching rules apply screen splitting or not. In case of a non-splitting rule, we calculate the overall estimated size by summarizing the size (space need) of each subtree (arrangement/layout of the subtrees is not considered yet, thus leading to an optimistic estimate). In case of a splitting rule, we take the size of the largest subtree as the estimated size of the current inner node. All rule combinations for communication model subtrees whose space need assumption does not fit in the screen, is discarded (i.e., not added to the list of possible rule combinations).

It is important that our space-need assumption is optimistic to guarantee that we can achieve an optimal GUI. Introducing this discard mechanism, the list of possible

GUIs will not grow dramatically for small screens. For large screens, however, this algorithm may need a huge amount of memory. Therefore, we excluded such screens from the scope of our current approach. The crossed out rule combinations in Table 2 are the removed because of the space-need assumption.

The list of fitting rule combinations at the root element of the discourse represents the solution space for the next steps.

3.4.2   Sort List of Possible Rule Combinations

After we have built a list of possible rule combinations that optimistically fit the screen during the first step, we now order this list according to our optimization objectives. Therefore, we represent the optimization objectives in a cost function, which we use to order the list of possible rule combinations. Each rule combination is classified according to the level of information loss and splitting that the applied rules cause. For the sorting of the list, we only use the first two objectives and do not include *minimum scrolling*, since this last objective is fulfilled by the extended transformation process itself. Our cost function guarantees, that we sort the list of rule combinations from minimum to maximum information loss before screen splitting is used. All rule combinations that apply screen splitting are ordered from minimum to maximum information loss, under the consideration of how many screens are split.

3.4.3   Generate the Structural UI Model

Taking the sorted list of possible rule combinations, the first one (i.e., the cheapest solution) is used to transform the communication model to a Structural UI Model. While the size calculated during the first step has been an estimate, we now create a valid layout for each screen, calculate the real space need and check if it still fits the given screen size. If it fits the given screen, an optimal UI according to our optimization objectives has been found. Otherwise the next possible rule combination from the list is tested. In case even the most expensive combination does not fit in the screen, we create the Structural UI Model for this combination and rely on scrolling.

3.5   Final UIs for Small Screens

Now let us illustrate the results after applying our approach to automatically generate optimized UIs for four target sizes and related resolutions. As input we use the communication model excerpt shown in Fig. 1.

Our first GUI is rendered for an *8.3" display* with a resolution of 640×480 pixels (see Fig. 4). The transformation rules with no information loss and no splitting are able to generate a GUI that fits such a screen. The rules applied are: {(N1,R1), (N2,R3), (N3,R1), (N4,R3), (N5,R4), (N6,R4) and (N7,R4)}. These are the same rules that have been applied in our basic transformation process. After having sorted the list of possible rule combinations according to their costs, we calculate the size

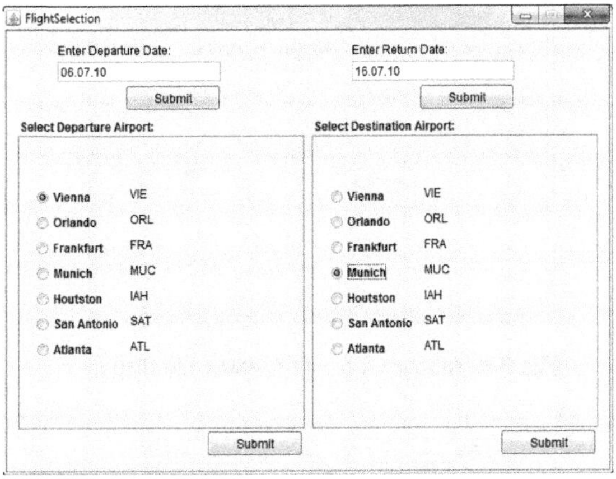

Fig. 4 Resulting UI for a 8.3", 640×480 display

for each panel in the corresponding Structural UI Model. We can place them next to each other without exceeding the screen. So, this GUI fits already and we trigger the model-to-code transformation.

Next, we generate a GUI for a *6" display* with a resolution of 480×320 pixels. The rule combination that gets applied and fits the screen is: {(N1,R2), (N2,R3), (N3,R2), (N4,R3), (N5,R4), (N6, R4) and (N7,R4)}, since the rule combination applied before has been ruled out by branch-and-bound. This rule combination uses the *Small Closed Question Rule* R2 instead of the Closed Question Rule R1 used for generating the GUI in Fig. 4. This rule matches the same source element (Question–Answer adjacency pair) as the Closed Question Rule, but has a *higher information loss* and, therefore, creates a GUI structure which occupies less space on the screen. A combo box element presents the content of the *Closed Question* communicative act to the user and a submit button is generated to confirm the selection of the user. The resulting GUI in Fig. 5 fits in the screen, using widgets with less space needs (combo boxes instead of radio buttons). However, the panels with the combo boxes do not fit next to each other. Therefore, the layouter arranges them vertically.

In a third run, we generate a user interface for a *4.8" display* with a resolution of 380×260 pixels. This time the rule combination that gets applied is: {(N1,R2), (N2,R3), (N3,R2), (N4,R3), (N5,R4), (N6,R4) and (N7,R5)}. Even after all rule combinations with more information loss have been tested, the generated GUI still does not fit. Therefore, we start using rule combinations that split the screen, implying an increase in the number of navigation clicks. In our example, this means that the *Small Joint Rule* is applied instead of the Joint Rule leading to the screen in Fig. 5. The Small Joint Rule matches the same source element (Joint relation) but creates a different GUI structure (a tabbed pane element instead of a panel). Fig. 6 shows the outcome for such a smaller screen. The *Small Joint Rule* and the *Small Closed Question Rule* have been applied, as well as the *Open Question Rule*, and the fitting GUI has been generated. This time, no layout modifications are necessary because each tab contains only one panel.

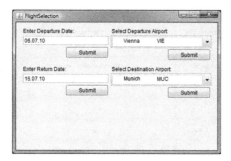

Fig. 5 Resulting UI for a 6", 480×320 display

Fig. 6 Resulting UI for a 4.8", 380×260 display

Fig. 7 Resulting UI for a 4.2", 320×240 display

Table 2 illustrates the execution of our optimization strategy for our example communication model in Fig. 1. It shows how the list of possible rule combinations is built for a device with a *4.2" display* and a resolution of 320×240 pixels. The resulting GUI is illustrated in Fig. 7. By eliminating the rule combinations that do not fit the screen during the calculation process, the solution space can be reduced significantly. The smaller the given screen, the more rule combinations can be ignored during the transformation process. The rule combination applied is: {(N1,R2), (N2,R3), (N3,R2), (N4,R3), (N5,R5), (N6,R5) and (N7,R5)}. This rule combination uses the *Small Joint Rule* R5 instead of the *Joint Rule* R4 for additional splitting of nodes N5 and N6 to fit the GUI in the screen. The information for the departure airport and the departure date are presented on separate tabs of a Tab Control.

The worst case in our extended generation process occurs if no more rule combinations are available and the generated screen still does not fit the given screen. In this case, we stop the optimization loop and rely on scrolling.

4 Related Work

A transformation system that fits Web pages automated and on-the-fly to screens of small devices is presented in [12]. The transformations are performed in order to minimize navigation and scrolling like in our approach. In contrast, however, this process alters an already existing UI.

Declarative user interface specifications are used as input for multi-target UI generation in [13]. The user interface adaption is treated as an optimization problem based on a user- and device-specific cost function. Compared to such user interface specifications, our interaction models are on a higher level of abstraction.

The model-driven approach for engineering multi-target UIs presented in [14] supports switching between predefined presentations during runtime. Our approach, in contrast, is intended to automatically generate GUIs for different screens of small size from a single discourse model.

An advanced approach for generating multi-device UIs is based on task models [15]. Such a Task Model specifies the temporal relations among tasks and has to be adapted according to the screen space available on the target device. Therefore, any optimization and screen splitting has to be done explicitly during the creation of the Task Model.

Parametric bidimensional semantic redesign is based on the MARIA framework as in [15], and is an approach that supports desktop-to-mobile UI adaptation [16]. Its starting point is an existing desktop HTML/CSS page that is reverse engineered in a first step. The subsequent redesign can be performed by the end user through definition of parameters (e.g., maximum and minimum font size, text limit, etc.) that influence the regeneration process of the Web page for small devices. In contrast to this approach, we do not use an existing UI as a starting point and we apply automated optimization to improve the usability of the GUI for small devices.

With respect to these approaches, we are not aware of any other approach that performs optimization in the course of model transformations. Neither are we aware of any model-driven GUI transformation process that takes optimization objectives for transformation rule selection into account.

5 Discussion and Outlook

Our optimization approach supports the automatic rendering of GUIs for small screens. The screen size is important for two reasons. First we do not (yet) optimize layout according to, e.g., aesthetic criteria, which becomes crucial if no optimization as defined in this chapter is needed. Second, the number of possible rule combinations rises exponentially. Depending on the number of discourse nodes and the number of transformation rules that match one node, this might lead to a memory problem if no combination exceeds the available space limit and cannot be discarded during the rendering process.

To solve the "layout-problem", we plan to apply heuristics and to give more control over the GUI generation to the designer [17]. Moreover, we plan to improve our algorithm by sorting our transformation rules in advance regarding to their estimated costs. This will allow us to combine them and to calculate the costs on the fly instead of calculating all the combinations first and the costs subsequently. This will make the algorithm more complex, but it will also improve another short-coming of our current version. The screen that is generated if no combination fits so far is the most "expensive" one. This is due to the fact that our algorithm does not consider each subtree of the discourse tree separately. Therefore, we plan to implement this in order to be able to optimize each screen separately.

Another layout optimization is to reduce the number of buttons on a screen. It would be sufficient if on each screen only one button for submitting all values is generated and not for each piece of information. This optimization cannot be solved by the model-to-model framework as it stands, it can only be done by analyzing the generated screens. Another point of analyzing the generated screens is to merge tab controls within tab controls to one tab control with more panels, if there is no semantic relationship implying a hierarchy between them.

6 Conclusion

In this paper, we address basic usability problems of GUIs for devices with small screens. Our new and extended approach introduces straight-forward optimization techniques into model-driven generation of GUIs to reduce such usability problems. This allows us to optimize generated GUIs for devices with small screens in such a way as to utilize the given space and to minimize navigation and scrolling.

We implemented this optimization approach by extending the straight-forward approach of model transformations through more flexible rule matching and execution. In this way, we introduce a GUI generation process that allows the same rule set to be used for generating GUIs for devices with small screens providing different amounts of space. Through the automatic calculation of space need, it may even have an advantage in this respect as compared to a human interface designer.

Acknowledgments

Part of this research has been carried out in the CommRob project, partially funded by the EU (contract number IST-045441 under the 6th framework programme), seehttp://www.commrob.eu. We also thank Points Management GmbH for sponsoring part of this research in the context of a project partially funded by the Austrian FFG.

References

1. Popp, R.: Defining communication in soa based on discourse models. In: OOPSLA 2009: Proceeding of the 24th ACM SIGPLAN conference companion on Object oriented programming systems languages and applications, pp. 829–830. ACM, New York (2009), DOI http://doi.acm.org/10.1145/1639950.1640035
2. Falb, J., Kaindl, H., Horacek, H., Bogdan, C., Popp, R., Arnautovic, E.: A discourse model for interaction design based on theories of human communication. In: Extended Abstracts on Human Factors in Computing Systems (CHI 2006), pp. 754–759. ACM Press, New York (2006), DOI
http://doi.acm.org/10.1145/1125451.1125602
3. Searle, J.R.: Speech Acts: An Essay in the Philosophy of Language. Cambridge University Press, Cambridge (1969)
4. Luff, P., Frohlich, D., Gilbert, N.: Computers and Conversation. Academic Press, London (1990)
5. Mann, W.C., Thompson, S.: Rhetorical Structure Theory: Toward a functional theory of text organization. Text 8(3), 243–281 (1988)
6. Popp, R., Falb, J., Arnautovic, E., Kaindl, H., Kavaldjian, S., Ertl, D., Horacek, H., Bogdan, C.: Automatic generation of the behavior of a user interface from a high-level discourse model. In: Proceedings of the 42nd Annual Hawaii International Conference on System Sciences (HICSS-42). IEEE Computer Society Press, Piscataway (2009)
7. Kavaldjian, S., Falb, J., Kaindl, H.: Generating content presentation according to purpose. In: Proceedings of the 2009 IEEE International Conference on Systems, Man and Cybernetics (SMC 2009), San Antonio, TX, USA (2009)
8. Kavaldjian, S., Bogdan, C., Falb, J., Kaindl, H.: Transforming discourse models to structural user interface models. In: Giese, H. (ed.) MODELS 2008. LNCS, vol. 5002, pp. 77–88. Springer, Heidelberg (2008)
9. Nilsson, N.: Principles of Artificial Intelligence. Springer, New York (1980)
10. Pearl, J.: Heuristics - Intelligent Search Strategies for Computer Problem Solving. Addison-Wesley, Reading (1984)
11. Kaindl, H.: Problemlösen durch heuristische Suche in der Artificial Intelligence. Springer, Heidelberg (1989)
12. Xiao, X., Luo, Q., Hong, D., Fu, H., Xie, X., Ma, W.Y.: Browsing on small displays by transforming web pages into hierarchically structured subpages. ACM Transactions on the Web 3(1), 1–36 (2009), DOI
http://doi.acm.org/10.1145/1462148.1462152
13. Gajos, K., Weld, D.S.: SUPPLE: Automatically generating user interfaces. In: Proceedings of the 9th International Conference on Intelligent User Interface (IUI 2004), pp. 93–100. ACM Press, New York (2004), DOI
http://doi.acm.org/10.1145/964442.964461
14. Collignon, B., Vanderdonckt, J., Calvary, G.: Model-driven engineering of multi-target plastic user interfaces. In: Proceedings of the Fourth International Conference on Autonomic and Autonomous Systems (ICAS 2008), pp. 7–14. IEEE Computer Society, Washington (2008), DOI http://dx.doi.org/10.1109/ICAS.2008.37

15. Paternò, F., Santoro, C., Spano, L.D.: Model-based design of multi-device interactive applications based on web services. In: INTERACT, vol. (1), pp. 892–905 (2009)
16. Paternò, F., Zichitella, G.: End-user customization of multi-device ubiquitous user interfaces. In: Proceedings of the MDDAUI 2010 Workshop on Model Driven Development of Advanced User Interfaces (2010)
17. Raneburger, D.: Interactive model driven user interface generation. In: Proceedings of the EICS 2010 Symposium on Engineering Interactive Computing Systems (2010)

Business Performer-Centered Design of User Interfaces

Kênia Sousa and Jean Vanderdonckt

Abstract. Business Performer-Centered Design of User Interfaces is a new design methodology that adopts business process (BP) definition and a business performer perspective for managing the life cycle of user interfaces of enterprise systems. In this methodology, when the organization has a business process culture, the business processes of an organization are firstly defined according to a traditional methodology for this kind of artifact. These business processes are then transformed into a series of task models that represent the interactive parts of the business processes that will ultimately lead to interactive systems. When the organization has its enterprise systems, but not yet its business processes modeled, the user interfaces of the systems help derive tasks models, which are then used to derive the business processes. The double linking between a business process and a task model, and between a task model and a user interface model makes it possible to ensure traceability of the artifacts in multiple paths and enables a more active participation of business performers in analyzing the resulting user interfaces. In this paper, we outline how a human-perspective is used tied to a model-driven perspective.

1 Introduction

User Interfaces (UIs) have been historically specified, designed, developed, and tested according to multiple design methodologies that have reflected a particular emphasis that was prevalent during a certain period. Each design methodology always adopted a certain viewpoint to drive the development life cycle. Over years, we witnessed the following viewpoints:

Kênia Sousa
Université catholique de Louvain, Louvain School of Management, Belgian Laboratory of Computer-Human Interaction, Place des Doyens, 1, 1348 Louvain-la-Neuve, Belgium
e-mail: kenia.sousa@uclouvain.be

Jean Vanderdonckt
Université catholique de Louvain, Louvain School of Management, Belgian Laboratory of Computer-Human Interaction, Place des Doyens, 1, 1348 Louvain-la-Neuve, Belgium
e-mail: jean.vanderdonckt@uclouvain.be

H. Hussmann et al. (Eds.): MDD of Advanced User Interfaces, SCI 340, pp. 123–142.
springerlink.com © Springer-Verlag Berlin Heidelberg 2011

Data-centered design: in this methodology, an interactive system is considered as a structured collection of data that will result into a data model, from which one or many UIs could be produced in order to properly manage this collection of data. The main advantage of this methodology was that deriving a UI for a particular data structure was straightforward. But the main disadvantage was that each data structure was then associated to a single screen in which the user has to carry out multiple functions that were not clearly identified [1]. It was then the responsibility of the end-user to properly execute the functions as expected in his/her tasks, thus resulting in several mismatches. In addition, data models did not initially consider the relationships between the concepts. In this case, the different interaction objects are derived from the information contained within the model, for instance, considering only the attributes of entities. It was clear at that point of the research that they needed to consider modeling functions and tasks [1].

Function-centered design: in this methodology, an interactive system is considered a collection of functions working on data identified in the aforementioned data model, that will result into a domain model. A domain model departs from a data model in that not only it contains the relationships between the data structures (e.g., as associations in a UML class diagram), but also its related constraints, and the functions associated to these data (e.g., the methods in a UML class diagram). The main advantage of this methodology was that deriving a UI for a particular function was possible to generate not only the layout of an interface, but also its dynamic behavior. The drawback of this approach was that only primitive functions were mainly supported (e.g., create, read, update, delete, list, search, print), thus forcing the end-user to re-interpret a task to be carried out in terms of such functions. Discovering, locating, and executing these functions was considered as a burden for end-users [2]. Therefore, researchers also acknowledged the need to consider task models for user interfaces with highly complex and flexible dialog structures.

Task-centered design: in this methodology, an interactive system is considered to support a collection of inter-related tasks that represent the user perspective of work, not the system perspective of work, thus resulting into a task model for every task of interest. A task model characterizes the way end-users carry out their effective task, not the prescribed tasks as found in manuals or procedures. In this way, it is expected that such a task model conveys a way of working that is close to the end-user. The main advantage of this methodology is that a UI derived from a task model is assumed to fit the end user's purpose since it should reflect his/her way of working. The difficulty of this approach is that many different UIs could be derived from the same task model and there is not enough effective knowledge today available that guides this derivation in order to ensure the quality of the result [3]. In addition, even though with some initiatives to consider user roles for a specific set of tasks in multi-user applications [4], it does not necessarily differentiate how user's profiles, skills and other aspects impact and differentiate these tasks and the design of user interfaces.

User-centered design: in this methodology, an interactive system is designed by gathering requirements directly from the end-user and by modeling these requirements in such a way that they can drive the rest of the development life cycle to maintain the end-user's perspective. Several ways exist in order to establish and follow a user-centered design, such as task modeling (as in the task-centered design), user modeling (e.g., through a user model), participatory design, contextual inquiry [5], etc. The main advantage of this methodology is that the UI resulting from the process is expected to be as close as possible to the end-user's expectations, abilities, and preferences. The difficulty with this methodology is that there is a wide range of instruments in order to conduct a user-centered design and, even with a high probability of success, there is no guarantee that a usable UI will be obtained. Indeed, a good instrument could be used in an inappropriate way. A second difficulty is that one task is examined at a time, thus posing some challenges in how to organize tasks in time and space. Indeed, an end-user is rarely working alone in his/her context of use. Rather, the end-user is incorporated in a series of interconnected tasks, some of these tasks could be collaborative, cooperative, competitive, or coopetitive. Therefore, there is a need to proceed with the user-centered design in order to encompass aspects that were not captured in the task model or in the traditional user-centered design in the context of complex business process applications.

Process-centered design: this methodology uses the business process model as "a structured, measured set of activities designed to produce a specific output for a particular customer or market" [6] in order to consider complex contexts. Different from the previous methodology, it does not start from the end-user's viewpoint. Although there are proven UI design methodologies, such as in user-centered design, process-centered design [7] differentiates itself by precisely focusing on business process intensive software which has not been the case with other UI design methodologies. More recently, a data-centered approach for business processes called artifact-centric business process models [8] puts business artifacts at the center of the approach. This approach focuses on key business-relevant entities, their lifecycles, and how and when services are invoked on these artifacts. It has concepts that are similar to traditional data models and business process models, but with augmented data records that correspond to business-relevant artifacts and richer semantic expressions for task conditions and consequences. Some recent works in this area propose aligning business processes with UIs with direct links between activities in processes and elements on the UIs. However, such strategies leave aside the consideration of the user interaction, which is much richer than what is specified in business processes. For this purpose, we introduce the following methodology:

Business Performer-centered design: in this methodology, it considers business processes, while not neglecting benefits brought by user-centered design by giving equivalent importance for business process performers (or simply business performers), who are, at the same time, end-users of enterprise systems [9]. This dual and balanced consideration is particularly challenging because end-users have been historically ignored by business process notations and methodologies by favoring a top-down approach when designing enterprise systems. Additionally to considering user-centered design on this proposal, we not only emphasize the global aspects of the work, but also individual aspects of each end-user, which is more precise than the attempt to summarize the human aspects using roles. Our main effort was to find out how user-centered design would be formally represented in this approach and, at the same time, keeping the compatibility with existing business process models. In our case, we propose that this merging point is a task model that serves as the cornerstone: the task model should be derived from the business processes that will in turn produce one or many UIs corresponding to the derived tasks. In this way, the expected win is that when a business process will change, the task model will change accordingly and so does the UI model corresponding to this task model, implementing a consistent alignment between business and user interfaces, and, consequently, providing traceability.

Considering these different viewpoints, several design methodologies have been defined over time with their specific purposes and aiming to be more thorough than the previous ones (see Fig. 1). In a timeline, Trident [10] automates user interface design from data models. In Mecano [2], each class in the hierarchy of the domain model is assigned to a window. In a task-based approach, a task model is given to identify UIs, for instance, CTT [11] recommends a task model where the interactive task is recursively and hierarchically decomposed into sub-tasks; and the UsiXML methodology [3] based on the Cameleon Reference Framework [12] has task and domain models at its center to specify user interfaces independent of implementation. In user-centered design, cognitive models of human users, known as user models, are used to predict human error and learning time, and can thus serve as a cheaper alternative to user testing, such as CogTool-Explorer [13]. Diamodl [14] takes a process centered design, which advocates to adapt BP modeling to include aspects of task modeling using BPMN for both BP and task modeling. While MDHI [15] is a design methodology and tool for the user interface life cycle that has business modeling as a starting point, including the business data. Finally, the UI-Business Alignment (or Usi4Biz) [9] considers business processes and their performers (end-users) to manage enterprise systems.

The remainder of this chapter is organized as follows: Section 2 will define the business performer-centered design as a way to align business process and UIs and introduces the concepts that are underlying to this design methodology. Section 3 will detail how this design methodology has been applied in a corporate environment, i.e. a very large telecommunication company, and how model-driven engineering has been used in order to support applying this methodology. Section 4 will discuss the potential advantages of this model-driven engineering as expected or observed in this case study, as well as identified shortcomings. Section 5 will conclude this chapter by highlighting the main contribution and by presenting some avenues of this research.

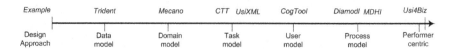

Fig. 1 Timeline of approaches

2 Going towards Performers and Users

One of the main goals that are aimed with the evolution of methodologies is to go beyond individual users or groups within a single organization. Emerging methodologies aim to consider the complex behaviors between people, among groups, among organizations, and between organizations and their environments. Fig. 2 depicts another perspective of the evolution of these different paradigms.

Despite the evolutions on these approaches and on the needs to address more complex behaviors, recent works [16, 17] still focus much more on how the artifacts are linked, handled and maintained than on the people who actually conceptualize and those who use enterprise systems. Thus, they end up failing to consider that these people are actually the ones who are key to making the organization work. Therefore, with a more human perspective, the business performer-centered approach considers the complexity of these relations intrinsic to business processes and adds the viewpoints of the business performers as active agents.

With that purpose, the UI-Business Alignment Methodology [9] considers business performers as active agents who open a new channel for business improvement by informing any sort of issues they face with systems. These identified issues may lead to changes on the processes, on the UIs or on both.

We rely on epistemological research to turn the recurring focus from business analysts and place it on business performers. This is in accordance with Giddens duality of structure theory [18], in which the organizational structure contains the behavior of professionals, but their behavior also makes the structure possible because these professionals have and apply their knowledge when acting, which may then change the organizational structure. Applying this theory to our methodology, business performers must adhere to the corporate structure following business processes, but they also bring changes to such structure since they think and behave differently.

Concerning the first state of the dual structure, in order to be able to adhere to defined processes, business performers must understand well how to perform these processes. However, it is common to find business processes defined at a high level that does not represent the tasks they should perform in their daily work. That is an important consideration to have task models with a lower level of granularity to specify performers' tasks. This way, there are fewer deviations from the tasks assigned to business performers. That is a reason for the growing interest from

Fig. 2 Evolution of approaches

organizations to know how specific agents, not generic roles, accomplish their work [19]. Therefore, we focus on actual users that we can identify within the organization since they are the ones who actually perform the process.

Looking at the second state of the dual structure, in order to enable business performers to bring changes to the corporate structure, they must play active roles by suggesting improvements on tasks defined at a low level of granularity, which is the manageable level of tasks corresponding to their work. Some works have emphasized the importance of involving users in process modeling [20]. But they had not yet realized how users can give more consistent contributions for business process improvement using their own knowledge, without having to acquire new skills (i.e. business analysis) before they are able to contribute.

In order to enable the active participation of business performers (a.k.a. end-users), the UI-Business Alignment methodology advocates different approaches, where different professionals can give their own contribution, depending on their skills and goals. These stakeholders can mainly contribute in the following manner:

- *Business analysts* can identify prospective improvements on business processes to address new corporate strategies;
- *UI designers* can identify improvements directly on the UI design to address specific interaction needs;
- *Usability experts* can identify better user interactive tasks that impact business operations;
- *Operation managers* can identify improvements on the performance of processes to address market opportunities that impact the processes and systems as a whole;
- *Users* can give suggestions towards improving user interaction and their productivity to be considered in the business context.

Each of these stakeholders contribute more precisely on specific approaches. The forward approach starts with business processes and stimulates the participation of operation managers and business analysts. The middle-out starts with interactive tasks and stimulates the participation of usability experts and UI designers. The backward approach starts with UIs and stimulates the participation of basically anyone in the organization, more precisely, UI designers and end-users.

UI-Business Alignment Methodology: The methodology proposes a strategy to map the core models related to enterprise systems and build a network of links that supports traceability and impact analysis when changes are requested in any of these models. The core actions to create the network of links can be applied in two main approaches: forward and backward:

Forward Approach simulates what could be the future user interaction to execute the process in situations where there is a process and there is no system.

Backward Approach uses navigation patterns in the system as a source of data to exploit business processes in situations where there is a system and there is no process.

The methodology is effectively adopted by starting with a critical process or system, which could be a great source of data to be analyzed in an initial project. After applying the methodology at the first time, a procedure is prepared to spread the methodology through other critical and non-critical processes and systems consi-dering the organizational context in other projects.

After the mappings are created, the models are managed through the execution of rules in three main approaches, as depicted in Fig. 3.

The **forward approach** starts with changes made on BP models, which can be done from a variety of reasons, including new or alternative ways of doing things, new business opportunities, organizational changes, new regulations; etc. When changes are made, rules are executed from the business process to the task model, persisting the changes on the task model, even if the task model does not yet exist, thus deriving a task model from the business process. Then, the rules are executed from the task model to the UI model, persisting the changes on the latter, assuming the UI model has been created beforehand.

The **middle-out approach** starts with changes made on task models, which can be done to perform new tasks that improve the user experience. In this approach, the rules are executed from the task model to the business process, persisting the changes on the latter, even if the business process model does not yet exist, thus deriving a business process from the task model. Then, the rules are executed from the task model to the UI model, persisting the changes on the latter, assuming the UI model has been created beforehand.

The **backward approach** starts with changes on UIs because of defects to be fixed, better user understanding of the systems' features, new technology, etc. In this case, rules are executed from the UI model to the task model, persisting the changes on the task model, assuming the task model has been created beforehand. Then, the rules are executed from the task model to the business process, persisting the changes on the latter, even if the business process model does not yet exist, thus deriving a business process from the task model.

There are no rules specified from the UI model to transform to the actual UIs of systems. There is a synchronization to indicate what has to be updated in the UIs directly by UI designers. This methodology considers that UI designers are relevant to create UIs for enterprise systems considering their human interpretation over user

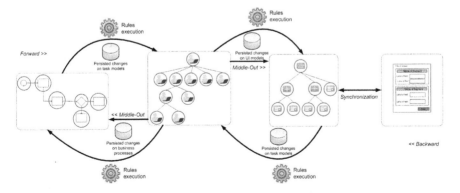

Fig. 3 UI-Business Alignment applying rules in different approaches

experience, user needs, and design ideas. The use of rules is a primordial aspect in this methodology because they enable tracing one element in the target model back to its causing element in the source model and provide transformations from source to target and vice-versa. But this tracing or transformation is useful only when people who perform the processes are active in analyzing and identifying bottlenecks in the business processes and user interfaces that support these processes.

For that reason, the backward approach is primordial to enable the participation of business performers. In this approach, end-users give suggestions based on their own experience with the systems. This solution is independent of how processes are designed and systems are developed. In most solutions in the market, business processes must be executed in specific engines and the system must be developed in a specific technology (e.g. web services) to allow collecting data as the system is used. Our solution is applicable in a wider range of corporate scenarios since we can monitor any kind of system that are representations of certain business processes (e.g. an order management system for provisioning products). In this approach, stakeholders do not need specific skills in order to be able to delineate which part of the system brings impediments for the successful completion of their goals. Therefore, we present how business performers can be active participants and the application of the rules aiming for better user interaction and improved process by presenting details of the model-driven perspective in the backward approach.

3   Model-Driven Perspective

The main models used in the UI-Business Alignment methodology are: Business Process Model, Task Model, User Interface Model. The UI-Business Alignment methodology is founded on Business Process Modeling Notation (BPMN) [21] for business process models and on the Cameleon Reference Framework and, more precisely on UsiXML for the definition of the task and UI models.

Business Process Model: This methodology is founded on BPMN that provides the standard for business process modeling. However, there are other business process notations that could be used with the UI-Business Alignment methodology. The main requirement to apply a business process notation in this methodology is that it is able to decompose activities in smaller parts, such as a sub-process in BPMN that can be decomposed in as many levels as needed to specify a complex activity.

Task Model: The types of UI Tasks in the task model are: (i) abstract, grouping of related tasks; (ii) user, task performed manually by a human being with no interaction with a system; (iii) interactive, task performed by the user interacting with the system; and (iv) system, task executed by the system itself. For the purpose of mapping business process activities that are to be performed by users when interacting with enterprise systems, we have delimited the scope to consider only interactive tasks in the traceability chain. Because we deal only with UIs, we do not need manual (user) tasks and automatic (system) tasks. Manual and automatic tasks by themselves do not involve the direct user interaction with a system. Thus, we have restricted our needs to interactive tasks only. Consequently, we simplify the task model with only one kind of task, which also contributes to increase the task model acceptance by providing simplicity.

User Interface Model: UI is a means by which users interact with the system. One of the main challenges of models aiming to formalize user interaction is to follow the fast technological evolution of devices and new kinds of interactions. This problematic has been our major motivation to investigate which model is the most appropriate to cover so many possibilities. In a survey comparing existing UI modeling languages [22], the abstract UI model seems to be the one that covers the broadest possible range of targets for the broadest possible range of delivery contexts. Therefore, we came up with an extension of the abstract UI model based on UsiXML. The difference is that the terms are not used literally because this UI model, for the purpose of UI-Business alignment, needs easy names and less UI components for simplicity. This simplification of the UI model aims to make it easily understandable by end-users when delineating the UI model. This different representation of the UI model does not substitute the language, which is used to guarantee interoperability. The UI model structure is comprised of UI components, which are components used for user interaction that start in an atomic level and are further composed in broader levels, namely: screen group, screen, screen fragment and screen element.

The core models have been structured with a set of elements that are primordial to be linked among them with the primary goal of UI-Business Alignment. In order to facilitate modifying how the models are structured, depending on the strategies adopted by the organization, an expert system approach based on production rules has been selected. This approach provides flexibility since it enables updating the rules whenever there is a change on how the models are structured and managed, without the need for direct maintenance of the platform that supports the methodology. This approach makes this framework adaptable to different organizational contexts by accepting that organizations may adapt their strategies to model processes and design user interfaces.

To define the knowledge of an expert system, it is necessary to specify the objects that are important to the domain, the properties of these objects and the relationships among them, and assertions about these objects, composing a *working memory* that is constantly changing during the operation of the system [16]. The format of our working memory is a graph with links among the model elements, forming the *network of links*.

Building the network of links is the process of mapping the elements of the core models of our methodology. These mapped elements form the working memory elements, called *objects*, that are instances of these model elements. These objects are of different types, represented by the *entities* of the models, such as BP activities, UI tasks, UI components.

For each entity of the models, there is a set of rules that verifies the integrity of the models when an event happens on any object of that entity. An *event* is any action that changes the state of the object, such as create, update, delete, and other types of operations performed in the models. Performing an event on any given object triggers the execution of rules for that object. Thus, when an event is done in any of the objects, a set of rules is executed in order to generate an impact report that lists all the elements on these models that have been impacted by the changes and the proposed changes to maintain consistency.

As a contribution for this research, we have defined rules that adhere to the basic properties of transformation rules [23] and follow the general format of production rules [16]. The rules have been written using the Drools Rule Language (DRL) because it is easy to understand, flexible, reusable, has a reasonable performance, independent lifecycle, can be easily embedded into existing applications, among other advantages of its declarative style solution [24].

To make the rules understandable by a larger range of stakeholders involved in managing the rules, such as non-technical stakeholders, it is productive to adopt human-readable rules using *Domain Specific Language* (DSL) [23]. A DSL is a computer language that is focused on a clearly definable problem domain, rather than a general purpose language that is aimed at any kind of software problem. A DSL file specifies the translation of sentences from the problem-specific terminology into rules. In Drools, a DSL file maps DSLR sentence (human-readable rule) to a DRL rule (rule in the Drools rule language). DSLR is useful to demonstrate an important reason for using rules; which is that rules can be customized by different stakeholders. Therefore, stakeholders can update and create new rules according to their approaches adopted for BP modeling, user experience, UI design, among other aspects.

To execute the rules, it is necessary to verify if the object matches specific conditions. For that, there are three main conditions that are checked, which are: if the object has been recently created, updated or deleted. The object is understood as recently created when its id is empty, since the id is generated automatically by the database only when the object is permanently persisted. The object is understood as updated when the id is different from empty, which means that the object already exists with a valid id. The object is understood as deleted when the reference to it is null, which means that the object does not exist anymore.

The Drools rule definition starts with the rule name; the condition and consequence sections follow. Drools keywords are *rule*, *when*, *then*, and *end*.

```
rule ''name of rule''
when
    conditions
then
    consequence;
end
```

The condition defines the patterns that the rule matches with. The consequence is a block of code that is executed when all of the patterns within the condition are matched. The rule condition can declare variables of an object type. The variable name starts with a $ symbol, it can be declared up front to be used later in the rule. The condition verifies if the object field matches a certain value, which can be of different types, such as predefined variable, string, regular expression, date, boolean and more. A condition can have multiple field constraints joined by additional keywords, such as an implicit *and* (i.e. a comma), *or*, *not*, *exists*, etc.

$$\$variable : Object\ (field_i == value_i, field_j == value_j)$$

In the rule consequence, Drools has convenience methods to be executed as simple actions: `modify`: to update existing facts in the working memory; `insert` to insert new facts in the working memory; `retract` to remove existing facts in the working memory.

Considering that each entity of the models has a set of rules that verifies the integrity of the models when an event happens on any object, we add the rule set name in the beginning of each rule definition. The rule set has the name of the entity to which it is related. The name of the rule follows this format: `impact on <<element>> when <<operation>> <<element>>`.

An example of a rule in the Drools rule language is presented as follows, which verifies when there is an element of type `activity` that has just been created (i.e. with a field id that is empty), then add to the working memory an element of type `UITask` related to this activity.

```
ruleset ''BP Activity''
rule ''impact on UITask when adding BP Activity''
when
    $activity: Activity(id == "")
then
    insert(new UITask($activity));
end
```

The execution of these rules follows a cycle of three steps [16] that uses the rules from a rule catalog, as follows:

- *recognize*: find the rules whose conditions are satisfied in the current working memory (e.g. rules for a BP activity);
- *resolve conflict*: among these rules recognized in the first step, choose the one that should be executed (e.g. rules that process the addition of a new BP activity that is not yet related to any UI task);
- *act*: perform the consequent actions of the rules selected in the second step to change the working memory (e.g. add the new UI task for this added BP activity).

This cycle continues until the conditions tested in the rules are false, which means that the models are supposed to be consistent at this point.

The rules that have been defined as pertaining to a rule catalog are explained and exemplified using a scenario from a case study at the telecommunications industry. The execution of the rules and its results are presented applying the backward approach.

Context of case study: This case study occurred in a customer-unit responsible for Business-to-Business transactions with twenty-three professionals, among managers, business analysts and IT professionals, who participated in meetings and interviews during four months.

The context under analysis is the provisioning of the Integrated Telephony Solution (ITS) products of the enterprise Voice over IP (eVoIP) solution for large enterprises that want to integrate their data and voice traffics on the same data network. From this context, we consider one category of these products that are determined by the quantity of dialing numbers (number of the physical phones) that the customer requires. Each dialing number may be associated to a package that represents voice service packages, such as call center, auto-attendant, receptionist, etc.

This case study is suitable to illustrate the backward approach since it did not have the business process modeled. For that reason, we start with UI model derivation from the UIs of the available system, followed by task model derivation and business process definition.

3.1   User Interface Model Derivation

A business analyst explained how the provisioning of ITS products works in practice and a system analyst presented how the provisioning is done using the system. After understanding the system, we observed 8 users interacting with the ordering system to provision eVoIP products.

During the observations, users mentioned that the selection of service packages was one aspect of the provisioning of products that was slowing them down. First, they selected voice service packages and then, they had to check if the packages remained the same after the attribution of dialing numbers. But since the attribution of numbers is an automatic process, this checking by users is unnecessary since they cannot interfere on those numbers, just on the packages that they have themselves selected previously.

Fig. 4 depicts exactly the two screens in which users first select service packages for eVoIP products that have not yet received the dialing numbers (i.e. Negotiate features). Once these products have the numbers, users can see the selected packages for each dialing number (i.e. Update features). Each screen uses a different way to display this information: the first one uses a tree and the second one uses a matrix.

This issue identified by end-users themselves decreases their productivity when managing the orders of customers. End-users proposed to merge these two UIs in one screen that is more efficient. Merging these UIs is done by selecting the most relevant UI components.

Based on the existing UIs of the ordering system, we have specified the UI model for the UIs. Fig. 5 depicts the UI model for the screen group to provide product, composed of several screens, but here the focus is on these two screens where users can select and check voice service packages. These screens have some screen elements in common (marked with dashed lines).

When two screens are merged, what happens is that a new screen is created with existing content. This change triggers a set of rules that supports deriving new UI tasks and updating the task model.

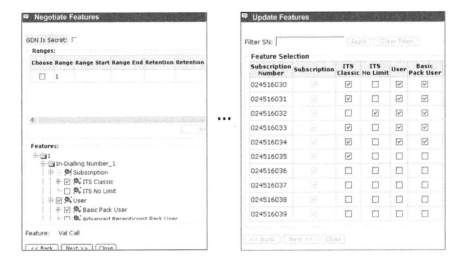

Fig. 4 Screens to select and check voice service packages

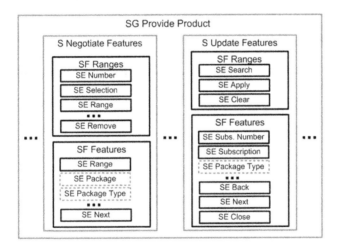

Fig. 5 UI model for the screens to select and check voice service packages

3.2 Task Model Derivation

Once the UIs were understood and the UI models created, the UI tasks in task models were derived from the execution of the rules. An extract of the task model to introduce products is depicted in Fig. 6.

Once this task model is created, whenever changes are made on its related UI model, this task model needs to updated accordingly.

For two screens that are merged, the working memory receives an instance of the new screen, of its pre-existing screen fragments and the UI tasks related to these

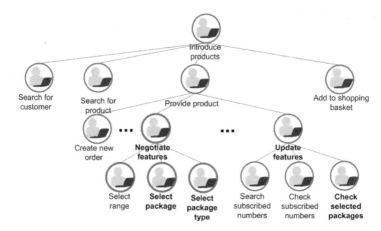

Fig. 6 Task model related to introducing products

screen fragments. The conditions that are verified in this case are: if there is a new screen with screen fragments, and this screen is not yet related to any UI Task, but its screen fragments are already related to UITasks. If this is the case, the task model needs to be updated. A set of rules related to Screen is triggered and the rule that positively addresses this condition is executed. The execution of the following rule creates a new UI task for this screen and creates sub-tasks for this UITask using the existing sub-tasks related to its screen fragments:

```
ruleset ''Screen''
rule ''impact on UI Task when merging Screens''
when
     The Screen has an empty id and does not have related
                UITasks
     The ScreenFragments have related UITasks
then
     create UITask for the Screen;
     modify this UITask with the association with
            sub-tasks related to the ScreenFragment;
end
```

Fig. 7 shows that a new screen is created with existing screen fragments from the two repeated screens. Since only the existing screen fragments are related to UI tasks, the rule results in the creation of a new UI task and associating it with the existing sub-tasks.

To delete the screens that have been merged, since a new screen is already substituting them, the working memory receives the instance of the deleted screen and of the UI tasks related to it. A set of rules related to screens are triggered and the rules that positively address the condition that verifies if a screen with related

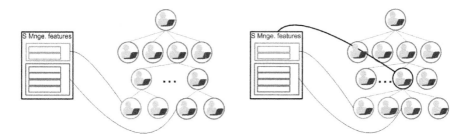

Fig. 7 UI model for the screens to select and check voice service packages

UI tasks was deleted is executed, thus deleting the related UI tasks through the following rule:

```
ruleset ''Screen''
rule ''impact on UI Task when deleting Screen''
when
     The Screen is null and
     There is an existing UITask
then
     remove UITask;
end
```

3.3 Business Process Definition

With the details of UI tasks, it was possible to specify the high level activities of the business process to provide product, depicted in Fig. 8. This business process model can be further refined by business analysts, checking accordance to business rules and strategies. This refinement is done depending on the levels of granularity adopted to model business processes: From an operational perspective, the activities are defined until the smallest action. From a process perspective, the activities specify what is performed and not details of how it is performed [25].

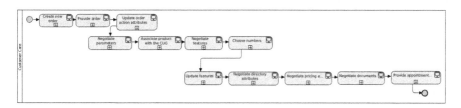

Fig. 8 Business process model to provide product

For each added UI task in the task model, the following rule was also executed to add the equivalent BP activities:

```
ruleset ``UITask''
rule ``impact on Sub Process when adding UI Task''
when
    The UITask has an empty id and does not have
                related activity
then
    create activity for UITask;
end
```

Once the business process is created, whenever changes are made on its related task model, this business process model needs to updated accordingly. Considering that some tasks were deleted because two screens were merged, some activities in the business process model need to be deleted. When UI tasks have been deleted, the working memory receives the instance of the deleted UI tasks and activities related to it. A set of rules related to UI tasks is triggered and the rules that positively address the condition that verifies if a UI task with related activities was deleted is executed, thus deleting the related activities through the following rule:

```
ruleset ``UI Task''
rule ``impact on Activity when deleting UI Task ''
when
    The UI Task is null and
    There is an existing Activity
then
    remove Activity;
end
```

This example has illustrated how the models are created and managed. Initially, the associations between business process models, task models and UIs is created, which builds a network of links. With this network built, it is possible to navigate in the network in any direction, which aids in identifying the impact of changes, supported by the execution of rules and updating the models according to the changes. This example particularly shows the analysis of the network of links starting with the UIs through suggestions of business performers taking into consideration their knowledge about the domain and expertise with the system.

4 Discussion

For the methodology to be efficiently applied, it is necessary to have a software platform to support the execution of these rules. The behavior of the platform is based on the methodology; accordingly, this platform can be used by different stakeholders, depending on their goal within the organization. To support the creation of the network of links, each stakeholder has a specific role.

Business analyst - When business analysts either create a new business process or update an existing one, they import the business process model into the platform as a starting point to create the network in the forward approach. Once this is done, the task model is automatically derived based on the imported business process.

Usability expert - Once a first version of the task model has been automatically created, most of the repetitious work is done and usability experts can focus on reviewing it and adding UI tasks that represent the user interaction.

UI designer - As the usability expert is working on the task model, the UI designer lists: the systems used to perform this business process, the users of these systems, and the UI components of each system. The level of detail given to the list of UI components depends on the level of detail expected for the result of the impact analysis. Once all these elements are listed and the usability expert finished updating the task model, the UI designer can associate the UI tasks with the listed UI components.

Operation Manager - When the network of links is created, the operation manager can request an impact analysis concerning a specific change that he/she prospects. When the operation manager, views the result of the impact analysis with the list of suggested changes, he/she can make a solid decision.

Each of these stakeholders is involved in managing specific models. We assume that the models created are correct, consistent and complete. They are complete considering that these models are designed in an iterative manner. Each iteration produces a version that is complete for the current context, but they are still open for changes and improvements. The platform is aimed to support stakeholders with information to help them maintain consistency between the models. However, the platform does not aim to indicate that a model is right or wrong because this is pertaining to the human abstraction skill. On the other hand, the platform indicates if a model is consistent or inconsistent, according to the conventions described in the rules. Being wrong may mean that it is different from reality or that it has a deadlock in the process flow, as an example of an error that stakeholders may make when modeling. As classified in [26], stakeholders normally fall in one of the seven sins of specification, namely: noise (i.e. irrelevant information), silence (i.e. lack of significant information), over-specification (i.e. specification of features out of scope), contradiction (i.e. incompatible definitions of a same feature), ambiguity (i.e. possibility to interpret a definition in different ways), forward reference (i.e. mention information before it is defined) and wishful thinking (i.e. lack of realistic aspects to validate the feature specified). Therefore, it is an assumption that stakeholders are confident in creating the models and that they at least try to maximize the correctness, consistency and completeness of the models.

The rules have been defined to provide flexibility to the platform since they can be updated whenever there is a change on how the models are managed, without the need for direct maintenance of the platform. The platform provides functionalities to make transformations from the business process into the task model, and backwards, avoiding creating models from scratch. The platform helps stakeholders to update UI tasks, delineate UI models and create the mappings and the rules are at the foundation of that support as they help maintain consistency between the models.

Besides the platform that can add productivity in the application of the methodology, there is also the return on investment that the methodology can bring to specific projects. For each project, the methodology can be evaluated to check that the benefits of applying it outgrow its costs, thus proving its feasibility in a corporate setting and motivating stakeholders to continue applying it. Besides the profit that the methodology might bring from resulting improvements on business processes, the human perspective in this methodology makes end-users become active agents in the company. The methodology enables a free channel where they can give their opinion about user interaction. This opinion is translated into business processes so operation managers can ponder on their impact. When end-users' suggestions are put into practice and these changes improve their work, they are motivated to collaborate. The more an end-user's suggestions helps other end-users, the stronger is their reputation within the group (e.g. customer representative department) and higher is the trust between people.

5 Conclusion

This methodology is aimed for enterprise systems in organizations with extensive business processes and hundreds of users using thousand of user interfaces. The main goal is to keep enterprise systems aligned with business processes from the point of view of business process performers and business process designers, offering a complementary approach to existing solutions of IT-Business alignment. These complementary solutions are more concerned with requirements and implementations, while we focus on UIs, the part effectively in use by business performers (who are also end-users).

Because of this concern with business performers, this methodology becomes human-centered since it is concerned with the people who perform the business processes and use enterprise systems; more than merely on technological or methodological aspects, supported by the theory of structuration [18].

To demonstrate the effectiveness of the business process perfomer-centred approach, the methodology has been quantitatively analyzed using sensitivity analysis [27] to evaluate the cost-benefit analysis of its application in a telecommunications company. This quantitative analysis has demonstrated that applying it brings up to 60% of return on investment related to process improvement and user experience.

To further develop the human-centered aspects of this methodology, the authors are analyzing techniques to be used by business performers to aid them in giving suggestions about the user interaction and how they collaborate with others to achieve this goal. Another important aspect to be analyzed is how well business process models are understood by different stakeholders, how data is handled in the execution of business processes, etc. In the current state of the methodology, it does not control the business process in execution time, especially since it is risky to execute the rules and change the models at runtime. But for guidance and visualization purposes, a solution for stakeholders to be aware of the state of the process in execution time would be to change corporate applications to store information when users interact with specific UIs to know where they are in the process by looking at the mappings. Consequently, there are other requirements that can be considered as an extension of this methodology.

Overall, this research has achieved good results both in the academia and in the industry and it is differentiated by considering a human perspective for UI-Business Alignment, which had not yet been addressed in the literature neither in the industry. Its characteristic of being multi-disciplinary and complementary to existing IT-Business alignment strategies opens new themes for collaboration with researchers and practitioners from other communities.

Acknowledgements. We acknowledge the support of the ITEA2 Call3 UsiXML project (under reference 20080026).

References

1. Janssen, C., Weisbecker, A., Ziegler, J.: Generating User Interfaces from Data Models and Dialogue Net Specifications. In: Proc. of InterCHI 1993, pp. 418–423. ACM Press, Amsterdam (1993)
2. Puerta, A.R., Eriksson, H., Gennari, J.H., Musen, M.A.: Beyond Data Models for Automated UI Generation. In: Proc. of HCI 1994, pp. 353–366. Cambridge Univ. Press, Cambridge (1994)
3. Vanderdonckt, J.: A MDA-Compliant Environment for Developing User Interfaces of Information Systems. In: Pastor, Ó., Falcão e Cunha, J. (eds.) CAiSE 2005. LNCS, vol. 3520, pp. 16–31. Springer, Heidelberg (2005)
4. Mori, G., Paterno, F., Santoro, C.: CTTE: Support for Developing and Analyzing Task Models for Interactive System Design. IEEE Transactions on Software Engineering 28, 797–813 (2002)
5. Beyer, H., Holtzblatt, K.: Contextual Design: Defining Customer-Centered Systems. Morgan Kaufmann, San Francisco (1998)
6. Davenport, T.: Process Innovation: Reengineering work through information technology. Harvard Business School Press, Boston (1993)
7. Henry, P.: Process-User Interface Alignment: New Value. From a New Level of Alignment. Align Journal (2007)
8. Hull, R.: Artifact-centric business process models: Brief survey of research results and challenges. In: Meersman, R., Tari, Z. (eds.) OTM 2008, Part II. LNCS, vol. 5332, pp. 1152–1163. Springer, Heidelberg (2008)
9. Sousa, K., Mendonça, H., Vanderdonckt, J.: A Model-Driven Approach to Align Business Processes with User Interfaces. International Journal of Universal Computer Science, Special issue on Human-Computer Interaction 14, 3236–3249 (2008)
10. Bodart, F., Hennebert, A.M., Leheureux, J.M., Vanderdonckt, J.: Computer-Aided Window Identification in Trident. In: Nordbyn, K., Helmersen, P.H., Gilmore, D.J., Arnesen, S.A. (eds.) Proc. of 5th IFIP TC 13 Int. Conf. on Human-Computer Interaction Interact 1995, pp. 331–336. Chapman & Hall, London (1995)
11. Paterno, F.: Task Models in Interactive Software Systems. In: Chang, S.K. (ed.) Handbook of Software Engineering & Knowledge Engineering. World Scientific Publishing Co., Singapore (2001)
12. Calvary, G., Coutaz, J., Thevenin, D., Limbourg, Q., Bouillon, L., Vanderdonckt, J.: A Unifying Reference Framework for Multi-Target User Interfaces. Interacting with Computers 15, 289–308 (2003)

13. Teo, L., John, B.E.: Towards Predicting User Interaction with CogTool-Explorer. In: The Human Factors and Ergonomics Society, 52nd Annual Meeting, New York (2008)
14. Traetteberg, H.: UI Design without a Task Modeling Language Using BPMN and Diamodl for Task Modeling and Dialog Design. In: Forbrig, P., Paternò, F. (eds.) HCSE/TAMODIA 2008. LNCS, vol. 5247, pp. 110–117. Springer, Heidelberg (2008)
15. Sukaviriya, S., Mani, S., Sinha, V.: Reflection of a Year Long Model-Driven Business and UI Modeling Development Project. In: INTERACT, vol. 2, pp. 749–762 (2009)
16. Brachman, R.J., Levesque, H.J.: Knowledge Representation and Reasoning. Elsevier, San Francisco (2004)
17. Stolze, M., Riand, P., Wallace, M., Heath, T.: Agile development of workflow applications with interpreted task models. In: Winckler, M., Johnson, H. (eds.) TAMODIA 2007. LNCS, vol. 4849, pp. 2–14. Springer, Heidelberg (2007)
18. Giddens, A.: The Construction of Society. Political Press, London (1984)
19. Zacarias, M., Caetano, A., Magalhaes, R., Sofia Pinto, H., Tribolet, J.: Adding a Human Perspective to Enterprise Architectures. In: DEXA - WEISE 2007 - International Workshop on Enterprise Information Systems Engineering, pp. 840–844 (2007)
20. Stoitsev, T., Scheidl, S., Flentge, F., Muhlhauser, M.: From Personal Task Management to End-User Driven Business Process Modeling. In: Dumas, M., Reichert, M., Shan, M.-C. (eds.) BPM 2008. LNCS, vol. 5240, pp. 84–99. Springer, Heidelberg (2008)
21. OMG, Business Process Modeling Notation Specification, v. 1.2. (2009), http://www.omg.org/spec/BPMN (accessed September 10, 2010)
22. Souchon, N., Vanderdonckt, J.: A Review of XML-Compliant User Interface Description Languages. In: Jorge, J.A., Jardim Nunes, N., Falcão e Cunha, J. (eds.) DSV-IS 2003. LNCS, vol. 2844, pp. 377–391. Springer, Heidelberg (2003)
23. Kleppe, A.: Software Language Engineering: Creating Domain-Specific Languages Using Metamodels. Addison-Wesley, Reading (2008)
24. Bali, M.: Drools JBoss Rules 5.0 - Developer's Guide. Packt Publishing, Birmingham (2009)
25. Bhattacharya, K., Caswell, N., Kumaran, S., Nigam, A., Wu, F.: Artifact-centric Operational Modeling: Lessons learned from customer engagements. IBM Systems Journal 46, 703–721 (2007)
26. Meyer, B.: On Formalism in Specifications. IEEE Software 3, 6–25 (1985)
27. Krajewski, L., Ritzman, L., Malhotra, M.: Operations Management Processes and Value Chains, 8th edn. Pearson International Edition, NJ (2007)

A Formal Model-Based Approach for Designing Interruptions-Tolerant Advanced User Interfaces

Philippe Palanque, Marco Winckler, and Célia Martinie

Abstract. Due to the omnipresence of multitasking features in modern working environments, interruptions become commonplace as users must temporarily suspend a task to complete unexpected intervening activities. Interruptions are unpredictable and cannot be usually disregarded by users. They are quite often associated with negative effects (e.g. resuming to task after interruptions is difficult and is time consuming) but also with positive ones (e.g. alert systems shift our attention to matters that require immediate care to perform adequately a monitoring task). As users are facing more and more sources of information competing for attention, it is important to understand how interruptions affect user abilities to complete tasks. Despite multitasking environments are not new, interruptions are rarely considered explicitly in the design phases of interactive systems. In this chapter, we present how to integrate system models, task models and interruption models within a Model-Driven Approach (MDA). We show how formal descriptions of system and tasks can be used for simulation purposes while assessing system performance and how such simulations can be exploited to understand the consequences of interruptions on users' work. These aspects are illustrated by a case study demonstrating that these simulations can support the assessment of various interaction techniques according to interruption rates. An application of such concepts is also presented in the case of dynamic reconfiguration of the user interface (after hardware or software failures for instance).

1 Introduction

Task analysis is widely recognized as one fundamental way to focus on the specific user needs and to improve the general understanding of how users may

Philippe Palanque · Marco Winckler · Célia Martinie
ICS-IRIT, Université Paul Sabatier Toulouse 3
118, route de Narbonne, 31062 Toulouse Cedex, France
e-mail: {palanque,winckler,martinie}@irit.fr

H. Hussmann et al. (Eds.): MDD of Advanced User Interfaces, SCI 340, pp. 143–169.

interact with a user interface to accomplish a given interactive goal [22]. In many modern working environments, interruptions are commonplace and users must temporarily suspend their current task in order to complete unexpected (or unplanned) activities [24, 62]. Interruptions are unpredictable and quite often unavoidable in working environment. Web page pop-ups, emails, phone calls, instant messaging and social events can also be disruptive when people need to concentrate on specific tasks. In this context, users are responsible for accomplishing multitasking (i.e. two or more tasks at the same time) and being able to do so is now identified as a desired skill for most job functions [58].

Interruptions raise questions of both practical and theoretical significance [48]: How many interruptions occur at work? How performance is affected by various interruption characteristics, such as complexity, duration, timing and frequency? Who takes benefit of the interruption? How disruptive are interruptions for the main task? What can be done to mitigate the disruptive outcomes? Most of the current research has tackled these questions by conducting empirical studies with users either under controlled conditions (i.e. usability labs) or within working environments (e.g. ethnographical studies). The work reported in this paper brings a new perspective for the research in that field by employing analytical modeling techniques to simulate disruptive effects of interruptions on user performance. This work proposes a model-based approach for the specification of interactive systems making it possible to reason about properties that emerge from the disruptive effects of interruptions. Our ultimate goal is to explore the role that these properties play in terms of making interactive systems more resilient to unexpected and unavoidable interruptions. We employ a tool supported formal description technique for the design and development of interruptions-tolerant user interfaces. The justification of using formal description techniques is twofold: i) the behavior of interruptions, tasks and system can be defined in a complete and unambiguous way; ii) it makes it possible to reason about models in order to assess the interruptions' behavior (e.g. simulation and models co-execution). In addition the formal description technique we use offers interactive prototyping capabilities so that it is possible to adjust models according to different parameters associated to interruptions (i.e. frequency and duration).

We begin by presenting a comprehensive state of the art of the research on interruptions in the field of Human Computer Interaction (HCI). This state of the art structures related work in terms of anatomy of interruptions, sources and types factors influencing disruptiveness while users are interacting with computing devices or more generally in a working environment. Then, we discuss modeling aspects of interruptions in general. We present a set of abstract models describing user tasks, system behavior, and interruption behavior. The underlying idea around these models is to identify useful abstractions highlighting the aspects that should be considered when designing interactive applications with an explicit focus on interruptions. This work is grounded on the formal description techniques ICO (for the system and interruption models) [9] and HAMSTERS [6] (for the tasks models). The information related to user internal behavior (motor, perceptive and cognitive) is embedded as additional information in both tasks and systems models. We have defined a correspondence pattern for connecting system and task models that are in fact two different views on the same world. Such connection makes it possible to use the user additional information for assessing the overall performance of the connected models. Lastly, this paper reports on a preliminary method that can be used to analyze and predict the disruptive effect of interruptions taking into account different frequency and duration of interruptions. Using stochastic modeling it is then possible to measure the disruptive effects of interruptions when using different interaction techniques (or interaction styles) to perform a specific task. This method aims at producing an estimation of the level of resilience that could be reached by the interactive systems under unpredictable and unavoidable interruptions.

2 Overview on Multitasking and Interruptions in HCI

Literature about human interruption addresses this design problem from one the following different perspectives: a) psychology of human interruption [2, 3, 4, 14, 49]; b) technologies for improving the quality of interruption generation [20, 30]; c) HCI methods for brokering interruptions [23, 56, 57, 59, 64]; d) the effects of interruptions in work settings [21,49]; and e) case studies describing the results of introducing technologies into the workplace in an attempt to improve coordination performance [31, 39,59]. This section summarizes the main advances made for the understanding of the nature of interruptions in working environments.

2.1 The Anatomy of Interruptions

There are relatively few reported task analyses including interruptions. However, a number of simple task analyses have been conducted across several different domains to capture the critical aspects of the tasks [56, 57]. As depicted by Fig. 1, a person is working on a primary task, which can be thought of as similar to the complex, long-lasting task [21]. Next, an alert for a secondary task occurs. Alerts come in different forms—for example, a phone ringing, a person coming into the room to ask the person a question, or a fire alarm. During the interruption lag, the person has a moment (or longer) before turning his or her attention to the interrupting task. Then, the person starts the secondary task. After the secondary task is completed, the person must resume the primary task. During the resumption lag, the person must figure out what he or she was doing during the primary task and what to do next. Finally, the person resumes the primary task. From this task analysis and the real-world examples, it is clear that different aspects of the cognitive system are relevant to the study of interruptions and resumptions. First, executive control is very important for all interruption/resumption tasks. Second, upon completing the secondary task, the person's main goal is to remember what task he or she was working on and what to do next (though in some real-world situations, new task demands occur or the environment may have changed so that significant re-planning may need to occur). Third, people may or may not use some sort of cue in the environment to actively help them remember what they had been doing.

Fourth, there may or may not be a link between the primary and secondary tasks. Fifth, in some situations (e.g., an emergency), cues may not have been thought about—there may be relatively different preparatory processes that occur.

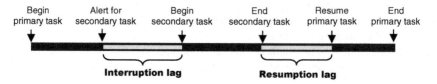

Fig. 1 Time line: anatomy of an interruption (based on Trafton et al [56]).

2.2 Sources, Types and Taxonomy of Interruptions

Sources of task interruptions can be either external when caused in the environmentor internal when users decide to break the current task flow due. Internal interruptions are very difficult to detect; in some cases, they should be considered normal deviations on the user scenario, for example when the user gives up to reaching the initial goal. External sources are many and vary, ranging from social events from the environment (ex. phone calls) to alarms and notification systems.

Some interruptions are beneficial such as warnings and alerts, reminders, notifications and suggestions. Waliji et al. [64] provide examples in a healthcare context, although these types of interruptions would also exist in other domains:

- **Warnings and alerts:** are usually a sign or signal of something negative occurring, or a notice to be careful. They are intended to make people aware of an impending danger or difficulty. They are designed to interrupt the current task, and alert to a potential adverse event. Although such warnings may be critical in preventing errors, it is found that in practice such warnings are often ignored or overridden, suggesting the need for better designed warnings. Warnings and alerts are often urgent and need to be handled quickly.

- **Reminders:** is a form of interruption that causes an individual to remember or recall an event. Decision support systems often remind users of standard tests or procedures that conform to practice guidelines. Although the urgency or importance of reminders may vary, many will include an explicit associated action. For example, go to a meeting occurring in 15 minutes.

- **Suggestions:** are ideas or proposals that are propagated to individuals. For example, patients often receive suggestions and recommendations from their physicians during appointments. Suggestions are unlikely to be of high urgency or importance. But effective suggestions may occur in due time and associated actions that are recommended.

- **Notifications:** are usually described as the process of informing. Notifications are defined as the most generic type of interruption, with the least degree of importance or urgency. A notification may purely be informational in purpose with no explicit instruction for action.

A few researchers have attempted to define interruptions and establish a taxonomy that describes the different issues surrounding interruptions. McFarlane [36] developed taxonomy of human interruption, as a tool for answering interruptions research questions. McFarlane's taxonomy lists eight dimensions of human interruption including: source of interruption, individual characteristics of person receiving interruption, method of coordination, meaning of interruption (e.g. alert, reminder, etc), method of expression, channel of conveyance, human activity changed by the interruption, effect of the interruption. Despite the fact the limited number of studies on interruptions taxonomy, there have some evidence of its usefulness to report human errors (due to interruptions). Brixey et al. (2004) [13] report taxonomy of task interruption in healthcare systems as a tool to identify how the introduction of a technology might introduce new interruptions, by contributing to an avoidable medical error or changing the work of clinicians.

2.3 Factors Influencing Disruptiveness

Interruptions will ultimately affect our ability to complete tasks but their disruptive effect varies according to the type of interruption [3, 4, 15, 26]. Quite often, interruptions are associated with negative effects: resuming to task after interruptions is difficult and can take a long time [57], interrupted tasks are perceived as harder than uninterrupted ones [5, 37], interruptions cause more cognitive workload and they are quite often annoying and frustrating because they disrupt people from completing their work [5]. Interruptions can also lead to incidents due to human error. According to Trafton & Mon [56], pilots experiencing interruptions during preflight checklists have been blamed for multiple aviation crashes [40, 42]. In addition, recent studies have shown that interruptions may be an important factor in driving [38], emergency room care [17], and nursing errors [62]. Indeed, frequent interruptions can reduce user performance, however not all interruptions bring negative impact: awareness systems such as alarms and alert systems effectively shift our attention to matters that need immediate care [13, 32] and, at least for simple tasks, interruptions may actually increase performance [61].

Gillie and Broadbent [26] describe a series of experiments aimed at elucidating features of interruptions that make them more or less disruptive to an ongoing computer task. They manipulated interruption length, similarity to the ongoing task, and the complexity of the interruption. They showed that being able to rehearse one's position in the main task does not protect one from the disruptive effects of an interruption. In addition, they discovered that interruptions with similar content could be quite disruptive even if they are extremely short.

McFarlane [34] examined four methods for deciding when to interrupt someone during multitasked computing. He explored several interruption policies such as requiring an immediate user response, letting users to choose when to attend, delegating to an intelligent agent the decision on when to interrupt, and interrupting at pre-arranged time intervals. It was found that performance was affected by the method used for coordinating interruptions, but there was no one best method for all performance measures.

Other studies focused on timing of interruptions, and how a warning can allow a person to anticipate an interruption [23, 57, 38, 28, 33]. These studies have shown that the interruption lag created by warnings can reduce the disruptive effects of interruptions, primarily by reducing reorientation time to the primary task after the interruption task is completed and thereby reducing overall performance time of the primary task. Interruption lags in these studies allowed participants to either finish what they were working on before attending to the interruption, or encode retrieval cues to allow for better task resumption following the interruption. Most of these studies have focused on computerized work, where an automated computerized system must intermittently interrupt a user for input, while the user is focused on other tasks. However, it is important to note that in safety critical environments, such as a hospital, it may not be possible for health care workers to anticipate interruptions and have a substantial interruption lag.

2.4 Solutions and Design Support

Although the research on interruptions is still relatively new, and much work still needs to be done at both theoretical and applied levels, there are some evidences on how to make interactive systems more resilient and how to reduce the disruptive effects on user tasks. These strategies include *human training*, *guidelines for design* and *tool support*.

Human training is one of the most striking findings in many studies as it has been shown that trained users scan rehearse or use environmental clues to mitigate the disruptive effects of interruptions [26]. Training people on the task itself would reduce the disruptiveness of the interruptions. However, if people are learning how to resume, then training on interruptions and resumptions should be built into current training programs. It has been found that interruptions became less disruptive over time with experience and practice on the resumption process itself; experience on the primary task alone (without interruptions) did not reduce the disruptiveness of interruptions.

Based on empirical findings, some *guidelines* for reducing effects of interruptions have been proposed [56, 57]. For example, within the prospective memory framework, McDaniel et al. [33] found that the use of a blue dot cue could improve performance upon resumption of the task. This suggests that providing an external mnemonic may greatly benefit performance. Using the Long Term Working Memory (LTWM) perspective, Oulasvirta and Saariluoma [26] also made several applied suggestions. Based on the results of their experiments, they suggested that system designers should keep "interaction chains" (the number of interface actions that lead to a goal or subgoal) quite short. The amount of time does not seem to be theoretically determined, but 20 s seems to be a heuristic used by some designers. They also suggested preventing interruptions on tasks that require large amounts of encoding time (e.g., certain checklists that airline pilots go through). Finally, they suggested that user control of interruptions is beneficial (consistent with McFarlane [35]) because it allows the person to have control over the encoding time, which is critical under their framework.

Other solutions include the development of specialized *tools*. Based on theoretically grounded applied research principles [21], Czerwinski's group at Microsoft Research has developed on a prototype tool called GroupBar that allows people to save and retrieve applications and window management setups, which can be extremely useful when switching tasks. Bailey and his colleagues also have built several tools based on empirical work [5]. They suggested that the best place to interrupt people is between "coarse" breakpoints between tasks. They have used an empirical approach to explore the linkages between traditional task analytic approaches (e.g., goals, operators, methods, and selection rules, or GOMS) and pupil size as a measure of mental workload. They have created a tool that is able to automatically detect times of high and low workload. They have suggested that interrupting people at times of low workload is best. They currently have several demonstration systems that perform components of this task.

3   A Model-Based Approach for Dealing with Multitasking and Interruptions

There are several attempts to formalize cognitive models describing the impact of interruptions in the human behavior [1, 57, 59, 61]. However, only a few works in the literature have addressed formal description techniques to describe the occurrence of interruptions in system specifications [28, 65]. This section proposes a design process for the design and assessment of interruption-tolerant systems. Fig. 2 presents the iterative process of the construction of models using formal description techniques. In the beginning of the process, a preliminary model is constructed that is then analyzed in order to assess what kind of properties it fulfils. According to the result of the analysis process, it can be decided that the model has to be modified. In [49], the interested reader can find a detailed explanation on how to perform such verification in the field of interactive systems, in order to deal with that complexity. As the ultimate goal of a safety critical system is to allow operators to perform their goals in an efficient and error free manner, we have previously presented a process integrating tasks modeling and system modeling. The process made it possible to assess the compliance of the tasks and system models [43]. That paper presented, on a case study, how iterations are performed, how models compatibility can be checked and what kind of properties can be proven. The

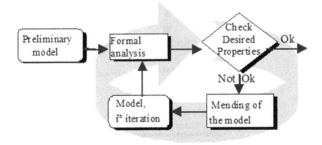

Fig. 2 Iterative process for building a model.

current paper extends that previous work to exploit performance evaluation technique to compare the interruption-tolerance of systems.

The basic assumption, in this design process, is that the interruptions are considered as an independent system (called Interruptions Source) located in the environment of the interactive system under consideration. Here again, the modeling activity starts with a preliminary model that is subject to modifications according to the analysis results or to further understanding of the behavior of the Interruptions Sources. Indeed, while we imply that there is only one interruption model there can be several whose behavior are integrated in a single model. It is important to note that the model of the Interruptions Sources only triggers elements of the system and tasks models. However, it can also be the case that the model of Interruptions Sources can be accessed from the system model. This can only be the case if one of the Interruptions Sources provides an (Application Programming Interface) API for interfering on the predefined behavior of the Interruption Source.

3.1 Modeling Activities

In the safety critical domain, Interruptions Source can be both computing resources (such as an alarm (as, for instance, a Ground Collision Avoidance System (GCAS) in a cockpit) and socio-technical resources (as an Air Traffic Controller sending a clearance to the pilot of an aircraft). For sake of brevity, and as it does not have an impact on the approach we propose, we consider that interruptions are only part of an external system model and will thus be modeled independently.

Fig. 3 presents the extended process exhibiting system, tasks and interruption models. A task model is the description of the sequence of tasks that have to be performed by the user to reach a particular goal. A critical point in the process is the consistency assurance activity (centre of the diagram). Indeed, it is important

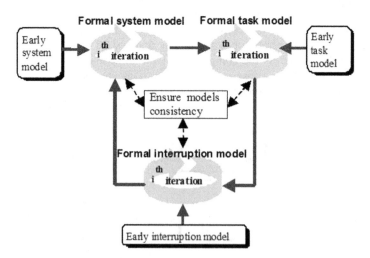

Fig. 3 Iterative process involving system, tasks and interruptions models

to ensure that the three models are compliant as they represent 3 different views of the same world i.e. the operator (task model) interacting with a system (system model) while external sources (Interruption Sources model) can interfere with that activity.

As the goal of the approach is to assess the interruption-tolerance, Fig. 4 presents the process for performing such assessment on two different systems and in a relative way. The two boxes on the right-hand side of the figure correspond to them (system A on top and System B on the bottom). Both systems are aimed at supporting the same user goals and at receiving the same perturbations from the Interruptions Sources and, consequently, the interruptions model is the same in both cases.

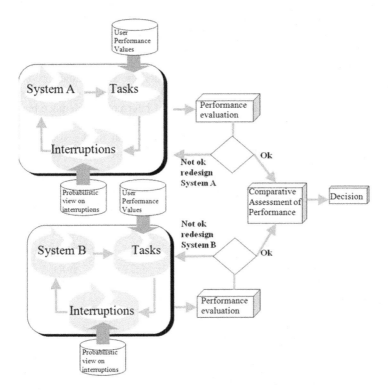

Fig. 4 Process for assessing the impact of interruption on user performance for two different systems

3.2 Values Injections

In order to be able to compute performance evaluation of the systems, performance values are inserted in the models. User performance values and cognitive theory are used to enrich and extend the task model to obtain a comprehensive model of user behavior according to the type of the tasks (motor, cognitive or perceptual). Such values correspond to information available in the field of HCI such as Fitts' law data for motor values [25], Human processor for cognitive and perceptual performance values [17] and ICS (Interacting Cognitive Subsystems) [7]. For instance, Human processor model states that cognitive processor cycle time has a mean of 70 ms (max-min being 25-170 ms). Other, more recent data can also be used as the field is evolving quickly and more research is regularly performed especially providing data for prediction related to interaction techniques as [1] for constraint movement and [11] for zoomable interfaces.

The validity of such data is critical when performance evaluation of the triplet (system, tasks (extended with user values), interruption) is concerned. This phase is represented by the boxes labeled "performance evaluation" in Fig. 4 and Fig. 5. The results of the phase will be used as a re-design driver in order to decide (in the case of performance lower than required/expected) to modify the elements: the system (by for instance, by changing the interaction technique), the tasks (for instance, by modifying the training of the operators and, by consequence the tasks they have to perform), the interruption (if it is possible to influence that "external" element). However, it is important to note that the exact value of data is not important per se, as far as the comparative assessment is concerned, and the same values are chosen to model activities that the interaction techniques have in common. Indeed, such assessment does not provide an absolute measure of interruption-tolerance but a comparison of two systems. Therefore, as the same (sub-)tasks are modeled by the same values, the actual values have no influence on the result of the assessment. This argument however does not hold if the interaction techniques are not similar.

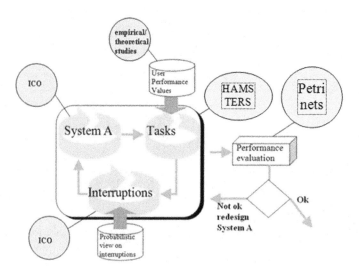

Fig. 5 Instantiation of the process presented in Figure 5.

3.3 Instantiation of the Approach

Fig. 5 presents the instantiation of the process of Fig. 4 including the notations and the values presented above. The light grey circles contain the underlying theories from which data are produced and the notations used for building the various models. For instance, System and interruption models are described using the ICO notation. Performance analysis is performed using the Petri nets performance analysis tools. As these tools require, as input, only Petri nets, transformation needs to be defined from enriched HAMSTERS specification into the Petri nets. At this stage, the process remains theoretical making it applicable to a large set of interactive systems from various application domains. Even though critical for interactive systems assessment, this performance analysis process is not further developed in the paper as we focus on the modeling aspects and more precisely on the multiple views (tasks, system and interruption) integration. The next section sketches how this approach can be instantiated on a case study, presenting the various models and their integration.

3.4 Modeling Interruptions in Task Models

In multitasking environments, interruptions should be seen just as a break in the current task execution that causes a (unexpected or intended) deviation on the control flow. This problem is well known in the domain of Operational Systems where several programs can run in parallel (i.e. multitasking). Previous work [60] has demonstrated that systematic description of all deviations on the system control flow is almost impossible as it would lead to an exponential and unpredictable number of states. The unpredictability of interruptions would favor the use of declarative models to describe what should be accomplished by the user system (whatever it happens) rather than describe the steps required (i.e. control flow) to accomplish it [54]. Notwithstanding, in some cases an interruption should be considered as part of the user goals as, for example, to cancel document printing. Indeed, some task model notations such as Concur Task Tree (CTT) [53] and HAMSTER [6] explicitly provides the operator *suspend/resume* (i.e. |>) that allow explicitly modeling between tasks as presented by Fig. 2. Similarly, West and Nagy [65] have added theoretical structures to the notation GOMS in order to overcome its limitations for analyzing interruptions when task switching are common.

Jambon [28] has analyzed the idiosyncrasies of relationships between tasks (such as *parallelism, interlacing and sequence*) thus providing a formal semantics for interruptions in notations like MAD, UAN and Petri Nets. For example, if two tasks are specified for running in sequence, the interruption of one task could be interpreted as an definite disruption (e.g. starting task *t2* will cancel the task *t1*) or an interlacing among tasks with an less disruptive effect on human activity (e.g. starting task *t2* will interrupt task *t1*, but *t1* could be resumed after task *t2* has finished). Tasks resumption could be done at different steps on the task execution (i.e. restarting from the beginning, resuming the task at the point before interruption occurs, resuming at the end of the task assuming it has been accomplished).

Hereafter, we provide a brief description of the task model notation HAMSTER that will be used in the case studies.

Modeling with HAMSTERS

HAMSTERS can be defined as a graphical and hierarchical notation to describe task models. It is delivered as part of a tool supporting edition and simulation of

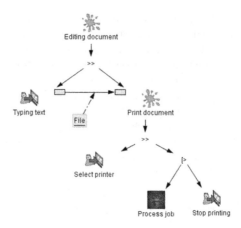

Fig. 6 Example of task modeling with interruption operator "I>" in HAMSTER.

task models. In a nutshell, HAMSTERS is open source, featuring a task simulator and provides a dedicated API for observing editing and simulation events. The main need that has triggered the design of these notation and tool is to have an extension of the current task modeling approaches making possible the synergistic support of task and system modeling activities. The notation is inspired from existing notations, especially from CTT [53] and has thus been designed to remain compatible with CTT (from the point of view of people building the models) as models are hierarchical, graphical with operators between the tasks.

Table 1 Illustration of the task type within HAMSTERS

Task type	Icons in the task model			
Abstract Task	Abstract task			
System Task	System task			
User Task	User task	Cognitive task	Perceptive task	Motor task
Interactive Task	Interactive task	Input task	Output task	InputOutput task

The elements of task models described by HAMSTER are illustrated by Table 1 and include:

- Abstract task is a task that involves sub tasks of different types.
- System task is a task performed only by the system.

- User task is a generic task describing a user activity. It can be specialized as a Motor task (e.g. a physical activity), a Cognitive task (e.g. decision making, analysis), or Perceptive task (e.g. perception of alert).
- Interactive task is an interaction between the User and the System; it can be refined into Input task when the users provide input to the system, Output task when the system provides an output to the user and InputOutput task is a mix of both but in an atomic way.

As in CTT, each particular task of the model can be either iterative, optional or both types (see Fig. 7):

- Iterative: concerns a task that can be executed 1 or more times. It can be interrupted or suspended by another task. It should not be a subtask of an ENABLE operator but of an INTERRUPT or SUSPEND_RESUME operator.
- Optional: An optional task is a task that does not necessarily needs to be executed. During the simulation, an optional task will be proposed with the following task(s) to be executed.

Fig. 7 Illustration of an Optional task Iterative task and of a task both iterative and optional

Again, as in CTT temporal relationship between tasks is represented by means of operators as described by Table 2a.

Table 2 Illustration of the operator type within HAMSTERS

Operator type	Symbol	Description
Enable	>>	ENABLE operator shall allow its tasks and/or task group and/or operator groups to execute one after another, from left to right on the model. ENABLE operator can have more than 2 branches.
Concurrent	|||	CONCURRENT operator shall allow tasks and/or tasks belonging to task groups and/or operator groups to execute at the same time in any order. CONCURRENT operator can have more than 2 branches.
Choice	[]	CHOICE operator shall allow the user to select the first available task to execute of each available branch. When a task is executed, HAMSTERS should disable all the branches that don't contain the executed task. CHOICE operator shall have 2 and only 2 branches.
Disable	[>	DISABLE operator shall deactivate the execution of the first branch when a task is executed on the second branch. DISABLE operator shall have 2 and only 2 branches.
Suspend-resume	|>	SUSPEND-RESUME operator shall suspend the execution of the first task or branch when task is executed on the second branch.
Order independent	|=|	ORDER INDEPENDENT (2x) operator shall allow its tasks and/or task groups and/or operator groups to execute one after another, in any order. ORDER_INDEPENDANT operator can have more than 2 branches.

In HAMSTERS, the notion of objects represents the part of the world managed by the tasks. HAMSTERS offers two types of relationships between tasks. The first one describes how tasks are related to other tasks (using the temporal operators presented above) and the second one represents the information flow between tasks (as illustrated by Fig. 8 where the PIN entered in the first task is conveyed to the next task by means of input and output ports).

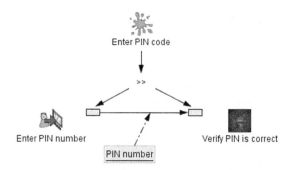

Fig. 8 Input and output flow between tasks in HAMSTERS

Modeling interruptions with HAMSTERS

As illustrated by Fig. 6, it is possible to represent in HAMSTERS the occurrence of interruptions that are related to user's goals. Unpredictable interruptions (such as user errors that are not related to the goal) are outside of the scope of task models and should be represented as independent models. Following our approach, such unpredictable interruption models are represented using the ICO formalism (described in the following section) instead of HAMSTER. By combining task models and interruption models, we create a so called *task model decorated with interruptions* that can be used for assessing the impact of interruptions on tasks performance and to redesign the system or the tasks to better tolerate interruptions.

3.5 Interactive System Modeling Using ICOs

Hereafter, we present the main features of the Interactive Cooperative Objects (ICO) formalism which is dedicated to the formal description of interactive systems. We encourage the interested reader to look at [45] for a complete presentation of this formal description technique.

ICOs are dedicated to the modeling and the implementation of event-driven interfaces, using several communicating objects to model the system, where both behavior of objects and communication protocol between objects are described by the Petri net dialect called Cooperative Objects (CO). In the ICO formalism, an object is an entity featuring four components: a cooperative object which describes the behavior of the object, a presentation part (i.e. the graphical interface), and two functions (the activation function and the rendering function) which make the link between the cooperative object and the presentation part.

- **Cooperative Object:** Using the Cooperative Object formalism, ICO provides links between user events from the presentation part and event handlers from the Cooperative Objects, links between user event availability and event handler availability and links between state in the Cooperative Objects changes and rendering.
- **Presentation part:** The presentation of an object states its external appearance. This presentation is a structured set of widgets organized in a set of windows. Each widget may be a way to interact with the interactive system (user → system interaction) and/or a way to display information from this interactive system (system → user interaction (3x)).
- **Activation function:** The user → system interaction (inputs) only takes place through widgets. Each user action on a widget may trigger one of the Cooperative Objects event handlers. The relation between user services and widgets is fully stated by the activation function that associates each event from the presentation part with the event handler to be triggered and the associated rendering method for representing the activation or the deactivation.
- **Rendering function:** the system → user interaction (outputs) aims at presenting the state changes that occurs in the system to the user. The rendering function maintains the consistency between the internal state of the system and its external appearance by reflecting system states changes.

ICOs are used to provide a formal description of the dynamic behavior of an interactive application. An ICO specification fully describes the potential interactions that users may have with the application. The specification encompasses both the "input" aspects of the interaction (i.e. how user actions impact on the inner state of the application, and which actions are enabled at any given time) and its "output" aspects (i.e. when and how the application displays information relevant to the user).

An ICO specification is fully executable, which gives the possibility to prototype and test an application before it is fully implemented [46]. The specification can also be validated using analysis and proof tools developed within the Petri net community and extended in order to take into account the specificities of the Petri net dialect used in the ICO formal description technique. This formal specification technique has already been applied in the field of Air Traffic Control interactive applications [47], space command and control ground systems [51], or interactive military [6] or civil cockpits [8]. The example of civil aircraft is used in the next section to illustrate the specification of embedded systems. To summarize, we provide here the symbols used for the ICO formalism and a screenshot of the tool.

- States are represented by the distribution of tokens into places
- Actions triggered in an autonomous way by the system are represented as and called transitions
- Actions triggered by users are represented by half bordered transition

ICOs are supported by the Petshop environment that makes it possible to edit the ICO models [10], execute them [52] and thus present the user interface to the user and support analysis techniques such as invariants calculation [49].

3.6 Interruptions Modeling Using ICOs

As discussed in the previous sections, any interruption that is not part of users' goal should be represented as an individual model. For that very purpose, we employ ICO formal description technique. Using the same formalism to model interruptions and the system it is possible to run both models in parallel to observe the counter effects between them. Moreover, the ICO formalism support unique characteristic that is very useful for modeling interruptions, as follows:

- Support for time-based modeling (systematic occurrence of interruptions based on temporal evolution), simulating, for instance, the occurrence of instant messenger popup;
- Notification based modeling (the system state has evolved and the interruption model is notified and then triggers an interruption) – interruptions are related to system's evolutions;
- Information based modeling (some values have reached a certain threshold then an interruption occur)

These features all illustrated in the next section.

4   Case Study

In order to exemplify the approach described above, we introduce a simple case study. The objective of the case study is to present the various phases of the approach on a simple but realistic application.

4.1 Informal Description of the Case Study

Fig. 9 presents the user interface of the case study. In the application, a set of icons is presented in a window on a grid. The icons can be moved to different locations and deleted.

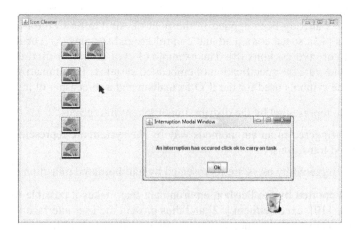

Fig. 9 User Interface of the case study

The user's tasks are thus limited to the one presented in Fig. 10. The user's goal (upper task in the tasks model) is to remove all the icons on the user interface. This can be achieved by doing, in any order, the selection of an icon and the triggering of a deletion command. In order to reach the goal, users have to perform iteratively the selection and deletion of icons (represented in the model by the * symbol next to the upper abstract task "Clear Icons".

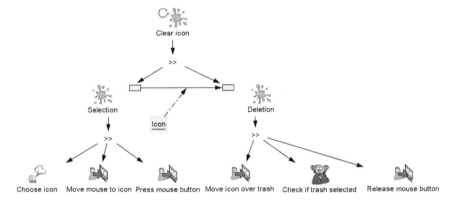

Fig. 10 Task model refined to be conformant with Drag & Drop behavior (system model A)

To support this goal, two different systems have been constructed. System A (called Drag & Drop) features an interaction technique of type Drag and Drop. Icons on the user interface can be selected by moving the mouse cursor over them and pressing the left button. Once selected, icons can be dragged in the window at any new position. If the mouse button is released when the icon is positioned over the icon of the trash, then the icon is deleted. System B (called Speak & Click) features a multimodal interaction technique involving speech recognition

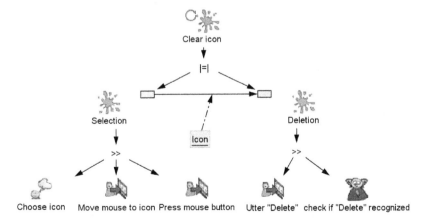

Fig. 11 Task model refined to be conformant with Speak & Click behavior (system model B)

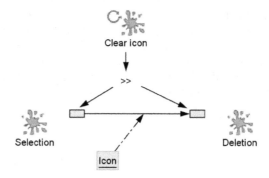

Fig. 12 Abstract tasks model expressed in HAMSTERS

(for the deletion command) and gesture (for icon selection). Systems and tasks models related to these two systems are presented in the next sections.

4.2   Formal Modeling of the Case Study

Modeling System A (Drag & Drop)

The behavior of System A has been fully modeled using the ICO notation and is presented in Fig. 13. Indeed, the model contains all the preconditions about the current state of interaction as well as the set and sequences of events that are available to the user.

According to Fig. 3, system and task models need to be kept consistent as the system has an impact on how the tasks can be performed by the user. Thus going

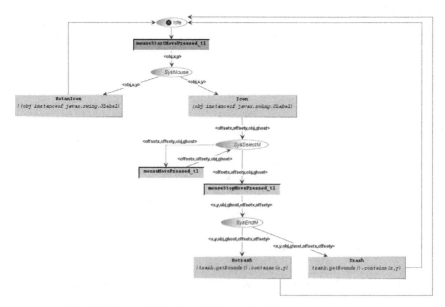

Fig. 13 ICO model of system A (Drag & Drop interaction technique)

from an abstract description of the tasks to a detailed one (fitting with a given system), the tasks models are different. According to the description of System, the abstract tasks model presented in Fig. 12 has to be refined as presented in Fig. 10. Indeed, Selection and Deletion tasks can be now refined more precisely. Selection is performed first by deciding the icon to be deleted then by moving the mouse cursor on the icon and by pressing the mouse button. Deletion is performed by moving the selected icon over the trash icon, verifying that trash icon is highlighted and releasing mouse button.

It is interesting to note that the temporal operator order independence between tasks Deletion and Selection is more constrained in the refinement as it has been replaced by a sequence operator. Adding constraints is allowed in the refinement process, as what is allowed in the refined model remains compliant with the abstract description. Relaxing constraints is not allowed as it would make it possible for the users to trigger sequences of action (in the refined model) not accepted by the abstract model.

Modeling System B (Speak & Click)

As for System A, System B has been fully described using the ICO formalism and is presented on Fig. 14.

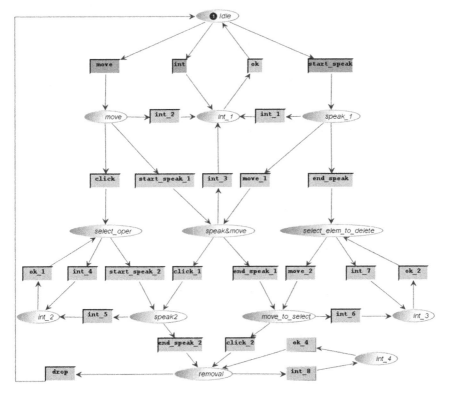

Fig. 14 ICO model of system B (Speak & Click interaction technique) composed with the behavior of the interruption source

This model allows users to either start by a speech command "delete" and then selecting an icon or selecting first an icon to be deleted and then uttering the word "delete". That model is a refinement of the ICO model describing the application. It includes the interruption sources behavior and excludes manipulation errors or recognition errors. In any case, interaction must start either by the user moving the mouse (this is represented by the transition **move** on the upper part of the model) or by uttering a word (**start-speak**). As has been done for System A, the abstract tasks model presented in Fig. 12 has to be refined in order to be compliant with System B. Fig. 11 presents the refined task model. It is interesting to note that this task model is less constrained as it accepts Deletion and Selection in any order (modeled by using the *concurrent* operator at the first level).

Modeling Interruptions

According to the approach presented in Fig. 3, the last model to be built is the model describing the behavior of the Interruption Sources. While the state of the art section has explained the anatomy of interruptions and the various research results (especially in psychology about the impact of interruptions on users' activity), we present in this section the simplest model of interruptions possible. Indeed, this paper is devoted to the description of a process integrating tasks, systems and interruptions models and how the resulting models can be used to compute performance evaluation on that triplet. We are currently integrating this process in the area of interactive cockpits, extending previous work in the re-configuration of cockpit applications when part of the hardware side of the user interface has failed [44]. Such failures and re-configurations are intrinsically perceived by the operators as interruptions and assessing pilot performance in such a context is critical.

The interruption taken into account here behaves as follows. Each time an interruption occurs, a modal window occurs featuring an Ok button (see window in the center of Fig. 9) is displayed and the user has to click on it to be able to carry on the initial task. Fig. 15 presents such behavior using the ICO notation. In the initial state, the interruption model is idle (there is a token in the place *Interrupt*) waiting for an interruption to occur.

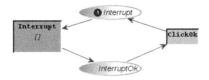

Fig. 15 ICO model of Interruption Source

This is modeled by transition Interrupt which is triggered according to a temporal evolution (represented by the symbol []). When the interruption has occurred, the token in place Interrupt moves to place InterruptOk and the transition ClickOk becomes available. This transition is connected to the Ok button, i.e. when the event is triggered by the user, the transition is fired and the model comes back to its initial state.

Such interruption model is extremely simple as it does not convey any pertinent semantic about the interruptions it describes. The fact that we are using the ICO notation for the description of interruptions makes it possible to describe more complex behaviors but also to have several interruptions models interacting with a system at the same time. This is when simulation and prototyping aspects are very important as it makes it possible to define in a complete and unambiguous way how such intertwined interruptions impact the usage of an interactive system. This impact can be assessed at the interaction technique level (as presented in [11]) and even at the dialogue level exhibiting classical human errors such as "strong habit intrusion" or "over shooting a stop rule" (when the interruption is not taken into account).

However, interruptions can also arise not as an external event (and thus represented by a specific model), but from the system itself (for instance, when a failure occur) resulting in functions or information not being available anymore to the user. Such interruptions are very similar to service availability in the area of dependability [18] and thus arise typically from a malfunction at the system level. We already addressed such issues in the field of interactive cockpits [44] where user interfaces reconfigure themselves after a system failure. For instance, in the case of a display unit (sort of screen in a cockpit) failure, the interactive applications presented on that display may be re-allocated to other display units if they are critical for the current flight phase. In such a case, the crew tasks have to be re-organized according to the reconfigured interactive system. That reallocation is known by the crew (by means of training) and can be considered as an interruption. This is an interesting kind of interruption where users have to react to autonomous systems. The ICO notation is able to fully represent such interruptions behavior (not presented here due to space constraints).

4.3 Co-execution of System Models, Task Models and Interruption Models

While previous research activities done on the topic of interactive systems modeling made ICO mature enough to be the basis of the proposed framework, they pointed out the need of an extension of current task modeling approaches making it possible to support in a synergistic way tasks and system mode-ling activities. With Hamsters, we propose a notation and a tool to answer these needs, making it an independent tool supporting task modeling activities, and enhancing it to be part of the framework (by means of interactive input and output tasks, explicit artifacts, dedicated API …). A snapshot of such integration is presented in Fig. 16.

The integration framework presented in this paper allows for property checking during verification and validation phases of the development process as described by Hix and Hartson [27]. Validation phase relates to the question "do we have modeled the right system?" while the verification phase addresses the question "do we have modeled the system right?" At notation and tool level, our approach provides the

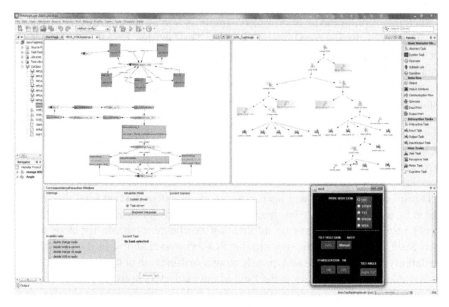

Fig. 16 Case tool integration of HAMSTERS and PetShop

first bricks for the validation and verification of the synergistic exploitation of task
and system modeling:

- It is possible to assess the structural compatibility between models while
  editing the correspondences between them.
- It is possible to verify if particular scenarios are playable on the system model.
  This makes it possible to highlight or verify system behaviors that ensure the
  non-occurrence of particular tasks scenarios as this impossibility could be required in the system (ex. Getting card before getting cash using ATM to avoid
  post completion errors or ensuring that an accident scenario cannot reoccur).
  This work could be extended to automatically extract scenarios from the task
  models and assess automatically to their compatibility with the system model.
- It is possible to execute the system model driven by the simulation of the task
  model and it is possible to build scenarios driven by the system execution, but,
  even if the framework makes it possible, we did not present the complete co-
  execution of the two models due to space constraints. One of the possible use of
  such complete co-execution could be to enhance the user providing contextual
  help at runtime:

  – While interacting with the system, it is possible to identify the current task
    in the task model, it is thus possible to provide the user with information
    about this task (for instance, how many actions and which actions are still
    required to reach the goal).
  – A scenario from task model can drive the execution of the system model, it
    is thus possible to extract scenario that illustrates how to perform a task,

and play it on the system to interactively show to the user how to achieve her goal (as training material for instance).

Such model checking is part of the role of the correspondence editor that notifies any inconsistency between the HAMSTERS and the ICO specifications. More information about these tasks-systems relationship can be found in [40] for the architectural aspects and in [6] for the usability aspects and simulation aspects.

5 Conclusion and Perspective

This paper has presented a tool supported approach for bridging the gap between tasks, system and interruptions views in the design of interactive systems. To this end, we have briefly introduced a new notation called HAMSTERS for the description of tasks models. For the system side, we used the ICO notation supported by the CASE tool PetShop.

While in earlier work [43] the bridge between task models and system models was performed in an asynchronous way by means of scenarios, the current paper has presented the principles of full integration of two dedicated tools and how this can support by various means the design interruption tolerant interactive systems. The interruption models are used for assessing the capability of both user and system to manage their work within a "real-life" context, i.e. when interruptions of any type occur on a regular basis.

The work presented here belongs to a longer term research program targeting at the design of resilient interactive systems using model-based approaches. Future work aims at exploiting these two models to support the usability evaluation of interactive systems and to provide task-based training material in the field of real-time command and control systems including cockpits and satellite ground segments. In such contexts, interruptions are of primary importance as they can result in accidents or incidents and in putting human life at stake.

References

1. Accot, J., Zhai, S.: Beyond Fitts' law: models for trajectory-based HCI tasks. In: Proc. of ACM CHI 1997, pp. 295–302 (1997)
2. Altmann, E.M., Trafton, J.G.: Memory for goals: An activation-based model. Cognitive Science 26(1), 39–83 (2002)
3. Altmann, E.M., Trafton, J.G.: Timecourse of Recovery from Task Interruption: Data and a Model. Psychonomics Bulletin and Review 14(6), 1079–1084 (2007)
4. Bailey, B.P., Konstan, J.A., Carlis, J.V.: Measuring the effects of interruptions on task performance in the user interface. In: IEEE International Conference on Systems, Man, and Cybernetics 2000, vol. 2, pp. 757–762 (2000)
5. Bailey, B.P., Konstan, J.A., Carlis, J.V.: The effects of interruptions on task performance, annoyance, and anxiety in the user interface. In: Proceedings of INTERACT 2001, pp. 593–601. IOS Press, Amsterdam (2001)

6. Barboni, E., Ladry, J., Navarre, D., Palanque, P., Winckler, M.: Beyond modelling: an integrated environment supporting co-execution of tasks and systems models. In: Proceedings of the 2nd ACM SIGCHI Symposium on Engineering interactive Computing Systems. EICS 2010, pp. 165–174. ACM, New York (2010)

7. Barnard, P.J., Teasdale, J.D.: Interacting cognitive subsystems: A systemic approach to cognitive-affective interaction and change. Cognition and Emotion 5, 1–39 (1991)

8. Bastide, R., Navarre, D., Palanque, P., Schyn, A., Dragicevic, P.: A Model-Based Approach for Real-Time Embedded Multimodal Systems in Military Aircrafts. In: ICMI 2004 - Sixth International Conference on Multimodal Interfaces, pp. 243–250. ACM Press, New York (2004)

9. Bastide, R., Palanque, P., Le, D., Munoz, J.: Integrating rendering specifications into a formalism for the design of interactive systems. In: DSV-IS 1998. Springer, Heidelberg (1998)

10. Bastide, R., Navarre, D., Palanque, P.: A model-based tool for interactive prototyping of highly interactive applications. In: CHI 2002 Extended Abstracts on Human Factors in Computing Systems, pp. 516–517 (2002)

11. ter Beek, M., Faconti, G., Massink, M., Palanque, P., Winckler, M.: Resilience of interaction techniques to interrupts - A formal model-based approach. In: Gross, T., Gulliksen, J., Kotzé, P., Oestreicher, L., Palanque, P., Prates, R.O., Winckler, M. (eds.) INTERACT 2009. LNCS, vol. 5726, pp. 456–472. Springer, Heidelberg (2009)

12. Bourgeois, F., Guiard, Y., Beaudouin-Lafon, M.: Multi-scale pointing: Facilitating pan-zoom coordination. In: ACM SIGCHI Conf. on Human Factors in Computing Systems, CHI 2002, pp. 758–759. ACM Press, New York (2002)

13. Brixey, J.J., Walji, M., Zhang, J., Johnson, T.R., Turley, J.P.: Proc. 6th International Workshop on Enterprise Networking and Computing in Healthcare Industry. Proposing a Taxonomy and Model of Interruption, pp. 184–188 (2004)

14. Brudzinski, M.E., Ratwani, R.M., Trafton, J.G.: Goal and spatial memory following interruption. Paper presented at the 8th International Conference on Cognitive Modeling, Ann Arbor, MI (2007)

15. Cades, D.M., Trafton, J.G., Boehm-Davis, D.A., Monk, C.A.: Does the difficulty of an interruption affect our ability to resume? In: Proc. of the Human Factors and Ergonomics Society 51th Annual Meeting, Santa Monica, pp. 234–238 (2007)

16. Caffiau, S., Girard, P., Scapin, D., Guittet, L., Sanou, L.: Assessment of object use for task modeling. In: Forbrig, P., Paternò, F. (eds.) HCSE/TAMODIA 2008. LNCS, vol. 5247, pp. 14–28. Springer, Heidelberg (2008)

17. Card, S.K., Thomas, T.P., Newell, A.: written at London, The Psychology of Human-Computer Interaction. Lawrence Erlbaum Associates, Mahwah (1983); ISBN 0898592437

18. Cervantes, H., Hall, R.S.: Autonomous Adaptation to Dynamic Availability Using a Service-Oriented Component Model. In: Proceedings of the 26th International Conference on Software Engineering, May 23 - 28, pp. 614–623. IEEE Computer Society, Washington (2004)

19. Chisholm, C.D., Collison, E.K., Nelson, D.R., Cordell, W.H.: Emergency department workplace interruptions: Are emergency physicians "interrupt-driven" and "multitasking"? Academic Emergency Medicine 7, 1239–1243 (2000)

20. Czerwinski, M., Cutrell, E., Horvitz, E.: Instant Messaging and Interruption: Influence of Task Type on Performance. In: Paris, C., Ozkan, N., Howard, S., Lu, S. (eds.) OZCHI 2000 Conference Proceedings, Sydney, Australia, December 4-8, pp. 356–361 (2000)

21. Czerwinski, M., Horvitz, E., Wilhite, S.: A diary study of task switching and interruptions. In: Proceedings of the SIGCHI Conference on Human Factors in Computing Systems CHI 2004, Vienna, Austria, April 24-29, pp. 175–182. ACM, New York (2004)

22. Diaper, D., Stanton, N.A. (eds.): The Handbook of Task Analysis for Human-Computer Interaction, 650 p. Lawrence Erlbaum Associates, Mahwah (2004)

23. Diez, M., Boehm-Davis, D.A., Holt, R.W.: Model-based predictions of interrupted checklists. In: Proceedings of the 46th Annual Meeting of the Human Factors and Ergonomics Society, pp. 250–254. Human Factors and Ergonomics Society, Santa Monica (2002)

24. Dix, A., Ramduny-Ellis, D., Wilkinson, J.T.: Analysis: understanding broken tasks. In: Diaper, D., Stanton, N. (eds.) The Handbook of Task Analysis for Human Computer Interaction, Lawrence Erlbaum Associates, Mahwah (2004)

25. Fitts, P.M.: The Information Capacity of the Human Motor System in Controlling the Amplitude of Movement. Journal of Experimental Psychology 47, 381–391 (1954)

26. Gillie, T., Broadbent, D.: What makes interruptions disruptive? A study of length, similarity and complexity. Psychological Research 50(4), 243–250 (1989)

27. Hix, D., Rex Harston, H.: Developing User Interfaces: ensuring usability through product and process. Wiley, Chichester (1993); 978-0-471-57813-0

28. Horvitz, E., Apacible, J.: Learning and reasoning about interruption. In: Proceedings of the 5th International Conference on Multimodal Interfaces, ICMI 2003, November 5-7, pp. 20–27. ACM, New York (2003)

29. Jambon, F.: Formal modelling of task interruptions. In: Human Factors in Computing Systems: Proceedings of CHI 1996, Conference Companion, pp. 45–46. ACM Press, New York (1996)

30. Iqbal, S.T., Bailey, B.P.: Effects of intelligent notification management on users and their tasks. In: Proceeding of the Twenty-Sixth Annual SIGCHI Conference on Human Factors in Computing Systems, CHI 2008, April 5-10, pp. 93–102. ACM Press, New York (2008), http://doi.acm.org/10.1145/1357054.1357070

31. Kapoor, A., Horvitz, E.: Experience sampling for building predictive user models: a comparative study. In: Proceeding of the Twenty-Sixth Annual SIGCHI Conference on Human Factors in Computing Systems, CHI 2008, Florence, Italy, April 5-10, pp. 657–666. ACM Press, New York (2008),
http://doi.acm.org/10.1145/1357054.1357159

32. McCrickard, D.S., Chewar, C.M.: Attuning notification design to user goals and attention costs. Communications of ACM 46(3), 67–72 (2003)

33. McDaniel, M.A., Einstein, G.O., Graham, T., Rall, E.: Delaying execution of intentions: overcoming the costs of interruptions. Applied Cognitive Psychology 18(5), 533–547 (2004)

34. McFarlane, D.C.: Comparison of four primary methods for coordinating the interruption of people in human-computer interaction. Human-Computer Interaction 17, 63–139 (2002)

35. McFarlane, D.C.: Coordinating the interruption of people in human-computer interaction. In: Sasse, A., Johnson, C. (eds.) Proceedings of Human-Computer Interaction, INTERACT 1999, pp. 295–303. IOS Press, Amsterdam (1999)

36. McFarlane, D.C.: Interruption of People in Human-Computer Interaction: A General Unifying Definition of Human Interruption and Taxonomy (NRL Formal Report NRL/FR/5510-97-9870), US Naval Research Laboratory, Washington (1997)

37. Mark, G., Gudith, D., Klocke, U.: The cost of interrupted work: more speed and stress. In: Proceeding of the Twenty-Sixth Annual SIGCHI Conference on Human Factors in Computing Systems, CHI 2008, Florence, Italy, April 05-10, pp. 107–110. ACM, New York (2008), doi= http://doi.acm.org/10.1145/1357054.1357072

38. Monk, C., Boehm-Davis, D., Trafton, J.G.: Recovering from interruptions: Implications for driver distraction research. Human Factors 46, 650–663 (2004)

39. Morris, D., Brush, A.B., Meyers, B.R.: SuperBreak: using interactivity to enhance ergonomic typing breaks. In: Proceeding of the Twenty-Sixth Annual SIGCHI Conference on Human Factors in Computing Systems. CHI 2008, pp. 1817–1826. ACM, New York (2008)

40. Navarre, D., Palanque, P., Barboni, E., Mistrzyk, T.: On the Benefit of Synergistic Model-Based Approach for Safety Critical Interactive System Testing. In: Winckler, M., Johnson, H. (eds.) TAMODIA 2007. LNCS, vol. 4849, pp. 140–154. Springer, Heidelberg (2007)

41. National Transportation Safety Board (1968). Aircraft accident report: Pan American World Airways, Inc., Boeing 707-321C, N799PA, Elmendorf Air Force Base, Anchorage, Alaska, December 26 (NTSB/AAR-69/08). Washington, DC (1969)

42. National Transportation Safety Board (1987). Aircraft accident report: Northwest Airlines, Inc.,McDonnell Douglas DC-9-82, N312RC, Detroit Metropolitan Wayne County Airport, Romulus,Michigan, August 16 (NTSB/AAR-88/05).Washington, DC (1988)

43. Navarre, D., Palanque, P., Bastide, R., Paternó, F., Santoro, C.: A tool suite for integrating task and system models through scenarios. In: Johnson, C. (ed.) DSV-IS 2001. LNCS, vol. 2220, p. 88. Springer, Heidelberg (2001)

44. Navarre, D., Palanque, P., Basnyat, S.: Usability Service Continuation through Reconfiguration of Input and Output Devices in Safety Critical Interactive Systems. In: Harrison, M.D., Sujan, M.-A. (eds.) SAFECOMP 2008. LNCS, vol. 5219, pp. 373–386. Springer, Heidelberg (2008)

45. Navarre, D., Palanque, P., Ladry, J., Barboni, E.: ICOs: A model-based user interface description technique dedicated to interactive systems addressing usability, reliability and scalability. ACM TOCHI 16(4), 1–56 (2009)

46. Navarre, D., Palanque, P., Bastide, R., Sy, O.: Structuring Interactive Systems Specifications for Executability and Prototypability. In: Paternó, F. (ed.) DSV-IS 2000. LNCS, vol. 1946, p. 97. Springer, Heidelberg (2001)

47. Navarre, D., Palanque, P., Bastide, R.: Reconciling Safety and Usability Concerns through Formal Specification-based Development Process. In: HCI-Aero 2002. MIT, USA (2002)

48. O'Conaill, B., Frohlich, D.: Timespace in the workplace: Dealing with interruptions. In: Human Factors in Computing Systems, CHI 1995, pp. 262–263. ACM Press, New York (1995)

49. Oulasvirta, A., Saariluoma, P.: Surviving task interruptions: Investigating the implications of long-term working memory theory. Int. J. Hum.-Comput. Stud. 64(10), 941–961 (2006)

50. Palanque, P., Bastide, R., Sengès, V.: Validating Interactive System Design Through the Verification of Formal Task and System Models. In: Proc. of EHCI 1995, Garn Targhee Resort, Wyoming, USA, August 14-18. Chapman et Hall, Boca Raton (1995)

51. Palanque, P., Bernhaupt, R., Navarre, D., Ould, M., Winckler, M.: Supporting Usability Evaluation of Multimodal Man-Machine Interfaces for Space Ground Segment Applications Using Petri net Based Formal Specification. In: Ninth International Conference on Space Operations, Rome, Italy, June 18-22 (2006)

52. Palanque, P., Ladry, J.-F., Navarre, D., Barboni, E.: High-Fidelity Prototyping of Interactive Systems can be Formal too. In: Schaefer, R., Cotta, C., Kołodziej, J., Rudolph, G. (eds.) PPSN XI. LNCS, vol. 6239, pp. 145–156. Springer, Heidelberg (2010)

53. Paterno, F., Mancini, C., Meniconi, S.: ConcurTaskTrees: A Diagrammatic Notation for Specifying Task Models. In: Proc. of Interact 1997, pp. 362–369. Chapman & Hall, Boca Raton (1997)

54. Pinheiro da Silva, P.: User Interface declarative models and Development environments: A survey. In: Paternó, F. (ed.) DSV-IS 2000. LNCS, vol. 1946, pp. 207–226. Springer, Heidelberg (2001)

55. Ratwani, R.M., McCurry, J.M., Trafton, J.G.: Predicting post completion errors using eye movements. In: Computer Human Interaction, CHI 2008 (2008)

56. Trafton, J.G., Monk, C.A.: Task Interruptions. Reviews of Human Factors and Ergonomics 3, 111–126 (2007)

57. Trafton, J.G., Altmann, E.M., Brock, D.P., Mintz, F.E.: Preparing to resume an interrupted task: Effects of prospective goal encoding and retrospective rehearsal. International Journal of Human-Computer Studies 58(5), 583–603 (2003)

58. Tsukada, K., Okada, K., Matsushita, Y.A.: Cooperative Support System Based on Multiplicity of Task. IFIP Congress (2), 69–74 (1994)

59. Rukab, J.A., Johnson-Throop, K.A., Malin, J., Zhang, J.: A Framework of Interruptions in Distributed Team Environments. Journal on Studies in Health Technology and Informatics, Part 2 107, 1282–1286 (2005)

60. Silberschatz, A., Galvin, P., Gagne, G.: Operating Systems Concepts. John Wiley & Sons, Chichester (2008); ISBN 0-470-12872-0

61. Speier, C., Vessey, I., Valacich, J.S.: The effects of interruptions, task complexity, and information presentation on computer-supported decision-making performance. Decision Sciences 34(4), 771–797 (2003)

62. Su, N.M., Mark, G.: Communication chains and multitasking. In: Proceeding of the Twenty-Sixth Annual SIGCHI Conference on Human Factors in Computing Systems, CHI 2008, Florence, Italy, April 5-10, pp. 83–92. ACM, New York (2008)

63. Tucker, A.L., Spear, S.J.: Operational failures and interruptions in hospital nursing. Health Services Research 41, 643–662 (2006)

64. Walji, M., Brixey, J., Johnson-Throop, K., Zhang, J.: A theoretical framework to understand and engineer persuasive interruptions. In: Proceedings of 26th Annual Meeting of the Cognitive Science Society, CogSci 2004 (2004)

65. West, R.L., Nagy, G.: Using GOMS for Modeling Routine Tasks Within Complex Sociotechnical Systems: Connecting Macrocognitive Models to Microcognition. Journal of Cognitive Engineering and Decision Making 1(2), 186–211(26) (Summer 2007)

Dynamic Distribution and Layouting of Model-Based User Interfaces in Smart Environments

Dirk Roscher, Grzegorz Lehmann, Veit Schwartze, Marco Blumendorf, and Sahin Albayrak

Abstract. The developments in computer technology in the last decade change the ways of computer utilization. The emerging smart environments make it possible to build ubiquitous applications that assist users during their everyday life, at any time, in any context. But the variety of contexts-of-use (user, platform and environment) makes the development of such ubiquitous applications for smart environments and especially its user interfaces a challenging and time-consuming task. We propose a model-based approach, which allows adapting the user interface at runtime to numerous (also unknown) contexts-of-use. Based on a user interface modelling language, defining the fundamentals and constraints of the user interface, a runtime architecture exploits the description to adapt the user interface to the current context-of-use. The architecture provides automatic distribution and layout algorithms for adapting the applications also to contexts unforeseen at design time. Designers do not specify predefined adaptations for each specific situation, but adaptation constraints and guidelines. Furthermore, users are provided with a meta user interface to influence the adaptations according to their needs. A smart home energy management system serves as running example to illustrate the approach.

1 Introduction

The developments in computer technology in the last decade change the ways of computer utilization. The emerging smart environments make it possible to build ubiquitous applications that assist users during their everyday life, at any time, in any context. This requires the applications to adapt themselves to the current

Dirk Roscher · Grzegorz Lehmann · Veit Schwartze · Marco Blumendorf
Sahin Albayrak
DAI-Labor, TU-Berlin, Ernst-Reuter-Platz 7, 10587 Berlin, Germany
e-mail: `firstname.lastname@dai-labor.de`

H. Hussmann et al. (Eds.): MDD of Advanced User Interfaces, SCI 340, pp. 171–197.
springerlink.com   © Springer-Verlag Berlin Heidelberg 2011

context and provide a usable and suitable interaction at all times. In [4], five properties of ubiquitous user interfaces (UUIs) have been identified:

1. Shapeability – to address different layouts for users, devices and usage contexts
2. Distribution – the capability of being distributed across multiple interaction devices
3. Multimodality – for being accessible through various input and output modalities
4. Shareability – to support cooperative interaction of multiple users
5. Mergability – the interoperability of different applications

The availability of a variety of multimedia and interaction devices, sensors and appliances makes the development of UUIs for smart environments a challenging and time-consuming task. Furthermore, it is very complex to predefine adaptations of an application for every possible context. UUIs also have to respond to contexts-of-use unforeseeable at design time. This leads to the need for automated adaptations of the user interface intelligently handling changes of the context.

Since the developer is no longer present while an application adapts to a context at runtime, she cannot guide the adaptation process directly. Hence a system must take over her role and the developer needs a language to stay in control over the adaptation results. Two main building blocks are needed to

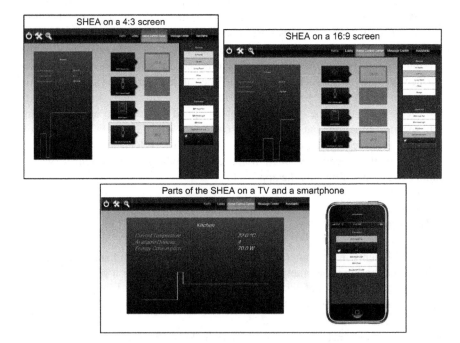

Fig. 1 Example layout and distribution adaptations of the SHEA for different interaction devices

address this: 1) a runtime system, dynamically handling the context specific interaction and automatically adapting the application based on design time information from application models; 2) a language that allows the developer to describe UUIs by providing relative hints or constraints guiding the automated adaptations, rather than specifying concrete adaptations.

In the next section, we describe a smart home application with a ubiquitous user interface. Throughout this chapter, it will serve as an example of an adaptive application, very difficult to implement with traditional development technologies.

1.1 Example Application and Scenario

The Smart Home Energy Assistant (SHEA) is a home automation application with a special focus on energy consumption. In accordance with the current energy conservation and smart metering trends, the SHEA helps the users to save energy by providing them with energy usage information about their home appliances. By analyzing and comparing the energy consumption of their appliances, the users become aware of existing saving potentials.

An example smart home environment, in which the SHEA could be deployed, consists of three networked interaction devices: a smartphone, a PC in the home office and a digital TV in the living room. Each device features a different combination of input and output modalities, e.g. the PC provides a standard mouse and keyboard input interface, the smartphone is equipped only with a touch surface and the TV with a remote control. While all interaction devices provide a display, the interaction capabilities of the displays vary in terms of screen size, ratio and resolution. An example scenario highlights the adaptation capabilities of the SHEA:

- **Step 1:** The user starts the interaction with the SHEA in the office, by saying "SHEA". SHEA's user interface appears on the interaction device near the user's position – in this case the PC. The UI layout adapts to the PC display (*SHEA on a 4:3 screen* in Fig. 1).
- **Step 2:** After checking the power consumption charts of some appliances, the user decides to continue the interaction in the living room. The user enables a "Follow Me"-mode and the SHEA seamlessly follows through different rooms by migrating from one interaction device to another, across platforms. The UI adapts to the current combination of interaction resources (IRs) on-the-fly. As the user walks into the living room, the UI follows from the 4:3 PC screen to the 16:9 HD-TV. The UI adapts to match the new screen ratio and resolution (*SHEA on a 16:9 screen* in Fig. 1)
- **Step 3:** Although the UI adapted correctly to the current context, the user wishes to reconfigure the SHEA by migrating a part of it to the smartphone. Through a configuration wizard ("Meta-UI"), the user moves SHEA's device controls to the smartphone, but leaves the power consumption chart on the big screen of the TV for better readability.
- **Step 4:** With the device list and controls on the smartphone, the user walks around the living room and checks the power consumption of the devices. As

the user nears a device, the device list on the smartphone is reshuffled and the UI element representing the nearest device is put on the top of the list.

In this chapter, we present how the adaptation capabilities exemplified in the above scenario can be defined in a model-based user interface development approach and implemented by a runtime architecture.

1.2 Contribution

This chapter deals with issues related to the adaptation of UUIs. On basis of the SHEA example, we show how runtime user interface models enable the provision and adaptation of UUIs. We focus on three of five ubiquitous user interface properties: shapeability, distribution and multimodality. We show how user interface distribution and layout algorithms can be designed to automatically handle the adaptation along these axes at runtime. The Multi-Access Service Platform (MASP) is presented as a user interface runtime architecture implementing the proposed algorithms. Thereby, information from the models defined by the user interface developer is utilized at runtime. We describe how the developer and user can influence the automatic adaptations and what impact the context information from the environment has on it. On basis of the SHEA example, we show how user interface models move away from absolute to relative specifications, giving free room for automatic adaptations at runtime.

In the next section, we give an overview of related work in the area of model-based user interface development. Afterwards we describe the MASP, a user interface runtime architecture enabling the generation and delivery of UUIs. The details of the underlying user interface models follow in the next section. Step-by-step, we describe the models on the basis of the SHEA example. In the section thereafter, we describe how the combination of architecture and models enables a ubiquitous interaction with smart home applications. We elaborate the automated distribution of the user interfaces and discuss the dynamic layout of the graphical user interface. Afterwards, we describe how the described scenario is realized with the distribution and layout adaptations. Finally, we conclude our chapter and give an outlook on future work.

2 Related Work

Model-driven engineering is a promising approach to the development of complex systems and applications. It is based on the notion of models as a basis for software engineering and represents the shift from object-oriented to model-driven thinking. Since its emergence, MDE has also been researched as a possible approach to reduce the complexity of user interface development [41]. Based on the Cameleon Reference Framework [10], model-based user interface engineering aims at expressing different aspects of the user interface using models on different levels of abstraction at design time. Utilizing these formal user interface models takes the design process to a computer-processable level, on which design decisions become understandable for automatic systems. User interface description languages like UsiXML [25] and TERESA [31] utilize this approach to generate user interface code from formal models at design time.

Smart environments require the user interfaces to adapt dynamically to contexts-of-use, most often unforeseeable at design time. To address this issue, the use of user interface models at runtime has been proposed [38]. Runtime models make the design information available during the execution of the application. At runtime, the information in the models can be used for reasoning about the decisions of the designer, who is no longer available. The utilization of models at runtime is therefore a common approach for the design and adaptation of large, (self-)adaptive systems, like [39] and [20]. The designed adaptations are performed on the running system by transforming the models of the system. [36] proposes the Cumbia platform as a runtime system to execute runtime models, aiming at the provisioning of reusable monitoring and control tools. Other approaches, like [2], utilize models at runtime to debug and validate applications at runtime.

Several user interface development approaches utilize models at runtime. [12] extends the DynaMo-AID design process with context data evaluated at runtime, supporting UI migration and distribution. Knowledge about the tasks the user is pursuing and the context the tasks are executed in can drive optimizations of output presentation and input processing [13]. In [17], the authors describe FAME, a model-based Framework for Adaptive Multimodal Environments, that utilizes a set of models to control an adaptation engine and create multimodal user interfaces. [24] deals with the execution of CTT-based user interface models. These approaches mainly aim at the utilization of static models to support the generation of user interfaces at runtime. But the creation of UUIs requires a more flexible approach and utilization of the models. Such user interfaces are distributed across multiple interaction devices (with different input and output modalities), while providing a presentation shaped to the properties of the user, device capabilities and the current context-of-use.

The distribution of user interfaces to different IRs supporting various modalities has been a topic of various research activities, ranging from the characterization of distributed UIs [16] to development support for specifying distributed UIs [30]. The approach of Elting and Hellenschmidt [18] supports simple conflict resolution strategies when distributing output across graphical UIs, speech syntheses and virtual characters. The main goal is the semantic processing of input and output in distributed systems. The dynamic redistribution and definition of dynamic UI models have thus not been the focus of the approach. The I-AM (Interaction Abstract Machine) system [3] presents a software infrastructure for distributed migratable UIs. It provides a middleware for the dynamic coupling of IRs to form a unified interactive space. The approach supports dynamic distribution across multiple heterogeneous platforms, but does not support the arbitrary recombination of IRs and is limited to graphical output as well as mouse and keyboard input. Our approach utilizes the modeled design information at runtime to dynamically adjust the combination of the used IRs.

Such distributed graphical user interfaces and the heterogeneous and dynamic smart environments require a very flexible layout generation at runtime. Different to other approaches like [26], we shift the decision about which interpretations are relevant to support a specific context-of-use scenario from design time to runtime so we can flexibly adapt the layout to consider new device capabilities, user demands and user interface distributions. Some approaches like PUC [32] generate graphical user interfaces from a device description. Different to PUC, we are not focusing on control user interfaces, but on a domain independent layout model that specifies the containment, the orientation and the size of all individual user interface elements.

Layouting adaptations for different context-of-use scenarios have been topic of various research activities. There are approaches ranging from adaptations of graphical user interfaces to mobile devices, like in [28], to adaptations depending on the user's capabilities [21]. In most of these approaches, the adaptations are defined at design phase and no adjustments at runtime are possible. In [22], the authors describe an approach, to allow the user to (re-)layout virtual maps for a museum guide by dragging and dropping icons to the map and define routes. The tool provides an easy way to create a museum guide for users without programming experience, but the user interface adaptation for the used large screen and the mobile device are pre-defined. In difference, we provide a way for the end-user to adjust and adapt the layout model to different situations at runtime.

The described approaches provide partial solutions for the considered aspects of UUIs. There are approaches for handling distribution of user interfaces (e.g. [16] [30]), and others that deal with the definition of dynamic and adaptive user interface layouts ([21], [28] or [32]). However, to provide UUIs an integrated approach covering the distribution, layouting and multimodality at runtime is required. The recent shift of user interface model utilization from design time to runtime is a promising approach for handling the dynamic interaction capabilities of smart environments. In the following, we present the Multi-Access Service Platform (MASP), which aims at the provision of UUIs by utilizing user interface models at runtime. We have used the MASP to implement the example SHEA application. A detailed description of its models is provided in the section thereafter.

3 Multi-access Service Platform

Aiming at the creation of UUIs for smart home environments, we have identified the need for a runtime architecture that provides support for the common properties of such interfaces and that can be used and configured by the designer as well as by the user. We thus applied a model-based approach, integrating user interface models with a runtime system, to separate shared logic and application specific properties. This leads to the implementation of the MASP, an architecture to enable distributed multimodal interaction, and its flexible adaptation to the current needs and the context-of-use [7]. The core of the MASP is a set of executable user interface models representing the interaction on different levels of abstraction, according to the well-accepted Cameleon Reference Framework [10] (including task & domain, abstract, concrete & final UI models).

At design time, the developer specifies the user interface as a set of models which comprises task-, domain-, service-, context- and interaction-model. The developed set picks up findings from other model-based approaches (Cameleon-RT [1], DynaMo-AID [11], ICARE [9], the Framework for Adaptive Multimodal Environments (FAME) [17], Tycoon [27], SmartKom [35]), but puts a strong focus on the issues arising during the runtime interpretation of user interface models. In an additional mapping model, the developer defines mappings that interconnect the models. At runtime, the MASP generates the user interface based on the information from the models and context information held in a runtime context model. Rather than relying on pre-compiled user interface code, the MASP creates the final user interface on-the-fly, taking the current state of the environment into account. As the interaction with the user progresses, the MASP enriches the models of the UI with state information. This way, the models dynamically evolve over time and describe the application, its current state and the required interaction as a whole instead of providing a static snapshot only. The approach of utilizing dynamic, executable models enables the MASP to adapt the applications by means of model reconfiguration at runtime.

Fig. 2 shows an overview of the MASP architecture comprehending the set of models, their relationships as well as components to provide the dynamic adaptation of the interaction at runtime. Each model describes a different aspect of the UI. While the service model allows interaction with backend systems, the task and domain model describe the basic concepts underlying the user interface. Based on the defined concepts, the interaction models (abstract interaction-, concrete input- and concrete presentation model) define the actual communication with the user. The abstract interaction model thereby defines abstract interactors aiming at a modality and device independent description of interaction. The concrete input- and concrete presentation model substantiate the abstract interactors by specifying concrete interactors targeting specific modalities and device types. Furthermore, the interaction model provide support for the definition of multimodal interaction. A context model provides interaction-relevant context information. It holds information about the available interaction resources and allows their incorporation into the interaction process at runtime. Additionally, it provides information about users and the environment and comprises context providers, continuously delivering context information at runtime. The model is continuously updated at runtime to reflect the current context-of-use of the interaction.

The different models are connected by mappings as described in [6]. The mappings are also defined in a model (mapping model) and provide the possibility to interconnect the different models and to ensure synchronization and information exchange between models. By linking the task model to service and interaction models, the execution of the task model triggers the activation of service calls and interactors. While service calls activate backend functions, active interactors are e.g. displayed on the screen and allow user interaction. They also incorporate domain model elements in their presentation and allow their manipulation through

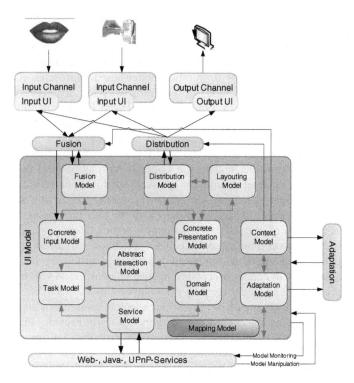

Fig. 2 The MASP runtime architecture, comprising interaction channels, fusion, distribution, layouting and adaptation components and a comprehensive user interface model

user input as defined by the mappings. The context model finally also influences the presentation of the interactors that are related to context information. Thus, the execution of the task model triggers a chain reaction, leading to the creation of a user interface from the defined user interface model. The structure underlying this approach also opens the possibility to add additional models or change existing models in the future.

The whole concept of the MASP is based on a client-server architecture with the MASP server managing multiple IRs with different interaction capabilities and modalities. The resources are connected via channels and each user interface delivered to a resource is adapted according to the capabilities of the resource and the preferences of the user. For this purpose, the MASP runtime architecture, also depicted in Fig. 2, combines the models and the related mappings with a set of components. While the models reflect the state of the current interaction and the UI, the components provide advanced functionality.

An adaptation component allows the utilization of an adaptation model to directly adapt the user interface models according to the context-of-use (including device, user and environment information). Based on this adaptation model, an application can e.g. support mobile and static devices by adapting the user interface accordingly. Flexible multimodal interaction is supported by a distribution component, segmenting the user interface across multiple modalities and devices if necessary. Achieving a suitable presentation of the possibly distributed user interface, is the task of a layouting component and finally a fusion component matches and interprets input from different modalities. All components utilize the underlying user interface model allowing the configuration of the components.

In contrast to other multimodal approaches, we do not aim at the semantic analysis of any user input, but at the provisioning of a multimodal user interface guiding and restricting the possible interaction. As mentioned above, the connection of the IRs to the MASP is done via channels. The channels identify the connection to IRs and provide related APIs allowing their direct incorporation into the user interface delivery and creation process. The activation of different combinations of channels also allows changing the currently supported modalities during the interaction. A channel-based delivery mechanism is used for the delivery of the created final user interfaces to the interaction devices [5]. The combination of multiple devices allows combining complementary devices to enhance the interaction and support multiple modalities and interaction styles. A common example for this feature is the utilization of a mobile device as a remote control for a large display. This is possible by distributing an application across the two devices. Additionally, voice support can be added via a third device. Fig. 1 shows this combination of mobile and static clients as an example on the very top of the image.

4   MASP Models

To actually use the architecture described above, the models are the core part that provides the application specific configuration of the whole system. The interface developer makes use of these models to express the design of the application and the underlying interaction. In the following, we illustrate the utilization of these models, by describing the models underlying the SHEA example application. Step-by-step we will present the models of the application. Due to space constraints we will limit our example to SHEA's device visualization and control part. For each device available in the home environment, the SHEA visualizes its status, functionality and, most importantly, its energy consumption over time. Additionally it enables the direct control of each appliance, e.g. by means of dimming of lights or configuring the heating program. All models are available at runtime during the execution of the application. A top of the models, we have implemented algorithms that utilize the information specified by the designer to optimize the adaptation process.

4.1   Task and Domain Models

The creation of a MASP application typically starts with the definition of a task tree describing the tasks that a user and the system need to perform during their interaction. The task tree models of MASP applications are based on the CTTE notation [34] extended with some constructs necessary for their runtime interpretation.

Fig. 3 shows the subtree of SHEA's task model, defining the user-system interaction for the device control and visualization part. There are four types of tasks in the subtree. *Abstract* tasks are refined by more concrete children tasks, *Application* tasks that are performed by the application, *InteractionIn* tasks, in which the user provides some input to the system, and *InteractionOut* tasks in which the system displays some information without user's interaction. Additionally, the tasks are annotated with information about the accessed domain objects. There are three types of access: *R* for reading an object, *C* for creating an object and *M* for modifying an existing object.

The abstract *DeviceControlAndVisualization* task is the root task of our subtree and has four children tasks:

- *DeviceProgramming* – enables the user to re-program a device (change dim level in case of lights or temperature in case of heating systems). First, the user must input a new program (*InputProgram InteractionIn* task) and then, the system programs the device accordingly (*ProgramDevice Application* task).
- *ProvideDeviceInformation* – in this *InteractionOut* task, the system provides the user with information about the device (its type, state, current power consumption, etc.).
- *DeviceStateControl* – enables the user to turn the device on or off.
- *EnergyConsumptionAnalysis* – provides the user with an energy consumption chart. The system creates a chart for the device (*GenerateChart Application* task) for a given time span (defined in the *timeSpan* object). The chart is then made available for the user in the *InteractionOut ProvideChart* task. The user may modify the chart's time span in the *ConfigureChart InteractionIn* task, which restarts the *EnergyConsumptionAnalysis*.

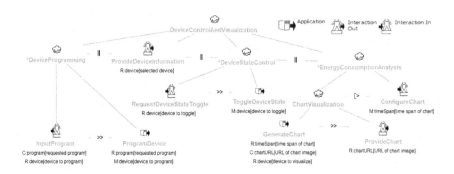

Fig. 3 SHEA task subtree for the interaction with home appliances

The MASP provides developers with a graphical editor for the task models. A task tree simulator integrated with the tool enables to simulate the execution of the created task trees. Using the simulator, the developer can verify the possible task performance sequences in an early design stage before proceeding with the definition of the user interface.

At runtime, the MASP interprets the task tree of each application and on-the-fly generates a UI for the current combination of tasks that can be performed (the so called enabled tasks set). For each activated *Application* task, the MASP executes an associated service call, defined in a service model of the application. For the *InteractionIn* and *InteractionOut* tasks, a user interface is generated on basis of abstract and concrete user interface models.

4.2 Service Model

In the service model, the developer refines the application tasks defined in the task model by specifying backend service calls performed by the application. The service model is thus the glue between the user interface and the backend service logic.

The service calls of the SHEA device visualization and control tasks are *ToggleDeviceState*, *ProgramDevice* and *GenerateChart*. Every call has parameters (corresponding to the input objects of the tasks) and properties (describing the execution of the call). Additionally, each service call is associated with a service adapter, responsible for its execution. The MASP currently provides adapters for Java, Webservice and UPnP service calls.

4.3 Abstract User Interface Model

On the abstract user interface (AUI) level, the designer refines interaction tasks with device and modality independent AUI interactors. As explained in [7], there are five types of AUI interactors in the MASP's AUI model:

- *OutputOnly* – when the computer presents the user information without requiring feedback or input (e.g. images or text).
- *FreeInput* – when the user inputs (unstructured) data into the system (e.g. providing a name or a password).
- *Command* – when the user sends a signal to the system ordering it to perform an action (e.g. OK and Cancel buttons).
- *Choice* – provides a list to the user and denotes the possibility to choose one or several options from this list.
- *ComplexInteractor* – allows the aggregation of multiple abstract interaction objects into a more complex type. This provides e.g. logical grouping facilities.

In our example SHEA application, there are five interaction tasks – two *InteractionOut* and three *InteractionIn*. The *InteractionOut* tasks are always mapped to *OutputOnly* interactors, because the user does not provide any input to the system while performing them. In the SHEA, the user is provided with an energy consumption chart in *ProvideChart* and with information about the device in *ProvideDeviceInformation*. Both tasks are mapped to *OutputOnly* interactors. The task *RequestDeviceStateToggle* is refined with a *Command* interactor, because by performing it, the user urges the system to perform an action. In *ConfigureChart* and *InputProgram* tasks, the user selects an item from a set of alternatives (new time span for the chart and new program for the device respectively), so the tasks are represented by *Choice* interactors on the AUI level.

4.4 Concrete User Interface Model

The concrete user interface model allows refining the AUI interactors with different modality specific representations. In contrast to other approaches, the MASP concrete user interface (CUI) model is split into two parts – concrete presentation- and concrete input model. This is the basis for supporting a flexible combination of input and output capabilities. The details of both have been described in [7]. For this chapter, it should be sufficient to say that the concrete presentation model contains graphical elements like buttons, labels, text fields or images, signal interactors for haptic, sound and visual output and natural language and text output interactors for text and speech output. On the CUI input side, there are interactors describing gestures, natural language or text as well as signal or pointing input.

Furthermore, both models support the definition of relationships between the concrete interactors by means of the CARE properties (Complentarity, Assignment, Redundancy, Equivalence) [15]. Thereby, the developer can specify how the related interactors can be used for multimodal interaction. Defining multimodal relations with the CARE-properties is similar to the ICARE software components [8]. In contrast to ICARE however, the components and thus the multimodal relationships are not statically related at design time, but can be freely configured between arbitrary modalities through the integration in the model and evaluated at runtime. The relationships make it possible to perform multimodal fusion and fission of the user interface and influence the behavior of the MASP distribution and fusion components.

Although the information from the CUI model makes it possible to create a user interface, the results may suffer from the typical weakness of model-based user interfaces – their generic character. To overcome this issue, the MASP enables the designer to customize the user interface with special details on the final user interface level.

4.5 Final User Interface Layer

On the final user interface (FUI) level of the Cameleon reference framework, the user interface is specified in a platform-dependent language and is thus executable on the target platform. The MASP currently supports HTML and Media Resource Control Protocol (MRCP) platforms, as well as a non-standardized gesture recognition platform developed as a part of a student project. Depending on the runtime distribution of the user interface between the available interaction devices, the MASP generates the FUI and delivers it to the target devices via so called channels. The generation of the FUI is based on the Velocity Template Language (VTL)[1] and can happen twofold:

---

[1] http://velocity.apache.org

- The FUI can be automatically generated from the CUI model of the application by means of generic mappings between the CUI model and the FUI elements available on the platform. The MASP provides default VTL templates for the supported platforms (e.g. mapping CUI *Image* elements to *<img>* tags for the HTML platforms).
- The developer may customize the FUI generation process by overwriting the generic templates with application-specific VTL templates. The MASP uses a Velocity engine and merges the application-specific templates at runtime. This way, the developer has the possibility to customize the resulting FUI and avoid its generic character.

The models defined so far describe the basics of the dialog between the user and the system and provide details about the interaction capabilities of the application, as well as its communication with the backend services. In the following section, we present how the models are used to guide the automatic distribution and layout of the user interface at runtime.

5 Adaptation: Distribution and Layouting

The so far described models of the example SHEA application are independent of any static IR or modality combination, nor are they bound to a fixed context-of-use. To simplify the development of UUIs, the MASP provides automated adaptation capabilities. Based on the information in the user interface models and the context data gathered from the environment, the MASP is capable of dynamically distributing and layouting the user interface to the current context-of-use. However, automated algorithms are not always feasible. On the one side, the user interface developer may wish to provide some custom context-bound behavior in her application, e.g. define diverse UI layouts for different user types. On the other side, the user may wish to configure the application to best match her current mood or goal (which can hardly be detected at runtime and incorporated into adaptation algorithms). In order to provide the developer and user a possibility to influence the automatic user interface adaptation, the MASP supports three layers of adaptations:

1. Automatic adaptations: Based on the user interface models and the information about the context-of-use, the MASP provides automatic adaptation capabilities. In the following sections, we describe how a default user interface distribution and layout are calculated for the currently available IRs. The decisions made by the automatic algorithms have the lowest priority and can be overwritten by statements of the developer and the user.
2. Adaptations specified by the developer: In cases where custom, application-specific adaptation behaviour is needed, the designer specifies distribution and layout guidelines. Rather than defining absolute statements about the user interface (e.g. *the button B must be 100 pixels high*), the designer provides relative specifications (e.g. *the button B must be twice as big as the label L*).

This way, the MASP still has some free room for automatic adaptation within the boundaries set by the developer.

3. Adaptations specified by the user: The MASP provides the users with a so called Meta–User-Interface (Meta-UI). While hiding the technical details, the Meta-UI enables the user to influence the adaptation mechanisms of the MASP and configure them according to their preferences. The user can e.g. reconfigure the distribution of the user interfaces in her environment or disable some layout adaptations. It should be noted that the decisions made by the user have the highest priority for the MASP (e.g. the user may reconfigure a user interface distribution even if it was pre-defined by the developer).

In the following subsections, we explain in more details how the MASP calculates and adapts the user interface distribution and layout according to the layers presented above. In the subsection thereafter, the application of the distribution and layout for the example SHEA application are described.

5.1 Distribution

Distribution is one of the properties of UUIs and denotes the capability of UUIs to be distributed to several IRs. This also includes IRs with different modalities and from different platforms as well as changing IRs over time. Thereby, the capabilities of smart environments with their numerous interaction possibilities can be exploited and overcome the still predominant interaction with only one device at a time. But this also raises the need for choosing the interaction possibilities at runtime (when the context-of-use is known). We refer to the process of choosing the IRs and integrate them into a suitable interaction as *distribution*. Within the MASP architecture, the distribution component is responsible for this task. In accordance with the adaptation layers presented in the previous section, the distribution component includes the three different types of adaptation. The automatic algorithm, utilizing the currently available IRs as well as the user interface model is presented next.

5.1.1 Algorithm for Automatic Distribution

An overview of the distribution algorithm is depicted in (Fig. 4). The automatic distribution algorithm is triggered whenever a new set of active interactors or a new IR is available. The discovery and management of interaction devices providing the IRs is accomplished by MASP's context model. Besides the information about the active interactors and the available IRs, the distribution algorithm is influenced by additional variables: previously calculated distribution configurations or configurations specified by the user for the same set of interactors in a similar context-of-use (history). The algorithm thus checks for suitable distributions from the past and selects every distribution specified for the same set of concrete interactors. Furthermore, the situation describing the circumstances under which the distribution was established is compared to the current situation. Therefore, the relevant context information is retrieved from the

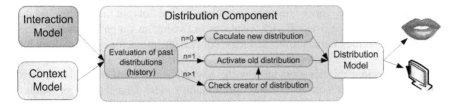

Fig. 4 Overview of the distribution algorithm

context model and compared to the saved context information from the selected distributions. All distributions where the context comprehends less or equal amount of information than the current context are marked as relevant for further consideration. These distributions were active when having at least the same "knowledge" as currently available and are thus relevant for further consideration.

One, more than one or no distribution can be found during the comparison process. If only one distribution is found, the distribution algorithm finishes and the distribution is set as current distribution. This triggers further UI generation steps, resulting in the rendering of the interactors on the IRs. If multiple distributions are found, the algorithm evaluates the creator of the distribution to determine the most suitable one. Distributions from the user are considered better than distributions of the application (which are based on constraints specified by the application developer) as user configurations are done by users to adapt the existing distribution to their needs. Similarly, application configurations are considered better than distributions calculated by the system as the application developer specifies distributions with a specific intention, which the system should not overrule. If the comparison of the saved distributions does not reveal any results, the current context comprehends more (detailed) information than the saved contexts. Thus, the distribution could probably be done with better certainty. The system then calculates a distribution based on information from the current context, properties of the user and constraints defined by the application developer as explained next.

At first, the IRs that the user may access must be determined. Therefore, the available IRs are queried from the context model together with information about the premises and localization and direction information. Based on the type of the IRs, the algorithm calculates if the resources are currently usable. E.g. displays are considered usable when they are within the visible to the user and haptical input. IRs are considered usable when they are within the range of the user. The resulting set of usable IRs determines the usable modalities and thus the types of concrete interactors that can be distributed. Next, the distribution algorithm matches the supported modalities to the available modalities of the available IRs by adhering to the following goals:

- Input: support as many (equivalent) input resources as possible while considering the specified CARE relations between the input elements. This aims at leaving the control about the used IRs to the user by supporting the widest possible range of input interactors.

- Output: find the most suitable combination of output resources while considering the specified CARE relations between the output elements. The algorithm decides between the different equivalent interactor combinations by selecting the one supporting the most modalities. This is based on the assumption that the designer utilizes the advantages of each modality, so that more modalities result in a better presentation. The Distribution of output interactors aims at utilizing the most suitable combination of IRs to convey the UI. The selection of IRs depends on their capabilities and context information like the resource location.

To achieve the above goals, the distribution algorithm first analyzes the CARE relations of the active concrete interactors. The specified CUI model contains trees of complex interactors with simple elements as leaf nodes. As only the leaf nodes have to be distributed, the relations defined by their parent complex interactors influence their distribution. Single interactors are automatically of type "assigned" and can thus be directly distributed if a corresponding type of IR is available. Interactors combined via complex elements of type complementary or redundant must be distributed together to reflect their meaning. This means that to make an interaction, defined as redundant, available to the user, all modalities addressed by the children of the complex interactor have to be available. The equivalence relation is used to specify different (combinations of) interactors that transport the same information in case of output or allow the user to provide the same information in case of input. This makes the system more reliable and reduces ambiguity and inconsistency. With respect to the distribution goals specified above, a different handling of the equivalency relation for input and output has been realized. For input, the distribution of as many equivalent interactors as possible results in more possibilities for the user to provide the needed input. For output, a selection of the most feasible interactors avoids confusion and unwanted redundancy.

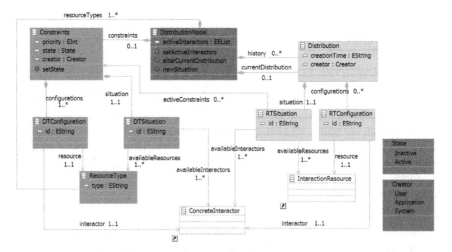

Fig. 5 The metamodel of distribution models for storing the distribution configurations of the user interface elements

5.1.2 Distribution Model for Developer-Defined Distributions

The metamodel, depicted in Fig. 5, provides a basis for the definition of distribution models. The models are used to store distribution constraints specified by the developer at design time (left part) as well as the runtime results, user settings and history of the distribution calculations (right part).

The application developer can specify certain distributions for specific situations in a distribution model and the user can change and store distributions via the Meta-UI. Both specifications are considered by the algorithm for an automatic distribution.

The design time configuration of distribution constraints allows the developer to specify application specific distribution hints. Constraints therefore contain configurations that map concrete interactors to IR types. This allows e.g. the assignment of a PDA display as preferred IR for one set of interactors and the definition of a fixed touch display for others. Situations acting as pre-condition for the constraint can be defined based on information modeled in the context model. Constraints are dynamically (de-)activated at runtime based on the fulfillment of the defined situation and only active constraints are considered throughout the distribution calculation.

At runtime, the distribution model mainly acts as storage for calculated- and user distributions. The current distribution is expressed as a set of configurations that map concrete interactors to specific resources, based on the current context situation. This situation also contains the currently active constraints as this configuration can change and lead to a new distribution. Each applied distribution is also defined by a timestamp of its applications and the creator of the distribution (user, application, and system can also directly assign interactors to resources). A history stores all applied distributions for later consideration within the algorithm.

Storing the current distribution within the model also makes this information available to the interaction model. A mapping can transport the information of the currently used IRs to variables in the interaction model. The storage of a new distribution configuration also triggers the layouting process of the MASP. Furthermore, the distribution model provides the basis for the user to change the distribution according to her needs as explained next.

5.1.3 User-Defined Distribution via the Meta User Interface

In addition to the distribution configurations specified by the developer and those calculated automatically by the MASP, the user also has the possibility to configure the distribution according to her needs. The manifold possibilities of combining different devices in numerous situations also make this a very useful and required addition for such flexible interaction. Users need a configuration tool that satisfies their specific needs, while hiding the underlying technical details. In case of the distribution, this results in providing high-level functions and not only the concrete interactor and IR tuples available in the distribution model. We have developed a Meta-User-Interface (Meta-UI) that provides configuration options to adapt the distribution according to the possible changes defined e.g. by Coutaz [14]. At any point of time, the user can access the Meta-UI and redistribute UI elements to different IRs (at interactor level). The user has the possibility to move or clone interactors, migrate parts or the complete user interface to an IR, as well remould the existing user interface on one IR by adding or removing UI elements.

In the current version of the Meta-UI, we distinguish four features the user can utilize to configure her interactive space. (1) The migration feature provides possibilities to migrate a service UI from one IR to another to e.g. transfer the UI to another screen better viewable from the users' current position. Through the distribution feature (2), the user can distribute parts of the user interface to other IRs. Thereby, the user can also specify if the selected parts should be cloned or moved to the target IR. The third configuration feature is called multimodality (3) and provides possibilities to configure the utilized modalities within the interaction. This allows users to e.g. switch off audio output of the MASP if it is currently disturbing the user. The adaptation feature (4) allows the user to configure further functions of the MASP. E.g. the MASP supports a so called "FollowMe" modus which can be configured through the adaptation feature. The activation of the "FollowMe" modus leads to an automatic configuration of the interactive space by the MASP over time. The MASP monitors the available IRs of the user and reconfigures the interactive space according to the new resource combination.

After creating a new distribution configuration via one of the three different possibilities, the layouting is responsible for generating a coherent presentation. Thereby, the layouting has to handle the dynamic distribution of user interface parts to different IRs, which makes it impossible to predefine layouts for every situation at design time.

5.2 Layouting

This section describes our layouting approach to generate adaptive layout for the numerous possible combinations of heterogeneous interaction resources in smart environments. Like the distribution, the layouting supports the automatic calculation of the presentation based on the user interface models of the application and provides configuration possibilities for application developers and users. The basis of our approach is a layout model that constrains and defines the presentation of the user interface.

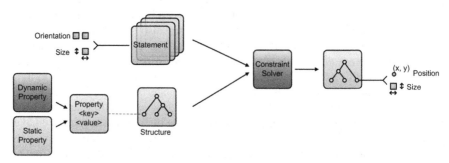

Fig. 6 Layout model overview

The model contains a structure of all user interface elements and related statements defining the design characteristics of the elements like containment, orientation and size. From the model, a constraint system is extracted from which the specific positions and sizes of the concrete interactors are calculated by a constraint solver. We shift the decision about which of the statements are applied from design time to runtime to enable flexible context-of-use adaptations of the user interface layout. This allows us to describe new context-of-use adaptations of the layout without the need to change the application itself just by describing the layout characteristics of a new platform or a new user profile. At design time, an initial layout model is automatically generated from the already specified information in the user interface models. The developer can then adapt this model by defining application specific statements with the support of a tool. At runtime, the layout influenced by the context-of-use and the distribution of the user interface is generated automatically from the model. The user can also adjust the layout according to her needs.

5.2.1 Layout Model

The layout model shown in Fig. 6 consists of the structure of the user interface and statements affecting the layout characteristics (containment, orientation and size). In the following paragraphs, we describe the two different parts of the layout model (structure and statements) and the automatic creation of the initial layout model in detail.

The automatic generation of the initial layout model uses a logical structure of the user interface and semantic information annotated to the nodes to respect basic design rules defined in [40] to create a good initial layout. The user interface structure consists of containers and elements. Container consists of a set of nested containers and nested elements. Elements are the visible parts of the user interface structure and present information to the user. The initial structure of the layout model is retrieved from the user interface models. The task model is used to generate an initial hierarchy. Afterwards, the corresponding refinements of the abstract user interface model are attached as leafs and then the user interface elements from the concrete user interface models.

For the example of the SHEA, the root task *DeviceControlAndVisualisation* is transformed into the root container of the user interface structure. Iteratively, the child nodes of the next level are attached if they are abstract or interaction tasks. In the end, abstract tasks only having one interaction task are replaced with this interaction task. The created structure has only interaction tasks as leafs and is extended with information derived from the representations of the abstract- and concrete user interface models.

The elements of the tree structure can be configured by so called statements, which are the building blocks of the constraint system. They are divided into Node- and Type statements. Node statements affecting specific nodes of the user interface structure and influence their size or orientation. Type statements affecting an amount of user interface nodes with a specific characteristic defined within another user interface model like the representation at the concrete user interface model (e.g. all elements with type Button). The dimensions which can be influenced are containment, orientation and size. The containment characteristic describes the relation of elements as a nested hierarchy by abstract containers that can contain other abstract containers or UI elements and thus influence the structure of the layout. The orientation distinguishes between elements that are oriented horizontally or vertically to each other. Finally, the size specifies the width and height of containers and UI elements relative to other UI elements or abstract containers.

For the initial layout model, default values for the statements are set as explained with the SHEA example. The algorithm moves from the container *DeviceStateControlandVisualization* of the structure to the leaf elements. The children nodes of the first layer (*InputProgram, ProvideDeviceInformation, RequestDeviceStateToogle, EnergieConsumptionAnalysis*) are vertical orientated because information normally needs more horizontal than vertical space. This follows from the behavior of textual information shown in [23] by the relation between the font size and the width and height of the text containing shape. The node *ProvideDeviceInformation* is moved to the top, because of the representation at the abstract user interface level. Information often describes actions user has to perform and depending on the reading direction (in Europe top-left to bottom-right) this element must be read first. The space allocation depends on the amount of inherent elements of each child. Every child gets the percentage of space of the relative between its number of elements and the total number of elements of its parent. For example, the *DeviceStateControlandVisualization* has 7 elements in total and its child node *EnergyConsumptionAnalysis* has 4 elements resulting in 4/7 amount of the total space for the child node. To optimize the ratio between the width and height for each element, the algorithm uses an alternating orientation at each level. As a result, the children of the node *EnergyConsumptionanalysis* should be orientated horizontal. Because the representation at the concrete user interface model of the nodes *ProvideChart* and *ConfigureChart* is well-defined, this information is used to change the orientation for these two nodes. The *OutputOnly* characteristic of the node *ProvideChart* and the *Choice* representation of the node *ConfigureChart* lead to the vertical orientation. Additionally, the original resolution of the image showing the chart is used to generate a constraint, assure that the constraint system respects the aspect ratio. In Fig. 7, the result of the automatic layout generation process is shown. The picture combines the tree visualisation of the user interface structure and spatial relations between the container and elements.

Affected by the discussion about automatic layout generation for graphical user interfaces [33] and approaches like [29] to support the design process, we have developed a tool [19] for the definition of statements and the simulation of situations and effects to the user interface. The designer can manipulate the pre-generated layout to match his aesthetical requirements by adding statements that relate information of the design models with a layout characteristic of a UI element. The layout editor supports this process though the interpretations of the user interface model and domain model information. In our example, the layout algorithm recommends to group the device control elements *InputProgram* and

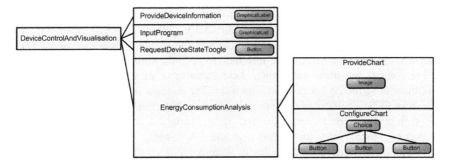

Fig. 7 Automatic layout generation result for the SHEA application

DeviceStateToggle to define a more abstract "control widget" container because both manipulate the domain object. The object representing the selected device is changed by both user interface elements, so the grouping function adds a description for the created *ControlDevice* node (element with the dashed border in Fig. 8) to give a hint for the end user about the motivations of the designer. This element additionally denotes an unsplittable node which means that the end user can only distribute the node *ControlDevice* to a different device. Because the graph of the energy consumption depends on the actual state of the devices, the designer arranges the node *ControlDevice* to the left side of the *ProvideChars* element. To realize the emerging free space, the layout editor adds a blank element to the container *DeviceStateControlandVisualization Node*. The result of the user interface design process is shown on the right side of Fig. 8.

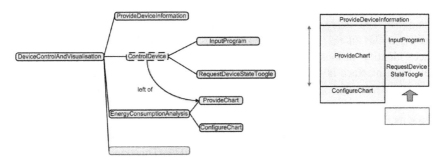

Fig. 8 Application specific design process

To complete the design of the user interface, the designer defines style definitions statements for members of an element type (e.g. a button or a menu bar) or a specific user interface element. Because the style definition is bound to a statement, the designer can define different styles for specific characteristics of a platform or disabilities of the user.

The layout algorithm is customizable for different situations. The designer creates statements affecting the orientation and size as well as the font size and color of the elements. For each platform the font size is created depending on the display's size and aspect ratio. Additionally, other dependencies like the interaction possibilities influence the size and the visual appearance of the user interface elements. To adapt the interface to specific situations, the designer can define context sensitive statements, these statements are only active for specific situations described by context information. The concept of situation adaptation is shown in [37]. The situation contains a function describing the relations between the different contexts variables and these variables are bound to dynamic properties stored into the context model. According to type statements, a recalculation is triggered if the value is changed.

5.2.2 Context Sensitive Layout Adaptations

The broad range of possible user interface distributions and the diversity of available interaction devices make a complete specification of each potential context-of-use scenario difficult during the application design. Necessary adaptations require flexible and robust (re-)layouting mechanisms of the user interface and need to consider the underlying tasks and concepts of the application to generate a consistent layout presentation for all states and distributions of the user interface. Our previous work is described in [19] and here we want to show some examples to adapt the control elements of the SHEA application to characteristics of the user. First, we define a situation depending statement, which supports left handed users by changing the position of control elements. While the user switches the device, the energy consumption isn't longer disguised. The statement uses the information stored into the abstract user interface model to identify affected user interface elements.

Another adaptation is described in [37] and adapts the interface to specific situations. The designer can define context sensitive statements to prioritize specific nodes of the user interface structure. In a smart environment, different places identify various situations. Applications can consider these spots to adapt their user interface layout to focus on those parts of the UI that are identified as most important for a certain spot. The algorithm allocates the space according to the weight (contained elements), so the increase depends on the amount of other elements. For example, if the algorithm prioritizes one of three nodes at the same level, so the algorithm adds a statement ensures that the selected node gets two-thirds of the available space for the parent node. This kind of statement can improve the usage for a device overview, in this case, the algorithm prioritize the nearest device to control.

5.2.3 User-Defined Layouts via the Meta User Interface

Like for the distribution, the user is given the possibility to influence the layout adaptations through the Meta-UI. On the one hand, the Meta-UI provides the user with control over the automatic layout adaptations. At any time, the user can disable or enable the adaptations, for example the spot-based layouting described in the previous section. On the other hand, the user can enhance the layout configuration for individual interactors. In its current state, the Meta-UI enables the resizing and repositioning of the interactors. This way the user can reorganize the layout of her applications according to her preferences or desires. A possible adaptation could be the enlargement of button elements to simplify the control via touch displays [42].

The layout configuration performed by the user is stored in the layout model in form of new statements with the highest priority. It is thus assured that the user configuration is always applied to the user interface, regardless of the configurations provided by the application developer or the automatic layout algorithm.

5.3 Distribution and Layouting in SHEA

In the introduction, we sketched the scenario of the SHEA being used through different devices with different interaction capabilities. This section describes, how the scenario is implemented using the MASP by explaining each step of the scenario from the MASP point of view.

Step 1: The user starts the interaction with the SHEA by saying the word "SHEA" via a microphone in the office. This triggers the MASP's distribution algorithm to determine the interaction resources that should be used for the current status of SHEA's interaction model. As no distribution for the current context-of-use exists in the history of the distribution model, the MASP calculates a new UI distribution across the interaction devices in the office. First, the available interaction resources are queried from the context model. In the next step, input and output interaction resources are selected, with the goal of supporting as many modalities as possible. In this context, the PC-monitor and the PC-loudspeaker are selected as output devices, the microphone (used by the user for the "SHEA" command), the mouse and the keyboard of the PC are used as input interaction resources.

After the distribution calculation, the layouting is triggered to calculate the presentation. Therefore, the size and aspect ratio of the PC-monitor are requested from the context model and the constraint solver calculates the sizes and positions of the concrete user interface elements based on the defined layout model. Afterwards, the concrete user interface elements are transformed to the final user interface representation and sent to the interaction resources via the channels.

The user can now interact with the SHEA and selects the light from the device overview with the mouse. The gathered input results in updates of the interaction model which in turn results in updates of the input possibilities and presentation. Thereby, the distribution is not changed as the context-of-use is not changing, but the layouting has to calculate the presentation whenever the set of concrete interactors changes.

Step 2: The user decides to continue the interaction in the living room and thus enables the "FollowMe"-mode via the Meta-UI. Thereon, the distribution component monitors the context model for changes in the position of the user and check if a redistribution is needed. When the user walks into the living room, the distribution determines that other interaction resources are available for the user and triggers the distribution algorithm.

Step 3: The user calls the MASP Meta-UI again and accesses the distribution menu. Through it, the user selects the smartphone as target interaction resource and clicks on the UI elements, which are immediately redistributed. The configuration is stored in the distribution model and will be reused every time the user calls the SHEA in the living room in the future.

Step 4: The automatic resizing of UI elements representing the appliances near the user is implemented in form of context-dependent layout statements specified by SHEA's developer. The statements query information from the context model and influence the position and size of the UI elements. As soon as the user comes close to a specific light, the situation specific layout statement is activated and prioritizes the user interface element representing the device.

6 Conclusion and Outlook

In this chapter, we have presented an approach for the development of multimodal and distributable user interfaces, which dynamically adapt to unforeseen contexts-of-use and combinations of interaction resources. Our approach combines a user interface runtime architecture and runtime user interface models. The architecture (called Multi-Access Service Platform) dynamically handles context information from the environment and adapts the user interfaces based on automatic adaptation algorithms. The algorithms are influenced by the adaptation guidelines defined by designer and the preferences specified by the user. In particular, we elaborated the distribution and layout algorithms. Using the example of a Smart Home Energy Assistant application we have shown how MASP applications are defined in form of models. We have also explained how the MASP utilizes the design information contained in the models for adapting the user interfaces at runtime to the context-of-use.

The presented approach focuses on the provision of UUIs supporting multimodality, distribution and shapeability. In the future, we plan to extend the MASP architecture with support for the remaining two properties of UUIs: shareability (cooperative interaction of multiple users) and mergability (interoperability of different applications). For this purpose, we intend to explore further adaptation algorithms. Another issue, which we wish to explore in the future, is the evaluation of the runtime adaptations. Therefore, we currently pursue the idea of linking the adaptation algorithms with an automatic usability evaluation. The basic idea here is to simulate different adaptation alternatives, evaluate the usability of the resulting user interfaces and select the adaptation producing the best usable user interface. On the side of the MASP modeling language, we are considering the definition of a multimodal widget set that would reduce the efforts necessary to build user interfaces based on the different levels of abstraction in the interaction models.

References

[1] Balme, L., Demeure, A., Barralon, N., Coutaz, J., Calvary, G.: Cameleon-rt: A software architecture reference model for distributed, migratable, and plastic user interfaces. In: Markopoulos, P., Eggen, B., Aarts, E., Crowley, J.L. (eds.) EUSAI 2004. LNCS, vol. 3295, pp. 291–302. Springer, Heidelberg (2004)

[2] Balz, M., Striewe, M., Goedicke, M.: Embedding state machine models in object-oriented source code, pp. 6–15 (2008)

[3] Barralon, N., Coutaz, J., Lachenal, C.: Coupling interaction resources and technical support. In: Stephanidis, C. (ed.) UAHCI 2007 (Part II). LNCS, vol. 4555, pp. 13–22. Springer, Heidelberg (2007)

[4] Blumendorf, M.: Multimodal Interaction in Smart Environments A Model-based Runtime System for Ubiquitous User Interfaces. Ph.D. thesis, Technische Universität Berlin (2009)

[5] Blumendorf, M., Feuerstack, S., Albayrak, S.: Multimodal user interaction in smart environments: Delivering distributed user interfaces. In: Mühlhäuser, M., Ferscha, A., Aitenbichler, E. (eds.) AmI 2007. LNCS, vol. 4794, Springer, Heidelberg (2007)

[6] Blumendorf, M., Lehmann, G., Feuerstack, S., Albayrak, S.: Executable models for human-computer interaction. In: Graham, T.C.N., Palanque, P. (eds.) DSV-IS 2008. LNCS, vol. 5136, pp. 238–251. Springer, Heidelberg (2008)

[7] Blumendorf, M., Lehmann, G., Roscher, D., Albayrak, S.: Ubiquitous User Interfaces: Multimodal Adaptive Interaction for Smart Environments. In: Multimodality in Mobile Computing and Mobile Devices: Methods for Adaptable Usability, pp. 24–52. IGI-Global (2009)

[8] Bouchet, J., Nigay, L., Ganille, T.: Icare software components for rapidly developing multimodal interfaces. In: Proceedings of the 6th International Conference on Multimodal Interfaces, ICMI 2004, pp. 251–258. ACM Press, New York (2004)

[9] Bouchet, J., Nigay, L., Balzagette, D.: Icare: A component-based approach for multimodal interaction. In: Proceedings of the 1st French-speaking conference on Mobility and Ubiquity Computing, UbiMob 2004, pp. 36–43. ACM Press, New York (2004)

[10] Calvary, G., Coutaz, J., Thevenin, D., Limbourg, Q., Souchon, N., Bouillon, L., Florins, M., Vanderdonckt, J.: Plasticity of user interfaces: A revised reference framework. In: TAMODIA 2002: Proceedings of the First International Workshop on Task Models and Diagrams for User Interface Design, pp. 127–134. INFOREC Publishing House, Bucharest (2002)

[11] Clerckx, T., Luyten, K., Coninx, K.: Dynamo-aid: A design process and a runtime architecture for dynamic model-based user interface development. In: Feige, U., Roth, J. (eds.) DSV-IS 2004 and EHCI 2004. LNCS, vol. 3425, pp. 77–95. Springer, Heidelberg (2005)

[12] Clerckx, T., Vandervelpen, C., Coninx, K.: Task-based design and runtime support for multimodal user interface distribution. In: Proceedings of Engineering Interactive Systems 2007, EHCI-HCSE-DSVIS (2007)

[13] Clerckx, T., Vandervelpen, C., Luyten, K., Coninx, K.: A task-driven user interface architecture for ambient intelligent environments. In: IUI 2006: Proceedings of the 11th international conference on Intelligent user interfaces, pp. 309–311. ACM Press, New York (2006)

[14] Coutaz, J., Calvary, G.: HCI and Software Engineering: Designing for User Interface Plasticity. In: Sears, A., Jacko, J. (eds.) Human Factor and Ergonomics series, 2nd edn., ch. 56, pp. 1107–1125. Taylor & Francis/CRC Press (2008), ISBN 9780805858709, http://www.isrc.umbc.edu/HCIHandbook/

[15] Coutaz, J., Nigay, L., Salber, D., Blandford, A., May, J., Young, R.M.: Four easy pieces for assessing the usability of multimodal interaction: The care properties. In: INTERACT 1995, pp. 115–120 (1995)

[16] Demeure, A., Sottet, J.S., Calvary, G., Coutaz, J., Ganneau, V., Vanderdonkt, J.: The 4c reference model for distributed user interfaces. In: The Fourth International Conference on Autonomic and Autonomous Systems, ICAS 2008, Gosier, Guadeloupe. IEEE Computer Society Press, Los Alamitos (2008)

[17] Duarte, C., Carriço, L.: A conceptual framework for developing adaptive multimodal applications. In: IUI 2006: Proceedings of the 11th International Conference on Intelligent User Interfaces, pp. 132–139. ACM Press, New York (2006)

[18] Elting, C., Hellenschmidt, M.: Strategies for self-organization and multimodal output coordination in distributed device environments. In: Workshop on Artificial Intelligence in Mobile Systems 2004 In conjunction with UbiComp 2004 (September 2004)

[19] Feuerstack, S., Blumendorf, M., Schwartze, V., Albayrak, S.: Model-based layout generation. In: Bottoni, P., Levialdi, S. (eds.) Proceedings of the Working Conference on Advanced Visual Interfaces, ACM, New York (2008)

[20] Fleurey, F., Dehlen, V., Bencomo, N., Morin, B., Jézéquel, J.M.: Modeling and validating dynamic adaptation. In: Chaudron, M.R.V. (ed.) MODELS 2008. LNCS, vol. 5421, pp. 97–108. Springer, Heidelberg (2009), http://dx.doi.org/10.1007/978-3-642-01648-6

[21] Gajos, K., Weld, D.S.: Preference elicitation for interface optimization. In: Proceedings of the 18th Annual ACM Symposium on User Interface Software and Technology, UIST 2005, pp. 173–182. ACM Press, New York (2005)

[22] Ghiani, G., Paternò, F., Spano, L.D.: Cicero designer: An environment for end-user development of multi-device museum guides. In: Pipek, V., Rosson, M.B., de Ruyter, B., Wulf, V. (eds.) IS-EUD 2009. LNCS, vol. 5435, pp. 265–274. Springer, Heidelberg (2009)

[23] Hurst, N., Marriott, K., Moulder, P.: Minimum sized text containment shapes. In: Proceedings of the 2006 ACM Symposium on Document Engineering, DocEng 2006, pp. 3–12. ACM, New York (2006)

[24] Klug, T., Kangasharju, J.: Executable task models. In: Proceedings of TAMODIA 2005, pp. 119–122. ACM Press, Gdansk (2005)

[25] Limbourg, Q., Vanderdonckt, J., Michotte, B., Bouillon, L., López-Jaquero, V.: USIXML: A language supporting multi-path development of user interfaces. In: Bastide, R., Palanque, P.A., Roth, J. (eds.) DSV-IS 2004 and EHCI 2004. LNCS, vol. 3425, pp. 200–220. Springer, Heidelberg (2005), http://dx.doi.org/10.1007/11431879_12

[26] Lutteroth, C., Weber, G.: User interface layout with ordinal and linear constraints. In: Proceedings of the 7th Australasian User Interface Conference, AUIC 2006, pp. 53–60. Australian Computer Society, Inc., Darlinghurst (2006)

[27] Martin, J.C.: Tycoon: Theoretical framework and software tools for multimodal interfaces. In: Intelligence and Multimodality in Multimedia interfaces. AAAI Press, Menlo Park (1998)

[28] Martinez-Ruiz, F.J., Vanderdonckt, J., Arteaga, J.M.: Context-aware generation of user interface containers for mobile devices. In: Proceedings of the 2008 Mexican International Conference on Computer Science, ENC 2008, pp. 63–72. IEEE Computer Society, Washington (2008)

[29] Meskens, J., Vermeulen, J., Luyten, K., Coninx, K.: Gummy for multi-platform user interface designs: shape me, multiply me, fix me, use me. In: Proceedings of the Working Conference on Advanced Visual Interfaces, AVI 2008, pp. 233–240. ACM, New York (2008)

[30] Molina, J., Vanderdonckt, J., González, P., Fernández-Caballero, A., Lozano, M.: Rapid prototying of distributed user interfaces. In: Proceedings of 6th Int. Conf. on Computer-Aided Design of User Interfaces, CADUI 2006, pp. 151–166. Springer, Heidelberg (2006)

[31] Mori, G., Paternò, F., Santoro, C.: Design and development of multidevice user interfaces through multiple logical descriptions. IEEE Trans. Softw. Eng. 30(8), 507–520 (2004)

[32] Nichols, C.A.J., Myers, B.A., Higgins, M., Hughes, J., Harris, T.K., Rosenfeld, R.: of Computer Science Carnegie Mellon, M.P.S.: Generating remote control interfaces for complex appliances. In: UIST 2002: Proceedings of the 15th annual ACM symposium on User interface software and technology, pp. 161–170. ACM Press, New York (2002), http://citeseer.ist.psu.edu/602919.html

[33] Omojokun, O., Dewan, P.: Automatic generation of device user-interfaces? In: PERCOM 2007: Proceedings of the Fifth IEEE International Conference on Pervasive Computing and Communications, pp. 251–261. IEEE Computer Society Press, Washington (2007)

[34] Paternò, F.: Model-Based Design and Evaluation of Interactive Applications. In: Applied Computing. Springer, Heidelberg (1999)

[35] Reithinger, N., Alexandersson, J., Becker, T., Blocher, A., Engel, R., Löckelt, M., Müller, J., Pfleger, N., Poller, P., Streit, M., Tschernomas, V.: Smartkom: Adaptive and flexible multimodal access to multiple applications. In: ICMI 2003: Proceedings of the 5th International Conference on Multimodal Interfaces, pp. 101–108. ACM Press, New York (2003)

[36] Sanchez, M., Barrero, I., Villalobos, J., Deridder, D.: An execution platform for extensible runtime models. In: 3rd Int. Workshop on Models at Runtime at MoDELS (2008)

[37] Schwartze, V., Feuerstack, S., Albayrak, S.: Behavior-sensitive user interfaces for smart environments. In: HCII 2009 - User Modeling (2009)

[38] Sottet, J.S., Calvary, G., Favre, J.M.: Models at runtime for sustaining user interface plasticity. presented at Models@run.time workshop (in conjunction with MoDELS/ UML, conference) (2006)

[39] Staikopoulos, A., Saudrais, S., Clarke, S., Padget, J., Cliffe, O., Vos, M.D.: Mutual dynamic adaptation of models and service enactment in alive*. In: Proceedings of the Models@Runtime workshop at Models 2008, pp. 1–10 (September 2008), https://www.cs.tcd.ie/publications/ tech-reports/reports.08/TCD-CS-2008-56.pdf

[40] Tognazzini, B.: TOG on Interface. Addison-Wesley Longman Publishing Co., Inc., Boston (1992)

[41] Vanderdonckt, J.: Model-driven engineering of user interfaces: Promises, successes, failures, and challenges. In: Proceedings of ROCHI 2008 (2008)

[42] Schwartze, V., Marco Blumendorf, S.A.: Adjustable context adaptations for user interfaces at runtime. In: Proceedings of the Working Conference on Adnvanced Visual Interfaces, pp. 321–325 (2010)

Model-Driven Development of Interactive Multimedia Applications with MML

Andreas Pleuss and Heinrich Hussmann

Abstract. There is an increasing demand for high-quality interactive applications which combine complex application logic with a sophisticated user interface, making use of individual media objects like graphics, animations, 3D graphics, audio or video. Their development is still challenging as it requires the integration of software design, user interface design, *and* media design.

This chapter presents a model-driven development approach which integrates these aspects. Its basis is the *Multimedia Modeling Language (MML)*, which integrates existing modeling concepts for interactive applications and adds support for multimedia. As we show, advanced multimedia integration requires new modeling concepts not supported by existing languages yet.

MML models can be transformed into code skeletons for multiple target platforms. Moreover, we support the integration of existing professional multimedia authoring tools into the development process by generating code skeletons which can be directly processed in authoring tools. In this way, the advantages of both – systematic model-driven development *and* support for creative visual design – are combined.

1 Introduction

With the evolution of end-user oriented applications in the last years – like the advancements in web applications, mobile applications, entertainment, or infotainment area –, it has become widely accepted that a sophisticated user interface can significantly contribute to an application's success. Such user interfaces are often highly interactive, provide a sophisticated user interface, and – depending on the

Andreas Pleuss
Lero, University of Limerick, Ireland
e-mail: andreas.pleuss@lero.ie

Heinrich Hussmann
University of Munich, Germany
e-mail: hussmann@ifi.lmu.de

H. Hussmann et al. (Eds.): MDD of Advanced User Interfaces, SCI 340, pp. 199–218.
springerlink.com

purpose – make use of multimedia capabilities. Typical reasons for multimedia usage are 1) to enhance efficiency and productiveness of the user interface, 2) to achieve more effective information and knowledge transfer, and 3) to provide enhanced entertainment value [10].

This work deals with the development of interactive multimedia applications. While the application areas mentioned above are typical for multimedia usage, multimedia user interfaces can be found in almost any application area today. Traditionally, the term multimedia has been understood as a composition of continuous (like audio, video, and animations) and discrete media elements (like 2D and 3D graphics, text, and images) into a logically coherent unit [2]. However, from the viewpoint of application development, the main difference today is much more the integration of *non-standard* media objects into the application. This requires specific experts and tools, like for graphics design, video production, or 3D design. Thus, here we understand the term "'multimedia application'" in a broad sense as *any kind of interactive application integrating individual media objects* (like graphics, animations, audio or video) *to an extent relevant for its development.*

The development of multimedia applications still lacks a systematic development approach. Traditional approaches from multimedia domain provide extensive support for media creation but neglect the application logic and Software Engineering principles [9, 15, 12]. On the other hand, existing approaches from software engineering do not support user interface and media aspects yet (see Section 2).

In our opinion, the most important differences between the development of multimedia applications and conventional application development (as considered in Software Engineering) are:

1. *Interdisciplinary development:* Multimedia application development involves three different kinds of design: 1) *Software Design*, as in conventional software development, for developing the application logic 2) *User Interface Design*, as usability is strongly important for multimedia applications, and 3) *Media Design* as creation of media objects requires usually specific knowledge and tools. Thus, different developers groups, tools, and artifacts have to be integrated into the development process.

2. *Importance of non-functional requirements:* Requirements like entertainment value, usability, and aesthetics, are strongly important for multimedia applications. Thus, visual authoring tools focusing on the creative, artistic visual design, like *Adobe Flash* or *Adobe Director*[1], have been established as development tools [3, 7].

In our work, we aim to address these challenges by a model-driven development approach which integrates the different developer groups and the artifacts they produce. For this, we provide a modeling language that integrates software design, user interface design, and media design into a single, consistent language. The models hence provide a kind of contract between the different developer groups, so that all developed artifacts will fit together.

---

[1] http://www.adobe.com/

From the models, we then automatically generate code skeletons. As our modeling language is platform-independent, it is possible to generate code for any target platform. In particular, to integrate the existing established authoring tools, we support them as target platforms and generate code skeletons which can be directly processed within these tools. In this way, the development process becomes much more systematic while still leveraging these established tools for the final user interface and media design.

The remainder of this chapter presents our modeling language for multimedia applications. The language integrates concepts from areas of Software Engineering and model-based user interface development and extends them by new concepts required for advanced multimedia integration.

For the purpose of this chapter, we use a 2D racing game application as a running example. Gaming applications are well-suited examples because they are commonly understood and make use of both, 1) a very complex and individual user interface and 2) complex application logic. Nevertheless, it is important to note that our approach is not restricted to any specific application domain and has already been applied to many other kinds of multimedia applications (see Section 9).

Our language supports five kinds of models: The *Task Model* describes the user tasks to be supported by the application. It uses the existing *ConcurTaskTree* notation [16] and is thus not further discussed in this chapter. The other models are the *Structure Model*, the *Scene Model*, the *Presentation Model*, and the *Interaction Model*, which are explained in the following. Afterwards, we give an overview on the language, the interrelations between the different models, and the modeling process. Finally, we describe the existing tool support and the basic concepts for the code generation.

2   Related Work

This section briefly presents related approaches. As interactive multimedia applications integrate different aspects – application logic, user interface, and media –, it is related to various existing modeling approaches.

To model the application logic, the *Unified Modeling Language* (*UML*) [14], can be used. However, UML on its own is not sufficient for multimedia applications as it does not cover neither the user interface aspect nor media types.

The user interface aspect is addressed by various approaches from the area of *Model-based User Interface Development* (*MBUID*) [24] (including model-driven approaches as described in this book). Their main concepts can be summarized as follows [4]: The *Task Model* specifies the user tasks supported by the application, e.g., specified as ConcurTaskTrees [16]. It is usually complemented with a *Domain Model*, which can be a conventional UML class diagram. Based on the Task Model and the Domain Model, the *Abstract User Interface Model* (*AUI*) specifies the user interface in terms of *Abstract Interaction Objects* (*AIOs*) which are platform- and modality-independent abstractions of user interface elements. The *Concrete User Interface Model* (*CUI*) refines the AUI for a concrete target platform.

Currently, a large amount of approaches from this area exist which nowadays have evolved towards the model-based and model-driven approaches described in this book, considering advanced user interface issues like specific target devices or context-sensitivity. However, as existing approaches address user interfaces built from standard widgets, they on their own are not sufficient for interactive multimedia. However, they provide the basic concepts for the user interface aspect in MML.

The area of *Web Engineering* [11] targets model-driven development of web applications. Typical models, besides a *Domain Model*, are the *Hyperlink* or *Navigation Model* which shows the links and navigation structure of the application, and the *Presentation Model* which specifies the look and feel of the user interface and sometimes also its behavior. While earlier approaches mainly address applications with HTML-based user interfaces, latest work focuses on Rich Internet Applications [5, 25, 23]. However, they still address user interfaces made of standard widgets while individual multimedia user interface are not supported yet.

Finally, a few modeling approaches exist which already address multimedia. However, most of them [8, 26, 2] focus on multimedia documents but do not cover interactive applications. An exception is OMMMA [6] which supports interactive multimedia applications as considered in this chapter. However, OMMMA does not integrate the results from MBUID area and also lacks of the advanced concepts we discuss in Section 3. Nevertheless, it provides substantial basic concepts which have been included into MML.

First concepts of MML have been presented in [18, 17]. However, as discussed in [20], there is a need for advanced modeling concepts for Media Components, like different abstraction layers, inner structure, and variations (see Section 3). Moreover, the language has evolved based on the experience from its usage in several student projects (see Section 9). In this chapter, we present the resulting integrated version of MML. A full language reference can be found in [19].

3   MML Structure Model

The MML Structure Model describes the structure of the application. Fig. 1 shows an example of a racing game application and is used throughout this section to illustrate the introduced concepts.

The Structure Model contains the Domain Classes for the application logic. They are described like in a conventional UML class diagram. For instance, a racing game might contain classes Race, Car, Player, and Track. A Track contains Obstacles and Checkpoints (like the start and the goal). Domain Classes have properties and relationships like in conventional UML class diagrams (Fig. 1).

In addition, the media elements are basic assets of the application as well and their production can require much effort, specific experts, and specific tools. In addition, the usage of a specific kind of media content can be an essential requirement for the application. For instance, the customer might want the racing game application to use 3D graphics or an e-learning application to contain videos. For these

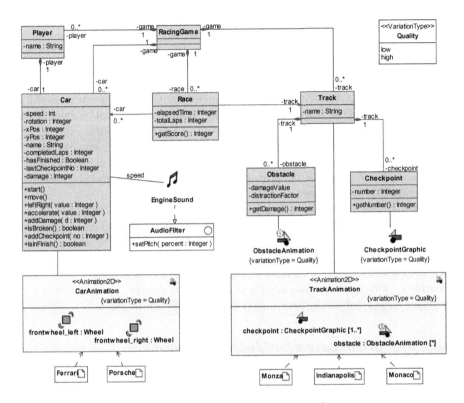

Fig. 1 MML Structure Diagram Example

reasons, the media elements are modeled in MML as first-class entities in the Structure Model.

In interactive applications, media content is often associated with some functionality to render and control the media content. For instance, a video is usually shown in a video player which allows to play, stop, rewind, etc., the video. Thus, in MML, the media content is encapsulated together with basic playing and rendering functionality as a *Media Component*. Each Media Component is of a certain media type which can be *Audio*, *Video*, *2D Animation*[2], *3D Animation*, *Graphics* (i.e., vector graphics), *Image* (i.e., raster graphics), or *Text*.

A Media Component is denoted in MML similar to a Component in UML as a rectangle with several optional compartments for additional properties. Like UML, MML allows to choose between different alternative notations. The media type is denoted by an icon and/or a keyword. In Fig. 1, the Media Components CarAnimation and TrackAnimation are displayed with a compartment showing their inner

---

[2] "Animation" here refers to any kind of change over the time, like changing its position on the screen or changing its shape.

structure (explained below). The Media Components EngineSound, ObstacleAnimation, and CheckpointAnimation are denoted in collapsed notation with an icon only.

Media Component are associated with Domain Classes which they represent. This is specified in MML by a *Media Representation* relationship between a class and a Media Component. In the example, the Domain Class Car is represented by CarAnimation and EngineSound. Obstacle and Track are represented by animations as well (ObstacleAnimation and TrackAnimation) while Checkpoint is represented by static graphic (CheckpointGraphic). To specify that the Media Component represents a specific property or operation of the class, Media Representation relationship is marked with the name of the property or operation. For example, EngineSound represents the property speed of Car.

MML defines some standard operations for each media type, which have not to be modeled explicitly and can be used in the Interaction Model (see Section 6) to specify a Media Component's behavior. For instance, a 2D Animation provides operations to access its coordinates on the screen and its size. It is also possible to define custom operations for Media Components in terms of Interfaces (like UML Interfaces) which can be associated with Media Components. An example is the interface AudioFilter which is associated with EngineSound in Fig. 1.

3.1 Abstraction Layers for Media Components

In [20], we have discussed advanced concepts for modeling Media Components in interactive applications that have not been addressed so far. An important finding is that different abstraction layers have to be considered: Media Components, like CarAnimation, are abstract constructs which might be realized by multiple concrete artifacts, like Porsche and Ferrari. It is beneficial to consider them as abstract elements, instead of dealing with the concrete artifacts only, because in this way, all kind of cars can be handled in the same way. Moreover, the concrete artifacts are often unknown in early phases, because it is not decided yet how many different cars the final application will provide. In fact, in some cases the concrete artifacts are not known at all at the design time, because they are dynamically loaded from a server or because the user creates them himself dynamically at runtime (e.g., using a "car editor" delivered with the application). Even when the concrete artifacts are known, it might be desired not to model all of them, because their number is too large and they will be loaded from a database later.

On the other hand, if the concrete artifacts are already known, there should be a way to specify them in the model. Thus, we introduce *Media Artifacts* which can be used to optionally specify concrete artifacts. In the example, CarAnimation is manifested by two Media Artifacts Porsche and Ferrari and TrackAnimation by three Media Artifacts Monza, Indianapolis, and Monaco.

One should note that there is a third abstraction layer for Media Components which are the concrete instances of Media Components on the user interface (see Section 5). Of course, a Media Component can be instantiated multiple times, like in a racing game where usually multiple cars take part. Again, it is possible to specify the concrete Media Artifact used for a Media Instance but not mandatory; sometimes they might be decided at design time (e.g., in the first level of the racing game the user has always to use the Porsche) while sometimes it might be decided at runtime (e.g., the user can select the car herself).

3.2   Inner Structure of Media Components

A second important finding from [20] is the need to define the inner structure of Media Components. This is in particular important for interactive multimedia applications: For instance, let us consider, that the CarAnimation's front wheels should turn when the car drives through a turn. Then, the media designer needs to know that the car's front wheels have to be designed as own (graphical) objects which can be accessed and modified by the application logic. The software designer in turn needs to know how to access them (e.g., the names assigned by the media designer). Thus, it is necessary to specify such inner structure in the model as a kind of contract between the developers.

It is important to note that it is not intended in MML to model the complete (visual) structure of the car. The inner structure is modeled only when it should be accessed by application logic. This happens either when some media parts should be accessed or modified, like in the example above, or when an event listener should be attached to a media part (like, for instance, that the user can trigger some action by clicking on the car's wheels).

Again, the different abstraction layers have to be considered in a consistent way. In MML, a *Media Part* represents an (abstract) part of a Media Component, like *Wheel*. Each Media Part has a type depending on the Media Component it belongs to. For instance, a video can consist of *Audio Channels* and *Image Regions* while a 3D animation consists of *3D Objects, Transformations, Light*, etc. 2D animations, like in the racing game example, consist just of graphical objects which we call *SubAnimations*.

A Media Part can be instantiated multiple times, acting in multiple roles, similar like properties in a conventional UML class. For instance, a car has multiple wheels like frontwheel_left and frontwheel_right[3]. These instances are called *Inner Properties* (to distinguish them from other properties of the Media Component).

An Inner Property can also be an instance of another Media Component, like in TrackAnimation, which contains multiple instances of ObstacleAnimation and CheckpointGraphic. As shown in the example, a multiplicity can be specified for each Inner Property. The software developer can then access the single instances in a way similar to arrays, e.g., 'wheel[1]'.

Analogously to Media Components, it is optionally possible to specify a concrete artifact for a Media Part, called *Part Artifact*, which can be useful if the developer wants to distinguish explicitly between PorscheWheel and FerrariWheel or to

---

[3] Note that the back wheels have not to be modeled here as they need not to be accessed by application logic.

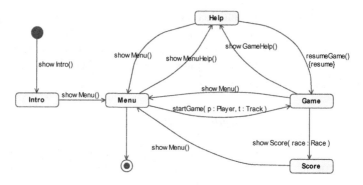

Fig. 2 MML Scene Diagram Example

express that all car types reuse the same artifact for their wheels (specified by marking an Inner Property with the keyword unique) (see [20] for in-depth discussion of all possible cases).

3.3 Variations of Media Components

A third concept, not discussed in previous work so far, is the need for an efficient way to specify different variations of Media Components. For instance, Media Components frequently have to be provided, e.g., in different qualities or different languages. Therefore, in MML, the modeler can introduce in MML a *Variation Type* (like *Quality* in Fig. 1) and specify different *Variation Literals* for it, like high and low. This means that each Media Component, where the Variation Type is assigned to, must be created in each possible variation. For instance, all visual Media Components in the example have assigned the Variation Type Quality which means that the media designers have to provide them in the two different variations high and low. Basically, the variations could also be combined with mechanisms for context-sensitive user interfaces from MBUID (see Section 2), e.g., to select the appropriate variation automatically at runtime based on the application context.

4 MML Scene Model

The Scene Model describes the application's coarse-grained behavior or navigation in terms of *Scenes*. A Scene represents an application state associated with a corresponding user interface. For instance, in the racing game, the scenes are Intro, Menu, Help, Game, and Score. The Scene model shows the Scenes and the transitions between them using an adapted notation of UML State Charts (Fig. 2).

An important multimedia-specific aspect of Scenes is their dynamic character. One the one hand, this is caused by dynamic behavior of time-dependent media instances (audio, video, animations) in the Scenes. On the other hand, user interfaces are often generated dynamically at runtime, like the number of cars taking part in a racing game or the track chosen by the user. Thus, Scenes can be generic and receive parameter values. Therefore, each Scene has *Entry Operations* and *Exit Operations*. Entry Operations are used to initialize the Scene and pass parameters to it. Exit Operations are used to clean up a Scene and invoke another Scene.

As shown in Fig. 2 for the racing game example, the Scenes are denoted as states with the possible transitions between them. The transitions are annotated with the names of Entry Operations executed in the target Scene when performing the transition. Exit Operations need not to be modeled explicitly as their names are by convention derived from the transitions in the diagram.[4].

By default, executing an Entry Operation initializes a Scene. However, sometimes a Scenes has already been active before and its previous state should be resumed. This is specified by attaching the keyword resume to the Entry Operation. For instance, when the user calls the Help during the Game he/she probably wants to resume the game after the consulting the help. Thus, the Entry Operation resumeGame() is marked with this keyword (Fig. 2).

Beside Entry and Exit Operations, it is also possible to define additional properties and operations for a Scene. Moreover, Media Components can not only represent Domain Classes, as explained for the Structure Model, but also Scenes. For instance, a Media Component HelpText would probably not be associated with one of the Domain Classes but with the Scene Help. Analogously to the Structure Model, this is specified by a Media Representation relationship between the Media Component and the Scene.

5   MML Presentation Model

The MML Presentation Model specifies the user interface for each Scene. It is initially modeled using Abstract Interaction Objects as common in the MBUID area (see Section 2). However, as we deal with multimedia applications, in a second step, the instances of the Media Components from the Structure Model come into play.

5.1   Abstract User Interface

In MML, each Scene is associated with a *Presentation Unit*. A Presentation Unit is an abstraction from a screen in a graphical user interface. It contains *Abstract Interaction Objects* (*AIO*) which are platform- and modality-independent abstractions of user interface elements. For instance, an *InputComponent* enables the user to input some data, an *Output Component* presents some data to the user, an *Edit Component* combines input and Output Component, and an *Action Component* allows the user to trigger an action. It is also possible to apply further concepts from MBUID here, like modeling the layout of the AIOs, but this is not further discussed here.

---

[4] The names are composed of a prefix 'exitTo', the name of the target scene, and the name of the target Entry Operation, separated by _, e.g. exitTo_Menu_showMenu().

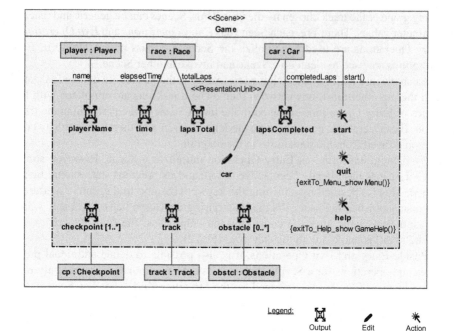

Fig. 3 AIOs in the MML Presentation Model for the Scene **Game**.

Fig. 3 shows as an example the Presentation Unit for the Scene **Game**. The Scene acts as the overall container. It contains *Domain Objects*, which are instances of the Domain Classes from the Structure Model, and a Presentation Unit containing the AIOs. The Presentation Unit in the Scene **Game** contains, for instance, several Output Components to show the track, the obstacles, and the checkpoints. The player's car is represented by an Edit Component as it presents the current state of the car which is also manipulated by the user. There are some Output Components for additional information, like the playerName, time, and lapsCompleted, and some Action Components to start the race or to navigate to the help or back to the menu.

Each AIO represents a Domain Object as specified by *UI Representation* relationships. Analogous to Media Representation relationships in the Structure Model, it is possible to annotate the name of a property or operation to specify that this specific property or operation is represented by the AIO. For instance, the Output Component playerName represents the property Name of player. AIOs not associated with a Domain Object represent the Scene itself. In this case, the name of a Scene's property or operation represented by the AIO is denoted directly below the AIO (in curly braces), like for the Action Component quit which triggers the Scene's Exit Operation exitTo_Menu_showMenu() (see Section 4).

Due to the possible dynamic character of multimedia user interfaces, it is possible to specify a multiplicity for an AIO (like for obstacle) as their number is calculated dynamically at runtime. Also, the Interaction Model can be used to specify that

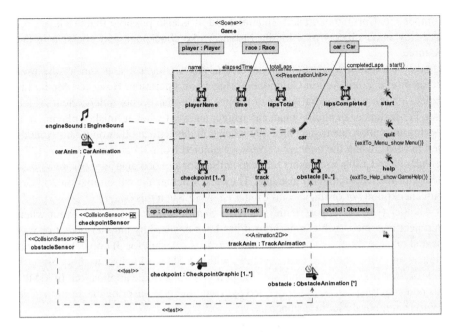

Fig. 4 MML Presentation Diagram enhanced with Media Instances and Sensors for the Scene Game

AIOs are added or removed from the user interface. To indicate that an AIO is initially invisible on the user interface and becomes visible at runtime, the keyword invisible can be attached to the AIO.

5.2 Multimedia User Interface

As we deal with multimedia applications, some of the AIOs can be realized by media objects. Therefore, the respective AIO is connected with a *Media Instance* by a *UI Realization* relationship. Its semantics is that the AIO is implemented by the Media Instance. In turn, the Media Instance must provide the interaction concepts defined by the AIO. For instance, if an animation should realize an Action Component, this means that, e.g., clicking on the animation triggers some action. Thus, not any type of Media Instance can realize any AIO (see discussion in [18]). AIOs which are not realized by a Media Instance are intended to be implemented in conventional way, i.e. using standard widgets.

Media Instances are instances of Media Components from the Structure Model. So, a Media Component can be used in different Scenes. For instance, the CarAnimation is not only used in the game itself, but also in the menu where the user can select between different cars.

Fig. 4 shows the Presentation Model for the Scene Game enhanced with Media Components. For instance, the AIO car is realized by instances of the Media

Components CarAnimation and EngineSound. It is also possible that AIOs are realized by inner objects of a Media Instance, like checkpoint and obstacle in the example.

Like in existing MBUID approaches, the AIOs trigger events during the user interaction; e.g., an Action Component triggers an operation. However, Media Instances of temporal media type can trigger additional events independent of the user. For instance, an audio object can trigger an event when it finishes playing or a moving animation can trigger an event when collides with another one. This is modeled in MML using the concept of *Sensors* adapted from 3D graphics domain [27]. In Fig. 4, two Collision Sensors (checkpointSensor and obstacleSensor) are associated with the CarAnimation instance. They test whether the car animation collides with checkpoints or obstacles and trigger an event when this occurs.

Another type of sensors is the *Visibility Sensor* which triggers an event when an object becomes visible, e.g., after it has been covered by another object or was located outside the screen. A *Proximity Sensor* is relevant for 3D objects only and triggers an event when the user navigates within a 3D world close to this object. A *Time Sensor* triggers an event at specific points of time in the application. In MML, this points in time can be either defined by fixed time interval or by one or more *Cue Points* of temporal Media Instances.

A *Cue Point* (not shown in the example) can be defined for any temporal media object and allows to refer to a specific point in time on the media object's time line. This can be used to specify synchronization between temporal media objects. Let us consider that the racing game application shows as introduction a video and some animated text. The text should appear after the first scene in the video is finished. Therefore, a Cue Point can be defined, like "firstSceneFinished". Using a Time Sensor it is now possible to specify that, when firstSceneFinished occurs, an operation is triggered on the Media Component for the text, like setVisible(). The advantage of Cue Points compared to concrete time values is their abstract character as often the concrete duration of the video is still unknown or may change later according to the aesthetic considerations of the media designer.

6 MML Interaction Model

The Interaction Model specifies the user interaction and the resulting behavior of the Scene. The core idea is to specify how events initiated by the user interface trigger operations of Domain Objects or of user interface elements (AIOs or Media Components). In that way, the Interaction Model specifies the interplay between the elements defined in the foregoing models. The behavior of Domain Class operations itself is not part of the MML models as it is often quite complex and usually specified directly in a programming language – in particular, as the operations in a multimedia application (like moving the car in a realistic way) often require much trial and error and cannot be specified in advance.

Existing work in MBUID often uses Task Models to describe the interaction. As mentioned in the Section 1, MML supports Task Models as well. They are sufficient

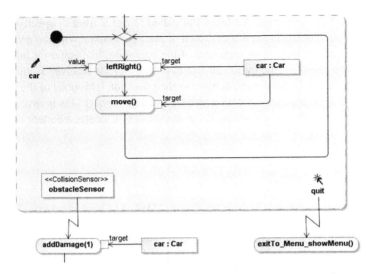

Fig. 5 Simplified extract from the Interaction Model for the Scene Game

to specify the interaction for less dynamic Scenes, like the Menu in the racing game. However, dynamic multimedia Scenes, like the Scene Game, often require a more detailed modeling of temporal behavior. Therefore, such Scenes are modeled using the MML Interaction Model which is an adapted UML Activity Diagram. As shown in existing work [1], extended UML Activity Diagrams can also be used to specify similar operations like in Task Models, while on the other hand, as sometimes used in UML, they also allow to model very detailed object-oriented behavior.

The objects which can be used in a Scene's Interaction Model are the Domain Objects, AIOs, Media Instances, and Sensors owned by the Scene as defined in the Scene's Presentation Model. Additional objects can be passed as parameters of the Scene's Entry Operations. An *Action* in the Interaction Model refers to an operation call (like UML *CallOperationActions*) on one of the objects owned by the Scene. In this way, by restricting the Activity Diagram to defined objects and operation calls, it is possible to directly generate code from the model.

As mentioned before (Section Section 3), MML defines some standard operations for Media Components, like start, stop, play() for videos. Analogously, some standard operations are predefined by MML for the AIOs (e.g., disable(), setVisible()) to save the modeler defining them manually.

Beside the operation calls, the Interaction Model contains events triggered by AIOs and Sensors to model the interaction. They can be used analogous to *AcceptEventActions* in UML, e.g., in combination with *InterruptibleActivityRegions* whose execution terminates when they are left via an interruptible edge. In this way, it can be specified that, e.g., some user input interrupts the current program flow (i.e. terminates tokens) and starts another one.

Fig. 5 shows an simplified extract from the Interaction Model for the Scene Game. Like in UML Activity Diagrams, Actions have *Input Pins* to specify the parameters for an operation. An Input Pin called target is used to specify the object on which the operation call is executed. Input Pins marked with the name of an operation argument receive an argument of the operation, like value for leftRight(). In the simplified model, the input value to control the car is received from the Edit Component car, and passed as parameter to the operation leftRight() of the Domain Object car. Afterwards, the operation move() is called on car. This is executed in a loop until an interruption occurs by the collision sensor obstacleSensor or by the ActionComponent quit.

7 Overall Approach

Fig. 6 shows the overall modeling process with MML. The horizontal axis shows the different developer roles involved in the process, i.e. software design, user interface design, and media design. The vertical axis represents the temporal dimension. The center shows the different MML models and the interrelations between them.

The modeling process is performed during the design phase of the application. It starts after the requirements analysis, which is performed in the usual way and not further considered here. The Task Model reflects the user tasks to be supported by the application from the viewpoint of user interface design. They have to be derived from the requirements specification. In parallel, the Structure Model is specified which consists of Domain Classes and Media Components. Domain Classes can be derived from the requirements specification similar to conventional object-oriented development.

The Media Components are derived from the requirements specification as well, as far as they are specified therein. Domain Classes and Media Components are related through Media Representation relationships. Thus, adding Media Components can require additional Domain Classes which represent associated application logic. In turn, for each Domain Class can be considered whether it is useful to represent it by a Media Component. The Structure Model should be created in cooperation between Software Designer and Media Designer as it defines how application logic can access Media Components and how those must be structured for this purpose.

The Scene Model describes the Scenes and the navigation between them. The decomposition into Scenes influences the application's usability and is thus specified by the user interface designer. The Scenes can be identified based on the Task Model, for instance, using an approach like in [13].

For each Scene, a Presentation Model is defined by the user interface designer. It specifies the AIOs which can be derived from the Task Model as well. The AIOs are associated with Domain Objects which are instances from the Domain Classes in the Structure Model. In the next step, the Presentation Model is complemented with Media Components and Sensors. At this point, the user interface designer and the media designer have to cooperate. The Media Instances refer to Media Components in the Structural Model. During these steps, missing Domain Classes and missing Media Components can be identified and added. In addition, the user interface designer and the media designer can add Sensors to Media Components. Basically, it is

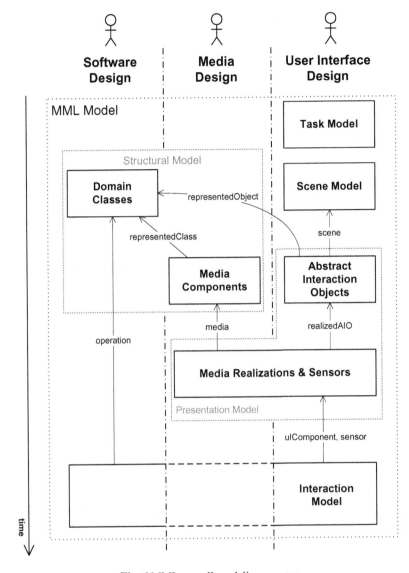

Fig. 6 MML overall modeling process

also possible to refine the Presentation Model in terms of a Concrete User Interface Model as in existing MBUID approaches.

Finally, the Interaction Model is specified in cooperation between the software designer and the user interface designer. It specifies how user interface events and Sensor events trigger operation calls on domain objects. Missing model elements, like missing objects in the Scene or missing class operations, can be identified and

added. The user interface designer is responsible for the interaction which can –
at least to some degree – be derived from the Task Model. The software designer's
knowledge is mainly required for specifying the more complex behavior of dynamic
Scenes like the Game Scene in the racing game.

It is not mandatory to follow the modeling process always as described here.
Basically, it is possible to start with any kind of MML model or to specify the model
in several iterations. For example, it is possible to start the process with the Scene
and Presentation Models and to create the Structure Model on that base. Indeed,
it is also possible that all three developer groups iteratively specify all models in
cooperation or that there is an additional modeling expert who supports the different
developers in specifying the models.

8   Tool Support and Code Generation

MML is defined as a standard-compliant metamodel implemented with the *Eclipse
Modeling Framework (EMF)*[5]. The advantage of EMF is its integration with many
other existing tools from model-driven engineering, like tools for model transformation, validation, or model weaving[6]. As visual modeling tool for MML, we provide
an extension of the UML tool *Magic Draw*[7]. In addition, we provide a model transformation to transform the models from Magic Draw into EMF so that they can be
further processed by EMF-based tools. The advantage of using Magic Draw instead
of creating our own EMF-based visual modeling tool is that a professional modeling
tool provides a degree of usability and robustness which is difficult to achieve with
an implementation of our own.

After MML models have been transformed into the EMF-based format, it is possible to generate code skeletons for different target platforms. To this end, we provide several model transformations in the *Atlas Transformation Language (ATL)*[8].
The currently most mature transformation is one generating code skeletons for the
target platform Flash. A Flash application consists of *Flash documents* and associated code in the object-oriented programming language *ActionScript* which is part of
Flash. Thereby, we generate the Flash/ActionScript skeletons in such a way that they
can be directly loaded into the Flash authoring tool. The designers then can process
them using all the professional functionality of the tool. Other target platforms currently supported by prototypical model transformations are Java, SVG/JavaScript,
and Flash Lite for mobile devices.

The basic concepts for the Flash/ActionScript code generation are as follows:
The Domain Classes from the Structural Model are mapped to ActionScript classes,
analogous to existing mappings from UML class diagrams to Java code. The Media
Components are mapped to Flash documents containing placeholders according to
the Media Component's inner structure defined in the model. These placeholders

---

[5] http://www.eclipse.org/emf/

[6] http://www.eclipse.org/modeling/

[7] http://www.magicdraw.com

[8] http://www.eclipse.org/m2m/atl/

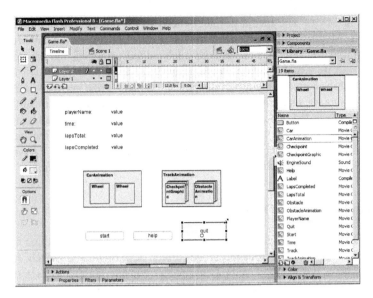

Fig. 7 Generated Skeletons for the Racing Game

then have to be filled out by the media designers using the Flash authoring tool. In addition, an ActionScript class is created for each Media Component providing predefined operations for the Media Component and skeletons for operations defined in custom interfaces (see Section 3).

Each Scene is mapped to an ActionScript class containing the Entry and Exit Operations defined in the model. The Exit Operations contain the code for the navigation between Scenes as defined by the transitions in the Scene Model. Additionally, each Scene is mapped to a Flash document containing the Scene's user interface. For the user interface, each AIO is mapped to a corresponding widget in the Flash document and an associated ActionScript class containing event listeners. For Media Instances, an instance of the generated Media Component is placed on the user interface. All instances on the user interface have a name by which they can be accessed from the code in the Scene's ActionScript class. Sensors are implemented by corresponding code in the Scene's ActionScript class, e.g., a Collision Sensor is implemented by an operation which tests whether two visual objects overlap each other on the screen. The Interaction Model is mapped to corresponding ActionScript code in the Scene.

It is possible to directly open the generated code skeletons in the Flash authoring tool. Fig. 7 shows a screenshot of the generated skeleton for the scene Game in the Flash authoring tool. It shows the user interface elements and the placeholders for Media Components (represented by simple rectangles) generated according to the MML model from Fig. 4. The application can also be directly executed to test the navigation between the generated Scenes.

To finalize the application, the developers have to complete the ActionScript code, mainly the bodies of the Domain Class operations, as those are not specified in MML. The media designers need to fill out the placeholders generated for the Media Components using the whole functionality of the authoring tool. The generated user interface can also be freely edited, arranged, and adapted in the tool using all its visual functionality (e.g., in Fig. 7 a button is resized). However, all relationships between the different application parts – like between an AIO and its Domain Object, its event handling code, and its Scene – are generated from the model. Moreover, the generated code is consistent and well-structured (using, e.g., design patterns, see [21, 19]). In this way, the advantages of both – 1) visual design of media and user interfaces using established authoring tools and 2) systematic development of well-structured application using model – are combined.

9   Conclusion and Outlook

In this chapter, we presented MML, a modeling language for interactive multimedia applications, and an associated model-driven development approach. It targets the needs for a systematic development process considering the characteristics of interactive multimedia user interfaces.

With respect to the main challenges for multimedia development from Section 1, we address the interdisciplinary development by integrating software design, user interface design, *and* media design into a single consistent modeling language. The MML models thus act as a kind of contract between the different developer groups. As discussed in Section 2, to our knowledge, none of the existing modeling languages covers all of these three aspects so far.

In particular, we show that modeling interactive multimedia requires new concepts like different abstraction layers (Media Components, Media Artifacts, and Media Instances) and modeling the (abstract) inner structure of Media Components. MML also demonstrates how to integrate these concepts into a consistent modeling approach. However, the general multimedia-specific concepts can also be used to extend other existing modeling approaches with multimedia support.

The need for visual, artistic design is addressed by integrating authoring tools through generation of code skeletons which can be directly loaded and processed within established professional authoring tools like Flash. This concept has been generalized beyond multimedia and Flash [22] and is an important aspect in practice as mature visual tool support is usually strongly important for user interface designers and media designers.

To validate the language as far as possible, it has been applied three times in a practical graduate course where students develop interactive Flash/ActionScript applications over three months in teams of four to seven students each. The developed applications were multi-player blockout games, multi-player jump and run games, and multi-player minigolf games. In addition, there were three student projects were a student developed a small or medium-size Flash/ActionScript application for a third party customer using MML. These were 1) an interactive multimedia application for a hairdresser, 2) an interactive visual help system for a professional customer relationship management system, and 3) an authoring tool for creating commercial interactive learning systems. In these cases, the final implementations made extensive usage of the code generated from the language. Some other kinds of applications have been created and implemented prototypically using MML, including a simple navigation system and a media player application. Although this validation can not provide quantitative evidence, it strongly contributed to revisions which lead to the version of the language as presented here.

For future work, it seems beneficial to combine the elaborated concepts with those from other modeling approaches, like mobile applications, context-sensitivity for multimedia user interfaces in ambient environments, or concepts from Web Engineering for Rich Internet Applications.

References

1. Van den Bergh, J.: High-level user interface models for model-driven design of context-sensitive user interfaces. Ph.d. thesis, Hasselt University, Diepenbeek, Belgium (2006)
2. Boll, S.: Zyx – towards flexible multimedia document models for reuse and adaptation. Phd, Vienna University of Technology, Vienna, Austria (2001)
3. Bulterman, D.C.A., Hardman, L.: Structured multimedia authoring. ACM Trans. Multimedia Comput. Commun. Appl. 1(1), 89–109 (2005), DOI
   `http://doi.acm.org/10.1145/1047936.1047943`
4. Calvary, G., Coutaz, J., Thevenin, D., Limbourg, Q., Souchon, N., Bouillon, L., Florins, M., Vanderdonckt, J.: Plasticity of user interfaces: A revised reference framework. In: Pribeanu, C., Vanderdonckt, J. (eds.) TAMODIA, pp. 127–134. INFOREC Publishing House, Bucharest (2002)
5. Carughi, G.T., Comai, S., Bozzon, A., Fraternali, P.: Modeling distributed events in data-intensive rich internet applications. In: Benatallah, B., Casati, F., Georgakopoulos, D., Bartolini, C., Sadiq, W., Godart, C. (eds.) WISE 2007. LNCS, vol. 4831, pp. 593–602. Springer, Heidelberg (2007)
6. Engels, G., Sauer, S.: Object-oriented Modeling of Multimedia Applications. In: Chang, S.K. (ed.) Handbook of Software Engineering and Knowledge Engineering, vol. 2, pp. 21–53. World Scientific, Singapore (2002)
7. Hannington, A., Reed, K.: Factors in multimedia project and process management–australian survey findings. In: ASWEC 2007: Proceedings of the 2007 Australian Software Engineering Conference, pp. 379–388. IEEE Computer Society, Washington (2007), DOI `http://dx.doi.org/10.1109/ASWEC.2007.22`
8. Hardman, L., Worring, M., Bulterman, D.C.A.: Integrating the amsterdam hypermedia model with the standard reference model for intelligent multimedia presentation systems. Comput. Stand. Interfaces 18(6-7), 497–507 (1997), DOI
   `http://dx.doi.org/10.1016/S0920-54899700014-7`
9. Hirakawa, M.: Do software engineers like multimedia? In: IEEE International Conference on Multimedia Computing and Systems, June 7-11, vol. 1, pp. 85–90 (1999), doi:10.1109/MMCS.1999.779125
10. Hoogeveen, M.: Towards a theory of the effectiveness of multimedia systems. International Journal of Human Computer Interaction 9(2), 151–168 (1997)
11. Kappel, G., Pröll, B., Reich, S., Retschitzegger, W. (eds.): Web Engineering - The Discipline of Systematic Development of Web Applications. John Wiley & Sons, Chichester (2006)

12. Lang, M., Fitzgerald, B.: New branches, old roots: A study of methods and techniques in web/hypermedia systems design. Information Systems Management 23(3), 62–74 (2006), DOI 10.1201/1078.10580530/46108.23.3.20060601/93708.7
13. Luyten, K.: Dynamic user interface generation for mobile and embedded systems with model-based user interface development. Ph.d. thesis, Transnationale Universiteit Limburg, Diepenbeek, Belgium (2004)
14. Object Management Group: OMG Unified Modeling Language (OMG UML), Superstructure, V2.2, Formal/2009-02-02 (2009)
15. Osswald, K.: Konzeptmanagement - Interaktive Medien - Interdisziplinäre Projekte. Springer, Berlin (2003)
16. Paternò, F.: Model-Based Design and Evaluation of Interactive Applications. Springer, London (1999)
17. Pleuß, A.: MML: A language for modeling interactive multimedia applications. In: ISM 2005, pp. 465–473. IEEE Computer Society, Los Alamitos (2005)
18. Pleuß, A.: Modeling the user interface of multimedia applications. In: Briand, L.C., Williams, C. (eds.) MoDELS 2005. LNCS, vol. 3713, pp. 676–690. Springer, Heidelberg (2005)
19. Pleuss, A.: Model-driven development of interactive multimedia applications. Ph.D. thesis, University of Munich, Munich, Germany (2009)
20. Pleuss, A., Botterweck, G., Hussmann, H.: Modeling advanced concepts of interactive multimedia applications. In: Proc. IEEE Symposium on Visual Languages and Human-Centric Computing VL/HCC 2009, pp. 31–38 (2009), doi:10.1109/VLHCC.2009.5295305
21. Pleuß, A., Hußmann, H.: Integrating authoring tools into model-driven development of interactive multimedia applications. In: Jacko, J.A. (ed.) HCI 2007. LNCS, vol. 4550, pp. 1168–1177. Springer, Heidelberg (2007)
22. Pleuss, A., Vitzthum, A., Hussmann, H.: Integrating heterogeneous tools into model-centric development of interactive applications. In: Engels, G., Opdyke, B., Schmidt, D.C., Weil, F. (eds.) MODELS 2007. LNCS, vol. 4735, pp. 241–255. Springer, Heidelberg (2007)
23. Preciado, J., Linaje, M., Morales-Chaparro, R., Sanchez-Figueroa, F., Zhang, G., Kroiss, C., Koch, N.: Designing rich internet applications combining uwe and rux-method. In: Proc. Eighth International Conference on Web Engineering, ICWE 2008, pp. 148–154 (2008), doi:10.1109/ICWE.2008.26
24. Szekely, P.A.: Retrospective and challenges for model-based interface development. In: Bodart, F., Vanderdonckt, J. (eds.) DSV-IS, pp. 1–27. Springer, Heidelberg (1996)
25. Urbieta, M., Urbieta, M., Rossi, G., Ginzburg, J., Schwabe, D.: Designing the interface of rich internet applications. In: Rossi, G. (ed.) Proc. Latin American Web Congress LA-WEB 2007, pp. 144–153 (2007), doi:10.1109/LAWEB.2007.4383169
26. Villard, L., Roisin, C., Layaïda, N.: An XML-based multimedia document processing model for content adaptation. In: King, P., Munson, E.V. (eds.) PODDP 2000 and DDEP 2000. LNCS, vol. 2023, pp. 104–119. Springer, Heidelberg (2004)
27. Vitzthum, A.: Entwicklungsunterstützung für interaktive 3d-anwendungen. Ph.D. thesis, University of Munich, Munich, Germany (2008)

Taking Advantage of Model-Driven Engineering Foundations for Mixed Interaction Design

Guillaume Gauffre and Emmanuel Dubois

Abstract. New forms of interactive systems, hereafter referred to as Mixed Interactive Systems (MIS), are based on the use of physical artefacts present in the environment. Mixing the digital and physical worlds affects the development of interactive systems, especially from the point of view of the design resources which need to express new dimensions. Consequently, there is a crucial need to clearly describe the content and utility of the recent models associated to these new interaction forms. Based on existing initiatives in the field of HCI, this chapter first highlights the interest of using a Model-Driven Engineering (MDE) approach for the design of MIS. Then, this chapter retraces the application of a MDE approach on a specific Mixed Interaction design resource. The resulted contribution is a motivated, explicit, complete and standardized definition of the ASUR model, a model for mixed interaction design. This definition constitutes a basis to promote the use of this model, to support its diffusion and to derive design tools from this model. The model-driven development of a flexible ASUR editor is finally introduced, thus facilitating the insertion of model extensions and articulations.

1 Introduction

From the birth of Augmented Reality systems [1] to the expression of Tangible Bits [2], through the proposition of Ubiquitous Computing [3], new interaction forms have been explored and have now started to integrate some common interactive spaces. Indeed research works that previously targeted specific, very demanding and restrictive application domains now apply to arts, knowledge transmission, communication, sale, etc., thus demonstrating their potentials [4]. Through a tight combination of physical and digital artefacts, or by having "Tangible Bits" becoming a reality, such interaction forms offer advantages: technology disappearance, better appropriation of concepts, low-learning phases, full-body involvement, large and complex motions, mobile situations, etc.

These potential benefits are in line with design philosophies coming from ecological design [5] and the definition of "calm technologies" [6]. In return, resulting interactions, which merge physical and digital worlds, must take into account the dimensions and the content of the physical environment: designing Tangible User

Guillaume Gauffre · Emmanuel Dubois
University of Toulouse – Tarbes, IRIT
31062 Toulouse Cedex 9, France
e-mail: {Guillaume.Gauffre,Emmanuel.Dubois}@irit.fr

H. Hussmann et al. (Eds.): MDD of Advanced User Interfaces, SCI 340, pp. 219–240.
springerlink.com   © Springer-Verlag Berlin Heidelberg 2011

Interfaces has to deal with the shape of the physical objects and the way they are manipulated or used to have an impact on digital data; with Augmented Reality systems, designers must handle the accuracy and the adequacy of the superimposition of digital data on the physical world; ubiquitous systems can integrate numerous sensors and their location and range are major concerns of the design, etc. Therefore, the design of these systems, hereafter referred to as Mixed Interactive Systems (MIS), has to take into account some specific dimensions and thus requires design resources able to manage them. To explore and better understand these specificities, two approaches coexist.

On the one hand, part of the HCI community is making great **technological advances**: many MIS prototypes are developed from scratch, thus solving technical issues, revealing and illustrating new possibilities. On the other hand, another branch of the community is focusing on **abstract approaches** for the design of these systems: technologies' independent design reasoning is thus promoted. The elicitation of such abstract models and taxonomies now enables the analysis and comparison of different forms of mixed interaction, and also contributes to structure and stimulate their design. However, numerous approaches adopt different points of view [4], tend to overlap and remain difficult to select, understand and use appropriately for none experts.

Practically, informal approaches, promoting participatory design and the use of scenarii or low-fi prototypes, are commonly adopted for the design of mixed interaction. But the gap remaining between a technological implementation and ideas or solutions informally expressed at the end of participatory design sessions is huge, thus requiring full expertise and experience to implement these systems. Therefore, structured and formalized expressions of design choices would help the transition to subsequent steps of the development: as a consequence using one of the above mentioned abstract approaches must be facilitated and no longer limited to expert. Concretely, their **content and syntax** must be made unambiguous and clearer to be used by none expert and increase their diffusion; their **role or purpose** must be clarified to express which aspects of the system can be described through the model; finally, their **range** has to be explained to facilitate their comparison and the selection of the most appropriate design resources, according to the design phase or specific facet of the system.

In this chapter, we adopt a Model-Driven Engineering (MDE) approach to make the ASUR model [7], a MIS-specific design model, compliant with these requirements. Indeed, recent developments in MDE demonstrated that MDE is a powerful approach to clearly describe the content and utility of models and their combination. The goal of this chapter is therefore to ease the understanding, visibility and diffusion of the ASUR model, and to demonstrate the benefit of MDE as a vector to reach these objectives.

The first section reviews the evolution of the use and content of models in HCI, then focuses on specific models, dedicated to advanced forms of User Interfaces. Given the complex nature of this domain, one unique model cannot be sufficient: a more global approach is required. Based on existing initiatives performed in HCI, we then highlight the interests of using Model Driven Engineering for the Design of Advanced User Interfaces. The second section introduces the ASUR metamodel, the corner stone of MDE approaches: the metamodel construct has been thought to promote and take advantage of the potential MDE benefits identified in the first section. All along the introduction of the metamodel, illustrations are provided on the design of a concrete system. Finally, the third section describes the way the metamodel was used to provide a tool enabling the management of ASUR models and states perspectives with regards to other modelling tools and resources.

2 Model-Based Design of Mixed Interactive Systems

The use of models in HCI is based on advances related to software engineering. This has resulted in the development of several models, expressing different specificities of interactive software engineering. However, with the emergence of new software technologies, such as component and services, light multiplatform systems, etc., these initial models are no longer discriminatory nor sufficiently helpful: additional models are required to more specifically support the design of interactive systems regardless of technological aspects.

This software engineering first influence has been complemented with cognitive and psychological considerations. For example, the action theory [8] describes the different steps of the input and output interaction and the associated users' capabilities: this layer-based description is central to the decomposition of an interaction modality as proposed in [9, 10]. Similarly, the interaction according to Arch [11] has a physical, a logical and a conceptual facet, the last one being in charge of the dialogue operated between the system and the users: this encourages the use of specific models for each aspect of the interaction, such as Statecharts or Petri nets to describe the interaction dialogue, hierarchical task models to represent links with users 'activity modelling, etc.

Finally, the development of interactive situations also triggered the apparition of new models. Models like GOMS [12], MVC [13] or ICO [14] were initially proposed and appeared to be useful to express the evolutions related to capabilities of the system-side of an interactive system (functional behaviour, rendering, metaphors, etc.). Current evolutions are now focusing on dimensions related to the user-side of an interactive system (physical environment, multimodality, ubiquity): specific models, that we are calling "interaction models", are thus required to cover the multiple facets of tactile input, direct manipulation, multimodal interaction and more recently mixed interactive systems (MIS) (see Fig. 1).

Fig. 1 From system-side enhancement to user-side enhancement of interaction capacities

MIS is one of the most recent forms of interactive systems: MIS takes advantage of the combination of the physical and digital worlds. In this context, the spaces and the elements that constitute an interactive situation have multiple scales, characteristics and roles; during design, the physicality of the interaction and the coupling of digital and physical elements therefore require a new set of models that recent works in MIS have explored.

2.1 Mixed Interaction Models

Among the works exploring the domain of MIS, many terms are used like pervasive, ambient or "everyware". Works identified as Tangible User Interfaces (TUI), Ubiquitous computing and Mixed or Augmented Reality, focus more particularly on the interaction design. Considering different but complementary aspects, they brought several interaction models. TUI emphasizes the physical artefacts and their association with digital elements through the MCRit model [15], the TAC model [16] and Fishkin [17] or Hornecker [18] taxonomies. Ubiquitous computing primarily addresses the notions of contextual data and technical environments, and generally adopts a software point of view as with UCM [19]. Mixed Reality describes an interactive space by focusing on the amount of digital and physical artefacts and qualifying their integration and relationships, as proposed by Trevisan [20]. Finally, these different aspects are also captured by models drawing an overview of the interaction with a MIS (e.g., RBI [21], MIM [22], ASUR [7]) or describing the underlying software required (e.g. FIIA [23]). Without being exhaustive, models mentioned in this section illustrate the interest of researchers in MIS on the use of models. The following sections extract the major dimensions covered by MIS models as well as the major capabilities they offer.

MIS Models' Dimensions. The review of these models led to a list of seven major dimensions that characterize MIS and that prevail during interaction design. Each dimension is totally covered ($\checkmark$), partially covered (p) or not addressed ($\times$) by the different models previously mentioned. Table 1 summarizes this characterization.

Description of entities. As they involve physical and digital entities, MIS models often describe the different entities involved during the interaction. Characterized by their nature (physical or digital, possibly mixed in MIM), their physical dimensions can be further characterized (e.g., TAC focus on physical entities), as well as the role played by digital entities (e.g., ASUR distinctions made between three forms of digital entities).

Physical relationships. The major originality of MIS is the insertion of physical entity in the user's interaction with the system. As their shapes and positions influence the interaction, expressing the physical relationships between them and the user is particularly relevant (e.g., TAC description of spatial constraints).

Digital-physical coupling. With MIS, the main objective is to associate digital and physical artefacts to get the best of their coupling. The appropriateness of the coupling can be based on their respective characteristics (e.g., Fishkin. Metaphors and MCRit tangible and intangible representations).

Interaction modalities description. MIS involves various and new forms of sensors and effectors, thus offering unusual input and output modalities. Among the models covering this dimension, some models pay a particular attention to the characterization of these modalities (e.g., ASUR and MIM), while others are limited to a list of devices (e.g., UCM), or a description of the manipulation types (e.g., Hornecker).

Context involvement. This difficult part aims at providing the clearest definition of the interaction context, and listing the elements not directly implied in the interaction. Since there is not a single description language, this element is not precisely characterized and is often limited to written document.

Actions triggering. Most of the models analyzed adopt static points of view on the interaction. However, they embed some elements used to describe the essential parts of the dynamics of the interaction (e.g., impact of an action on the system).

Interaction spaces. As the physical elements and space take importance with MIS, some models pay attention to it, to identify and characterize spaces (e.g., FIIA and Trevisan description of interaction spaces and their relationships).

Table 1 Models' coverage of MIS design dimensions

Models \ Characteristics	MCRit	TAC	Fishkin	Hornecker.	UCM	Trev.	RBI	MIM	ASUR	FIIA
Entities involved	x	p	x	x	✓	✓	x	✓	✓	✓
P/D coupling	✓	✓	p	p	x	x	x	✓	✓	x
Modalities description	x	x	x	p	p	x	p	✓	✓	p
Context	x	x	x	x	✓	x	✓	x	x	x
Physical relationships	x	✓	✓	✓	✓	✓	x	x	✓	x
Triggers	x	✓	x	x	✓	x	x	✓	p	✓
Shared spaces	x	x	x	p	x	p	x	x	x	✓

Models' Capabilities. Beyond the dimensions addressed by a model, the way it contributes to the development process is a second aspect of importance when dealing with models in MIS. We extracted four major types of capabilities that can be combined and proposed by MIS models. In the next paragraphs, we present these capabilities and mention models that offer them.

Conceptual framework. MCRit, RBI, Fishkins metaphors and Hornecker taxonomy highlight dimensions that are essential to understand such systems, some of their specificities and the challenges of their design. Their abstraction level presents the advantage to clearly indicate the benefits and issues of one design solution. They constitute frameworks for comparing and justifying design choices at high level, but do not precisely describe the structure and behaviour of the interaction, as opposed to what a notation could do.

Notational use. With TAC, MIM, ASUR, FIIA, UCM and Trevisan models, the authors provide notations to collect design results. MIM, FIIA, UCM and ASUR adopt graphical notations that depict the different facets of the user's interaction with digital entities and through physical ones. These graphical representations are also used to distinguish the different kinds of entities involved through iconographic representations. TAC and Trevisan model only provide textual notation, with tabular representations for TAC and n-uplet for the second one. In both cases, the precision of the collected design results can be adjusted according to the designer expertise with the model: the notation can be used with all or only a part of its attributes and elements.

Edition tools. Such tools are required to ease the manipulation and saving of models, representing existing MIS or design solutions: elements of the models are represented in menus or tools pallets, connexion rules can be embedded in the editors, attributes of the different elements can be listed, contextual help can be proposed, etc. According to our literature and web reviews, among the previously presented models only FIIA, ASUR and UCM provide such editing tools. An ASUR editor offers to create and edit models; but this editor does not include the latest updates of the model. UCM and FIIA also propose editors: they are directly connected to development environments.

Models' collaboration. This fourth models' capability consists in providing ways to link concepts of a model with other modelling resources or concepts of another model. Different ways of linking models have been explored and developed for different needs. For example, FIIA and UCM established links for implementation purposes; links have been defined between task model and the ASUR interaction model to promote the consistency between design choices expressed at the task analysis level and the interaction design level. Such links promote the collaboration between models and therefore contribute to increase the efficiency of the use of models: time spent to express the design decision in the form of a model constitutes the basis of subsequent steps of the design. However, frameworks to more easily define and operate such articulations must be developed: operating complex transformation cannot be efficiently performed by hand.

Outcomes of the Use of Models in MIS. The comparison of models' contents reveals the variety of dimensions and capabilities covered by a set of MIS models. It also highlights existing overlapping between them, thus illustrating the diversity and complexity of MIS. However the analysis is based on research papers, which do not necessarily reveal the whole aspects and details of the models. Research paper most often chose to emphasize specific considerations related to the model. As a result, it is difficult to get an entire view and understanding of these models, thus complicating the possibility to share them or position each one with regards to the other models. To overcome this limitation, a clear and standardized expression of the models is required to concisely express their objectives and content. Such a clarification would also allow a more comprehensive comparison of these resources and contribute to help designers in choosing the most appropriate one at different steps of the design process.

Furthermore, given the degree of maturity of MIS, additional models are still emerging. When proposing a new model that describes a specific aspect of a MIS, it seems rather hard to immediately provide all the capabilities identified in the previous section. Supporting the introduction of these capabilities into new models or facilitating the reuse of some of the already exiting capabilities would facilitate the introduction and use of new models in the domain of MIS.

In parallel to the evolution of the MIS domain, the contributions of the Model Driven Engineering (MDE) community are quickly developing and present some characteristics that are in line with the current needs and expectations of the MIS domain. The following section deeper analyses the benefits of MDE.

2.2 Model-Driven Engineering Benefits

MDE provides a framework to unify the different modelling technologies and to express the concepts necessary to their use and understanding [24]. It constitutes a development approach that takes advantage of descriptive and productive aspects of models. In particular MDE promotes the use and development of Domain-Specific Languages (DSL) that address specific design and development goals. DSLs use small and dedicated models to address a particular domain. This leads to the clear identification of multiple design dimensions in the domain, just as required in MIS. The corner stone of MDE approaches is the metamodel: a metamodel gives the opportunity to structure and document each model. Therefore, MDE also facilitates the understanding of the range of each model, the comparison of models, their articulation and diffusion.

The following sections highlight the potential of MDE with regards to MIS. These potentials are organized along the descriptive and productive supports offered by MDE. We then briefly review existing uses of these two aspects of MDE in the design of abstract user interfaces to motivate its applicability to MIS.

Descriptive Support. Models have the capability of describing specific aspects of a system. Rothenberg mentioned in **[25]** *"A model represents reality for the given purpose; the model is an abstraction of reality in the sense that it cannot represent all aspects of reality. This allows us to deal with the world in a simplified manner, avoiding the complexity, danger and irreversibility of reality."* In the case of MIS design, the concepts are innovative and unfamiliar. There is therefore a real need for a comprehensive presentation of these concepts to understand and manipulate them. MDE presents three potential benefits to support this first need:

- (B1: characterization) A metamodel contributes to **clearly identify and characterize** the different elements constituting a MIS. The grammar it defines will be closely adapted to the specific concepts of the domain. This is particularly required with MIS because they are complex systems involving many entities and there are many new systems that are hard to compare without a common solid reference language.
- (B2: documentation) The metamodel supports **documentation generation** of the design. For a given metamodel, different representations of a single model that conform to this metamodel, can easily be generated: XML/HTML/etc. documents can be produced as well as textual, graphical representations or structured web navigation. Given that designing MIS requires a multidisciplinary team, different representations are required to fit the abilities of each stakeholder and to facilitate its ability to understand the design. In addition, MIS models express unusual concepts that need to be well explained.

- (B3: evolution) MDE tools support the **evolution of a metamodel**. MDE facilitates further refinements and evolutions of a metamodel by enabling its rapid graphical edition and a clear decomposition of its constituting elements. This promotes a step by step definition of a metamodel. The domain of MIS is rich and complex and yet quite recent. Therefore it is still an open field that need further investigations which will raise additional design challenges and considerations. It is thus required to adapt, complement or further develop existing design models of MIS. Supporting this evolution is a crucial advantage for the domain.

These first set of benefits of MDE for the design of MIS contributes to the specification of the system by increasing the level of abstraction: better descriptions and analysis of this kind of systems are produced. A second set of benefits is driven from the ability of MDE to support the automation of some part of the development: this is the productive support of MDE.

Productive Support. Several models, expressing different considerations and/or related to different levels of abstraction, are most often required in a system development. This is especially true with MIS systems, which have to take into account device properties, available APIs, characteristics of physical artefacts, software structure, component definition, etc. MDE presents two major advantages to support these considerations:

- (B4: articulation) MDE offers tool-supports for model transformations that contribute to the **articulations of different design facets**. Early steps of a MIS design involve many different facets that need to be captured and understood: the manipulated domain objects, the resources of the environment, the users' abilities, the sequencing of the dialogue, etc. Through the use of transformations, one facet can be refined or can produce another one, even partially: for example, transformation can be used to ensure coherence between domain objects represented in task models and the corresponding interaction models.
- (B5: process) MDE also offers tool supported transformations to link models expressed at different abstraction levels of the development. This second form of transformation supports the **progression along the different development steps**. It leads to the articulation of design and implementation resources, for example, interaction design models and software architecture models. Such links constitute a map of design resources involved for designing MIS with a detailed specification of their interlacing. This is crucial in MIS because it allows a designer to decompose the design problem into different steps related to MIS specificities (e.g., physicality, software architecture and modalities design).

This second set of benefits of MDE for the design of MIS corresponds to an increase of automation and coherence in MIS developments. It allows the combination of different points of view in the design of MIS and then, higher-level models can be transformed into lower level models. These subsequent transformations can automatically or semi-automatically lead to the generation of components assemblies or code generation.

Previous sections have illustrated how the use of MDE, in terms of descriptive and productive support, can be fruitful for MIS design: it contributes to better structure and thus better understand design aspects of MIS, it supports the articulation of complementary design considerations and provides design tools based on modelling standards. The following section illustrates existing uses of MDE approaches in the field of HCI.

MDE and Abstract User Interfaces Design. Benefits of the descriptive and productive supports of MDE have already been explored and illustrated in HCI: indeed some works propose means to describe part of the interaction and then to derive executable prototypes from it. Such works essentially consider Abstract User Interfaces models (AUI) in order to address multi-platforms implementations and the reuse of former developments.

For example, on one hand, PervML [26] is used for pervasive systems development: it enables the description of services constituting the system and their communications. On another hand, CUIML [27], MRIML [28], and APRIL [29] are models used inside development frameworks for Mixed Reality or Augmented Reality systems and focus on the description of the elements underlying the interaction (view/controller distinction, type of widgets, etc.); However, they are tightly linked to the technologies embedded into these frameworks. Finally, UsiXML [30] proposes a set of metamodels to describe AUI but limits the possible interaction forms. In comparison to the two first sets of models presented above, UsiXML also proposes task, user and platform description with links between each of them, in order to use models at runtime for context adaptation.

These approaches mainly focus on a support to the software development underlying the interaction, instead of the design of the interaction itself. In addition, they do not easily support the expression of aspects related to the physicality of the user's interaction with a MIS. Therefore, based on these promising initiatives, additional resources are required to fit the expectations and requirements of MIS design, based on MDE.

Previous sections have shown how interaction models for MIS design remain experimental, difficult to seize and how hard it is to capture and understand their range. In addition, most of these models are not associated with tools for editing, manipulating and transforming them; for those being equipped with such environment, modelling standards are not used: this restrains their use with external and complementary design aspects. Considering the benefits of MDE approaches and the need for standardized and structured resources for MIS design we chose to exploit the promising link between MIS design and MDE with the ASUR model. The goal is twofold: first, it aims to structure and provide an explicit description of the ASUR model and second, it aims at using MDE frameworks to create tools based on modelling standards.

Next section presents the proposed metamodel of ASUR, according to its latest evolution [31], and justifies parts of the structure adopted in the metamodel construct. Then, we detail how an editor has been derived from this metamodel thanks to MDE tools.

3 Definition of a MIS-Specific Metamodel

The ASUR model is intended to support the reasoning and design of MIS. ASUR particularly emphasizes the physicality of the interaction, the nature of the interaction modalities and the existence of several design facets. Considering the design dimensions of MIS and the need for a clear description to ease their understanding, a metamodel has been created for ASUR: this metamodel offers a high-level design resource, technology independent.

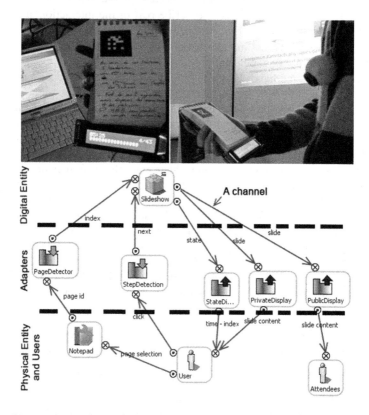

Fig. 2 The Notepad Assisted Slideshow prototype and its ASUR modelling

Among the current available metamodelling frameworks, the Ecore metametamodel [32] has been chosen to express the ASUR metamodel. The following sections present and motivate the content and structure of this metamodel and illustrate the ASUR concepts on a prototype used for interacting with slideshow presentation systems: the Notepad Assisted Slideshow (see Fig. 2 - top). This prototype is based on the use of a notepad as "remote control" and feedback source: each page of this physical notepad is associated to one digital slide of the presentation. The speaker can thus write his own comments on the notepad and easily access to the corresponding slide. Furthermore, potential animation steps of each slide are controlled through user's tap on the notepad. The corresponding ASUR model (see Fig. 2 - bottom) involves three *physical entities* (notepad, user, attendees). One *digital entity*, the slideshow, is represented at the top of the model and *adapter entities*, bridging the physical and digital worlds, are positioned in the middle of the model representation. The arrows represent the *interaction channels*, supporting data transfer; they are linked to entities with *connectors* (circles). These different *ASUR elements* are detailed in the following sections.

3.1 Structural Elements of the Interaction

To depict the interaction between two entities, such as the interaction between the *User* and the R_{Tool} "notepad" (see Fig. 2 - bottom), several concepts of the meta-model are required (see Fig. 3). Each concept, detailed in the following subsections, represents, describes and characterizes different elements of the interaction: the entities involved, the transmitted information, the way the emitter produces information and the way the receiver senses the information. These concepts are represented with distinct classes in the metamodel and each class displays its own attributes. This structure thus reinforces the visibility of the different forms of components involved in a MIS and their description. This is in line with the Benefit "B1: characterization" of use of MDE.

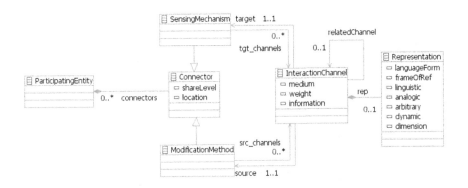

Fig. 3 Participating Entity, Connector, Interaction Channel and Representation elements

Participating Entities. The first main element, *participating entity (PE)* (see Fig. 3 - left), is used to represent an entity involved in the interaction; it can be physical or digital. Specific physical entities, *Adapters*, are used to interlace digital and physical worlds. To represent the decomposition of this class in the metamodel, the concept of class inheritance is used between elements as described in Fig. 4; this implies the existence of several abstract classes (e.g., physical entity and digital entity) to refine the role of each entity.

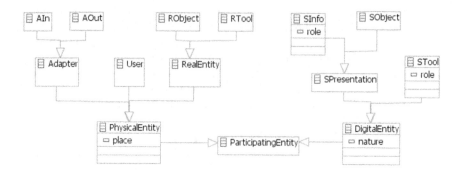

Fig. 4 Part of the metamodel describing Participating Entities

Interaction Channels. The second main element, *interaction channel (IC)* (see Fig. 3 - right), is used to represent information exchange between *Participating Entities*. This class of the metamodel contains two major attributes: *medium* (light, physical contact, infrared, air, etc.) and *information*. *Medium* describes the element carrying the data and *information* depicts the content and meaning, i.e. the concept to which is related the message carried on this *Interaction Channel*. In the fragment of the Notepad Assisted Slideshow illustrated on Fig. 5, the *Interaction Channel* between the "user" and the "notepad" transmits *information* related to a "page selection" and is based on "physical contact" as *medium*.

Representations. The third main element, *representation* (see Fig. 3 - right), is used to characterize the way the information is encoded on an Interaction Channel: it describes the elements that form the message carried along the interaction channel. The *representation* class of the metamodel refers to the *Interaction Channel* it is refining; it includes a list of attributes, which correspond to characteristics identified in ASUR and relevant to qualify an information flow. These attributes express the *language form* (how the elements are expressed), the *dimension* (2D, 3D, stereo ...), the *frame of reference* (point of view on the scene) and four Bernsen properties - *linguistic, analogical, arbitrary* and *dynamic*. These attributes can be progressively defined as the design of the system becomes more precise. In the fragment of the Notepad Assisted Slideshow illustrated on Fig. 5, the *representation* is named "pages folding" and characterized by the *language form* "move".

As only one *representation* may be associated to one *Interaction Channel*, all of its attributes could be part of the *Interaction Channel* class. But we considered the *representation* as an independent class in the metamodel, because this distinction clearly marks the difference between the coding scheme of the information carried (*representation* class) and the properties of a channel expressed in the *Interaction Channel* class. The characterization of a *representation* can therefore be reused for refining another *Interaction Channel*, either in another model or between two other entities of the same model. It thus promotes the reuse of design solutions and facilitates the evaluation of coherence among the forms of the data exchanges in a given model. This separation also allows further evolution of the *representation* that might need to include new characteristics, to refine some of them, or to introduce new kind of *representations* that would, for example, be specific to physical, visual or digital *mediums*. This is in line with the benefit "B3: evolution" of MDE and also facilitates the use of other models, as suggested by the benefit "B4: articulation".

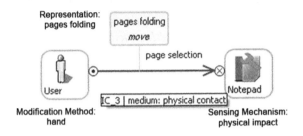

Fig. 5 Interaction between two Participating Entities

Sensing Mechanisms, Modification Methods and Connectors. The fourth main element of the metamodel is a set of three classes. Indeed, to complete the description of an information flow with ASUR, the source (emitter) and the target (addressee) of the *interaction channel* have to be characterized. Such elements are described in the metamodel respectively with the *modification method* to affect a medium used by an *Interaction Channel* and, the *sensing mechanism* for listening to the medium.

Each *Interaction Channel* thus includes a reference to one *sensing mechanism* and one *modification method*. These two anchors inherit from the class *connector* which includes two attributes (see Fig. 3 - left). *Share Level* indicates how many elements can be connected on this connectors. The *location* attribute depicts where the information is perceived (*sensing mechanism*) or affected (*modification method*). Considering the fragment of the Notepad Assisted Slideshow illustrated on Fig. 5, the "hand" of the user is the *modification method* which affects the channel; resulted modifications on this channel are captured through a "physical impact" (*sensing mechanism*) on the "Notepad".

The *connectors* thus complete the description of modalities. They also allow expressing and exploring the potential multimodal input/output capabilities of a *Participating Entity*: indeed, several *connectors* can compose a *Participating Entity* and can also be linked to several *Interaction Channels*. In that way, each connector describes one communicating faculty of a *Participating Entity*. It is therefore possible to identify a set of reusable *connectors*: human's *sensing mechanisms* (sensory organs - eye, ear, etc. -, skin), or APIs in the case of adapters.

3.2 Additional Design Considerations

With the introduction in ASUR of characteristics to better describe the physicality of the interaction [31], the notion of *interaction groups* has also been introduced.

Groups are intended to support the study of one property or specific design issue and to identify parts of the ASUR model required or involved in this consideration. Therefore, each *interaction group* can be considered as a specific dimension for analyzing a MIS design solution. For example, a group may enclose entities and channels related to a given feedback: this group will foster the design team to consider all the elements of the group simultaneously when reasoning about this feedback design. Given this informal definition of an interaction group and the core elements of the metamodel, *interaction groups* clearly appear as a composition of *Participating Entities* and *Interaction Channels*.

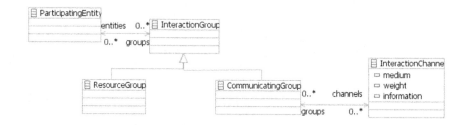

Fig. 6 Interaction Group composition

We further investigate this concept by identifying two forms of groups: *resource groups*, gathering *Participating Entities* only, and *communicating groups* gathering *Participating Entities* and *Interaction Channels* (see Fig. 6). In the metamodels, both forms of *communication groups* inherit from the *interaction group* superclass that references *Participating Entities*.

Resource Groups. This first kind of group, called *Resource Group*, contains *Participating Entities* only. A *resource group* referencing only *digital entities* is out of scope of this chapter, but might support the identification of constraints between digital elements: a link of composition or distribution constraints are such examples. Two other *resource groups* are presented and illustrated in Fig. 7.

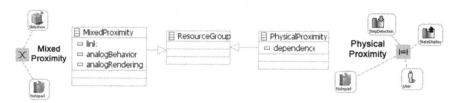

Fig. 7 Resource Groups and their attributes, illustrated on the case study

Physical proximity. Among the two *resource groups* defined in ASUR (see Fig. 7), the *physical proximity* group exclusively includes *physical entities*. This group is used to express the fact that several *Participating Entities* are grouped in the same physical location: they either compose a unique object or they are physically close during the user's interaction with the MIS. The attribute *dependence* specifies the kind of proximity the *Participating Entities* are sharing (close to each others, included in, one over the other, etc.).

Mixed proximity. This group contains *physical* and *digital entities* which are respectively physical and digital representations of the same concept involved in the task. The representation of this group in the metamodel is a class that contains three attributes: (1) the *link* can be established statically or dynamically during the interaction; (2) there can be an analogy between the *behaviour* of all entities of this group or not, and (3) there can be an analogy between the *appearance* of all entities or not.

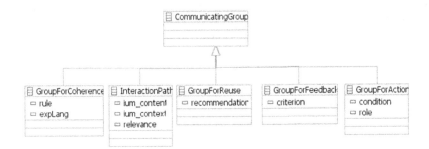

Fig. 8 Communicating groups and their attributes

Communicating Groups. This second kind of group, *Communicating Group* (see Fig. 8), also highlights concerns or specific issues to be explored when designing an interactive solution. It is complementary to the *Resource Groups* as it more specifically focuses on the way the interaction occurs and not only on the entities involved. Therefore, the class representing *Communicating Groups* also references *Interaction Channels* and may contain attributes. Based on reported experiences with the ASUR model, the metamodel currently includes five useful *Communicating Groups*. We briefly present them in the following paragraphs.

Interaction path. This group highlights elements of the models required to perform a specific part of the modelled task. *IUM-content* and *IUM-context* respectively express what the user is intending to perform and the context in which this can be performed.

Group for action. This group expresses a causal relation between *Participating Entities* of the model and a transfer of information. A *condition* will trigger the execution of the predefined *role* of the group.

Group for reuse. This group depicts an ASUR pattern, as defined in [7]. Such patterns can be stored for further reuse in other models. A *recommendation*, such as ergonomic criteria, can be added to precise the most suitable situations in which to use it.

Group for coherence. This group federates elements of the model that must be considered to evaluate a property on the model, such as the continuity of the interaction [2]. Each property to assess is an instance of this group. The *rule* expressed in the language *expLang* describes how the property is assessed.

Group for feedback. This last group reinforces the importance of a specific coupling between inputs and outputs with a MIS.

Resource Groups and Communication Groups are original elements considered in a model. They both highlight design considerations, without requiring an immediate focus on it: they can be marked but treated later in the process which is in line with the benefit "B5: process". In addition, the concept of group supports the use of complementary languages or models to better address these considerations (e.g., *expLang* may refer to another metamodel): this is in line with the benefit "B4: articulation". Finally, other kinds of *interaction groups* may be needed in the future. The structure of the metamodel enables to capture and characterize them easily: it is only required to add a class for each group, specify attributes and add references to existing elements of the metamodels. This is in line with the benefit "B3: evolution".

Based on this metamodel, it is now easier to correctly and entirely use the ASUR model for designing MIS. The specific point of view offered on the interaction as well as the elements taking part in a MIS, the way they interact and additional complementary facets are clearly documented and separated from each other. The metamodel itself offers a descriptive support to this design resource, structured with Ecore standards, and thus easing its understanding and promoting its diffusion. Increasing its use also rely on the existence of tools for manipulating ASUR models. Thanks to the efforts of the MDE community, such environments can be derived from the metamodel; it thus contributes to a rapid development of a tool and the possibility to embed "grammar" constraints in the tool itself. The next section presents the tool that has been derived using the frameworks of the Eclipse Modelling Project (EMP) [32].

4 Model-Driven Tools Derivation

Facilitating the use of a model, necessarily requires a clear documentation but also takes large advantage of a computer assisted support for its use. We first review existing environments for manipulating some of the already mentioned models and highlight the benefits of MDE for creating such an environment. We finally present GuideMe, an ASUR editor based on the metamodel previously introduced.

4.1 Existing Tools for Manipulating Models of MIS

In the specific domain of MIS, model-based design tools that focus on the interaction, independently of implementation resources, are not common. Actually, the rare ones are not based on a metamodel expressed with MDE standards and therefore, they cannot be updated according to the evolutions of the metamodels.

However, tools have been created for editing models previously introduced like MRIML [27], CUIML [28] or APRIL [29]. Standard functionalities of these editors enable the creation and modification of models and their storage as XML documents. But validation of models, storage with different technologies and export to different notations are not possible.

Efficient tools for rapid-prototyping have been proposed, too, like d.tools [33] or Artect [34]. Their functionalities offer to directly run a prototype from the current model designed, with adjustments of the software components at run-time. But their choice of developing the entire design environment without considering the potential need for collaboration with other models and technologies make them difficult to use and to extend: for example, proprietary software architecture may imply difficulties to use it on different platforms.

Finally, tools based on TopCased to support the UsiXML metamodel manipulation [30] give the possibility of creating models, validating and linking them with other tools. Developed in the context of critical applications and systems development, such an approach is more open to interconnection with other models and design or implementation resources.

Given that the design of MIS requires multiple resources and need to consider different facets, using standards and articulation facilities seem to be particularly adapted to the domain of MIS. Such facilities are supported by MDE tools based on the Eclipse Modelling Project (EMP). Indeed, EMP regroups efficient tools to create models editor that include the most common editors' functionalities. Furthermore, MDE tools can generate models editors on the basis of the definition of the corresponding metamodel, expressed in EMF with ECore; it results in a straightforward maintenance of the editor when the metamodel evolves. Moreover, the extension principles promoted by Eclipse facilitate the development of additional features (validation, export, etc.) on the basis of concepts and functionalities such as the notion of plugin. Therefore, even if existing tools have interesting functionalities, they do not offer the flexibility of those generated within EMP. Following this approach, the ASUR metamodel has been associated to an editor based on EMF and GMF for three main reasons: 1) the use of a Domain-Specific Language dedicated to mixed interaction design; 2) the perspective to support a development process based on the combined use of ASUR and other complementary metamodels; 3) the possibility to maintain these tools all along the evolution of ASUR, without having to pay attention to the development of the underlying framework (Eclipse) and constraints for supporting extensions.

4.2   Creation of a MIS-Specific Design Tool

The development of GuideMe [35] is based on the ASUR metamodel expressed with Ecore. It defines an Eclipse "feature" easily pluggable to any Eclipse environment thanks to its extension support. The core of the feature is generated with EMF, which produces two plugins in charge of manipulating the models. In addition, GMF is used to generate a third plugin that allows the graphical manipulation of the ASUR models. Following the MDE philosophy, GMF allows to define a graphical notation as a separate model. By mapping the Ecore elements constituting ASUR and the GMF notational elements, the framework generates almost automatically a specific plugin that will provide models creation and validation.

The resulting editor (see Fig. 9) creates ASUR model, expressed according to the XMI standard and thus easily shareable. Currently only one graphical representation is defined, i.e. one specific GMF plugin, but other ones can be easily developed to propose different visualisations of the ASUR models.

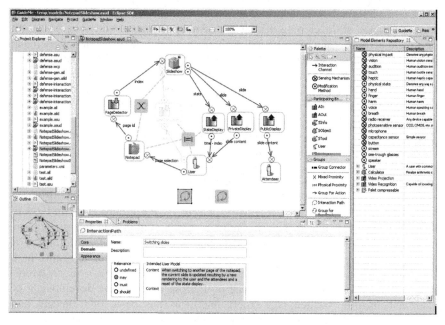

Fig. 9 ASUR model edition in GuideMe/Eclipse environment

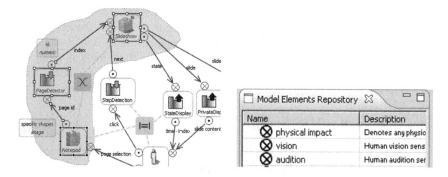

Fig. 10 Lasso selection tool and ASUR elements repository view

We developed additional tools based on model transformations to support the export to textual descriptions and HTML documents. Such functionalities are part of an extension that complements and modifies the default functionalities of GMF generated editors. This extension also contains a lasso-based selection facility to create ASUR groupings (see Fig. 10 - left), a panel for editing the attributes of

ASUR elements, with content proposals and operations on ASUR groupings (evaluation of rules for the Group for Coherence) and another panel to facilitate the reuse of existing ASUR elements stored in a repository (see Fig. 10 - right).

4.3 Design Features Additionally Required and Envisioned

The tool proposed remains in constant evolution because of the use of ASUR with other modelling resources. Therefore, additional features are required to edit other models and perform model-transformations. Currently, transformations between ASUR models, software architecture models and runtime environments dedicated to MIS are integrated into GuideMe [36].

Concerning the ASUR editor itself, its use in our research group allows to update its functionalities and to prepare the evaluation of both the ASUR notation and the editor's functionalities. If the existing functionalities require some evolutions to satisfy their uses and usability, other ones are also necessary to provide more efficiency when using models during design. The following evolutions will mainly focus on the management of several ASUR models, to easily create design alternatives and to compare or merge several ones. Another important perspective is to support the tracking of these evolutions along the design process. For that purpose, collaboration between the modelling resources used and models for design rationale is one solution considered.

As the works led around ASUR also imply informal approaches for design (coupling of ASUR and Focus-group), the modification of the interaction with GuideMe editor is also one of our major objectives. The goal is to enable collaboration between several designers around a more or less simplified version of the ASUR model, and with tabletop interactions for example. Configuring the level of details of the model provided to the stakeholders and the interactions offered to manipulate the editing environment will benefit from the facilities brought that MDE brings and that is now embedded into GuideMe.

5 Conclusions

Motivating the role of MDE in the context of the design of MIS and adopting a MDE approach to describe the ASUR design model for mixed interactive systems constitute the main contribution of this chapter. After reviewing the challenges of using design models in the context of MIS and some of the currently available models, this chapter highlighted how existing models are suffering from a lack of clear description and access. As a result, this chapter raised the need for the domain of MIS to ease model diffusion and use, as well as the need for an easier comparison between models of the domain. To contribute to this challenge, this chapter discussed how the MDE framework can be positively used to express the full definition of a metamodel dedicated to mixed interaction design. It resulted in an explicit description of the semantics and range of the ASUR model. Following the advances of MDE tools, this chapter finally introduced the way the metamodel has been used to create a pluggable and flexible editor to ASUR, a first step for its integration to different studies on the model-based development of MIS.

This work now opens perspectives to quantify and qualify the effects of using one given model during the design: such a structured reference can be used for supporting the comparison of models. It also constitutes a basis to clearly identify which aspects of which model are best suited to address which part of the complex design process of MIS: guidelines and prerogatives to the use of each model could then be identified. Finally, developing a detailed and clear breaking down of such models is also a first step toward the elicitation of complementary models for MIS developments.

References

[1] Caudell, T., Mizell, D.: Augmented reality: an application of heads-up display technology to manual manufacturing processes. In: Proc. of the Twenty Fifth Hawaii International Conference on System Science, pp. 659–669 (1992)

[2] Ishii, H., Ullmer, B.: Tangible bits: towards seamless interfaces between people, bits and atoms. In: Proc. of the ACM SIGCHI Conference on Human Factors in Computing Systems, pp. 234–241 (1997)

[3] Weiser, M.: The computer for the 21st century. In: Baecker, R.M., Grudin, J., Buston, W., Greenberg, S. (eds.) Human-Computer Interaction: Toward the Year 2000, 2nd edn. Morgan Kaufmann Publishers Inc., San Francisco (1995)

[4] Shaer, O., Hornecker, E.: Tangible User Interfaces: Past, Present, and Future Directions. Foundations and Trends in Human–Computer Interaction 3(1-2), 1–137 (2009)

[5] Gibson, J.J.: The Ecological Approach to Visual Perception. Lawrence Erlbaum Associates, Mahwah (1986)

[6] Weiser, M., Brown, J.S.: Designing calm technology. PowerGrid Journal 1(1), 75–85 (1996)

[7] Dubois, E., Gray, P., Nigay, L.: ASUR++: A Design Notation for Mobile Mixed Systems. Interacting with Computers 15(4), 497–520 (2003)

[8] Norman, D.A.: Cognitive engineering. In: Norman, D.A., Draper, S.W. (eds.) User centered system design. Lawrence Erlbaum Associates, Mahwah (1986)

[9] Foley, J.D., Dam, A.V.: Fundamentals of interactive computer graphics. Addison-Wesley Longman Publishing Co., Inc., Amsterdam (1982)

[10] Moran, T.P.: Command language grammar: a representation for the user interface of interactive computer systems. International Journal on Man-Machine Studies 15(1), 3–50 (1981)

[11] UIMS Workshop, A Metamodel for the Runtime Architecture of an Interactive System: the UIMS tool developers workshop. SIGCHI Bulletin 24(1), 32-37 (1992)

[12] Card, S.K., Moran, T.P., Newell, A.: The Psychology of Human-Computer Interaction. Lawrence Erlbaum, Mahwah (1983)

[13] Krasner, G.E., Pope, S.T.: A Cookbook for Using the Model-View-Controller User Interface Paradigm in Smalltalk-80. Journal of Object-Oriented Programming 1(3), 26–49 (1988)

[14] Bastide, R., Palanque, P.: A Visual and Formal Glue between Application and Interaction. Journal of Visual Languages and Computing 10(5), 481–507 (1999)

[15] Ullmer, B., Ishii, H.: Emerging frameworks for tangible user interfaces. IBM Systems Journal 39(3-4), 915–931 (2000)

[16] Shaer, O., Leland, N., Calvillo-Gamez, E.H., et al.: The TAC Paradigm: Specifying Tangible User Interfaces. Personal Ubiquitous Computing 8(5), 359–369 (2004)

[17] Fishkin, K.P.: A Taxonomy for and Analysis of Tangible Interfaces. Personal Ubiquitous Computing 8(5), 347–358 (2004)

[18] Hornecker, E., Buur, J.: Getting a grip on tangible interaction: a framework on physical space and social interaction. In: Proc. of the ACM Conference on Human Factors in Computing Systems CHI 2006, pp. 437–446 (2006)

[19] Blackstock, M., Lea, R., Krasic, C.: Toward Wide Area Interaction with Ubiquitous Computing Environments. In: Proc. of the First European Conference on Smart Sensing and Context, pp. 113–127 (2006)

[20] Trevisan, D.G., Vanderdonckt, J., Macq, B.: Designing Interaction Space for Mixed Reality Systems. In: Proc. of the International Workshop on Mixed Reality MIXER 2004, pp. 29–37 (2004)

[21] Jacob, R.J., Girouard, A., Hirshfield, L.M., Horn, M.S., Shaer, O., Solovey, E.T., Ziegelbaum, J.: Reality-Based Interaction: A Framework for Post-WIMP Interfaces. In: Proc. of the Twenty-Sixth Annual ACM SIGCHI Conference on Human Factors in Computing Systems CHI 2008, pp. 201–210 (2008)

[22] Coutrix, C., Nigay, L.: Mixed reality: a model of mixed interaction. In: Proc. of the ACM working Conference on Advanced Visual Interfaces AVI 2006, pp. 43–50 (2006)

[23] Wolfe, C., Graham, T.N., Phillips, W.G., Roy, B.: Fiia: user-centered development of adaptive groupware systems. In: Proc. of the ACM Symposium on Engineering Interactive Computing Systems, EICS 2009, pp. 275–284 (2009)

[24] Bezivin, J.: On the unification power of models. Software and System Modeling 4(2), 171–188 (2005)

[25] Rothenberg, J.: The Nature of Modeling. In: Widman, L.E., Loparo, K.A., Nielsen, N.R. (eds.) Artificial Intelligence, Simulation and Modeling. John Wiley & Sons, Inc., Chichester (1989)

[26] Muñoz, J., Pelechano, V.: Building a software factory for pervasive systems development. In: Pastor, Ó., Falcão e Cunha, J. (eds.) CAiSE 2005. LNCS, vol. 3520, pp. 342–356. Springer, Heidelberg (2005)

[27] Wittkaemper, M., Broll, W.: A Mixed Reality User Interface Description Language. In: Proc. of the International Conference on Computer Graphics and Interactive Techniques SIGGRAPH 2006 – Research poster, vol. 156 (2006)

[28] Sandor, C., Reicher, T.: CUIML: A Language for the Generation of Multimodal Human-Computer Interfaces. In: Proc. of the European UIML Conference, vol. 124 (2001)

[29] Ledermann, F., Schmalstieg, D.: APRIL: A high-level framework for creating Augmented Reality Presentations. In: Proc. of the IEEE International Conference on Virtual Reality, VR 2005, pp. 187–194 (2005)

[30] Limbourg, Q., Vanderdonckt, J., Michotte, B., Bouillon, L., López-Jaquero, V.: IXML: A language supporting multi-path development of user interfaces. In: Proc. of the Joint Working Conferences EHCI-DSVIS 2004, pp. 200–220 (2004)

[31] Dubois, E., Gray, P.: A Design-Oriented Information-Flow Refinement of the ASUR Interaction Model. In: Gulliksen, J., Harning, M.B., van der Veer, G.C., Wesson, J. (eds.) EIS 2007. LNCS, vol. 4940, pp. 465–482. Springer, Heidelberg (2008)

[32] Eclipse Foundation, Eclipse Modeling Project (2006), http://www.eclipse.org/modeling (accessed September 6, 2010)

[33] Hartmann, B., Klemmer, S.R., Bernstein, M., Abdula, L., Burr, B., Robinson-Mosher, A., Gee, J.: Reflective physical prototyping through integrated design, test, and analysis. In: Proc. of the 19th Annual ACM Symposium on User Interface Software and Technology, UIST 2006, pp. 299–308 (2006)

[34] Koleva, B., Egglestone, S.R., Schnädelbach, H., Glover, K., Greenhalgh, C., Rodden, T., Dade-Robertson, M.: Supporting the creation of hybrid museum experiences. In: Proceedings of the 27th International Conference on Human Factors in Computing Systems, CHI 2009, pp. 1973–1982 (2009)

[35] GuideMe, Editor of MIS specific models (2009),
     http://ihcs.irit.fr/guideme (accessed September 6, 2010)

[36] Gauffre, G., Charfi, S., Bortolaso, C., Bach, C., Dubois, E.: Developing Mixed Interactive Systems: A Model-Based Process for Generating and Managing Design Solutions. In: Dubois, E., Gray, P., Nigay, L. (eds.) The Engineering of Mixed Reality Systems. Springer Human Computer Interactions Series (2010)

T:XML: A Tool Supporting User Interface Model Transformation

Víctor López-Jaquero, Francisco Montero, and Pascual González

Abstract. Model driven development of user interfaces is based on the transformation of an abstract specification into the final user interface the user will interact with. The design of transformation rules to carry out this transformation process is a key issue in any model-driven user interface development approach. In this paper, we introduce T:XML, an integrated development environment for managing, creating and previewing transformation rules. The tool supports the specification of transformation rules by using a graphical notation that works on the basis of the transformation of the input model into a graph-based representation. T:XML allows the design and execution of transformation rules in an integrated development environment. Furthermore, the designer can also preview how the generated user interface looks like after the transformations have been applied. These previewing capabilities can be used to quickly create prototypes to discuss with the users in user-centered design methods.

1 Introduction

Using models to document the design of a user interface is not a novel approach. Nevertheless, using models just for documenting is not enough to tackle the challenges posed by the current situation in software development. Models are now supposed to drive the development as first order artifacts, as constructs of the user interface. This trend in user interface design has been pursued from the 90s in model-based user interface design community [19], but it is not until now that this technology is reaching a state mature enough to be widely adopted in industrial environments. This model-based user interface trend conforms to the general software development philosophy proposed by different organizations. Therefore, it supports the path towards a common technological ground for both business logic and user interface design.

A model can be as simple and informal as a paper prototype or as formal and complex as an algebraic representation. Using computable models, such as declarative models, supports using systematic approaches in the development of software, and user interface development is not an exception.

Víctor López-Jaquero · Francisco Montero · Pascual González
Laboratory of User Interfaces and Software Engineering (LoUISE)
Instituto de Investigación en Informática (I3A)
University of Castilla-La Mancha, 02071 – Albacete, Spain
e-mail: {victor,fmontero,pgonzalez}@dsi.uclm.es

H. Hussmann et al. (Eds.): MDD of Advanced User Interfaces, SCI 340, pp. 241–256.
springerlink.com

There are many variables that foster model driven approaches, and should prevent designers from using traditional approaches [11][22]: 1) Diversity of users: currently the profile of the users of software applications is shifting more and more towards a less advanced user profile. The traditional advanced user profile, usually even with some programming skills, has become a small percentage among the mass of users. 2) Richness of cultures: when an interactive application is going global, its user interface cannot remain the same for all languages, countries, and cultures. 3) Complexity of interaction devices and styles: there is a wide variety of interaction devices and styles to design to. 4) Heterogeneity of computing platforms: many different platforms are available, and they run different operating systems and have different capabilities. 5) Multiple target programming languages: depending on the platform the developer can choose what language to use during development, but it is not the case for many platforms. 6) Multiplicity of working environments: the devices are being used under different physical environmental conditions (light, noise, etc).

Taking into account all these variable parameters using traditional approaches for user interface design would require of different versions in order to couple with the many different parameter combinations that can arise. Nevertheless, creating several versions of the same application will easily result in version inconsistency and high monetary cost for maintenance.

Unfortunately, using model-driven approaches to user interface design is not perfect, and one of the main critics has been the claim that it lacks the required mechanisms to successfully imbue the model-driven design process with enough usability information. This is actually one of the main issues that still require more research efforts, although some solutions are starting to emerge. For instance, in [15] patterns at different levels of abstractions are proposed as a means to include design experience in model-driven approaches to produce more usable user interfaces.

Model-driven approaches to user interface design are based on the creation of different declarative models, staring with the more abstract ones (usually platform and computation independent) and transforming these models into more concrete ones until the user interface the user will interact with is generated.

In this paper, a tool to support the design of the transformation rules required to perform the model manipulations to generate a user interface is described. This tool is called T:XML. The paper is structured as follows. First, a description of the model-driven foundations underlying T:XML is provided for a better understanding of the tool. Next, a discussion of the different transformation approaches available in the literature is shown, to justify the transformation approach selected. T:XML is described in detail next, showing how it works and how it can be used. Finally, some conclusions and future work round up the paper.

2   User Interface Transformation Framework

When using a model-driven approach one first issue is to decide what models to use for the specification of the system. In T:XML we are currently supporting those models used in UsiXML [21]. A description of these models and their relationships can be found in [2].

The framework supported in the tool is described in [2] (see Fig. 1). In this framework the most abstract models are tasks and domain (concepts) models. These models are used for the generation of an abstract user interface independent from both modality and platform. Then, a concrete user interface is generated for each modality (but they are still platform independent). Lastly, the actual user interface (final user interface) is generated by using renderers for different platforms and languages.

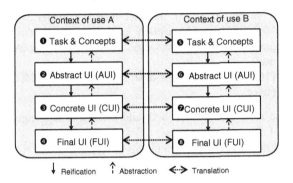

Fig. 1 User interface framework supported in T:XML

Three transformation operations are considered in the framework: 1) reification: a model can be reified into a more concrete model, 2) abstraction: a model can be abstracted into a more abstract model, and 3) translation: a model can be translated at the same level of abstraction to accommodate to changes in the context of use. These operations elaborate on the idea of having different entry points in the development process [8], i.e. the developer could start from an abstract mock-up of the user generated by using tools such as Guilayout++ [14].

As aforementioned, in the model-based approach to user interface design a set of models is used to specify the system. These models are transformed from the more abstract models to the more concrete ones. Nevertheless, a set of rules to specify how the models are transformed is required. These rules can be designed by using our tool T:XML, but what transformation approach should be used for the execution of the rules? In the next section, a review of current approaches is introduced, along with the motivation for our choice.

3 Transformation Approaches for Model-Driven Development

Many different approaches can be found in the literature regarding the transformation of models into other models or code. These different approaches are aimed at the development of general systems, but some of them are specific (or have been adapted) for their use in the development of user interfaces.

According to [3], the following generic approaches for model transformation are being used: (1) direct-manipulation approaches. (2) structure driven approach.

(3) relational approaches. (4) graph transformation based approaches. (5) template based approach. (6) operational approach. (7) hybrid approach. (8) other approaches: there are other approaches, such as XSLT (eXtensible Stylesheet Transformation Language) [24], that doesn't fall in any of the previous categories, but they are also commonly used in model transformation.

On the other hand, there are some approaches in user interface model transformation frameworks that adapt some of the aforementioned techniques. For instance, in [8], an adaptation of the graph transformation approach for the development of UIs can be found. In this approach, the user interface model expressed in terms of UsiXML [21] user interface description language is transformed by using the attributed graph grammars. To perform this transformation, the API provided by AGG tool [20] is used.

According to [16], there is a set of desirable features a model transformation approach should cover:

- Transformation rules: the approach should provide a language supporting the specification of transformation rules.
- Rule application control: a mechanism to control what rules to apply is required, since not every rule is applicable in a given context.
- Rule organization: reusing the transformations is a key feature. By reusing transformations we are not just reusing the time spent in creating the rules, but also the transformation rule design experience gathered during the development.
- Source-target relationship: it is the ability of the transformation approach to be able to generate several output models. This is important in user interface generation also, since usually several output files are required. For instance, if we would like to generate an HTML presentation out of a set of models, usually the formatting of the web page is done by providing a separate CSS (Cascade Style Sheet) file.
- Incrementally: because changes can occur both due to changes in the requirements and changes in the context of use, it is necessary to provide the ability to update an existing model.
- Directionality and tracing: ideally, the transformations should be bidirectional, and log of what transformations have been applied should be maintained. This feature supports a very important issue in transformation: undoing transformations.

These desirable features are applicable to user interface generation by model transformation.

Currently, the only approach covering all these features is QVT [17]. Nevertheless, the way QVT transformations are specified is complex, and it requires additional knowledge about OCL (Object Constraint Language). Furthermore, the application of the transformation using the current engines implies using a considerable amount of computing resources.

We have been using the graph transformation approach for some years now [8]. Although the way the transformations are specified if quite visual when using AGG tools [20], the amount of resources required for the transformation of an average user interface is somehow slow for its use in real-time environments. This is especially true when using mobile devices, whose capacities are much scarcer than desktop devices. Furthermore, some of these devices don't support the Java Runtime Environment required to run AGG engine. Graph transformation supports all the desirable features for a model transformation approach, except it does not support directionality and tracing.

On the other hand, XSLT is an approach very popular among software developers, and there are plenty of tools supporting both the design and the execution of XSLT. It provides a versatile tool to express the transformation rules. However, rule organization, rule application control and incrementally must be implemented by the developer. Furthermore, it does not support directionality and tracing.

4 Transformation Engine in T:XML

Because of our good experience in the design of transformation rules following the graph transformation approach, we have worked in the design of a transformation approach covering all our requirements. One requirement not usually considered in model transformation approaches is portability. Portability is paramount to user interface transformation, if run-time transformation should be supported. Thus, the transformation approach chosen must work for the different platforms the software was designed for, from desktop PCs to smartphones. This requirement can be overcome by using a client-server architecture, but it requires of a network connection constantly, that can eventually exhaust quickly the battery in portable devices.

Thus, in our approach, we are using a graph transformation approach to the design of transformations, but these transformations are internally converted by our tool to generate XSLT code. This code can be executed in almost every platform by using either Java-based implementations or Javascript-based implementations [1].

Nevertheless, by using this approach, we are not supporting directionality and tracing. To support directionality, we have implemented an undo layer on top of XSLT. This undo layer takes advantage of the information regarding the applied rules stored in the model transformed. This kind of information is stored by means of mappings (or links) [12] that express the relationships between the elements in the models being transformed and the elements created in the target models. These mappings are supported by user interface description languages (UIDL) such as UsiXML [21], XIML [23] or the Teallach approach [5].

Source-target relationship requirement for model transformation can be implemented in XSLT by using XSLT 1.1 or 2.0. In those versions of XSLT, several output files can be produced in a single transformation.

Next, a description of T:XML, the tool that tries to cover all the requirements enunciated throughout this section, is included.

5 T:XML: Visually Designing Transformation Rules

T:XML is a tool supporting the specification, organization and validation of transformation rules. This tool uses an approach for the specification of rules inspired on the graph transformation tool AGG [16]. Nevertheless, the visual notation used has been adapted for an easier specification of the user interface transformation rules.

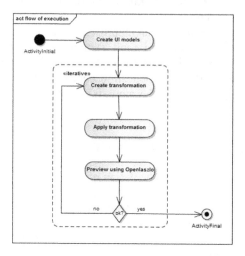

Fig. 2 Transformation design workflow in T:XML

Currently, the tool supports the definition of transformation rules that transform models specified in UsiXML language, but support for other user interface specification languages such as UIML [6] is planned, since the tool was designed as a generic transformation tool. Nevertheless, the dictionaries used for an easier editing must be updated for each language supported.

The aim of the tool is the generation of the specified transformation for different target transformation model languages, such as XSLT or QVT. By generating code for different transforming languages, we pursue maximizing the reuse and portability of the designed transformation. As a probe of concept, the tool currently supports the generation of XSLT code automatically for the visually designed transformations. Furthermore, the tool supports the generation of the final code of the user interface in OpenLaszlo language [18], for previewing and debugging the transformations designed. By doing so, the designer can easily discover unwanted effects or flaws in the designed adaptations.

In T:XML, the designer follows an iterative process that fits perfectly in user-centered design paradigm [7] (see Fig. 2). First, the designer should create the starting models. These models can be created either by hand (a very tedious job) or by using one visual tool such as IdealXML [13], GuiLayout++ [14] o grafiXML. The designer can also create or modify the source model by using the editor available en T:XML. Next, the designer creates transformations by creating transformation rules and composing them. Once the designer has finished a transformation, it can be previewed by using a renderer. This renderer will create a representation of how the actual user interface will look like. This rendered representation can be used as a hi-fi prototype, so the designer can discuss with the end-user to find any usability issues. The designer will iterate through this process until a final version is agreed with the customer or/and the end-users of the designed application.

5.1 Transformation Meta-model

Since our aim is supporting multi-path user interface development [8], with several different entry points, the transformation meta-model used does not force the designer to use a specific development process. This freedom in the process followed in the development process is positive since it supports multiple approaches. Nevertheless, the same freedom in the process can lead to the creation of transformations hard to reuse, and therefore losing one of the main benefits of model-driven development.

The transformation meta-model underlying our tool is depicted in Fig. 3. The transformation model consists of a series of transformation steps. Each one represents a stage in the development process, for instance, the transformation from abstract to concrete user interface. Nevertheless, in order to reduce the complexity of each step, they can be divided into other transformation steps. Each step also has a source input model and a target output model. A step consists of a set of ordered rules. The order of the rules represents the order in which the rules should be executed, within a specific step.

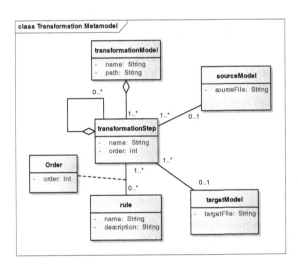

Fig. 3 Transformation meta-model supported in T:XML

The metaphor used in T:XML to represent this transformation meta-model is the project folder structure (see Fig. 4). A project includes as many steps as desired (represented as folders). In the example, there are two steps *Task2Abstract* and *Abstract2Concrete*. These folders can include other folders (substeps). Every folder can include XML input files (ATM.usi in the example). Finally, each input file includes some transformation rules that will be applied to this input file. By default, the input file for a step is the output from the previous one. Therefore, in the example, the ATM.usi file in *Abstract2Concrete* folder is generated by *Task2Abstract* step. The order in which steps and rules are executed is the same shown in the folder tree. It can be changed by using *drag & drop*.

Fig. 4 The folder metaphor for transformation meta-model

Next, a description of the functionalities provided by T:XML to designers is shown.

5.2 Designing Transformations in T:XML

When T:XML starts, the designer should create the structure of the project, that is, the steps that best fit the design process he is using. It can range from a single translation operation to accommodate the user interface to a new context of use to a full reification process starting from the most abstract levels or even an abstraction process to apply reverse engineering.

The development environment has a menu, as an alternative to toolbars options. The project structure is located at the leftmost part of the environment. The structure is a tree hierarchy where the designer can create/modify the structure of the project, reshuffle the order of the steps and the rules, create/delete/browse transformation rules and add/delete/create UsiXML input files.

5.2.1 The Graph Edition Area

When a UsiXML input/output file is double clicked, the file is open in the design area. The UsiXML input file is an XML-based specification. Nevertheless, since our tool relies on graph transformation visual syntax for the creation of the transformation rules, the UsiXML specification must be converted to a graph representation. To do so, every XML element in the specification will become a node in the graph, and implicit containment relationships will be used to create the hierarchical structure, i.e. if a *window* element has a *button* element inside its tag, then an edge will be created from the *window* node to the *button* one. The nodes from each model (task, domain, abstract user interface, ...) are drawn in different colors to help the designer. Furthermore, some extra work is required to accommodate the UsiXML representation to a graph representation. There are mapping relationships that establish inter-model relationships. These inter-model relationships are represented as an edge between the elements from the different models, i.e. if a *task* is performed in an *abstractContainer*, then the *isExecutedIn* mapping relationship will be represented as a link between the *task* and the *abstractContainer* involved. These mapping relationships are presented by light green edges, so the designer can distinguish them from regular edges.

To keep clean this design area, the designer can collapse or expand those branches not currently in use. The branches that have been collapsed are marked with a "+" sign (see *head* element in Fig. 5).

In the attribute edition area, the designer can modify any of the attributes of the elements in the model. Notice some nodes (see *window* element in Fig. 5) have a white tick within a green circle. This tick denotes that that element has an associated value in the resource model. This model is used in UsiXML to provide a separation of the contents from the presentation, supporting internationalization. For each context of use available in the model (see *context* elements in Fig. 5), a different instantiation of the resource can be provided. The resources can be modified in *Resources* tab.

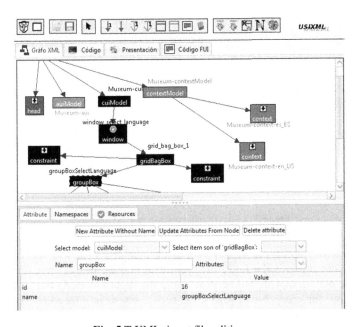

Fig. 5 T:XML: input file edition area

The designer can freely modify the XML input file by clicking the *code* tab. Nevertheless, to do this, designer must be very familiar with UsiXML XML schema. *Code* tab and the graph-based representation are always in synch. Thus, any change made in either the graph-based representation or the XML code representation will be automatically reflected on the other representation.

5.2.2 Transformation Rule Editing Area

When the user starts the transformation rule designer by clicking on the mask icon, the transformation design area appears. This area has four parts (see Fig. 6). It has a toolbar with buttons, and three areas for the specification of the transformation rule. To exemplify how transformation rules are created, a sample transformation rule will be created where a group of radio buttons is replaced with a dropdown list. This rule could be fired in different situations. For instance, a sensor could detect a change in the orientation of a mobile device when the user is switching from portrait orientation to landscape orientation. Since in landscape orientation the vertical space available is reduced, a set of radio buttons could be replaced with a dropdown list in order to decrease the screen space required to show the user interface. If the user switches back to portrait orientation, the reverse transformation could be done to restore the radio buttons. This rule could be triggered also in a desktop environment when the user resizes the window and the vertical space available is reduced. This rule shows the flexibility of using graph transformation graphical notation for the specification of transformation rules. Notice, this rule is dealing just with the aforementioned CUI level of abstraction of the. Furthermore, this transformation is a translation, since the transformation takes a CUI model and produces a new CUI model, but still at CUI level of abstraction.

The basic notion underlying graph transformation rules is the specification of patterns to be found in the original input graph, and then the specification of how those matching parts in the graph will be transformed to generate a new graph.

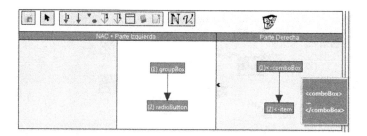

Fig. 6 T:XML: transformation rule edition area

The transformation edition area is split in three areas (see Fig. 6). The central area (in white color) is the *Left Part* specification area. In this area, the designer defines the pattern that should be matched in the input model. In our example, we are searching for *group boxes* with some *radio buttons* in it (see Fig. 6). The right most is the *Right Part* specification area. In this area, the designer specifies how to transform those nodes matching the left part. Those elements in the left part of the rule not present in the right part will be deleted from in the resulting graph. The usual way to create a rule is first the specification of the left part of the rule, then replicate the left part in the right part and start modifying it until the desire result is achieved. To make easier this process, when the left part is specified, the designer can select those parts that should be replicated in the right part and then click in the right part area to have it replicated in the right part.

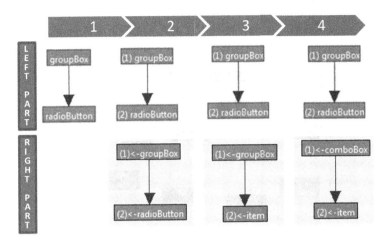

Fig. 7 Steps in the definition of a sample rule

In our sample rule, we start by specifying the pattern we are looking for, that is, a *radio button* that belongs to a *group box* (see step 1 in Fig. 7). Then, we have dragged the left part into the right part (see step 2 in Fig. 7). The matching numbers for *groupBox* and *radioButton* in both parts define a link between those nodes. In some way, it means that the element in the right and left parts with matching numbers is the same instance, and therefore, when we are changing the right part matched element, we are transforming the left part matched element into something else, i.e., we want to transform the *groupBox* into a *comboBox* and the *radioButtons* into *items* for the *comboBox*. Thus, in steps 3 and 4 in Fig. 7, we change the element type from *groupBox* to *comboBox*, and from *radioButton* to *item*. Therefore, all the parts of the model to be transformed matching the left part of the rule will be transformed into what we put in the right part.

If the rule is applied to the input graph model shown in Fig. 8a, the result would be the one shown in Fig. 8b. As can be seen in the figure, the *groupBox* has become a *comboBox*, and all the *radioButtons* have become *items*.

T:XML supports also the definition of variables. Variables can be used to apply arithmetic operations to the attributes in the model or to take the value of an attribute to set the value of another attribute. For instance, in the previous example, we could create a variable x for the *width* attribute of the *groupBox* element and then use this value to customize the value of the *width* of the *comboBox* created by assigning $x-10$ to the *width* attribute of the *comboBox* element in the right part of the rule. Thus, the actual width of the *comboBox* would be the width of the *groupBox* minus 10.

Finally, the leftmost part of the rule editing area is used to specify a NAC (*Negative Application Condition*). The NAC is used to specify situations in the input graph that prevent a transformation rule from being applicable.

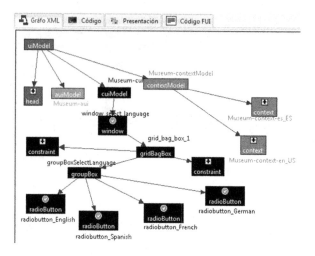

(a) Graph before transformation

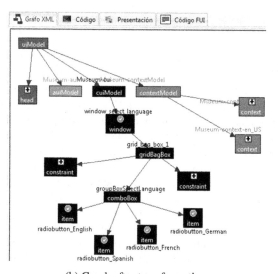

(b) Graph after transformation

Fig. 8 T:XML: graph representation before and after transformation

5.2.3 Previewing the Transformation Rule Results

After the transformation rule is created, it is ready to be saved and applied. T:XML generates the code for the target transformation language chosen. Currently, it generates a set of four XSL transformations. This XSL Transformations can be run in any of the many engines supporting this transformation language. Once the transformation rule has been applied, it can be previewed in T:XML by using a renderer for UsiXML to render the new UsiXML specification resulting from saving the graph. After the transformation rule into a user interface the user can directly interact with. The designer can configure the renderers and its parameters. By default, OpenLaszlo [18] language renderer is used. Thus, when the user clicks on the *Presentation* tab, T:XML automatically generates the preview for the graph currently displayed in the graph edition area. In the left part of Fig. 9, the preview for the input UsiXML specification used for the sample rule is shown. In the right part of the same figure, the presentation for the sample UsiXML specification after the transformation rule has been applied is shown.

Fig. 9 T:XML: previewing the presentation for input and output in transformations

6 Transformation Rule Design Issues

Using this approach for transformation raises some concerns regarding the feasibility of using this rule-based transformation paradigm for the development of the whole user interface, especially, when developing complex user interfaces.

The main issue behind rule transformation is scalability. Scalability issues appear as a consequence of rule chaining during the transformation of the models to produce other models. The designer of a transformation rule must consider the effects in the models produced by previous rules. This is a general issue in rule transformation, not just in user interface rule-based transformation development. Nevertheless, this problem can be partly mitigated, and it actually is in the approach proposed in this paper, by having a clear separation of concerns in the concepts and features represented at each model and level of abstraction. By adopting the framework proposed in [2], we are keeping a separation of concerns at the different levels of abstraction (Domain & Concepts, AUI, CUI and FUI). Nevertheless, this separation of concerns is not enough. The designer must get experienced in structuring the rules, as a programmer gets experienced in structured programming. Otherwise the reusability and feasibility of the approach are clearly compromised, as it is also compromised the development of a medium-size (or bigger) program when no structure is provided during the coding activities.

7 Conclusions and Future Work

The specification of model transformation rules is one of the most important issues in any model driven development method.

T:XML is presented as a tool that supports the specification of transformation rules for model-based development environments. This tool aims at providing the designers with a visual notation to create the transformation rules. Furthermore, it pursues also providing an integrated environment where the designer can manage, create, modify and preview the transformation rules.

T:XML is designed as a generic tool for model driven approaches where the models are expressed by using XML-based languages. Nevertheless, current version is focused towards the specification of transformation rules for UsiXML user interface description language.

Our tool supports model-to-model transformations, covering all the models that can be expressed in a model-based user interface development environment (tasks, domain, context, presentation, etc). Nevertheless, the development of a renderer that produces an XML interpretable language, such as XHTML, is possible with our tool.

As future work, we would like to add new user interfaces description languages, such as UIML or XIML. Furthermore, to improve the versatility of the tool we would like also to add support for other target transformation languages. We are currently working in the generation of QVT transformation language, since it is probably the most powerful transformation language currently available, apart from being one of the most widely used for general software development.

In the next version of the tool, we would like also to include predefined templates for different user interface development processes to help designers in the organization of their transformation rules.

Acknowledgments. This work is partly supported by the PII2I09-0146-8894 project funded by the region of Castilla-La Mancha and the Project TIN2008-06596-C02-01, funded by the Ministry of Science and Technology of Spain.

References

[1] AJAXSLT. Pure javascript implementation of XSLT and XPath, http://code.google.com/p/ajaxslt/

[2] Calvary, G., Coutaz, J., Thevenin, D., Limbourg, Q., Bouillon, L., Vanderdonckt, J.: A unifying reference framework for multi-target user interfaces. Journal of Interacting With Computer 15/3, 289–308 (2003)

[3] Czarnecki, K., Helsen, S.: Feature-Based Survey of Model Transformation Approaches. IBM Systems Journal 45(3), 621–645 (2006)

[4] Florins, M., Montero, F., Vanderdonckt, J., Michotte, B.: Splitting Rules for Graceful Degradation of User Interfaces. In: Proc. of 10th ACM Int. Conf. on Intelligent User Interfaces, IUI 2006, pp. 264–266. ACM Press, New York (2006)

[5] Griffiths, T., Paton, N.W., Goble, C.A., West, A., Barclay, P.J., Kennedy, J., Smyth, M., McKirdy, J., Gray, P.D., Cooper, R.: Teallach: A Model-Based User Interface Development Environment for Object Databases. In: Procs. of the 1999 User Interfaces To Data Intensive Systems, UIDIS. IEEE Computer Society, Los Alamitos (1999)

[6] Helms, J., Abrams, M.: Retrospective on UI description languages, based on eight years' experience with the User Interface Markup Language (UIML). Int. J. Web Eng. Technol. 4(2), 138–162 (2008)

[7] ISO/IEC 13407 Human-Centred Design Processes for Interactive Systems, ISO/IEC 13407 (1999)

[8] Limbourg, Q., Vanderdonckt, J., Michotte, B., Bouillon, L., López-Jaquero, V.: USIXML: A language supporting multi-path development of user interfaces. In: Feige, U., Roth, J. (eds.) EHCI-DSVIS 2004. LNCS, vol. 3425, pp. 200–220. Springer, Heidelberg (2005)

[9] López Jaquero, V., Montero, F., Molina, J.P., González, P., Fernández-Caballero, A.: A Multi-Agent System Architecture for the Adaptation of User Interfaces. In: Pĕchouček, M., Petta, P., Varga, L.Z. (eds.) CEEMAS 2005. LNCS (LNAI), vol. 3690, Springer, Heidelberg (2005)

[10] López Jaquero, V., Vanderdonckt, J., Montero, F., González, P.: Towards an Extended Model of User Interface Adaptation: the ISATINE framework. In: Gulliksen, J., Harning, M.B., van der Veer, G.C., Wesson, J. (eds.) EIS 2007. LNCS, vol. 4940, pp. 374–392. Springer, Heidelberg (2008)

[11] López-Jaquero, V., Montero, F., Real, F.: Designing User Interface Adaptation Rules with T:XML. In: Proceedings of the 14th International Conference on Intelligent User Interfaces, IUI 2009, Sanibel Island, USA. ACM, New York (2009)

[12] Montero, F., López Jaquero, V., Vanderdonckt, J., González, P., Lozano, M.D.: Solving the Mapping Problem in User Interface Design by Seamless Integration in Ideal XML. In: Gilroy, S.W., Harrison, M.D. (eds.) DSV-IS 2005. LNCS, vol. 3941, pp. 161–172. Springer, Heidelberg (2006)

[13] Montero, F., López Jaquero, V.: IdealXML: An Interaction Design Tool and a Task-Based Approach to User Interface Design. In: 6th International Conference on Computer-Aided Design of User Interfaces, CADUI 2006, Bucharest, Romania, June 6-8 (2006)

[14] Montero, F., López Jaquero, V.: GUILayout++: Supporting Prototype Creation and Quality Evaluation for Abstract User Interface Generation. In: Workshop of ACM SIGCHI Symposium on Engineering Interactive Computing Systems, Berlin, Germany, June 20 (2010)

[15] Montero Simarro, F., Vanderdonckt, J.: Pattern-Based Design of User Interfaces in UsiXML. In: Workshop of ACM SIGCHI Symposium on Engineering Interactive Computing Systems, Berlin, Germany, June 20 (2010)

[16] Navarro, E.: Ph.D Thesis, ATRIUM: Architecture Traced from Requirements by Applying a Unified Methodology, UCLM (2007)

[17] QVT. MOF Query/Views/Transformations final adopted specification. OMG Document pct/05-11-01 (2005)

[18] OpenLaszlo. Rich Internet Applications framework,
     http://www.openlaszlo.org

[19] Puerta, A.R.: A Model-Based Interface Development Environment. IEEE Software 14(4), 40–47 (1997)

[20] Taentzer, G.: AGG: A Tool Environment for Algebraic Graph Transformation. In: Münch, M., Nagl, M. (eds.) AGTIVE 1999. LNCS, vol. 1779, pp. 481–488. Springer, Heidelberg (2000)

[21] UsiXML. USer Interface eXtensible Markup Language,
     http://www.usixml.org
[22] Vanderdonckt, J.: A MDA-Compliant Environment for Developing User Interfaces of
     Information Systems. In: Pastor, Ó., Falcão e Cunha, J. (eds.) CAiSE 2005. LNCS,
     vol. 3520, pp. 13–17. Springer, Heidelberg (2005)
[23] XIML. eXtensible user Interface Markup Language, http://www.ximl.org
[24] XSL Transformations (XSLT), version 1.0 W3C recommendation (November 16,
     1999), http://www.w3c.org/TR/xslt

Formalising Interaction Patterns

Paolo Bottoni, Esther Guerra, and Juan de Lara

Abstract. The use of patterns as a way to refer to common solutions in the field of interface design is becoming widespread. However, contrary to the situation for software patterns, definitions of interaction patterns do not enjoy a common standard yet. Moreover, patterns are developed for design aspects as diverse as: user experience, layout, action coordination, or specification of entire widgets, reflecting the complexity of the field. As a consequence, research on formalisation of interaction patterns is not developed, and few attempts have been made to extend techniques developed for design pattern formalisation. We show here how an extension to an approach to pattern formalisation recently proposed by the authors can be usefully employed to formalize some classes of interaction patterns, to express relations like subtyping and composition, and to detect conflicts.

1 Introduction

Patterns in the field of Human Computer Interaction (HCI), often called *interaction* (or *HCI*) *patterns*, capitalize on best practices in User Interfaces (UI) design, concerning aspects as diverse as layout, navigation, coordination, and user experience. Several collections of such patterns are available, presented in books [31, 34] or dedicated websites [19, 36, 39].

The movement towards patterns in HCI started under the influence of their success in Software Engineering (SE) [18], but had to face the specific problem

Paolo Bottoni
Università di Roma "Sapienza", Rome, Italy
e-mail: bottoni@di.uniroma1.it

Esther Guerra
Universidad Autónoma de Madrid, Madrid, Spain
e-mail: Esther.Guerra@uam.es

Juan de Lara
Universidad Autónoma de Madrid, Madrid, Spain
e-mail: Juan.deLara@uam.es

H. Hussmann et al. (Eds.): MDD of Advanced User Interfaces, SCI 340, pp. 257–276.
springerlink.com © Springer-Verlag Berlin Heidelberg 2011

of the conflict between the designer's view of patterns (as typical forms of collaborations among software components) and the user's view (where users are interested in reusing their experience from familiar widgets, layouts or navigation strategies) [16]. Hence, while the components of a pattern presentation are usually the same (for example, the Pattern Language Markup Language [14] provides a comprehensive list of elements with *name, context, problem, forces, solution, diagram, implementation*, among others), there is no common notation to specify the solution. In most cases, on the contrary, the solution is presented through examples and explanatory text, leaving it to the developer to code its details. Hence, it becomes hard to answer questions like: "Is **X** a new pattern or just a variation of **Y**, or even **Z** in disguise?", "Can I use **X** and **Y** together?", or "Does the use of **X** depend on using **Y** in the same interaction?". A pattern formalism able to support this kind of reasoning would therefore be useful to designers and users alike.

As HCI patterns can refer to layout, behaviour of individual components and their coordination, or even to the domain model, presenting them only via examples makes it hard to separate what is essential to the pattern and what is a feature of the application domain. This hinders the definition of a "real" pattern language in which not only to give names to patterns, but also to express pattern composition, sub-typing, dependency and conflict, thus supporting pattern-based design. In particular, in the field of Model-Based UI Development (MBUID), techniques for completing models with respect to patterns (see e.g. [5]) can support the automatic generation of UI components from design knowledge expressed with patterns.

In this paper, we propose an approach to the foundation of a notion of HCI pattern languages by extending our recently proposed algebraic formalisation of a general notion of pattern [4], with applications beyond SE design patterns. We consider a pattern as emerging from the synchronisation of specifications of different aspects involving entities in different domains. To this end, we define mappings between components of an abstract UI specification and the roles played by these components in the pattern, thus developing effective methods to establish if a particular implementation is an instantiation of a pattern, to construct interface parts from specialisations of patterns, and to reason about the compatibility between patterns which should share some component. We base our abstract interface specification on the UsiXML meta-model [37]. Moreover, we extend the theory presented in [4] to describe relations between patterns, in particular pattern subtyping, conflict and composition, following the developments in [5, 6].

Organisation. After revising related work in Section 2, we introduce interaction patterns in Section 3 and present our formalisation in Section 4. Section 5 formalizes relations among patterns, and Section 6 draws conclusions and points to future work.

2   Related Work

Most research on pattern formalisation originates from describing design patterns via diagrams from the Unified Modeling Language (UML). France et al. extend

UML class and sequence diagrams with roles and constraints, checking conformance of a model to a pattern as the standard relationship between model and meta-model [17]. To avoid immediate reference to UML diagrams, Kim and Carrington add stereotypes to the UML meta-model and use Object-Z for structural aspects [21]. Constraints are enforced in [35] via pattern-specific high-level transformations.

UML profiles are extended with stereotypes and tagged values in [12] in order to visualize roles of elements in UML class and communication diagrams, and to allow instance-based pattern composition. The proposal in [33] uses subsets of First Order Logic for structural aspects and Temporal Logic of Actions for behavioral ones. It also supports pattern combinations. In [24], rules are applied to abstract syntax trees to annotate the found pattern instances, while in [28], models are transformed to conform to patterns, exploiting graph queries that detect needs for transformations.

Attempts to formalize HCI patterns are more limited, even though literature on HCI patterns is expanding. For example, studies on usability have met architectural patterns to include interaction mechanisms early in the design process [20]. Folmer et al. relate architectural choices to usability patterns by identifying usability requirements which might have an impact on the architecture [15]. These are not expressed in terms of classes and relations, but define sets of problems the architecture has to solve. In this line, van Welie et al. [16] propose *bridging patterns* to provide information, in typical SE notation, on how to implement usability patterns, illustrating possible solutions to the requirements from interaction designers. Support to pattern selection and to generation of code from pattern templates is offered by the Pattern-Driven and Model-Based UI approach, exploiting UsiXML models and XUL code [1]. This approach is related to architectural levels in [32].

Although no standard exists for presenting HCI patterns, several researchers have started publishing patterns in a structured Alexandrian style, aiming at the foundation of a pattern language for HCI and interaction design. In particular, Borchers [3] proposes a notion of pattern language as a directed acyclic graph, where nodes are patterns and edges describe references from a pattern to another. However, the description of individual patterns relies on text and illustrations, not on a formal characterisation, so that the existence of a relation between two patterns must be explicitly stated and cannot be derived from their analysis.

Categorisations of HCI patterns enable understanding and problem-based selection of patterns. Mahemoff and Johnston [22] identify *task-related*, *user-related*, *user interface element* and *system-based* patterns, while van Welie and Trattenberg [40] classify end-user patterns under terms such as: *Visibility*, *Natural Mapping*, *Affordance*, etc., drawn from HCI principles and heuristics. However, patterns present different aspects, making it difficult to assign them to a unique category. In this paper, we identify pattern roles pertaining to specific dimensions of the interaction design, where patterns may require roles from several dimensions.

In the area of MBUID, Schattkowsky and Lohmann propose an abstract definition of interface as a composition of platform-independent widgets and views, to be mapped to platform-dependent realisations [29]. An abstract view of components of interactive systems is also at the core of the UsiXML proposal, combining approaches to model-driven platform-independent UI design [23] and abstract notions of interface objects [8]. Pribeanu and Vanderdonckt present a methodology which exploits abstract interaction objects to derive interaction patterns from analysis of domain and task models (e.g., patterns for creating/deleting/modifying entities, or drawing associations between them) relating them to specific interaction and presentation techniques [27]. The templates are partially defined in a formal way, but the proposed methodology does not support the definition or evaluation of relations among different patterns. A direct extension of the UsiXML model to describe patterns is provided in [41]. The proposal facilitates automatic generation of interfaces from patterns, but does not support formal reasoning on patterns.

With Interaction Patterns for Rich Internet Applications, platform specific transformations map both abstract patterns – described through a meta-model and an interaction semantics – and their concrete counterparts to code, based on platform-specific transformations [38]. Pattern concepts are described through a meta-model. An interaction semantics, specifying what must happen when the pattern is applied, can be given using textual descriptions or additional models.

The Wisdom model [25] reduces HCI design elements to UML through stereotypes extending the UML meta-model; the CanonSketch model integrates this model by taking into account presentation aspects and mapping to code [9]. Finally, Almendros-Jiménez and Iribarne specialize UML use-case and class diagrams [2].

In general, although several lines of research converge towards defining HCI patterns, a solid formal foundation for their specification, composition and analysis is still missing, thus hindering the possibility of pattern reuse independently of their specific realizations, in the context of MBUID. The limitations of the current situation are discussed in [7]. In the rest of the paper, we propose such a foundation.

3   Interaction Patterns

As a full coverage of all the aspects of UI design is beyond the scope of this paper, we focus on three axes in the interaction design space for visual interfaces, that we deem *Domain*, (static) *Presentation*, and *Dynamics*, as shown in Fig. 1.

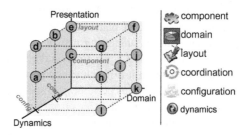

Fig. 1 Interaction design space

We can thus categorize specific concerns of interaction design (and the related patterns) with respect to positions in this space. In particular the domain axis refers to the application data, while the presentation axis organizes aspects related to components' appearance, static configuration (i.e. interface composition), and layout. While design can be concerned with data and presentation aspects alone, the dynamics can only be defined with respect to the other two axes.

Hence, we identify an *application-dependent* (or component) dynamics, completing the definition of the domain space, and a *layout* dynamics, pertaining to the modification of the visual arrangement of the components on the screen. Moreover, components dynamics presents two aspects: *coordination* refers to the dependencies between the states of the elements (hence their aspect), e.g., switching between enabled and disabled states, while *configuration dynamics* specifies which components have to be created or destroyed as interaction proceeds. As examples of classification, we deem *Visual Framework* as a purely presentational pattern (i.e. with design choices involving nodes c and e in Fig. 1); *Clear Entry Points* associates specific tasks with components in the initial interface (nodes a and h); *Form* supports user's specification of values for a complex task, relating data with component configuration and layout (nodes c, f and j), while *Left Aligned Labels* specializes layout (node e); *Command Area* and *Button Group* relate component configuration and layout to task or data dynamics, usually with specific requirements on layout and coordination (nodes b, e, i and l). Fig. 2 offers a reminder of the first five patterns.

Left Aligned Labels

Form

Clear Entry Points, Visual Framework

Command Area

Fig. 2 Examples of pattern realisations

We exploit the conceptualization in Fig. 1 to characterize roles of elements in a pattern with respect to these axes. This is done by using as stereotypes combinations of the icons shown to the right of the figure. Moreover, although independent of concrete technologies, this organisation of the design space can be easily mapped to the models of the UsiXML meta-model, namely *transformation*, *task*, *domain*, *aui* (abstract UI) and *cui* (concrete UI) models, with the first two models related to presentation dynamics and domain dynamics, respectively, the third modeling data, and the last two pertaining to static presentation. In the rest of the paper, we will express presentation aspects of the discussed patterns mainly with reference to the abstract interaction objects populating the *auiModel*, occasionally expressing additional constraints on implementation via elements from the *cuiModel*.

4   Formal Model of Interaction Patterns

In general, a pattern expresses a complex relation among elements playing specific roles and collaborating to provide experimented solutions to recurring problems. For instance, in SE design patterns, collaborations are realized through message exchanges, and roles are played by structural elements. In HCI patterns, collaborations can be implicit and simply recognized by the users, and roles can be played by any typed element populating the interaction space. In any case, we separate the definition of a *pattern vocabulary* introducing the roles, from that of possible role realizations. Moreover, we allow for different types of collaborations by specifying a pattern as a collection of synchronized diagrams, with a designated *structuring* diagram – usually the one regarding presentation – introducing the roles, and other diagrams showing different features of their collaboration [4]. Also, diagrams contain *variability regions* constraining the number of elements which can play the same role in any given realization of the pattern. For example, the *Button Group* pattern only makes sense when there are 2 or more buttons to be presented together.

As the resulting notion of pattern is domain-independent, domain-specific concepts can be used to express roles and to specify the elements realising them. In our approach, diagrams result from the annotation of model elements, typed on the UsiXML meta-model, with roles from the HCI pattern vocabulary. In addition, patterns are equipped with constraints (invariants), expressing contextual conditions that must hold for the correct application of the pattern and which, to some extent, express some of the consequences and intentions of the pattern.

Next, Section 4.1 introduces the meta-models for UsiXML and for the roles vocabulary. Then, Section 4.2 presents the main concepts of our formalization.

4.1   A Meta-model for Interaction

We adopt the UsiXML meta-model as representative of the interaction domain and relate its elements to pattern roles through a specific correspondence layer. UsiXML provides a collection of modeling entities for the abstract and concrete definition of interactive systems. The UsiXML meta-model allows a description of an interactive system as composed of several models, in which an abstract user interface is realized through concrete elements and is connected to domain objects and workflow descriptions. Fig. 3 presents a fragment of it, relevant to the patterns we show.

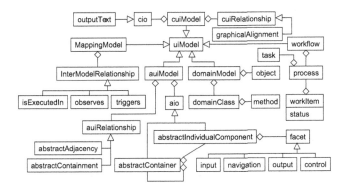

Fig. 3 Fragment of the UsiXML meta-model

In addition, we identify a vocabulary of roles composed of instances of the class `PatternRole` defined in Fig. 4. In order to keep the domain and vocabulary models mutually independent, we adopt triple graphs [30], where a *correspondence graph* contains maps to relate the graphs, called *source* and *target* graphs, specifying the two models. This is similar to a weaving model [11] that relates elements in the UsiXML and Vocabulary (roles) models and offers two advantages. First, we can exploit any implementation of the domain specific meta-model, as we do not need to modify it to accommodate pattern roles. Second, any meta-model for interaction can be used, without affecting role definition. Roles are recognizable by their name, and are attributed with a list of labels defining their focus, as taken from the *Focus* enumeration type, according to the classification given in Section 3. Different UsiXML classes play different roles as given by the role maps in the correspondence meta-model, for which we use abbreviations in Fig. 4. From left to right, we have therefore *Presentation*, *Affordance*, *Layout*, *Action*, *Container* and *Element* maps.

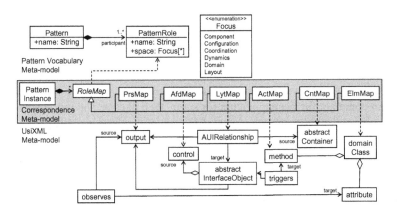

Fig. 4 A fragment of the triple meta-model for the definition of Interaction Patterns

4.2   Pattern Specification

In its simplest form, a pattern consists of one structure, called *root*, with the mandatory part that any pattern realization must contain, and a number of *variable* parts or
variability regions defining additional structures that can be replicated several times
for each instance of the root [4]. In order to represent root and variable parts, we use
the symbolic graphs proposed in [26], where the set of data nodes is replaced by a
finite set of sorted variables and a formula γ constraining the possible values taken
by the variables. For simplicity, we first present them without role annotations.

Variable parts can be nested: a nested part can only be instantiated by adding
structures to an instance of its parent. In addition, for each part, a variable name with
values ranging on *integer* is used in equations restricting the allowed number of its
replicas. Equations may contain relations between the allowed replicas of variable
parts, and the number of times a pattern can be instantiated in a model is restricted
by equations on the variability of the root. If the set of equations has no solution in
the natural numbers, then the pattern cannot be instantiated.

Defintion 1 (Pattern). *A pattern is a construct* $VP = (P, root, Emb, name, var)$,
where:

- $P = \{V_1, ..., V_n\}$ *is a finite set of non-empty graphs, where each* V_i *is called*
  variable part,
- $root \in P$ *is a distinguished element of* P,
- *Emb is a set of morphisms* $v_{i,j} : V_i \rightarrow V_j$ *with* $V_i, V_j \in P$, *s.t. it spans a tree rooted*
  in root with all graphs $V_i \in P$ *as nodes and the morphisms* $v_{i,j} \in Emb$ *as edges,*
- *name:* $P \rightarrow L$ *is an injective function assigning each variable part a name from*
  a set of variables L, *of sort* $\mathbb{N}$,
- $var \subseteq T_{AlgIEq}(name(P))$ *is a set of equations governing the number of*
  possible instantiations of the variable parts, using variables in $name(P) \subseteq L$,
  arithmetic operations, and the $<, \leq, =, >, \geq$ *relation symbols. We call this sig-*
  nature "Algebraic Inequalities" (Σ_{AlgIEq}); $T_{AlgIEq}(name(P))$ *is the term-algebra*
  with variables in $name(P)$.

Example. Fig. 5 shows a simple version of the *VisualFramework* pattern. The graph
V_{VF} is the *root* and V_{Vars}, V_{VarCmp}, and V_{Fix} are the variable parts, using UsiXML
types from the aui model (see Fig. 3). The pattern models a visual framework
through the presence of an abstract container f, contained in all the occurrences of
the main container for the application (or set of Web pages). The morphisms identify the object f in the root with objects f in each of the three variable parts. f may
contain an arbitrary number of interaction objects, forming the *Fix* region. On the
other hand, as defined by the *vars* region, each occurrence of the main container can
also present another abstract container, with a set of elements in a *VarCmp* region.
The occurrence of the container for the varying part of the interface is related to the
container for the fixed part through some abstract adjacency relation (typically preventing their overlapping). For compactness, rather than this direct representation of
the formal definition, we adopt the notation shown in Fig. 6, where a coloured area
represents a variable part and region nesting is represented by containment. Note

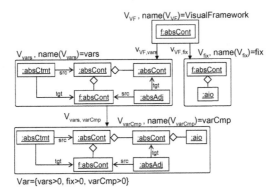

Fig. 5 *VisualFramework* pattern in theoretical form

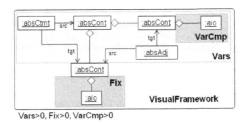

Fig. 6 *VisualFramework* in compact form

that a morphism $v_{i,j} : V_i \rightarrow V_j$ represents a "graph difference", or an embedding of V_i in V_j. We represent this visually by a colored polygon enclosing the elements of V_j not mapped from elements of V_i. Hence, in the example, the root contains only the object f, and we depict with two disjoint regions (*Vars* and *Fix*) the elements of the two variable regions different from the element in the root. In a similar way, region *VarCmp* includes the elements in V_{VarCmp} not present in V_{Vars}. The equations below govern the number of times each variable part is allowed to be replicated.

The semantics of a pattern is given by the set of all valid expansions of its variability regions.

Defintion 2 (Expansion). *The expansion set $EXP(VP)$ of a pattern VP is given by the set of colimits $\{C_i\}$ of all possible diagrams α obtained by replicating the graphs in P, and the morphisms in Emb, s.t.: (i) the diagram α is consistent with the morphisms in Emb, which means that if $V_i \rightarrow V_j$ is included in α, then there is a morphism $v_{i,j} : V_i \rightarrow V_j$ in Emb; and (ii) the number of replicas in each path from root to C_i satisfies the equations in var.*

Example. Fig. 7 shows the construction of one of the diagrams in the expansion set $EXP(VisualFramework)$. In particular, the variable regions *Vars* and *VarCmp* are expanded once, and *Fix* twice. The expansion C results by glueing all graphs through the elements identified by the morphisms.

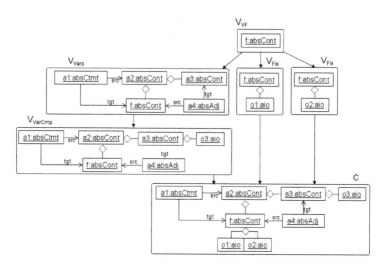

Fig. 7 One possible expansion of the *VisualFramework* pattern

A model satisfies a pattern when some pattern expansion is found in the model.

Definiton 3 (Satisfaction and Semantics). *Given a pattern VP and a graph G, G satisfies VP, written $G \models VP$, iff $\exists C_i \rightarrow G$ injective with $C_i \in EXP(VP)$. The semantics of VP, $SEM(VP) = \{G \mid G \models VP\}$ is given by the set of all graphs that satisfy it.*

As the definition of HCI patterns involves several models, in particular the *aui* and *cui* models from UsiXML, the problem of checking whether a model M of a UI satisfies a pattern VP has to take care of this fact. In particular, M could specify only some components, say only an abstract UI model, leaving the choice of concrete widgets to developers. Vice versa, one could have available only the specification at the level of concrete UI model, while a pattern could only involve a specification at an abstract level. In particular, when one has a pattern VP defined with types from the *aui* model (but not from the *cui* model) and an interface model M expressed in terms of the *cui* model (without reference to an *aui* model), a virtual *aui* model $AM = virt(M)$ can be reconstructed, using rules such as the following:

- for each element $ae \in AM$ there exists an element $ce \in M$ and an instance *arc* of an `isAbstractedInto` relationship with $arc.src = ce$ and $arc.tgt = ae$;
- if ce is an input element, ae has a facet `input`;
- if ce is an output element, ae has a facet `output`;
- if ce is a graphical container, ae is of type `abstractContainer`.

We say that M *virtually satisfies* VP ($M \models_m VP$) if $virt(M) \models VP$.

We discuss now the annotation of the elements in the graph with the roles they play in the pattern, thus using triple graphs, as introduced in Section 4.1, instead of graphs as objects in the set P. In our approach, the source graph represents a model in a given domain-specific language (e.g. UsiXML), while the target graph contains nodes with the different roles the elements can take. The assignment of roles to elements is made through the nodes in the correspondence graph, which have morphisms to source and target nodes, as shown in Fig. 4.

Example. To the left of Fig. 8, roles are added to the *root* of the *VisualFramework* pattern via a triple graph. The lower compartment depicts the UsiXML model, while the upper part contains the involved roles. The middle section is the correspondence graph, linking elements in the domain with their roles. Node `PatternInstance` aggregates the different maps of the same pattern instance to facilitate their recognition. As the formalization is given categorically, all definitions remain the same when replacing graphs by triple graphs. The right part of the figure shows the compact notation for patterns with roles, where roles and focus are given as stereotypes, roles being visualized as text, and focus via small decorations. In this case, all roles are referred to the *Presentation* domain of Fig. 1.

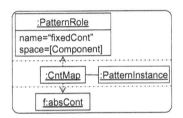 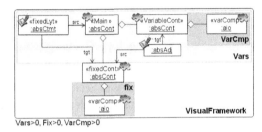

Fig. 8 Adding roles to the root of *VisualFramework* (left). Compact notation with stereotypes (right)

As the definition of a HCI pattern may extend over several diagrams, we introduce *synchronisation graphs*, to specify correspondences between elements in the variable parts of different patterns. In particular, we represent the synchronization between regions in distinct patterns by equality of their names, whereas the elements that overlap in regions with the same name are formalized in the notion of a *synchronization graph*, which factors out the common structure of the two patterns to be synchronized. In general, given n diagrams (i.e. n annotated patterns) to be synchronized with one structuring pattern, the n synchronization graphs are given by the intersections of those regions with equal name with respect to the roles (note that the diagrams to be synchronized share the same vocabulary model). Thus, the synchronization graph has one region for each two regions to be synchronized. Two elements in two annotated patterns mapped to the same role in two regions with same name, will be related through an element in a region of the synchronization graph. In [4], an algorithm is given for calculating the synchronization graph between a structuring pattern and any other annotated pattern.

Example. Fig. 9 shows the presentation elements for the *Wizard* pattern. In this pattern, a set of containers are presented one at a time (as indicated by the instances of the *mutualEmphasis* relationship) within a *main* container. For each *step* of the wizard, the specific container offers the user a set of *input* components, thus allowing the introduction of parameters for that step. Moreover, the main container has a control component to start the whole process, and each step container has a control element to indicate the completion of the step, *committing* the choices made.

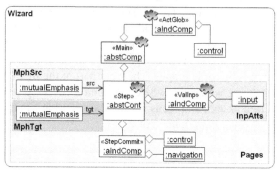

Wizard>=0, Pages>1, InpAtts>0, MphSrc=Pages-1, MphTgt=Pages-1

Fig. 9 The presentation diagram for *Wizard*

In Fig. 10, the dynamics associated with the pattern are given. A *global* process is composed of several tasks, each one connected with a step container, while the inputs assigned through the interface are associated with attributes manipulated by the task. The commit action can start one out of several tasks, depending on the application and the choices made, as indicated by the *Cmt* variable region. Note that only some of the components from the presentation (structuring) diagram are considered relevant to the dynamics and are marked with a bold **I** character, to indicate that they are part of the synchronization graph. Fig. 11 shows the analogous diagram expressing the navigational structure of the *Wizard* pattern, with an indication of the structuring elements defining the synchronization graph. Note that in both the navigation and the process diagram, the number of tasks which can be started, and correspondingly of the step containers which can be reached, or which can reach the current step, is limited by the global number of pages (i.e. step containers). The mutual exclusions between step containers induce an analogous constraint on the tasks: only one task at a time can be executed.

Patterns with Invariants. Patterns may include contextual conditions for their correct application, expressed as graph constraints and application conditions [13]. A *pattern with invariants* is a pattern with sets $PC(V_i)$ of *pattern constraints* defined over any of its variable parts V_i. An atomic constraint over V_i, noted $V_i \rightarrow X \rightarrow C_j$, consists of one *premise* graph X related to the variable part V_i it constrains, and a set of *consequence* graphs $C(X) = \{X \rightarrow C_j\}_{j \in J}$. As in logic, the intuition behind constraint satisfaction is: if the premise graph X is found in a model, then some of the consequence graphs C_j have to be found as well. More complex constraints can be

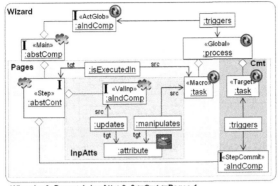

Wizard>=0, Pages>1, InpAtts>0, 0<=Cmt<=Pages-1

Fig. 10 The dynamics diagram for *Wizard*

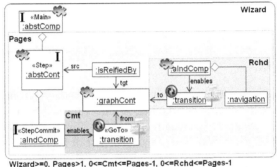

Wizard>=0, Pages>1, 0<=Cmt<=Pages-1, 0<=Rchd<=Pages-1

Fig. 11 The diagram defining the navigational structure for *Wizard*

formed by using boolean formulae over atomic constraints. In particular, a negative constraint is defined by forbidding the presence of any instance of X.

Example. Fig. 12 presents one of the constraints associated with the *VisualFramework* pattern. In particular, the relation of adjacency between the fixed and the varying containers must remain the same through all the occurrences of the main container. Fig. 13 shows another constraint associated with the root part of *VisualFramework*, demanding the fixed container to be always visible. Other constraints force equality of background colours, fonts, etc. for elements in the varying parts.

5 A Pattern Language

The proposed formalization allows the definition of several types of relations between patterns. In particular, in this section, we extend the formalism to handle pattern *subtyping*, *conflict* and *composition*, thus providing an effective basis for the construction of pattern languages.

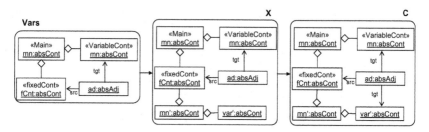

Fig. 12 Constraints on layout in *Visual Framework* (adjacency)

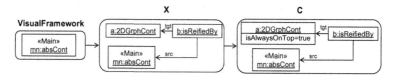

Fig. 13 Constraints on layout in *Visual Framework* (visibility)

5.1 Subtyping

In several interaction patterns, we can identify an abstract notion of *Unit* as the fundamental brick in pattern construction. A unit is formed by a *container* where some *individual components* contain messages providing explanations to the user and some others offer facets for user input. The left of Fig. 14 presents a unit as a pattern where role realizations are given via abstract elements from the *auiModel*.

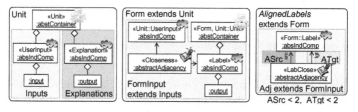

Fig. 14 Unit (left), Form as subtype of Unit (center), AlignedLabels as subtype of Form (right)

A common type of unit is a *Form*, characterized by the presence of labels adjacent to each user input. Hence, we define *Form* as a subtype of *Unit*, noted $Form \sqsubseteq Unit$, by adding new elements and describing their relation to the elements of *Unit* as shown in the center of Fig. 14. As formalized in Def. 4 below, subtyping can add new elements to a pattern, possibly introducing further constraints, or adding new variable parts as children of the root or of other existing variable parts. However, the subtype cannot relax the constraints on the parent type, nor can it introduce intermediate regions between the root and the original regions. We only show in the child those elements of the parent pattern needed for the extension (but as in OO programming, all elements of the parent are incorporated into the child).

Defintion 4 (Extension). *Given two patterns VP and VP', an injective morphism $Ext: VP \to VP'$ is defined as the tuple $Ext = (E = (E^V, E^E), f)$, where E is an injective morphism on trees that preserves the structure of the trees Emb and Emb' with:*

- $E^V: P \to P'$ *s.t.* $E^V(root) = root'$,
- $E^E: Emb \to Emb'$ *s.t.* $E^E(v_{ij}: V_i \to V_j) = E^V(V_i) \to E^V(V_j) \in Emb'$,

and $f = \{f_i: V_i \to E^V(V_i) \mid V_i \in P\}$ is a set of injective (triple) graph morphisms s.t. the square (1) in the figure below commutes, and $\forall V_i \to X \to C_j \in PC(V_i)$, $\exists E^V(V_i) \to X' \to C'_j \in PC(E^V(V_i))$ s.t. squares (2) and (3) in the figure below are pushouts and $|C(X)| = |C(X')|$. Regarding the set of equations var, we demand $E^V(var) \subseteq var'$ and that no formula of $var' \setminus E^V(var)$ contains variables in $E^V(P)$.

$$
\begin{array}{ccc}
V_i & \xrightarrow{f_i} & E^V(V_i) \\
{\scriptstyle v_{ij}}\downarrow & (1) & \downarrow{\scriptstyle E^E(v_{ij})} \\
V_j & \xrightarrow{f_j} & E^V(V_j)
\end{array}
\qquad
\begin{array}{ccccc}
V_i & \longrightarrow & X & \longrightarrow & C_j \\
\downarrow & (2) & \downarrow & (3) & \downarrow \\
E^V(V_i) & \longrightarrow & X' & \longrightarrow & C'_j
\end{array}
$$

Given patterns VP and VP', if $\exists Ext: VP \to VP'$ s.t. Exp preserves role names and focus we say that VP' extends VP, and we write it $VP' \sqsubseteq VP$.

The requirement of f for constraints of extended parts is that they should be provided exactly with the new elements added to the variable part they constrain (hence the pushouts) and they should not add new consequence graphs. However, VP' can add new premises X_k. The condition on the formula states that VP' cannot modify the formulae of VP, but can add equations involving new variable parts. In Fig. 14, if a variable part V_i of VP is extended by $E^V(V_i)$ of VP', we label the extended part as "$name'(E^V(V_i))$ extends $name(V_i)$".

The set-based semantics for patterns from Def. 2 provide the usual replaceability of supertypes by subtypes as subsetting of the respective expansions, as stated in Theorem 1, whose proof is immediate.

Theorem 1 (Subtyping). *Given patterns VP and VP', if $VP' \sqsubseteq VP$ then $SEM(VP') \subseteq SEM(VP)$.*

Example. Specific types of *Form* require labels to be in well-defined alignment relations with the inputs and between themselves. The Quince pattern repository distinguishes between the *Left Aligned Labels*, *Right Aligned Labels* and *Top Aligned Labels* patterns. To show their commonality, we introduce the abstract pattern *AlignedLabels* $\sqsubseteq$ *Form* (right of Fig. 14), by adding a role describing the adjacency between labels. Thus, each label is adjacent to one or two other labels (but labels at the beginning or the end have only one neighbour). Constraints on the realization can then be used to specify the type of alignment. Thus, all of *Left Aligned Labels*, *RightAlignedLabels* and *Top Aligned Labels* can be defined as subtypes of *AlignedLabels* by adding a set of suitable constraints. As an example, the left of Fig. 15 shows the constraints for left alignment. The pattern contains three constraints $X_i \rightarrow C_i$, presented as overlapping graphs, with nesting of a C_i area within a X_i area representing the morphism. The first constraint states that if the user input and the label are reified by concrete interaction object (*cio*) elements (X_1), those should be horizontally aligned (grphAlign indicates an instance of *graphicalAlignment*). The second constraint states that if the label has a closeness adjacency with another label (of an instantiation of another *AlignedLabel*), then the *cio* reifications of both should be vertically aligned. Finally, the third constraint states that if the output is reified by the concrete *outputText* element, this should be aligned to the left.

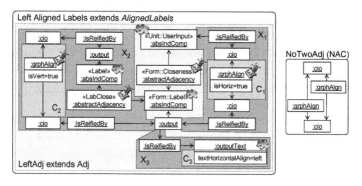

Fig. 15 Constraints for *LeftAlignedLabels* (left). Global Negative Constraint (right)

5.2 Pattern Composition

In order to compose two patterns, the idea is to select the elements to be identified in the root of both patterns, and then, to glue the roots through the identified elements (via a pushout construction) yielding the root of a new composite pattern. The process is repeated for the elements in the variable parts that one wants to identify. Concerning the variability equations, both merged variable parts receive the same name, hence, we perform the union of the original equations (after renaming) so as to consider the most restrictive ones. As an example, Fig. 17 shows a composition of the Quince patterns *Command Area* and *Clear Entry Points*.

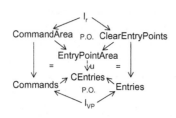

Fig. 16 Composition scheme

The first pattern groups commands together (modelled by variable part *Commands*) into a unified area of the interface (role *CommandArea*). The second pattern provides a set of clear entry points (region *Entries*) into an application or Web site, based on their most common tasks or destinations. The diagram in Fig. 16 shows the composition scheme. The resulting pattern is obtained by identifying the elements with roles *Main* and *HomePage* in the roots (graph I_r) as well as *Command* and *EntryPoint* (and linked object control) in the variable parts (graph I_{VP}). The composed pattern is built by the pushouts of the roots and the variable parts, where the embedding u of the resulting root is given by the universal pushout property. Altogether, the resulting pattern groups commands to entry points into a common area.

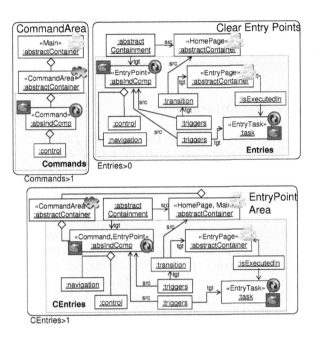

Fig. 17 Composing patterns

5.3 Conflicts

The introduction of constraints together with the notion of composition allow the identification of conflicts between patterns, when certain roles are identified with each other. These conflicts may arise between the constraints of the pattern, or be caused by incompatibilities with the integrity constraints of the domain specific language (i.e. constraints of the UsiXML meta-model in our case). In order to achieve a full management of such conflicts, one has to encode the meta-model constraints using graph constraints, and then detect incompatibilities statically by using composition. For example, the right of Fig. 15 is a negative constraint stating that two elements can only share one type of *graphicalAlignment* at most. Then, one can infer that all the *AlignedLabel* specializations are in conflict with each other. This is so, because if two pattern instantiations share a common UserInput, the constraint $X_1 \rightarrow C_1$ would demand two *graphicalAlignments*, in contradiction with the global constraint. Interestingly, these conflicts can be computed statically by applying the same procedure as for pattern composition. Once such conflicts are determined, then one can annotate the pattern with such information, thus providing a formal basis for the description of some of the consequences of pattern application.

It might also be the case that two patterns cannot be composed, due to conflicts, if certain identifications are performed, but a different set of identifications removes the cause for conflict. For example, a conflict can be detected between *VisualFramework* and *ClearEntryPoints* when we try to identify the abstract container playing the role of Home Page for *ClearEntryPoints* with the container for the fixed part in *VisualFramework*. Indeed, as the entry points must be present only in the home page, they cannot be fixed. On the other hand, one can force one occurrence of the varying container in the *Vars* region to host exactly the entry points, or provide a specialization of the visual framework to host entry points in the fixed part.

6   Conclusions and Future Work

The theoretical foundation of a notion of HCI pattern language is challenged by the heterogeneity of the aspects involved, from classical SE concerns to cognitive issues. Currently, the definition of pattern languages is based on structured textual descriptions of motivations, contexts and solutions, and exemplar realizations. Hence, relations between patterns cannot be properly identified, nor can it be determined if some implementation is a realizations of a known pattern.

In this paper, we have used a formal definition of pattern, based on triple graphs, to describe the solution component of a pattern. In particular, by identifying relevant roles in a pattern, from the point of view of the domain, presentation and dynamics aspects of interaction definition, we provide a basis for determining the existence of relations between patterns in particular, subtyping, conflicts and composition. Moreover, based on this formalization, a number of techniques becomes available, supporting pattern-based and model-based construction of UIs (see e.g. [10] .

The approach is being tested on existing collections of patterns and several examples have been presented in the paper. Among the expected outcomes of this exploration are the identification of common abstractions for families of patterns, and the exploration of the limitations of the current proposal. In particular, we envisage that imposing the structure of a directed acyclic graph, rather than of a tree, on the set of morphisms between variable parts will conquer more patterns to formalization. Another avenue of investigation regards the possibility of defining a notion of *satisfaction with respect to inheritance*, to consider cases where a pattern VP uses an element of some type T, and the model M uses elements which are instances of sub-types of T. A standard approach to this would be generating all the versions of VP where a type T is replaced by all its possible descendants T' [10]. More refined solutions can be studied, for example by distinguishing the notion of sub-typing in the definition of the pattern from that existing in the application model.

Acknowledgements. This work has been sponsored by the Spanish Ministry of Science and Innovation with project METEORIC (TIN2008-02081) and by the R&D program of the Community of Madrid (S2009/TIC-1650, project "e-Madrid"). This work was done during the research stays of the last two authors at the University of York, with financial support from the Spanish Ministry of Science and Innovation (grant refs. JC2009-00015, PR2009-0019 and PR2008-0185).

References

1. Ahmed, S., Ashraf, G.: Model-based user interface engineering with design patterns. Journal of Systems and Software 80(8), 1408 (2007)
2. Almendros-Jiménez, J.M., Iribarne, L.: An extension of UML for the modeling of WIMP user interfaces. J. Vis. Lang. Comput. 19, 695–720 (2008)
3. Borchers, J.: A Pattern Approach to Interaction Design. Wiley, Chichester (2001)
4. Bottoni, P., Guerra, E., de Lara, J.: Formal foundation for pattern-based modelling. In: Chechik, M., Wirsing, M. (eds.) FASE 2009. LNCS, vol. 5503, pp. 278–293. Springer, Heidelberg (2009)
5. Bottoni, P., Guerra, E., de Lara, J.: A language-independent and formal approach to pattern-based modelling with support for composition and analysis. Inf. Soft. Technol. 52(8), 821–844 (2010)
6. Bottoni, P., Guerra, E., de Lara, J.: Towards a formal notion of interaction pattern. In: Proc. VL/HCC 2010, pp. 235–239. IEEE CS Press, Los Alamitos (2010)
7. Breiner, K., Seissler, M., Meixner, G., Forbrig, P., Seffah, A., Klöckner, K.: PEICS: towards HCI patterns into engineering of interactive systems. In: Proc. PEICS 2010, pp. 1–3. ACM Press, New York (2010)
8. Calvary, G., Coutaz, J., Thevenin, D., Limbourg, Q., Bouillon, L., Vanderdonckt, J.: A unifying reference framework for multi-target user interfaces. Interacting with Computers 15(3), 289–308 (2003)
9. Campos, P., Nunes, N.: Towards useful and usable interaction design tools: Canonsketch. Interacting with Computers 19, 597–613 (2007)
10. de Lara, J., Bardohl, R., Ehrig, H., Ehrig, K., Prange, U., Taentzer, G.: Attributed graph transformation with node type inheritance. Theor. Comput. Sci. 376(3), 139–163 (2007)
11. Didonet Del Fabro, M., Valduriez, P.: Towards the efficient development of model transformations using model weaving and matching transformations. Software and Systems Modeling 8(3), 305–324 (2009)
12. Dong, J., Yang, S., Zhang, K.: Visualizing design patterns in their applications and compositions. IEEE TSE 33(7), 433–453 (2007)
13. Ehrig, H., Ehrig, K., Habel, A., Pennemann, K.-H.: Theory of constraints and application conditions: From graphs to high-level structures. Fundam. Inform. 74(1), 135–166 (2006)
14. Fincher, S.: PLML: pattern language markup language, http://www.cs.kent.ac.uk/people/staff/saf/patterns/plml.html (accessed September 14, 2010)
15. Folmer, E., van Gurp, J., Bosch, J.: A framework for capturing the relationship between usability and software architecture. Software Process: Improvement and Practice 8(2), 67–87 (2003)
16. Folmer, E., van Welie, M., Bosch, J.: Bridging patterns: An approach to bridge gaps between SE and HCI. Inf. Soft. Technol. 48(2), 69–89 (2006)
17. France, R.B., Kim, D.-K., Ghosh, S., Song, E.: A UML-based pattern specification technique. IEEE TSE 30(3), 193–206 (2004)
18. Gamma, E., Helm, R., Johnson, R., Vlissides, J.M.: Design Patterns. Elements of Reusable Object-Oriented Software. Addison Wesley, Reading (1994)
19. Infragistics: http://quince.infragistics.com (accessed September 14, 2010)
20. Juristo Juzgado, N., López, M., Moreno, A.M., Sánchez Segura, M.: Improving software usability through architectural patterns. In: ICSE Workshop on SE-HCI, pp. 12–19 (2003)

21. Kim, S.K., Carrington, D.: Using integrated metamodeling to define OO design patterns with Object-Z and UML. In: APSEC, pp. 257–264 (2004)
22. Mahemoff, M., Johnston, L.J.: Pattern languages for usability: An investigation of alternative approaches. In: Tanaka, J. (ed.) APCHI 1998, pp. 25–31. IEEE Computer Society, Los Alamitos (1998)
23. Mori, G., Paternò, F., Santoro, C.: Design and development of multidevice user interfaces through multiple logical descriptions. IEEE TSE 30, 507–520 (2004), DOI http://doi.ieeecomputersociety.org/10.1109/TSE.2004.40
24. Niere, J., Schäfer, W., Wadsack, J.P., Wendehals, L., Welsh, J.: Towards pattern-based design recovery. In: ICSE 2002, pp. 338–348 (2002)
25. Nunes, N.: Representing user-interface patterns in UML. In: Masood, A., Léonard, M., Pigneur, Y., Patel, S. (eds.) OOIS 2003. LNCS, vol. 2817, pp. 142–151. Springer, Heidelberg (2003)
26. Orejas, F.: Attributed graph constraints. In: Ehrig, H., Heckel, R., Rozenberg, G., Taentzer, G. (eds.) ICGT 2008. LNCS, vol. 5214, pp. 274–288. Springer, Heidelberg (2008)
27. Pribeanu, C., Vanderdonckt, J.: A transformational approach for pattern-based design of user interfaces. In: ICAS 2008, pp. 47–54. IEEE Computer Society, Los Alamitos (2008)
28. Radermacher, A.: Support for design patterns through graph transformation tools. In: Münch, M., Nagl, M. (eds.) AGTIVE 1999. LNCS, vol. 1779, pp. 111–126. Springer, Heidelberg (2000)
29. Schattkowsky, T., Lohmann, M.: Towards employing UML model mappings for platform indepedent user interface design. In: MDDAUI 2005. CEUR Workshop Proceedings, vol. 159, CEUR-WS.org (2005)
30. Schürr, A.: Specification of graph translators with triple graph grammars. In: Mayr, E.W., Schmidt, G., Tinhofer, G. (eds.) WG 1994. LNCS, vol. 903, pp. 151–163. Springer, Heidelberg (1995)
31. Scott, B., Neil, T.: Designing Web Interfaces: Principles and Patterns for Rich Interactions. O'Reilly, Sebastopol (2009)
32. Seffah, A., Taleb, M., Habieb-Mammar, H., Abran, A.: Reconciling usability and interactive system architecture using patterns. Journal of Systems and Software 81(11), 1845–1852 (2008)
33. Taibi, T., Ngo, D.C.L.: Formal specification of design pattern combination using BPSL. Inf. Soft. Technol. 45, 157–170 (2003)
34. Tidwell, J.: Designing Interfaces. O'Reilly, Sebastopol (2006)
35. Tourwé, T., Mens, T.: High-level transformations to support framework-based software development. ENTCS 72(4) (2003)
36. Toxboe, A.: Pattern library, http://ui-patterns.com (accessed September 14, 2010)
37. UsiXML: http://www.usixml.org/ (accessed September 14, 2010)
38. Valverde, F., Pastor, O.: Applying interaction patterns: Towards a model-driven approach for RIA development. In: IWWOST 2008 (2008)
39. van Welie, M.: Ui patterns, http://www.welie.com/patterns/ (accessed September 14, 2010)
40. van Welie, M., Trætteberg, H.: Interaction patterns in user interfaces. In: PLoP 2000, pp. 13–16 (2000)
41. Vanderdonckt, J., Simarro, F.M.: Generative pattern-based design of user interfaces. In: Proc. PEICS 2010, pp. 12–19. ACM Press, New York (2010)

Task Models in the Context of User Interface Development

Gerd Szwillus

Abstract. Task models are widely used in the field of user interface development. They represent a human actor's performance or the co-operation of a group of people on or together with a system. For considerable time, it was an open problem in the field how to switch from the analyzing step of task analysis and modeling to the synthesizing step of user interface design. In the meantime, interesting approaches have shown up dealing with this problem and helping to bridge the gap between task modeling and user interface development. In this chapter, some of these approaches are discussed, together with recent concepts used to improve the usability of user interfaces based upon underlying task models.

1 Introduction

Task modeling is an approach describing the behavior of one or more human actors grounded on rational consideration while explicitly pursuing specific goals. Within the context of model-driven development of user interfaces, task modeling is used for describing the users' actions while working with an interactive system. Task modeling is a semi-formal specification technique, combining formal elements for the specification of task structures and internal rules with informal task descriptions expressed in colloquial language.

Task modeling helps to understand and describe the way a human actor uses or will use an interactive system by concentrating on the sequence of actions performed by the user, based on his or her intentions and objectives. Hence, it supports the task analysis process, by documenting the tasks users fulfill in a current, running system, and it enables the designer to propose action steps to be performed with a new system. As such, task modeling or usage modeling [1] serves as a first design step of the functionality of an interactive system, by clearly stating the user's point of view on the task and his or her way of structuring it into subtasks and subsequent steps, referred to as the user's mental model of the task.

In the following, we will present basic common properties of the task modeling concept as such, and will discuss currently relevant task modeling approaches. Creating and maintaining realisticly-sized task models is laborious, hence we also cover tool support for this concept based on the partial formality of the models.

Gerd Szwillus
Institute of Computer Science, University of Paderborn, Fürstenallee 11, D-33102 Paderborn, Germany

H. Hussmann et al. (Eds.): MDD of Advanced User Interfaces, SCI 340, pp. 277–302.
springerlink.com   © Springer-Verlag Berlin Heidelberg 2011

When it comes to user interfaces, task models are used in two ways: First, they serve as a starting point for a transition into an actual dialogue, resp. a dialogue model. This has since long been identified as a non-trivial process [2] [3], but there exist some promising concepts now. Second, task models constitute a means to evaluate user interfaces in terms of task appropriateness, or usability. Although task models basically considered to deal with the user behavior on an abstract level, there are interesting approaches dealing with some usability issues as well. We discuss several of these approaches in the final part of this chapter.

2 Task Modelling Concepts

There are different task modeling approaches on the market which vary in several respects. Notwithstanding the differences, there is a common ground, however, supported by all these approaches, which can be considered to represent the essence of the task modeling concept.

2.1 Basic Elements of Task Modeling

Given the fact that the main purpose of task modeling is to document the way people understand and structure tasks, the dominant structure underlying all task modeling approaches is the decomposition of tasks into "smaller" subtasks, the task hierarchy. This hierarchy is in all cases depicted by a graphical representation of a tree structure. While the particular graphics differ, they all depict a task tree in some way or other. Hence, for instance, if the task "Sending a letter" includes the subtasks "Writing" (the letter), "Placing in envelope", and "Posting" (the letter) with "Posting" including "Adding stamp" and "Putting into mailbox", this would result in a structure as shown in Figure 1.

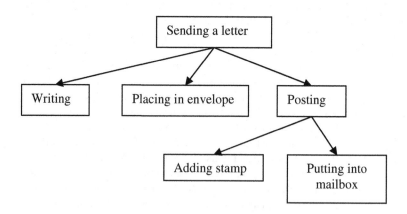

Fig. 1 Simple Task Model for the task "Sending a letter"

The hierarchy in itself only specifies the pure task-subtask-relations. More information is needed to properly model the user behavior when performing the task, most important being sequence information. Modeling the "Posting" task, for instance, would not be considered appropriate if it allowed the sequence of first doing "Putting into mailbox" and then doing "Adding stamp". Information like this is subsumed in the task modeling concept under the term of temporal relations. Again, different approaches vary in their choice of temporal relations and the way they are depicted in the hierarchy, but there is general accordance about the following types of temporal relations being indispensable. In many approaches, the temporal relations are specified as properties of the supertasks, a representation we will follow here as well. Given that A and B are subtasks of T,

- *sequence* denotes that first A and then B have to be performed to achieve T,
- *random sequence* denotes that A and B have to be performed one after the other to achieve T, but the order is irrelevant,
- *parallel* means A and B have to be performed simultaneously, meaning that there must be at least one point in time where A and B are both "running" at the same time,
- *unrestricted* means that A and B have to be performed, but there is no restriction whatsoever about their mutual timing, and
- *selection* means that only one of the subtasks needs to be done to perform T.

In addition, a task can be specified to be

- *optional*, hence it can, but need not, be executed,
- or an *iteration*, hence it can be repeated several times.

Figure 2 contains some additions specifying the necessary sequencing rules, and including the optional addition of a photograph to the letter, which can either be put into the envelope as first or as second step.

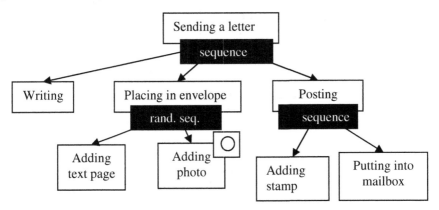

Fig. 2 Some temporal relations added to the "Sending a letter" task tree

This really small example can serve for illustrating three important points impacting the use of task models in real-world settings:

- *Validation*: The author of a task model must verify cautiously, whether the user's actions are described correctly, i.e. if the user really behaves in the way the model defines. This is by no means trivial, as a task model in most cases does not describe exactly one sequence of action, but typically allows several variants of execution sequencing. To evaluate the model, we need the user's expertise to assess whether the described behavior matches reality, but we cannot in general assume that users can read and understand task models. We will deal with this validation problem later in the chapter.
- *Granularity*: There is no universal rule at what level of detail the modeling process should end, as this depends on the objectives of the modeling process. The example of Figure 2 could easily be developed further, e.g., by refining the "Writing" task into "starting the computer", "invoking the text editor", "typing", and "printing". As we advocate the use of task models for specifying user behavior while using an interactive system, we should model deep enough to get a basic understanding of the functionality needed by the user when performing the task, without implicitly designing the future system already in the task model.
- *Variability*: A task model in general cannot take into account every eventuality happening during task execution. Quite the contrary, it should be seen as a typical, standard way of performing a task, representing frequent and important variations, but not every potential variant. Some authors refer to this as a typical "80/20-situation", meaning that 80% of the typical behavior is covered, while 20%, denoting the more special cases, are not. When task models are used for designing user interfaces, there is an obvious need to fully understand typical and frequent behavior, to allow the creation of an appropriate user interface for these cases. In the example of Figure 2, we could, for instance, modify the model such that the subtask "Adding stamp" could be performed at any time in the process, provided it is done before posting the letter. Technically, this would be correct, but the task model would then loose the property of describing the "usual", typical way of how the user structures and manages the tasks in semantically connected and clearly identifiable phases.

2.2 Additional Elements of Task Models

Task hierarchy and temporal relations have been identified as the basic building blocks of task models. There are, however, concepts, which are contained in single or several approaches, which have proven to be relevant additions to the concept of task modeling. There are good reasons, of course, to keep task models simple, especially when they are intended for different stakeholders to read and understand. In many cases, however, it is equally useful to include additional elements. The most important of these are the objects manipulated by tasks, conditions other than the temporal relations imposed on task performance, the distinction of different actors or roles, and events and context information. There exist huge differences with respect to these additional elements when it comes to single task modeling approaches.

2.2.1 Objects

In the concept as sketched out up to now that actual actions performed are simply stated in colloquial language as informal text (e.g. "Writing"). The objects being manipulated by the tasks are only mentioned as nouns in these short descriptions (e.g., "envelope", "text page"), if at all. Several task modeling approaches go further from here and allow the specification of the "things" used by tasks as formal elements. Typically objects are introduced as instances of classes, which define object attributes, as known from object-oriented programming languages. Objects can also own methods for attribute manipulation and a state concept. Within a task, it is possible to create, modify, and destroy objects. Also, this concept allows task execution results to be passed from one task to another.

In the example of Figure 2, for instance, the task „Writing" could create an object "text page", which is later used by "Placing in envelope". This last task could be specified as first modifying the state of "text page" from "unfolded" to "folded", then creating a new object of type "envelope" and changing its state from "empty" to "filled". Approaches differ in their descriptive power of object manipulations; typically, they are described as effects to be achieved after a task is completed.

It is obvious, that the remarks about granularity of the model apply to this modeling concept to a high degree. However, the concept allows the modeler to express object manipulation which later in the design process of a user interface should result in corresponding data displayed and edited by the user of the final system.

2.2.2 Pre- and Postconditions

Temporal relations specify the order in which subtasks are executed. However, this specification is limited to the subtasks of a common supertask; there is no means to express conditions holding between subtasks of different supertasks. Assume in our example model of Figure 2, for instance, that the task "Adding stamp" is influenced by the fact that a photograph is added to the letter (then we need 90 Cent) or not (then we need 55 Cent only).

Without the possibility to specify conditions, we could not describe that the user sticks the appropriate stamp on the letter, depending on the fact, whether a photograph was added or not. By modeling that "Adding photo" modifies the attribute photoAdded of the object Envelope e to true, we could specify the condition Execute only, if e.photoAdded = true as a *pre-condition* for the task "Glueing 90 Ct." and the inverse pre-condition to "Glueing 55 Ct.".

Apart from pre-conditions, some approaches use *post-conditions* as well, meaning that a condition must hold, before a task can be finished. Also, conditions can be used for defining under which circumstances an optional task is skipped, or if and how often a task should be iterated. Some approaches provide "world" conditions, i.e. conditions which are not influenced by the task model itself, but are set from the outside (e.g., "Sending a letter" could be dependent on the world condition "saturated" to avoid writing a letter while being hungry).

Conditions are a powerful structuring mechanism which add important rules to task models. In most cases, they represent domain knowledge the user must be aware of when performing the task. Hence, for eliciting the mechanics of task performance to be supported by an interactive system, conditions are extremely valuable and important. Sometimes they represent "tacit knowledge" from the application area, information that is taken for granted, and easily overlooked in system design processes. As conditions are typically not displayed in the graphical representation of the task hierarchy, they are a special challenge for the validation process.

2.2.3 Roles

Task models as described so far do not give any information about who performs the tasks at hand. Also, there is no distinction whether one person acts or a group of person co-operates. Some approaches explicitly deal with that situation.

In the simplest case, a task model distinguishes between tasks that

- the (one) human actor performs completely on his or her own ("*user task*"), and
- an action that the interactive system performs ("*system task*") for the user.

Additionally, there can be tasks, which the user performs together with the system ("*interaction task*"). For instance, while using a text processor, thinking of the text to enter is clearly a user task, creating a table of contents after the user issued the corresponding command is a system task, and entering the text is considered an interaction task. In these cases, we still think of **one** user using a system.

There are frequent work situations, however, where a group of persons co-operates together on performing a task. To cope with such a situation, some approaches support an explicit *role model*. Such a model contains typically a hierarchy of actors or roles, where rights and duties are inherited. The actor is the person (or system for that matter) performing a task. This can be a specific individual, or it can denote "one of a kind", a role, e.g., a pilot. A role is characterized by a set of responsibilities, denoted by the tasks, a role can or cannot perform. The co-operation of the roles can be captured in one big task model, where the tasks are annotated with the respective roles; or there might be a separate task model for each role and an extra one for the co-operation specification.

2.2.4 Events

Objects and conditions provide mechanisms to link tasks within a task model, even if they are far distant from each other, to each other. A special case of such a link is established via events. A task execution can be triggered from events happening "outside" of the model or as something "happening" within the model. Likewise, executing a task can trigger an event into the "world", or towards another task in the model. Similar to conditions, events represent important implicit domain knowledge, which should be detected during the task analysis phase and documented in the task model.

In the example of Figure 3, several implicit events and triggers are assumed, but not stated explicitly. After writing the letter, for instance, the task "Placing in Envelope" **can** be performed, and typically the user, as being aware of this action sequence, does so; otherwise writing the letter would not have been necessary in first place. Or, assume that in an organization there is one role responsible for writing a letter, but another person is responsible for posting it. In such a case, there must be a clear trigger from the task "Placing in Envelope" to the task "Posting", otherwise the letter might remain unsent. Again, information like this is very important for creating a correct design of an interactive system, which is modeled along the tasks performed by the users.

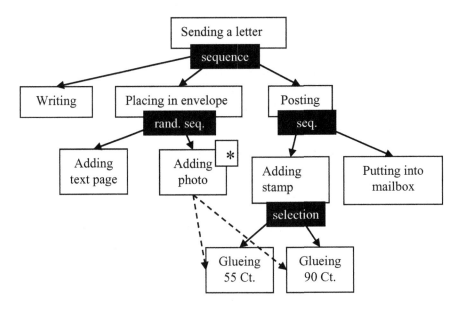

Fig. 3 Using conditions in task models (dependencies shown as dotted lines)

2.2.5 Context

With a task model, we want to specify how a human user performs a task with an interactive system. The purpose of the modeling process is to understand the action steps to be taken and the rules governing execution. Apart from the pure functional aspects covered so far, there can be a myriad of situational information relevant for the user's behavior. This applies to the physical situation (such as the physical conditions of the environmental situation), issues of timing (e.g., are there time constraints, is the user pressed, are the tasks executed rarely or frequently), organizational issues (such as whether the task is a single user task or a co-operative task), and user-specific properties (such as experience with the task, the application, the operating system, or computers as such). The sum of all these elements is referred to the task model context. For every task model either an explicit description of the context is given, or it is implicitly assumed. Just like for the design and implementation of every user interface context-information of this kind is extremely important for its success.

3 Current Task Modeling Approaches

In this chapter, we will give a short overview of six task modeling approaches. Of course, there are more (e.g., [4], [5]), but the ones discussed here cover the typical bandwidth of task modeling as it exists today. Interestingly enough, a recent approach named HOPS (Higher-Order Processes Specification language) [6] combines most elements of task modeling approaches as mentioned above in a unifying way, overcoming the dominance of the task hierarchy structure, coining the term of the "Situated Task Model" [7]. Within this chapter, we will take a look at the following approaches:

- HTA, the Hierarchical Task Analysis concept originating from the first paper on task models from Annett and Duncan in 1967 [8], and undergoing major modifications until today when it is supported by an appropriate tool,
- GTA, Groupware Task Analysis [9], an approach from the University of Amsterdam, Netherlands,
- CTT, the ConcurTaskTree concept [10] from CNR-ISTI in Pisa, Italy,
- K-MADe, the Kernel of Model for Activity Description environment [11] from INRIA, France,
- VTMB, the Visual Task Model Builder [12], and
- AMBOSS (Task Modeling for Safety-Critical Systems [In German: "Aufgabenmodellierung zur Bedienung von sicherheitskritischen Systemen"]) both developed at the University of Paderborn, Germany [13], and
- CTML (Collaborative Task Modeling Language) [14] from the University of Rostock.

3.1 Basic Elements

As mentioned above, there is a common understanding of task models as task hierarchies structured with temporal relations. Differences show up in the way temporal relations are dealt with.

- K-MADe, VTMB, AMBOSS and CTML apply the specification technique as used in the figures above, allowing roughly the same set of predefined temporal relations.
- GTA does so as well, only the temporal relations are not predefined, but are just (informal) text strings. This is less stringent, but gives the user more flexibility.
- HTA does not link predefined temporal relations to task nodes, but allows the explicit specification (as text) of how the different subtasks of a task are executed. This includes skipping, iteration, choice, but also conditions. Hence, it is the most flexible concept in that respect.
- CTT, as the most prominent and widely-used task modeling approach specifies temporal relations as a relation between neighboring subtasks. Its predefined set of temporal relation definitions is the most developed in the field. Figure 4, for instance, displays the top part of figure 1 in CTT notation, where the sequence of the three subtasks is expressed with the "enabling" operator >>.

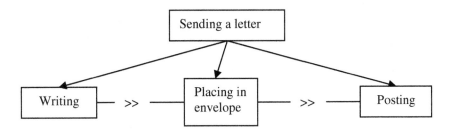

Fig. 4 Top part of Figure 1 rewritten with CTT

In the case of CTT, K-MADe, VTMB, AMBOSS, and CTML the set of prede-fined temporal relations assures that the models have well-defined execution se-mantics. Accordingly, the corresponding tools offer a simulation resp. animation of the models.

3.2 Additional Elements

When it comes to the additional elements of task models, identified above, the differences between the approaches are significant.

- **Hierarchical Task Analysis (HTA)** in its original form has concentrated on human operators' goal structures and their decomposition into subgoals. This included explicitly the distinction between a systematical plan for typical situa-tions and the coverage of untypical, exceptional situations, also treatment of erroneous behavior. Hence, an HTA model can include pre- and postconditions, also events, but does not cover manipulated objects or context information. The HTA tool existing now [15] is based on this original work, but includes a very rich environment to specify object, role, and context information of all kind.
- **Groupware Task Analysis (GTA)** explicitly contains two object hierarchies apart from the task hierarchy: an "is-a"-hierarchy (inheritance) and a "part-of"-hierarchy (aggregation). As such, GTA has the richest object model part from all approaches mentioned here. The user can specify in a very detailed way how objects are structured and used. But also with respect to all other additional elements, GTA is the most complete approach: The user can define roles (another hierarchy), assign responsibilities to roles, define who is allowed to or has to do which tasks, how a group co-operates on a task, define pre- and postconditions for tasks, can define the creation of and reaction to events, and has numerous possibilities to denote context conditions. A GTA model is a highly linked data structure which enables the user of the concept to define and interlink all relevant concepts.
- **ConcurTaskTrees (CTT)** stands out in its capacity to explicitly define how several actors together fulfill a task. The task-oriented behavior of every single role is defined in a task tree; then all these are linked by an additional tree. This is the most developed approach for co-operative tasks. In its original version,

CTT does not allow any specifications of objects, conditions, events, or context information. CTT is the most popular task modeling approach, sometimes referred to as de-facto-standard – the typical CTT trees can be found all over the task modeling literature.

- **K-MADe** explicitly covers roles, objects and events in its concept. The approach is highly detail-oriented and can be considered as being almost a programming environment, as transformations of objects and other calculations can actually be defined to full detail. Also, the approach explicitly covers time and timely behavior, which is an important aspect of context.
- The **Visual Task Model Builder (VTMB)** proposes a simple object model based on a class hierarchy, and incorporates pre- and postconditions, as well as effects of tasks, based on object attribute manipulation. It does not distinguish different roles, and does not cover events or context information. The approach concentrates on the decomposition of tasks and the sequence rules governing task performance.
- **AMBOSS** is a task model approach specifically targeted towards the analysis and documentation of safety-critical systems. Most of these are sociotechnical systems; hence, the definition of roles is essential. In addition, a hierarchical object system is included. Apart from that, several context parameters of task execution are captured, as they are relevant to safety issues. An important example is the communication between actors; others deal with spatial distribution of objects and actors, and barriers, protecting humans and material.
- **CTML** refines the behavior specification of single tasks, temporal relations and as such of the whole task model, by adding structured behavior to the single elements based upon a finite state machine. Task execution is not taken as atomic, but being subject to transitions between states such as "disabled", "enabled", "running", etc., thus allowing for a much more detailed behavior specification, which leads to a sophisticated specification concept for co-operation and task execution.

3.3 Tool Support

As seen above, there are big differences between the existing task modeling approaches with respect to the degree to which objects, conditions, roles, events, and context information are included. This has also consequences on the tool support existing for the approaches. First of all, the tool support is intended to release the designer from the editing and drawing load imposed by the use of task models. Second, however, task modeling tools can have tremendous impact on the use of task models by providing some way of visualizing the actual execution of a task model. There are basically two approaches to this: Either the graphical task tree is animated by dynamical, step-by-step annotations of the executed tasks (animation), or the set of currently executed tasks is visually represented by some dynamical graphics separate from the tree (simulation). In both cases, the designer can "see" the flow of actions, and can validate, if the model corresponds to reality.

- The historically "oldest" approach (HTA) was originally not supported by any tool. It was a pure pen-and-paper concept and its merit was in the ground-laying ideas of refining tasks into subtasks, governed by temporal relations. The ideas were later picked up by an institute[1] founded by the UK defense ministry, who developed the HTA tool to use the computer for creating and maintaining big HTA models. This tool, however, does not allow any kind of animation or simulation of the task model, as one of the most important building blocks, the plans, are specified as informal text to maintain utmost flexibility.

- Euterpe was[2] a tool supporting the GTA approach. It allowed the user to specify detailed information about the tasks into a highly interlinked structure, which could subsequently be printed as large graphics or be exported as a clickable website, showing both detail and context. Due to the fact that the temporal relations were not predefined there were no formally defined execution semantics, hence the model could only be documented, not simulated.

- CTTE is the environment to use CTT, and it provides sophisticated editors and a powerful animation of the model. A CTT model consists of one big task tree, which is used as the basis for a graphical animation process – currently activated tasks are depicted as "highlighted". A co-operative model combines several task trees into one construct, which can also be animated. This is a very powerful means to understand the mechanics of how several actors together work on a task. As a special highlight, CTTE animations can move forward and backward, thus allowing an easy way of exploring alternate routes.

- K-MADe comes with an even richer, sophisticated editing and simulation environment. It is close to being more of a programming environment, as a huge set of details can be specified which all are taken into account during simulation. While the approach's richness is astounding, the price paid is a big effort for specifying even small task models.

- VTMB has a simple-to-use editor component, which allows a quick construction of the task hierarchy with temporal relations. With a little more effort, objects and conditions can be included in the model, which enables the designer to define in a quite detailed way the human's behavior during task execution. Within the same tool the model can be simulated, which allows the user to watch task execution and corresponding object manipulation.

- AMBOSS comes with an editor and simulation environment as well. As the approach contains more detail than, e.g., VTMB, editing has to be "richer" with respect to object, roles, and safety-critical context information. The model can be simulated which takes into account most of the information specified. One of the strong points in modeling, the communication between actors, however, is not reflected in the simulation.

- CTML, finally, contains an editor and simulation environment. The task model specification is based upon the CTT concept and objects are described with UML, including a class hierarchy and object associations; the editor allows defining conditions and effects. A complete CTML model is compiled into a network of communicating state machines, which is interpreted by the simulator.

---

[1] HFI DTC – the Human Factors Integration Defence Technology Centre.
[2] We say „was", as it is no more available and was never completed.

The simulation is fine-grained with respect to the behavior and allows a detailed analysis of the model's execution mechanics, including visibility of single states, conditions, and effects.

As can be seen, all approaches have their strengths and weaknesses. Overall, the field of task modeling approaches and tools is still emerging, and largely in the hands of academia. Only CTT with its environment CTTE has found its way into industry to some degree as a de-facto-standard for task modeling.

4 Using Task Models for User Interface Development

There exists a rich literature on modeling user behavior with goal and action hierarchies, notably under the name of GOMS modeling [16]. This psychologically founded approach reflects the fact that rational human behavior can appropriately be modeled with hierarchies, decomposing user goals into subgoals down to atomic operations. Hence, to understand and document the user's way of planning, deciding, and acting, goal or task hierarchies such as in the approaches described above are proven to be adequate for this purpose.

Such a task model could be created for describing a current situation, i.e. the way a user acts with a currently existing system (current task model), or it can be used for specifying the intended user behavior for a new, envisioned system (envisioned task model). A current task model is created as a first step of the design team to understand how the work is done in the domain under consideration; with the help of this model, all stakeholders can make sure that the work situation has been properly understood. An envisioned task model aims at defining the way the work will be done with the new system; hence, in a model-based development approach, it is a first constructive step towards user interface design. This situation has also been described as the analysis-synthesis bridge model [17].

4.1 Multi-platform User Interface Development

When discussing the issue of granularity above, it was mentioned that the task model should concentrate on modeling the human operator's performing and organizing the tasks, and should reflect decisions and operation sequences referring to the task. At best, this should only relate to task properties and not to user interface properties. Only the user's cognitive process concerning the task to be achieved should be subject to contemplation, not the concrete actions within the user interface into which the human user has to translate the pursuit of his or her goals. Otherwise the task model would implicitly state properties of the future user interface. For instance, if a task is decomposed down to actions such as "Drag the file to the trash can and drop it there", this would imply that the user interface is designed as an object-oriented graphical user interface, which provides icons for files and the trash can usable in drag-and-drop-actions. Design decisions like this, however, should be postponed to the user interface design phase. As a rule of thumb, task models should not contain references to actual user interface elements, neither in the informal task descriptions nor as formal objects.

If the task model sticks to its proper designation, the model-based development approach also supports the growing problem of device-dependent design. No developer can afford to create dedicated individual applications or web pages for the wide range of interactive devices available, i.e. desktop computers with big screens, laptops, notebooks, smart phones, or cell phones. These devices differ widely in screen space and resolution, computing power, communication bandwidth, and storage capacity. Still, the user wants to be able to use all these systems concurrently and consistently, such as booking a hotel room in the Internet from the office, from home, or while on the road. While the user accepts variants in the layout, graphical extent, and richness of textual information when using these different devices, the basic flow of action which performs the task should be the same in all cases. Task modeling as the basis of the user interface design can serve as a unifying entity: If the task model is independent of the finally implemented user interface, then it can serve as a basis for different implementations for different devices, hence, the flow of actions will essentially always be the same.

In the following, we will discuss approaches supporting the development of dialogue models as a transitional step from task models, thus enabling the designer to create different device-dependent dialogue structures from a single task model. Dialogue models define the state space of a user interface, the valid inputs in any situation, the resulting outputs displayed to the user, and the occurring state transitions. A dialogue model, other than a task model, takes a system-oriented point-of-view. It defines the reaction of the system to any input in every situation, which will later on in the process be actually implemented by the software developer. Dialogue models come in different forms, such as state chart diagrams, transition networks, Petri nets, or event-oriented specifications; they are either specified explicitly as artifacts in an editing environment or are defined implicitly with the help of interface builders.

4.1.1 TADEUS

The TADEUS approach [18] as developed at the University of Rostock during the 1990s is covered here as typical example of one of the first developments of this type. It defines an explicit method for transforming a given envisioned task model into a dialogue structure. The starting point of the process is a task model, given as a task hierarchy with temporal relations, and a corresponding object model, describing the objects needed for and transformed by task performance.

As a first step, subparts of the task tree are identified as *dialogue views*, which the designer considers to be semantically linked functional units. The basic idea is that the tasks performed and the objects needed within this subpart of the task tree should be presented to the future user together in one view, such as a single dialogue box or a window, because they are highly semantically connected. Overall, a partition of all tasks in the task tree into disjoint dialogue views is created. One can imagine these to represent the different dialogue windows of the final user interface.

As the user's task performance sequence is described by the temporal relations within the task model, this enables the designer to define the transitions between different dialogue views accordingly. While the user is only performing tasks *within* a dialogue view, this view remains active and visible; when switching to a task within another dialogue view, this has to be presented to the user, e.g., by opening a corresponding dialogue box. Within the TADEUS approach, dialogue view transitions are specified as the so-called *N-graph*, where N stands for navigation, while the activities happening within a dialogue view, are described in a *B-graph*, where B stands for editing (in German "Bearbeiten").

Both N-graph and B-graph are formally based on Petri nets; hence, they contain places and transitions.

- Within **N-graphs** places represent the different views; distinctions can be made with respect to modality of views, or whether views can exist only once or in several independent instances. Views can be characterized as being active, visible, and/or manipulable, with rules governing the behavior of the transitions between views with respect to these categories. Transitions can be specified as being sequential (start view is closed on transition) or concurrent (start view remains open). The definition of the dialogue view and transition behavior has to be compatible with the temporal relations defined for tasks in the task model which lead from the corresponding tree partitions to the next. There exists significant freedom in defining the navigation behavior, but the designer has to make sure that the temporal relations as given within the task model are respected.

- A **B-graph** is created for defining the behavior in the inner part of a given dialogue view. Places represent the different tasks contained in the tree partition; they are referred to as abstract interaction elements, as they will later in the process be transformed into concrete interaction elements, allowing the user to input data, or trigger actions, which represent the corresponding task performance, and presenting the relevant objects to him, as specified in the task model. Again, these interaction elements are characterized as being active, visible, manipulable, and additionally as sensitive, with transitions describing the dependencies between them. These transitions have to be defined in accordance to the temporal relations defined in the task model within the corresponding tree partition identified as dialogue view.

Overall, the task model with its subtask structure, temporal relations, and related objects, is used to define a global navigation structure between different views. These views contain interaction elements allowing the single subtasks to be performed, by providing adequate input elements and display of the necessary objects, needed for the tasks. As the dialog definition process is based upon the envisioned task model, the designer can ensure that the resulting dialogue respects the task structure accordingly. Of course, the quality of the end result depends on the validity of the task model, the adequate partitioning of the model into dialogue views, and the correctness of the translation of the task structures into transitions between views and interaction elements.

Although TADEUS as environment is outdated, its basic approach for the transition from task to dialogue models is worthwhile to contemplate, as the idea of partitioning the task tree is in itself interesting and the basis for other approaches as well.

One of these efforts picked up the ideas and used them to create an editing and simulation environment based on the Java Eclipse IDE, thus applying up-to-date software technology to the early ideas [19]. In this approach, a task model represents the basis for the definition of the so-called dialog-graphs [20], which correspond to the N-graphs mentioned above. As in the original concept, the nodes of the dialog-graph represent views, which are connected to task partitions, and transition within and between views are defined in accordance to the temporal relations. The EMF- and GEF-frameworks are used within Eclipse to create powerful graphical editors to create and maintain the dialog-graphs [21].

In a second step, the nodes of the dialog-graphs are refined by the composition of dialogue elements on different abstraction levels, such as abstract "task execution" buttons, text input fields, complete structured dialogue boxes, or special components like video players. This more pragmatic approach replaces the B-graph notation mentioned above and is based on the XUL user interface specification language. As all elements are functional complete, the whole dialog-graph model can be simulated, even while still incomplete, thus allowing the designer to get an early feedback on the system behavior.

While the issue of creating device-specific user interfaces for the same tasks was not important when the TADEUS concept was created, this is different today. The dialog-graphs as discussed in the end of this chapter allows to re-use a large part of the design work (the task model and the associated dialog-graph) when user interfaces have to be re-implemented for different platforms. In fact, the revival of classical ideas such as developed in TADEUS was mostly due to the fact that multi-device design can significantly be reduced when applying model-based concepts. Typically, when re-arranging a user interface for a hugely different device, just exchanging the components of the single dialogue elements is insufficient. Changes have been made to the whole interaction strategy. The editor supporting dialog-graphs is implemented to allow for re-arrangement of dialog elements and to still conserve the link to the underlying task model. Ideally then, this method enables designers to re-use design results, and still "implement" the same task model.

4.1.2 TERESA

TERESA is a development environment [22] explicitly designed for creating user interfaces from task models. While in the beginning one was primarily interested in mastering this transition, recent developments in mobile device technology have increased the interest in such systems, as already mentioned. TERESA has been developed into a powerful environment for creating multi-modal, multi-device applications, based on underlying task models. With respect to the basic underlying concepts there are relevant and interesting differences to the view definition approach of the TADEUS type.

As TERESA was created by the inventors of CTT, the starting point for creating a user interface based on a task model is a ConcurTaskTree (CTT), i.e. a task hierarchy with temporal relations. The most important concept employed is the generation of so-called *presentation task sets* (PTS), which is the analogue to the partitioning process of the TADEUS type. At any moment in time while a task model is "running", there exists a well-defined set of tasks which are currently enabled, i.e. which can be executed. This set of *enabled tasks* (ETS) can be computed from the given temporal relations; in fact this computation is the core activity of every task model simulator. As the current ETS contains all next possible tasks, a user interface that behaves accordingly must provide the possibility to perform all tasks from the ETS to the user in this situation. The computed collection of all ETS is the basis for deriving the presentation task sets.

While the ETS can be computed automatically, the definition of PTS is a design decision. It has to be done manually, but can be guided by experience, captured in so-called heuristics. As the number of ETS can be very large as a result of combinatory explosion, the goal is to minimize the number of PTS by combining ETSs. An example of such a heuristic is the combination of single-element ETSs to one, if the tasks contained are semantically strong related. Overall, this process of reducing ETS to fewer PTS is the analogue to the view definition in the TADEUS type of approach. In [23], algorithms are presented which define the resulting automaton in a semi-automatic way under the term "Activity Chain Extraction".

Once a reasonable set of PTS is found, the elements within the PTS, which are task names from the task model, are arranged in a so-called abstract user interface representation. For this process, principles frequently found in user interfaces, such as grouping, ordering, or relating semantically close elements, are used. Again, these are design decisions, which have to take into account the temporal relations of the tasks under consideration, as defined in the task model. Subsequently, the task names in the PTS are replaced by appropriate interactors, which are suitable for the task. For instance, if a task represents some choice the user has to make, a selector interactor is chosen, with some basic parameters (such as single-choice or multiple-choice) adequately defined for the task.

The abstract user interface definition process is finalized by specifying the transitions from one PTS to the next. This is done by defining rules, which state, e.g., that control flows from some PTS 1 to some other PTS 2, when the user has performed task t within PST 1. These rules must, however, be defined such that the transitions respect the temporal relations of the underlying task model. This final step corresponds to the creation of the N-graph (navigation graph) within the TADEUS approach.

Once the process has reached this point, there exists a model of the user interface, which identifies the set of views that the user will see in the final interface, the set of proposed abstract interaction elements contained in every view, and a specification of which user action leads to the presentation of which other view. If all steps were carried out appropriately, it is assured that the user can operate with the user interface in the way the task model has defined.

In the subsequent process, the abstract interactors are replaced by concrete interactors which are dedicated to a special platform. The multi-device supporting property of TERESA, however, takes into account that this alone will not be sufficient to really create appropriately adapted user interfaces for such different devices as a desktop computer and a cell phone. To solve this, the underlying task model itself can contain device-dependent structures. In fact, it can be n models in 1, one for every platform (such as cell phone, PDA, desktop). This gives up the concept of one task model for all platforms, but has been found useful (and necessary) in practice. In addition, CTT was enhanced with a component to specify objects needed or manipulated by tasks individually for every platform, so the degree to which information is presented or not can be made dependent on device used.

Both TADEUS and TERESA start from an envisioned task model and combine subsets of the task model into groups, define their "content" and the transitions between them. This structure is taken as abstract user interface definition and can then be refined further into actual user interface implementations. Both approaches ensure that the user interfaces "behave" like the underlying task model, and provide different means to adopt the interfaces to device-dependent properties. Emphasis in these approaches is to bridge the gap between the description of intended user behavior and user interface construction. Recently, the European USIXML project has started picking up ideas like these and turning them into a complete working tool suite for model-based user interface development [24].

4.2 Task Models and Usability

Task models can also be helpful in dealing with usability issues. At first sight, this may sound as a contradiction to the fact that task models should not reflect elements of the user interface. Task models should certainly not deal with a large part of usability issues, such as the look & feel of user interfaces, button design, or font and color choices. However, the conceptual model of a system and its user interface are subject to usability considerations as well. The "dialogue logic" has to be "understood" by the user of the interactive system; or, in other words, the user's mental model of the application should match the conceptual model of the system, otherwise he or she would frequently be confused or irritated by the system's responses.

The user's view on the tasks is captured in the task model envisioning the future system. If the dialogue model is derived systematically from that task model, we ensure that the dialogue logic ultimately implemented matches the user's perspective on the tasks to be performed. Turning this argument upside down, it is possible to design the basic dialogue logic of an interactive system, by defining a corresponding envisioned task model. This model can be subject to critique and evaluation with respect to several usability issues.

Consider, for example, a train schedule information website, and a user who just wants to know how long a trip from A to B takes. The website may ask for the names of start and end point of a ride first, date and time as second information. For purposes of price calculation, it then requests the user to enter potential price reduction reasons, and asks about different train types and special needs for the trip. Only then does it return a list of train connections from A to B. One could model this behavior of the website as a task model without any reference to graphics, layout, or other visual information. But it would be easy to assess even on that pure task model level that the order of inputs required does not match the user's expectation about quick information on travel times.

Nielsen provided ten well-known usability heuristics [25] which can be seen as a generally accepted landmark for usability guidelines. It is obvious that a lot of violations of the usability heuristics can only be evaluated fully, when the concrete physical appearance of a user interface is defined. This holds for the heuristic "Speak the user's language", for instance, as without knowing what the user interface looks like in detail, we cannot tell whether the symbols shown and wording used make sense to the user. Other heuristics, however, can – at least partially – be taken into consideration even when a specification as abstract as a task model is given. This holds especially for the first heuristic "Use simple and natural dialogue", as the dialogue logic, the structure and ordering of the steps, is already visible in the underlying task model. Table 1 lists some of the heuristics and their potential applicability on task model level. Being vigilant on respecting these heuristics supports the implementation of a system and user interface which is better understood by the user. Faults in this area are hard to repair in the final system, as they concern the overall dialogue structure, much harder than "cosmetic" corrections of surface elements such as graphics, textual inscriptions, colors, or fonts.

Table 1 Applicability of Heuristics to Task Models

Heuristic	Applicability
Use simple and natural dialogue	Natural dialogue explicitly refers to the user's "natural" understanding of the task
Minimize memory load	Partly refers to task models when it comes to switching between tasks
Provide clear exit points	Task interruption or cancellation must be covered in the task model and must be appropriately handled by the user and/or the system
Prevent errors	Task models can ensure action sequencing which help to create fault-tolerance

We will discuss three approaches which connect usability issues to task modeling. We start with discussing the potential of directly assessing an (envisioned) task model underlying the definition of a web site. In the second approach, task model simulation information is used for making user interface design decisions towards better usability. Finally, we present some ideas for allowing experts to evaluate user interface usability, guided by the underlying task model.

4.2.1 Canonical Abstract Prototypes

In the following, we present a concept [26] for creating what Larry Constantine referred to as *canonical abstract prototype* [27] for a task model intended for describing the use of a website. The approach allows the designer of a task model to describe and simulate requested inputs and delivered outputs in an abstract way, such that it is possible to try and observe the sequencing of inputs and outputs. This enables a usability analysis and iterated improvements of the task flow, which will determine the dialogue logic of the final system.

The approach was implemented as a prototype system [28] in the wider context of a web development environment. The starting point of the development was a rich task modeling editor, which includes a detailed object model. While the user moves in the Internet, he or she typically inputs data, receives information, makes decisions based on this information and re-enters data. To be able to model this type of behavior, the task model is enhanced by additional information about which data a task provides to the user, which data the user delivers to the task, and which information is to be remembered (like "carried around" in a back pack) by the user within this session. These facts are added as so-called "actions" to the tasks. Actions can, for instance, request an input value from the user, or provide information to the user. Additionally, action objects can be used for definition of task conditions: the availability, as well as the absence of data can be specified, for instance, as necessary pre-condition for a task.

Enhancing the envisioned task model with this "action" and "condition" information is done very straightforwardly and typically only means to formalize the informal task description. In a case study of a web site selling train tickets, this involved the transition from a task named "define start point" to a task which receives a text object named "start point" from the user. Hence, defining the actions does not substantially change the task model but only states more precisely what is already there.

The objects formally included into the task with actions can be characterized in terms of their types (such as integer, boolean, date, time, text, password, email address) which frequently are used in the web. If the user is supposed to enter a value, an appropriate interaction element is included, such as a text input field or a dropdown list. Optional and default values can be defined, to enable a realistic simulation of the future behavior in the web.

Fig. 5 Situation during an abstract prototype simulation

Once this formalization step is done, the task model can be simulated and assessed by users knowledgeable in the domain. The visual representation has not undergone a specific design phase, all simulations created with the tool look alike (see Figure 5). The task representations contain the task names, optionally a description, the interaction elements specified for performing the actions on objects, and standard buttons, if applicable, to skip or finish a task. Only the tasks which are currently available are shown. Figure 5 shows a situation of the train ticket web site simulation, where the user has entered the start point "Dortmund", has selected "Bremen" as end point, and can optionally insert stopovers. At all times during the simulation, the user can enter comments about the flow of the simulation, by clicking on the small "add a comment" the right) contained in every task box. This information can later be systematically evaluated by the designer.

Overall, the concept starts from a conventional (envisioned) task model, and visualizes its behavior in terms of information provided to and required from the future users or an expert substituting the users. While doing so, the dialog logic can be experienced and thus validated. Once the underlying task model has iteratively been modified such that it is adequate for the tasks at hand, it can serve as a basis for implementing the final website. Important design decisions influencing the usability of the future system with relation to the heuristics mentioned in Table 1 can be supported by this simulation in a very early development stage.

4.2.2 The Key Task Concept

The primary purpose of a task model is to define the user's understanding of the task as such, independent from the details of a concrete user interface. If, however, a concrete user interface of some application supporting the tasks at hand is given and has to be analyzed with respect to its usability, we can let us guide by the task model to perform the analysis. Starting from the task model which is independent from the user interface (referred to as the abstract task model) we refine the tasks down to the level of single user interface actions, resulting in the concrete task model, which of course is dependent on the user interface. The creation of the concrete user interface is a laborious but not a complicated step.

Based on the concrete task model, a usability expert inspects this model, while executing the corresponding steps in the application under consideration. Every action the user performs in the application is reflected by a task within the model. For every such action, the usability expert is now challenged to inspect this step for the presence of potential usability problems, such as "missing feedback", "inappropriate metaphor", or having to deal with a large number of objects ("count"). Based on general usability experience or dedicated domain-specific experience, the usability expert works from an existing list of potential usability problems. Assuming that working around these problems takes a certain effort on the user's side, additional tasks (referred to as *key tasks*) are added to the task model describing these additional efforts to deal with the user interface deficiencies [29]; on the other hand, positive user interface properties, helping the user are also noted as key tasks.

Table 2 shows a list of key tasks found useful in the studies performed with the approach up to now. Key tasks can describe usability problems (negative), or usability properties actively helping the user (positive), but can also be neutral, i.e. having no positive or negative effect.

Table 2 Types of key tasks used

Name of the key task	Description
CONVENTION	A dialogue does (positive) or does not (negative) behave or look according to established conventions in the field
COUNT	The number of elements to understand is too big (negative) or acceptable (positive) for the user
EXIT	A dialogue does not have a clearly marked exit (negative)
FEEDBACK	The user is not informed appropriately about the status of an important action / process (negative)
GUIDE	The user is not guided through some options or input alternatives, but has to remember things (negative)
ICON	The user is irritated by a misleading icon (negative) or properly advised by an appropriate icon (positive)
MENU ORIENTATION	The user has to digest a big (negative) or appropriate (positive) menu
METAPHOR	An inappropriate metaphor confuses the user
ORIENTATION	A new page or dialogue asks considerable effort from the user to orientate (negative)
SCROLLING	The user has to scroll the page or dialogue to reach the necessary element (negative)
SHORTCUT	The system provides a shortcut to the user (positive)
WORDING	The language used here is appropriate (positive) or not (negative)

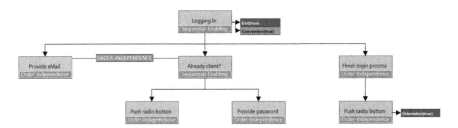

Fig. 6 Extract from a concrete task model describing a log-in process in the web with associated key tasks

Figure 6 shows a part of a concrete task model (grey boxes) with associated key tasks, as created and analyzed in the TEEAM prototype environment [30] to describe part of an electronic book shop in the web. In the visual representation, the key tasks are linked to the task where the usability issue shows up; they are not part of the task hierarchy. "Exit" was included as potential usability problem, as the web page does not include a clearly-marked exit from the log-in process; "Convention" was added as positive usability property because the web page sticks to certain conventions the user typically expects on log-in pages in the web; and the "Orientation" key task symbolizes that the user sees a new dialogue resp. web page for which considerable time is needed to scan its content and orientate himself on that page.

As can be seen from these examples, key tasks represent the effort on the user's side to fulfill the task in the corresponding dialogue element; this effort can have a negative effect, thus delaying or confusing the user, or a property of the dialogue can influence the user action in a positive, supportive way. In both cases, these effects can simply be existent or not, in which case a Boolean parameter is assigned to the key task defining whether the problem is present or not. Or the key task can depend on a numerical value, as, for instance, in the case of the key task "count": When the user is presented a large number of alternatives, such as a list of countries with 230 elements where he or she has to choose the own country from, then the key task "count(230)" can be specified. The user interface expert, on the other hand, can specify that a "count" with 1 to 20 elements is no problem, but a list with more than 20 is. On the other hand, providing a short cut to the user can be reflected as a positive usability property.

Name	Number of Occurences
Convention	9,115
Orientation	8,12
Exit	6
Count	1,5055
Wording	1
Icon	1
Count	1
Scrolling	1
Total Positive Occurences	**11,115**
Total Negative Occurences	**17,6255**

Fig. 7 Analysis results

During the analysis of an application, or a website, the analyst may discover facts, which are not described by any of the available key tasks. Hence, the editing tool allows creating new key tasks fulfilling the needs of the analyst, or modifying existing ones.

Once the concrete task model is created and enhanced with the key tasks the tool counts the occurrences of the key tasks within the model (see Figure 7). The count is based on assumed probabilities of choices and expected numbers of iterations which can be specified in the task model. As a result, the tool presents a list of positive and negative usability properties and their expected occurrences during the real execution. Based on this list, the analyst can assess the overall usability quality of the user interface with respect to the usability properties as captured in the key tasks. This result can be subject to targeted modifications, which then could again be annotated with key tasks, allowing a summative comparison between design variants.

4.2.3 The ReModEl Approach
At the University of Rostock, an integrated model-based development process was created, which builds on transformation processes between models, hence

supporting the complete user interface development cycle [31]. The approach uses task models, object models, user models, and environment models; the task models are refined by including abstract user interface objects, which are then transformed into concrete user interface elements dependent on the target platform. The transformation steps are not automated as they incorporate creative design steps, but they are supported by appropriate tools. Within this approach it is ensured that the transformational steps keep track of the elements manipulated or refined. Hence, the elements of the intermediate and finally reached user interfaces are linked to the underlying tasks structures.

The ReModEl system [32] is a simulating environment which can interpret such a chain of models on the (abstract) task model level, the level of abstract user interfaces, or the concrete user interface prototype. A concrete user interface prototype, for instance, can be employed in a usability test with "real" users, or it can be used by a domain expert for validating the chains of events, as offered by the tool. The ReModEl tool keeps track of the user actions and reports frequently performed tasks or transitions between tasks on task model level. The analysis results are presented in a heat map like style to the analyst. This visualization enables the analyst to identify certain situations which have to be taken into account for the final user interface design. For instance, if it is found that users frequently switch back and fourth between two tasks, it is recommended that these tasks are either presented together or can be reached easily from each other. Or, if a certain group of users frequently works in a special part of the task model, this hints at a special responsibility of the user group for these tasks. Also, wizard-like sequences or other typical patterns of actions can be detected. Apart from that, the link to the underlying task model can be used to specify expected, "correct" behavior and comparing it to actual behavior, either for guiding the user or learning something about potential orientation problems in the user interface.

5 Conclusions and Outlook

This book chapter has introduced several approaches for employing the concept of task modeling within model-based user interface design processes. On one hand, task models were advocated as a means for describing, documenting, and in fact designing natural task-oriented action sequences while performing certain tasks. On the other hand, there exist approaches to transform the task model information into a corresponding dialogue model which represents the underlying task model "logic" as dialogue logic presented to the user. Apart from this constructive use of task models in model-based user interface design, we proposed the assessment of important aspects of usability by creating and validating the performance of prototypes or the evaluation of user interface performance by enriching the task model with the usage details of a concrete interface.

In the area of multi-platform user interface development the model-based approaches have experienced a vivid renaissance, as they inherently provide a strong abstraction from device-dependent details. Especially the work on UsiXML [24] – a large European project which started in 2009 – looks promising, as for the first time it covers all aspects of user interface development, including the task model level. On the other hand, the work of Paterno and his group in Pisa, which started with classical task modeling and ultimately created the TERESA environment [22] for device-independent UI generation has a lot of potential. This is in particular stressed by the very recent publication of the MARIAE environment [33], which enhances the TERESA approach by incorporating web services into the design process.

References

[1] Meixner, G., Görlich, D.: Aufgabenmodellierung als Kernelement eines nutzerzentrierten Entwicklungsprozesses für Bedienoberflächen. In: Herausgegeben von Fachtagung Modellierung Berlin o. A, Workshop "Verhaltensmodellierung: Best Practices und neue Erkenntnisse" (March 2008)

[2] Bomsdorf, B., Szwillus, G.: From Task to Dialogue: Task-Based User Interface Design. In: Karat, C.-M. (hg.) Human factors in computing systems.: making the impossible possible, Workshop, April 18-23, p. 201. Addison-Wesley, Los Angeles (1998)

[3] Bomsdorf, B., Szwillus, G.: Tool Support for Task-Based User Interface Design. In: CHI 1999 Extended Abstracts on Human Factors in Computing Systems, pp. 169–170 (1999)

[4] Uhr, H.: Tombola: Simulation and User-Specific Presentation of Executable Task Models. In: Stephanidis, C. (hg.) Human-computer interaction: theory and practice II, Human factors and ergonomics: held jointly with Symposium on Human Interface, 5th International Conference on Engineering Psychology and Cognitive Ergonomics, 2nd International Conference on Universal Access in Human-Computer Interaction, Japan, Crete, Greece, vol. 2, pp. 263–267. Lawrence Erlbaum, Mahwah (2003)

[5] Meixner, G., Seissler, M., Nahler, M.: Udit - A Graphical Editor for Task Models. In: Meixner, G., Görlich, D., Breiner, K., Hussmann, H., Pleuss, A., Sauer, S., van den Bergh, J. (hg.) Proceedings of the IUI'09 Workshop on Model-Driven Development of Advanced User Interfaces, Sanibel Island, USA, February 8 (2009)

[6] Dittmar, A., Hübner, T., Forbrig, P.: HOPS: A prototypical specification tool for interactive systems. In: Graham, T.C.N. (ed.) DSV-IS 2008. LNCS, vol. 5136, pp. 58–71. Springer, Heidelberg (2008)

[7] Dittmar, A., Forbrig, P.: Task-Based Design Revisited. In: Calvary, G. (hg.) Proceedings of the ACM SIGCHI Symposium on Engineering Interactive Computing Systems incorporates he 16th International Workshop on the Design, Specification, and Verification of Interactive Systems (DSV-IS 2009)], Pittsburgh, PA, USA, July 15-17, pp. 111–116. ACM, New York (2009)

[8] Annett, J., Duncan, K.: Task Analysis and Training Design. Occupational Psychology 41, 211–221 (1967)

[9] van der Veer, G., van Welie, M., Chisalita, C.: Introduction to Groupware Task Analysis. In: Pribeanu, C. (ed.) Proceedings of the First International Workshop on Task Models and Diagrams for User Interface Design - TAMODIA 2002, Bucharest, Romania, July 18-19, pp. 32–39. INFOREC Printing House, Bucharest (2002)

[10] Paternò, F.: Model-based design and evaluation of interactive applications. Springer, Heidelberg (2000) (Applied computing)

[11] Baron, M., Lucquiaud, V., Autard, D., Scapin, D.: K-MADe: un environnement pour le noyau du modèle de description de l'activité. In: Proceedings of the 18th International Conference of the Association Francophone d'Interaction Homme-Machine, pp. 287–288. ACM, New York (2006)

[12] Biere, M., Bomsdorf, B., Szwillus, G.: Specification and simulation of task models with VTMB. In: CHI 1999 Extended Abstracts on Human Factors in Computing Systems, pp. 1–2 (1999)

[13] Giese, M., Mistrzyk, T., Pfau, A., Szwillus, G., von Detten, M.: AMBOSS: A task modeling approach for safety-critical systems. In: Forbrig, P., Paternò, F. (eds.) HCSE/TAMODIA 2008. LNCS, vol. 5247, pp. 98–109. Springer, Heidelberg (2008)

[14] Wurdel, M., Sinnig, D., Forbrig, P.: CTML: Domain and Task Modeling for Collaborative Environments. Journal of Universal Computer Science, 14 (2008)

[15] Farmilo, A., Whitworth, I., Hone, G.: Using THE HTA TOOL for Agile Mission Planning. In: Defense, D.o. (ed.) Proceedings of the 12th International Command and Control Research and Technology Symposium (2007)

[16] Card, S., Moran, T., Newell, A.: The Psychology of Human-Computer Interaction. Lawrence Erlbaum, Mahwah (1983)

[17] Dix, A., Ramduny-Ellis, D., Wilkinson, J.: Trigger Analysis: Understanding Broken. In: Diaper, D., Stanton, N.A. (hg.) The handbook of task analysis for human-computer interaction. Lawrence Erlbaum, Mahwah (2004)

[18] Schlungbaum, E., Elwert, T.: Dialogue Graphs - A Formal and Visual Specification Technique for Dialogue Modelling. Springer, Heidelberg (1996)

[19] Forbrig, P., Fuchs, G., Reichart, D., Schumann, H.: Modellbasierte Entwicklung mobiler multimodaler Nutzungsschnittstellen. In: Heinecke, A.M., Paul, H. (eds.) Mensch & Computer 2006, Mensch und Computer im StrukturWandel [Tagung "Mensch & Computer" 2006; Tagungsband], pp. 195–202. Oldenbourg, München (2006)

[20] Forbrig, P., Reichart, D.: Ein Werkzeug zur Spezifikation von Dialoggraphen. In: Gross, T. (ed.) Mensch & Computer 2007, Konferenz für interaktive und kooperative Medien, pp. 253–256. Oldenbourg, München (2007)

[21] Wolff, A., Forbrig, P.: Deriving User Interfaces from Task Models. In: Meixner, G., Görlich, D., Breiner, K., Hussmann, H., Pleuss, A., Sauer, S., van den Bergh, J. (hg.) Proceedings of the IUI 2009 Workshop on Model-Driven Development of Advanced User Interfaces, Sanibel Island, USA, February 8 (2009)

[22] Berti, S., Correani, F., Mori, G., Paternò, F., Santoro, C.: A transformation-based environment for designing multi-device interactive applications. In: Nunes, N.J. (ed.) International Conference on Intelligent User Interfaces, IUI 2004, Funchal, Madeira, Portugal, January 13 - 16, ACM Press, New York (2004)

[23] Luyten, K., Clerckx, T., Coninx, K., Vanderdonckt, J.: Derivation of a dialog model from a task model by activity chain extraction. In: Jorge, J.A., Jardim Nunes, N., Falcão e Cunha, J. (eds.) DSV-IS 2003. LNCS, vol. 2844, pp. 203–217. Springer, Heidelberg (2003)

[24] Limbourg, Q., Vanderdonckt, J.: Adressing the Mapping Problem in User Interface Design with UsiXML. In: Slavik, P., Palanque, P. (hg.) Proceedings of the 3rd Annual Conference on Task Models and Diagrams, pp. 155–163 (2004)

[25] Nielsen, J.: Usability engineering, 3rd edn. Acad. Press, Boston (1996) (print)

[26] Szwillus, G.: Modellierung aufgabenangemessener Abläufe im Web. In: Heinecke, A.M., Paul, H. (eds.) Mensch & Computer 2006. Mensch und Computer im Struktur Wandel, [Tagung "Mensch & Computer" 2006, Tagungsband], pp. 43–53. Oldenbourg, München (2006)

[27] Constantine, L.L.: Canonical abstract prototypes for abstract visual and interaction design. In: Jorge, J.A., Jardim Nunes, N., Falcão e Cunha, J. (eds.) DSV-IS 2003. LNCS, vol. 2844, pp. 1–15. Springer, Heidelberg (2003)

[28] Baule, D.: Konzept und Implementierung eines Prototypen zur Simulation aufgabenangemessener Abläufe im Web am Beispiel der Modellierungsumgebung WISE. Diplomarbeit, Institut für Informatik, Universität Paderborn (2008)

[29] Dabbert, J.: Aufgabenmodellierung als Hilfsmittel zur Usability-Evaluation am Beispiel eines kommerziellen Codegenerierungswerkzeuges. Masterarbeit, Institut für Informatik, Universität Paderborn (2009)

[30] Gerhard, M.:Konzeption und prototypische Entwicklung eines Tools für Usability-Untersuchungen an Aufgabenmodellen. Bachelorarbeit, Institut für Informatik, Universität Paderborn (2010)

[31] Forbrig, P., Wolff, A., Dittmar, A., Reichart, D.: Tool Support for an Evolutionary Design Process using XML and User-Interface Patterns. In: Proceedings of CUSEC 2006, Montreal, Canada (2006)

[32] Buchholz, G., Propp, S., Forbrig, P.: Methoden für Usability-Evaluationen auf Basis von Aufgabenmodellen. In: Röse, K. (ed.) Usability Professionals 2007. Berichtband des fünften Workshops des German Chapters der Usability Professionals Association e.V.; [vom 2. bis 5. September 2007 in Weimar], pp. 21–24. German Chapter der Usability Professionals Assoc., Stuttgart (2007)

[33] HIIS Laboratory: The MARIAE environment (2010),
      http://giove.isti.cnr.it/tools/Mariae

Author Index